Internal Frontiers

NEW AFRICAN HISTORIES

SERIES EDITORS: JEAN ALLMAN, ALLEN ISAACMAN, AND DEREK R. PETERSON

David William Cohen and E. S. Atieno Odhiambo, *The Risks of Knowledge*

Belinda Bozzoli, *Theatres of Struggle and the End of Apartheid*

Gary Kynoch, *We Are Fighting the World*

Stephanie Newell, *The Forger's Tale*

Jacob A. Tropp, *Natures of Colonial Change*

Jan Bender Shetler, *Imagining Serengeti*

Cheikh Anta Babou, *Fighting the Greater Jihad*

Marc Epprecht, *Heterosexual Africa?*

Marissa J. Moorman, *Intonations*

Karen E. Flint, *Healing Traditions*

Derek R. Peterson and Giacomo Macola, editors, *Recasting the Past*

Moses E. Ochonu, *Colonial Meltdown*

Emily S. Burrill, Richard L. Roberts, and Elizabeth Thornberry, editors, *Domestic Violence and the Law in Colonial and Postcolonial Africa*

Daniel R. Magaziner, *The Law and the Prophets*

Emily Lynn Osborn, *Our New Husbands Are Here*

Robert Trent Vinson, *The Americans Are Coming!*

James R. Brennan, *Taifa*

Benjamin N. Lawrance and Richard L. Roberts, editors, *Trafficking in Slavery's Wake*

David M. Gordon, *Invisible Agents*

Allen F. Isaacman and Barbara S. Isaacman, *Dams, Displacement, and the Delusion of Development*

Stephanie Newell, *The Power to Name*

Gibril R. Cole, *The Krio of West Africa*

Matthew M. Heaton, *Black Skin, White Coats*

Meredith Terretta, *Nation of Outlaws, State of Violence*

Paolo Israel, *In Step with the Times*

Michelle R. Moyd, *Violent Intermediaries*

Abosede A. George, *Making Modern Girls*

Alicia C. Decker, *In Idi Amin's Shadow*

Rachel Jean-Baptiste, *Conjugal Rights*

Shobana Shankar, *Who Shall Enter Paradise?*

Emily S. Burrill, *States of Marriage*

Todd Cleveland, *Diamonds in the Rough*

Carina E. Ray, *Crossing the Color Line*

Sarah Van Beurden, *Authentically African*

Giacomo Macola, *The Gun in Central Africa*

Lynn Schler, *Nation on Board*

Julie MacArthur, *Cartography and the Political Imagination*

Abou B. Bamba, *African Miracle, African Mirage*

Daniel Magaziner, *The Art of Life in South Africa*

Paul Ocobock, *An Uncertain Age*

Keren Weitzberg, *We Do Not Have Borders*

Nuno Domingos, *Football and Colonialism*

Jeffrey S. Ahlman, *Living with Nkrumahism*

Bianca Murillo, *Market Encounters*

Laura Fair, *Reel Pleasures*

Thomas F. McDow, *Buying Time*

Jon Soske, *Internal Frontiers*

Internal Frontiers

*African Nationalism and the Indian
Diaspora in Twentieth-Century South
Africa*

❧

Jon Soske

OHIO UNIVERSITY PRESS ❧ ATHENS, OHIO

Ohio University Press, Athens, Ohio 45701
ohioswallow.com
© 2017 by Ohio University Press
All rights reserved

First published 2017 in the United States of America by Ohio University Press, Athens, OH 45701

Published 2017 in Southern Africa by the University of Witwatersrand through its Wits University Press

Printed in the United States of America
Ohio University Press books are printed on acid-free paper ∞ ™

27 26 25 24 23 22 21 20 19 18 17   5 4 3 2 1

Library of Congress Cataloging-in-Publication Data
Names: Soske, Jon, 1977- author.
Title: Internal frontiers : African nationalism and the Indian diaspora in twentieth-century South Africa / Jon Soske.
Other titles: New African histories series.
Description: Athens, Ohio : Ohio University Press, 2017. | Series: New African histories | Includes bibliographical references and index.
Identifiers: LCCN 2017036213| ISBN 9780821422830 (hc : alk. paper) | ISBN 9780821422847 (pb : alk. paper) | ISBN 9780821446102 (pdf)
Subjects: LCSH: South Africa--History--20th century. | South Africa--Politics and government--20th century. | East Indians--South Africa. | East Indian diaspora. | South Africa--Ethnic relations.
Classification: LCC DT1924 .S67 2017 | DDC 968.05--dc23
LC record available at https://lccn.loc.gov/2017036213

For Kate Elizabeth Creasey
Benim kafadarim

Contents

Preface and Acknowledgments

In July 2004, I visited Durban for the first time, where one of my guides was the late and dearly missed historian Jeff Guy. After finishing lunch, he introduced me to his children, Joe and Heli, who had arrived at the same café. He suggested that we speak, since I had expressed interest in postapartheid social movements and they had been active in some of these campaigns. The next day, we met for a coffee at a seaside café and, among many other things, they talked about the way that the local African National Congress (ANC) invoked historical inequalities between Africans and Indians in order to undercut service delivery protests in Indian townships such as Chatsworth, in effect using racial divisions to attack the very kinds of activism that had helped bring the ANC to power. After our conversation, I walked through the Grey Street neighborhood in downtown Durban, absorbed in the markets, shops, colonnades, mosques and minarets, and curry stalls. In a very hazy and undeveloped fashion, I started to wonder about the place of this Indian Ocean city in the history of South Africa and the significance of the Indian diaspora, as well as Indian and African racial divisions, for the development of the liberation struggle and African nationalism.

The research that I finished in 2009 sought to integrate Indian and African histories in Durban within a single narrative while providing a critical account of how the antiapartheid struggle addressed the question of the also-colonized other. Strongly influenced by Walter Rodney's seminal *History of the Guyanese Working People*, I felt the conviction that the ANC had failed to overcome—and perhaps exacerbated—racial divisions by building a superficial alliance from above rather than class unity from below. Against an official rhetoric and historiography that stressed nonracialism, my research spent considerable time uncovering Natal's fraught racial histories and the currents of racial thinking within the liberation organizations. Nationalism, I believed, was inevitably haunted by the specter of race. While this research informs the present book, I draw rather different conclusions in the account that follows. While Natal's racial divisions were (and remain) stark, they form only one part of a more complex and interesting story about how race was lived in black communities in the early days of apartheid. Moreover, my research did not fully appreciate the awareness within the ANC of both these racial dynamics and the dangerous entanglements between racial and nationalist thinking. There was a philosophical audacity to the ANC's vision of inclusive African nationalism that—in the current age of managerial multiculturalism—is easy to misrecognize. While still critical in its approach, *Internal Frontiers* is far more interested in the power of African nationalist thought and the ANC's attempt to rethink the meaning of nation in the midst of life and death struggles. As I attempt to show, the effort to reimagine African nationalism in radically open terms was one of the twentieth century's major intellectual achievements.

I conducted my research in the Department of History at the University of Toronto. Given Toronto's location within a geography etched by the British Empire, the city was a fertile space to begin to reflect on these questions. Not only did I benefit from the mentorship and advice of a wonderful community of Africanist scholars, my colleagues, friends, and collaborators also invited me to think through my project in relationship to parallel and connected histories across South Asia, the Caribbean, and Palestine. I am deeply grateful to Alissa Trotz, Michelle Murphy, Melanie Newton, Ritu Birla, Rick Halpern, Jens Hanssen, Shivrang Setlur, Brian Beaton, Doris Bergen, John Saul, Natalie Zemon Davis, Lauren Dimonte, Richard Iton, Ato Quayson, Christopher Linhares, Terrance Ranger, Melanie Sampson, Dickson Eyoh, J. Edward Chamberlin, Ian Hacking, Lorna Goodison, Luis Jacob, Chris Curreri, Lauren Lydic, and Antoinette Handley. Sean Hawkins was a generous and supportive mentor who insisted on the ethical stakes of the historian's craft. Choosing to study with him was one of the best decisions of my life. Melissa Levin listened and argued with me patiently over the course of a decade. Her friendship has improved every word of this book. While finishing my research, I had the opportunity to collaborate with Hillina Seife, Haema Sivanesan, and Tejpal Ajji on the *South-South: Interruptions and Encounters* exhibition. Their friendships, and other opportunities to work with the South Asian Visual Art Centre, have greatly enriched my understanding of the issues explored in these pages.

Since my first research trip to South Africa in 2006, I have found a generous and welcoming community of scholars at the University of the Witwatersrand. During this and subsequent trips, I was repeatedly humbled by the willingness of South African colleagues to share their knowledge, research, and resources. Through the friendships of Ronit Frenkel and Pamila Gupta, I was introduced to the discussions regarding South Africa–India connections and Indian Ocean studies that eventually evolved into the Centre for Indian Studies in Africa (CISA), where I was Postdoctoral Fellow from 2009 to 2011. These conversations were crucial to the development of this project. I would like to thank Ronit, Pamila, Juan Orrantia, Natasha Erlank, Zen Marie, Phillip Bonner, Noor Nieftagodien, Madhumita Lahiri, Achille Mbembe, Dan Ojwang, Bhekizizwe Peterson, Shireen Hassim, Rehana Ebrahim-Vally, Thembinkosi Goniwe, Kelly Gillespie, and Kevin "Owl" Heydenrych. As director of CISA, Dilip Menon provided institutional support and, more importantly, our conversations enriched my understanding of intellectual history. This book is much stronger due to the comments and criticisms of Arianna Lissoni over the course of several years. Liz Gunner's knowledge of Natal and Zulu culture have been an inexhaustible resource. Lungile Madywabe helped me with isiZulu translations. Working on the film *African-Indian Odyssey* with Hina Saiyada was a vital experience. I hope that my many discussions with Sarah Nuttall, and the influence of her scholarship, are evident in the pages that follow.

Isabel Hofmeyr, mentor extraordinaire, deserves her own paragraph. Since my first conference paper, she has been able to see—far beyond me—the potential of this project and gently encouraged me to go further. If not for her wisdom, brilliant insights, and scholarly example, this book would not have been written.

I had the opportunity to present two of the book's chapters, 3 and 4, at the history seminar at the University of Kwa-Zulu Natal. For a historian of Durban, the seminar was an invaluable space, an opportunity for comment and critique from scholars who have dedicated their careers to Natal and its history. In addition to Jeff, I owe debts to Catherine Burns, Julie Parle, Goolam Vahed, Keith Breckenridge, Gerhard

Mare, Vukile Khumalo, Vishnu Padayachee, and Thembisa Waetjen. Bill Freund, who hosted me during research trips to Durban, has been a wonderful friend and teacher. His boundless erudition and seminal research on Natal have been central to my education.

In addition to Bill, several other scholars read and commented on my manuscript. This book has gained significantly from the insights of Thomas Blom Hansen, Aisha Khan, Surendra Bhana, Sharad Chari, Mark Hunter, and Joseph Lelyveld.

In 2014, I received a Mellon Fellowship to spend a semester at the Center for Humanities Research (CHR) at the University of the Western Cape, where I completed the process of conceptualizing this book. The CHR is a peerless space and the opportunity to participate in its discussions has been invaluable. Heidi Grunebaum, who invited me to CHR, helped me think through the idea of a global moment of Partition. In numerous discussions, Patricia Hayes deepened my understanding of the aesthetic dimensions of resistance politics. I am grateful for the exmaple and scholarship of Suren Pillay, Ciraj Rassool, Uma Dhupelia-Mesthrie, Helena Pohlandt-McCormick, and Gary Minkley. More than any other historian, Premesh Lalu's work has shaped how I understand the problem space of African nationalist thought. My debt to him is immense.

Since moving to Montreal, I have enjoyed the advice and support of Subho Basu, Laura Madokoro, Elizabeth Elbourne, Gwyn Campbell, Tassos Anastassiadis, Lorenz Lüthi, Daviken Studnicki-Gizbert, Rachel Berger, Andrew Ivaska, Rachel Sandwell, Monica Patterson, Suzanne Morton, Allan Greer, Malek Abisaab, Monica Popescu, Laila Parsons, Catherine Desbarats, Catherine Lu, Elena Razlogova, and Selin Murat. Renee Saucier, Yasmine Mosimann, and Lauren Laframboise provided research assistance. Working with Rajee Paña Jeji Shergill on the Info Bomb exhibition greatly enriched my understanding of Partition. Thank you to Jim Morris for his friendship in the last days of finishing this project.

Antoinette Burton, who read two versions of this manuscript, was unstintingly generous in her feedback and criticisms. One of the great joys of this project was thinking through some of its questions in collaboration with her. Paul Landau vetted material, answered queries, and (most importantly) his scholarship helped me understand the great historical depth of the inclusive tradition within African political culture.

While finishing this book, I have been inspired by the courage and philosophical conviction of Rashad Ramazanov and Konul Ismayilova.

Over the past ten years, I have received advice, encouragement, and support from too many people to list. I am deeply grateful to Phiroze Vasunia, Marcus Rediker, Vijay Prashad, Giancarlo Casale, Gabeba Baderoon, Sean Jacobs, Dan Magaziner, T. J. Tallie, Neelika Jayawardane, Sana Aiyer, Alex Lichtenstein, David William Cohen, Marissa Moorman, Farzanah Badsha, Christopher J. Lee, Allison Schachter, James Brennan, Centime Zeleke, Frank Wilderson III, Teresa Barnes, Orhan Esen, Zuba Wai, Franco Barchiesi, Timur Hammond, Clapperton Mavhunga, Souleymane Bachir Diagne, Sarah Balakrishnan, Shannon Walsh, Serhan Lokman, Robert Vinson, Prabhu Mohapatra, Suraiya Faroqhi, Erdem Kabadayı, Robin D. G. Kelley, Imraan Coovadia, Derek Peterson, Jean Allman, Gail Gerhart, Peter Limb, Allen Isaacman, Nima Fahimian, Alicia Weisberg-Roberts, Kelyn Roberts, Peggy Kamuf, Quincy R. Lehr, Anna Norris, Octavio Guerra, *Chimurenga* Magazine (especially Ntone Edjabe, Stacy Hardy, and Achal Prabhala), South African History Online (Mads Nørgaard, Jeeva Rajgopaul, and many others), Şiirci Kafe, Maia Woolner, Ashraf Jamal, Christopher Cozier, Tsitsi Jaji, Jill Kelly, Nafisa Sheik, Nick R. Smith, Meghan Healy-Clancy, Jo Soske, and the Otolith Group (Anjalika Sagar and Kodwo Eshun).

Most importantly, I have received guidance and wisdom from individuals who participated in the organizations discussed in this book and encountered their intellectual worlds as living traditions of struggle. More than anything else, these conversations helped me see past political texts, as important as these are, and understand ideas as embodied in organizational cultures, symbolism, personal relationships, and ways of being. Raymond Suttner read some of my early writing on Luthuli and provided encouragement and generative insight. Bobby Marie and Phumi Mtetwa, in a crucial conversation, complicated my rather American understanding of South African racial dynamics. I have learned important things from Ahmed Kathrada, Jay Naidoo, Shamim Meer, Joe Phaahla, Amina Cachalia, Ebrahim Ismail Ebrahim, Elinor Sisulu, Zwelakhe Sisulu, Jerry Coovadia, David Hemson, Tony Mpanza, Derek Powell, Ismail Nagdee, and Tom Manthata. Bhekisizwe Ngwenya introduced me to Pan-Africanist Congress veterans in Soweto, helped me with isiZulu, and watched my back.

Although comrades from the Black Consciousness Movement might disagree with some of my conclusions, I owe much to them. Thank you to Sadeque Variava, Anver Randera, Karen Randera, Saths Cooper, Jerry Waja, Zithule Cindi, Lybon Mabasa, Yosuf Veriava, and all the supporters of the Abu Asvat Institute for Nation Building.

In 2006, I interviewed Billy Nair at his favorite restaurant on a beachfront near Tongaat, north of Durban. Early the next morning, he woke me with a phone call in order to observe that I did not appreciate the symbolic power of the 1955 Freedom Charter. He asked me to imagine what it was like for him, a young Indian trade unionist in his mid-twenties, to travel from Durban to Johannesburg and stand on the stage of the Congress of the People on 26 June 1955. In front of the most representative gathering in South Africa's history, and surrounded by comrades of every conceivable background, Nair spoke on behalf not of Indians, but of all South Africa's working people. This story has stayed with me while writing this book. So has a very different anecdote from the indomitable Phyllis Naidoo. While selling the *Guardian* newspaper with an African comrade, Phyllis and her companion got caught in the rain. She insisted that he come home, take off his soaking clothes, and then warm up in a bath. She waited for him to emerge and eventually, after almost an hour had passed, knocked on the door to see what was wrong. Phyllis was surprised by the privilege revealed by her shock at the response. "I never imagined," he moaned, "that this thing would feel *so* good."

This book would not have been finished without the friendship and mentorship of Omar Badsha. As a trade unionist, antiapartheid activist, photographer, and historian, Omar has been thinking about these questions for over five decades. At each stage of writing, I shared sections with Omar, always to receive sharp-eyed criticism and his version of encouragement: "It raises the right questions." Eventually I grew frustrated: When was I going to find some answers? As I finish this book, I believe I understand what he was saying to me. A definitive history is a dead history. The historian's job is to take a story—sometimes familiar, sometime new—and make it resonate in the urgency of the present. If I have managed to accomplish this task in the least, it is due to Omar's example.

Finally, I dedicate this book to Kate Elizabeth Creasey. In and between Toronto, Johannesburg, Istanbul, Cape Town, Los Angeles,

Durbin, and Montreal, our life together runs like an invisible thread through these pages. Her strength, courage, love, brilliance, and forgiveness have made me better in every way.

Note on Language

This is a book about permutations of race. Race appears as a set of social relationships, as a way of talking about and understanding the world, and as an object of intellectual debate and political struggle. As part of its argument, I analyze the production of an African-Indian racial divide by a number of mechanisms, including colonial policies, regimes of urban space, nationalist rhetoric, and everyday social practices. Yet even as this book tracks the far-reaching consequences of this division, it argues against attributing homogeneity to "Africans" and "Indians" as groups or assuming that these categories are adequate for understanding the complexity of identity and social life in mid-century Natal. In depicting both the power and limitations of racial categories, I have given considerable attention to the importance of language. When this book refers to African or Indian newspapers, stores, neighborhoods, political organizations, and individuals, it is marking the effects of how social life was organized and coded in racialized terms. When this book discusses groups as the object of stereotype or racial fantasy, it refers to "the Indian" or "the merchant" in the singular. Because language tends to reify complex historical processes, it is important to reflect—continuously—on the work that description is doing. I ask that the reader keep this challenge in mind.

This is also a book about ideas. I have reconstructed intellectual debates by analyzing the terms employed by contemporaries and, when possible, I have relied on texts produced during the period in question rather than interviews or memoirs from later moments. Some of these terms were critiqued and displaced by later generations of activists. "Non-European," which was widely used during the 1940s–'50s, was rejected by the Black Consciousness Movement of the 1960s–'70s on the basis that it reduced black identity to a mere negation. An epithet in North America, Coloured is used in South Africa to refer to

Afrikaans-speaking communities of "mixed" racial background. Some see both terms as colonial holdovers. In their place, later generations employed the term Black in a capacious sense to designate all communities oppressed by apartheid racial structures. While I am strongly sympathetic to these arguments, importing this language into my text would have been anachronistic and obscured the precise contours of debate during the period in question. On a few occasions, I do employ Black to interrupt the excessive reiteration of other racial categories. Hopefully, this use will be clear in context.

Histories of the antiapartheid struggle are sometimes filled with dozens of acronyms for different political organizations. For the uninitiated reader, these can be intimidating and confusing. In order to increase the accessibility of this book, I have tried to avoid acronyms as much as possible, for example by using Indian Congress for NIC (Natal Indian Congress) or Communist Party for CPSA (Communist Party of South Africa, which was banned in 1950 and reformed in the early 1950s as the South African Communist Party, SACP). I have made this choice advisedly. An organization's name is a banner of struggle — some activists understandably interpret getting it wrong as a sign of disrespect. I hope that the greater readability of this text will serve to justify this decision.

The Internal Frontier of the Nation-State

ON 19 February 1948, the Pietermaritzburg-based journal *Inkundla ya Bantu* (The people's forum) published a lengthy piece of news analysis entitled "Bambulaleleni Ugandhi?" or "Why did they kill Gandhi?" At one level, the article offered a disarmingly simple answer: the culprit in question was the Indian people as a whole. India murdered Gandhi because he represented the ideal of Hindu-Muslim equality within a single nation. (The author's failure to name Gandhi's assassin, Nathuram Godse, reinforced this attribution of collective responsibility.) According to the article, Gandhi had argued that the Hindu and Muslim "tribes" (*uqobo*, segments or parts of a totality) should unite in the struggle for independence, but Muslims began to agitate for a separate country when they realized that the Hindu majority would come to power, reducing them to "slaves." Asserting their right to rule, a younger generation of Hindus began to attack Muslims and, after Gandhi attempted to reconcile the two sides, murdered their former leader as a traitor to their national aspirations. The author apportioned blame equally: Gandhi's vision had been undermined by the secessionist politics of an anxious minority and the violent retaliation of a majority in ascendance. Consequently, the country—as both a people and a political project—stood under judgment before the court of global opinion. However, if the article initially summoned its readership to identify with this international tribunal, it then shifted perspectives and projected Africans into the position of the defendant. Directly addressing its readership, it admonished Africans to draw from the lessons of division and violence: "The wages of stabbing each other is death. It is a way of running away from the truth." At this point, the article presented Partition and Gandhi's death as foreshadowing Africa's own future, or at least one possible scenario. The world should not, it argued, condemn Indians: "given the opportunity, they can build a great nation." With these words, the author defended not only the viability of Gandhi's vision of plural nationhood, but the very possibility of national sovereignty beyond the West and its norms.[1]

This piece was one of hundreds, if not thousands, of items about India that appeared in newspapers written by and for black South Africans in the 1940s. And this profusion of coverage, centered on the changes sweeping the British Empire and their implications for South Africa, was only one moment in a much longer conversation that began in the late nineteenth century and continues to the present. From Gandhi's first political campaign in Johannesburg in the 1890s to today's BRICS (Brazil, Russia, India, China, and South Africa) group of emerging economies, India has served as an essential reference point for South African politics and black political thinkers. If Gandhi's twenty-one years in South Africa are the most well-known episode in this history, they form only one strand of a larger and considerably more complex story. Other major figures of the Indian independence struggle traveled to South Africa, including Indian National Congress president Gopal Krishna Gokhale (who toured the country in 1912), the iconic poetess and nationalist politician Sarojini Naidu in 1924, and a young Indira Nehru during the 1940s. South African journalists, writers, and students journeyed in the other direction; for example, the African National Congress (ANC) leader S. S. Thema (Gandhi advised him that the ANC should abandon Western pretensions and go "about with only a tiny clout around your loins"[2]), the future president of the ANC Albert Luthuli, and Fort Hare professor D. D. T. Jabavu, who published a book on his experiences in isiXhosa titled *In India and East Africa*.[3] Journeys by intellectuals and anticolonial militants occurred against the backdrop of the legacy of indentured Indian labor in the South African province of Natal, political and administrative linkages between the colonies, and the mass circulation of newspapers, books, spices, religious icons, films, and other culture-bearing commodities.[4] Most significantly, the two countries were bound by the communities of Indian descent that built lives and homes across South Africa.

These connections provided a reference and resource for the antiapartheid struggle. In November 1980, the acting president of the ANC, Oliver Tambo, accepted the Jawaharlal Nehru Award for International

Understanding on behalf of Nelson Mandela, then imprisoned on Robben Island. Speaking in New Delhi, Tambo praised "the striking role of India in the development of the struggle for national and social liberation in South Africa," including labor actions carried out by indentured workers in nineteenth-century Natal, India's case against South Africa's racial policies at the first meeting of the United Nations (UN) General Assembly in 1946, and Nehru's statement of solidarity with Africa—Asia's "sister continent"—at the 1955 Afro-Asian Conference held outside of Bandung, Indonesia.[5] If Tambo's remarks conflated the diaspora, the Indian anticolonial struggle, and the postcolonial state by attributing them a single historical agency, they also made India integral to a narrative of South African history based on anticolonial nationalism. Paying tribute to this relationship, Mandela adapted the title of his 1994 biography *Long Walk to Freedom* from an essay by Nehru that he first read as a student in the 1940s. When Mandela met E. S. Reddy (the chair of the UN Committee against Apartheid and an Indian citizen) shortly after his release from prison, he was still able to recite long passages of Nehru's writings from memory.[6] Tambo's remarks and Mandela's allusion both produced a twinning effect: they configured South African and Indian histories as simultaneously distinct and inseparable. They also, both historically and symbolically, incorporated this twinning into the ANC's understanding of nation.

Internal Frontiers tells the story of this relationship. It argues that it played a fundamental role in shaping the intellectual trajectory of the ANC and the South African antiapartheid struggle during the crucial conjuncture of the 1940s and '50s. At the moment of Indian independence and the emergence of the Third World, African intellectuals confronted the question of the also-colonized other. Simultaneously oppressed and privileged by the framework of white domination, the Indian diaspora posed a fundamental challenge to the political practice and philosophy of African nationalism. If African nationalism excluded Indians from the antiapartheid struggle and its conception of political community, it risked defining 'nation' in racial terms and therefore recapitulating colonialism and apartheid's dehumanizing categories. However, the inclusion of the diaspora threatened to fragment the territorial unity of the nation or, perhaps more seriously, displace the centrality of the African political subject by subordinating the struggle for national liberation to another politics (for example, the universalizing discourses of Cold War liberalism or Marxism). What conceptualization of nation could incorporate, but *not* assimilate, a diasporic group that was tied to Africans through colonial oppression, but divided by culture and language, state-sanctioned privileges, and a history of misunderstanding and resentments? Responding to this dilemma, a group of intellectuals, centered in the Indian Ocean port city of Durban, attempted to rethink the idea of nation by privileging a relationship negotiated across difference. What would the practice of African nationalism look like if, rather than presupposing the end points of sovereignty and homogeneity, it began with an open-ended relationship with the also-colonized other?

AFRICAN NATIONALISM AND UNCANNY INDIA

Internal Frontiers examines the intellectual history of the South African liberation struggle from the founding of the ANC Youth League in 1944 to the 1960 Sharpeville Massacre through three distinct (and sometimes converging) lenses. First, it explores the ways that Indian anticolonial nationalism and the events surrounding Indian independence, including the partition of India and Pakistan, helped shape the political thinking of African intellectuals, especially their imagination of sovereignty. If the Indian National Congress and the Quit India Movement of the 1940s provided a new generation of African intellectuals with an important reference point for conceptualizing their own struggle, Partition illuminated the dangers inherent to the assertion of self-rule, including the schismatic and oppressive potentials of majoritarian nationalism. The considerable influence of India, however, was both mediated through and complicated by the sizable population of Indians in South Africa. This is the second lens employed by this book. It follows the debate that emerged among African intellectuals (including, it should be underlined, South African Indians) in the mid-1940s over the role of Indians within the liberation struggle and, ultimately, their place within South Africa. Initially posed in terms of the relationship between the ANC and Indian political organizations, this discussion evolved into a wide-ranging reconsideration of the struggle's ideological foundations and framed the ANC's ambitious attempt to rethink the concept of nation in the 1950s. Though these two discussions—one over India as a model and the other over Indians as a group—sometimes ran in parallel, at other times they intersected in complex ways, raising questions about both the internal and external boundaries of the nationalist political project. At crucial points, they were also interrupted and reconfigured by interventions from "below." The third lens of this book focuses on vernacular discourses of race, including a powerful current of anti-Indian populism among many Africans, which consolidated in Durban as migration reconfigured urban space from the 1930s. While new racial dynamics generated a sense of African-Indian antagonism on an unprecedented scale, they also coexisted with the intimacies and anonymous solidarities of urban life. Multiple relationships, in ways that were both highly visible and unremarkable in their ordinariness, crosshatched the hardening divide. In confronting this fractured and contentious landscape, African intellectuals navigated and later theorized the existence of a profound division between the colonized that, as they knew well from their own life experiences, failed to exhaust the complexities of identity in Natal.

By exploring the interplay between these three lenses, *Internal Frontiers* argues that India and the Indian diaspora were decisive questions—and at certain moments *the* decisive question—during the crucial period when the ANC first emerged as a mass political organization and fully developed its conception of African nationalism. Since its foundation in 1912, the ANC (then called the South African Native National Congress) had countered the settler dystopia of a white South Africa with the demand for inclusive citizenship based on individual capacity (a qualified franchise and "equal rights for all civilized men"). By the mid-1940s, a series of factors—increased African militancy, the publication of the *Atlantic Charter*, and the closing of wartime prospects for reform—led a new generation of intellectuals, including figures as different as Dr. A. B. Xuma and Anton Lembede, to demand universal citizenship rights based on African nationalism. In the wide-ranging debate that emerged over the nature of this nationalism (it involved not only intellectuals within the ANC, but liberals, Communist Party members, and the heterodox Marxist Non-European Unity Movement), India provided a reference point for all sides. For South African observers as well as many others around the world, the decolonization of India and Pakistan announced the transition from empire to the sovereign nation-state as the foundation of the global system. When Xuma argued for transforming the ANC into a mass movement in the early 1940s, he invoked the Indian National Congress in much the same way that Youth League members, including Mandela and Tambo, would list the actions of Gandhi and Nehru when arguing against Xuma's cautious approach at the end of the decade. While Lembede quoted Nehru in his celebration of nationalism as the spiritual expression of racial genius, his fellow ANC Youth League activist H. I. E. Dhlomo stressed India's importance in terms of the postwar system of nation-states and the human rights framework of the United Nations. Marxists of various stripes cited India as an example of a successful alliance between Communists and the forces of anticolonial nationalism as well as a betrayal of the revolution by political elites tied to the Indian bourgeoisie.

Across these competing appropriations, the figure of India served a common purpose: it authorized a claim of self-determination in the present. The ANC's earlier leadership had, with brief exceptions, envisioned the gradual incorporation of Africans into colonial society under the leadership of the black middle class. By and large, they accepted that democracy presupposed a common social existence ("Western civilization") based on property ownership, education, the nuclear family (including its heteronormative vision of gender relations), Christianity, and the rule of law.[7] Intellectuals within the ANC did not, of course, reproduce this framework passively. At various points, they challenged one or more of the precepts of civilization and critiqued their underlying racial assumptions. They asserted Pan-African origins for the universal values that Europe claimed to exemplify.[8] They struggled to build independent black institutions—the African press, schools like John Dube's Ohlange Institute, and the ANC itself—that would provide the basis for a self-consciously modern political life outside of white control.[9] They championed the cause of African workers in order to extend the reach and criteria for participation in civil society.[10] And, as Robert Vinson argues, many black South Africans looked to African Americans as both examples and allies in the "regeneration" of Africa: an alternative path to modernity that would bypass colonial trusteeship.[11]

The Indian independence struggle, in contrast, did not symbolize a desired future. It instantiated democratic self-government in a diverse, polyglot, and religiously divided country whose leadership, moreover, asserted continuity with two ancient civilizations, Hinduism and Islam. A world historic event, it had philosophical as well as political ramifications. Indian independence not only challenged the fact of foreign rule, it negated a common assumption of colonial ideology and important strands of liberal political theory: that a developed political economy, experience in modern institutions, and common loyalty to a shared identity—in other words, the normative attributes of 'nation' in liberal thought—were the necessary foundations of a sovereign and democratic state.[12] Transported and translated into South African intellectual life, India provided African intellectuals with a vehicle to begin to think (both empirically and theoretically) about possible foundations of nationhood beyond empire and settler civil society. This transformed temporality of politics—conveyed most powerfully by Lembede's slogan "freedom in our lifetime"—created a new conceptual "problem space."[13] In claiming sovereignty on behalf of a subaltern and socially heterogeneous people, the 1940s generation of nationalists inaugurated a new intellectual horizon within which African thinkers would reimagine the grounds and meaning of nation.

THE INTERNAL FRONTIER OF THE NATION-STATE

If Indian independence suggested a new model for the thinking of nation, the Indian diaspora interrupted a central precept of this worldview: the envisioning of nation—to subvert Benedict Anderson's famous phrase—in homogenous, empty space.[14] The postwar map may have been composed of "liberated sovereignties," emerging states that would ostensibly realize and guard the promise of universal human rights, but this map was far from empty.[15] It was transversed by older geographies of empire, capitalism, and the oceanic worlds created by the movement of people, cultures, and ideas.[16] These dense histories posed a fundamental problem for the new nationalisms. When anticolonial intellectuals conceptualized the people as sovereign over a territory, they confronted the question of translating these alternate geographies into the imaginary of the nation-state. The "other than national" had to be rendered internal (and therefore governable by an entity with territorial jurisdiction) or foreign—a more ambiguous and exceptional status. The Indian diaspora resisted both determinations. A deterritorialized and geographically dispersed entity, diaspora served as an internal frontier of the imagined political community, a site where the principle of nationhood (however it was articulated) confronted other scales and forms of identity. Things "Indian" permeated the sociopolitical landscape of Natal and, to a lesser degree, other parts of the country. They appeared both in everyday life and material culture (from the *atchar* sold by the local shopkeeper to the grand minarets of Grey Street's mosques) and in great events that shaped the course of South Africa's history (such as Gandhi's campaigns). India was ubiquitous, part of the very fabric of South Africa. The ambiguity of the term "Indian," which named both a distant country and a variety of familiar people and places, intensified this uncanny effect.

In his important book *Enlightenment in the Colony*, Aamir Mufti suggests that eighteenth- and nineteenth-century arguments regarding the place of Jews within Europe—the famous "Jewish question"—prefigured the dilemma faced by ethnic minorities within the postcolonial nation-state. [17] According to Mufti, the secular state, based on the categories of national identity and citizenship, produced the Jewish diaspora as doubly anomalous. On the one hand, the Jew functioned as a figure of premodern, religious particularity that disrupted the universalizing ideal of individual and secular citizenship. On the other hand, the diasporic and cosmopolitan character of Jewishness, which European nationalist intellectuals frequently associated with the elusive attributes of transnational capitalism, threatened the Romantic ideal of a solidly rooted and holistic national identity. Reading the place of the Muslim in contemporary India through these earlier debates, Mufti concludes that the contradictory imperatives of secular nationalism, rather than demography, produce the cultural-political status of the minority. If nationalism institutionalizes a territorial identity through the establishment and policing of external boundaries, the category of minority allows the nationalist project to replicate this structure of demarcation *within* its territorial body: the minority group is included inside the space of the nation in such a way as to protect both the putative universalism of citizenship and the underlying exclusivity of a singular (cultural, linguistic, or racial) national subject. This mode of incorporation renders the minority precarious and vulnerable. In the process of unifying a collective territorial subject, nationalism "makes large numbers of people eminently unsettled. More simply put, whenever a population is *minoritized*—a process inherent in the nationalization of peoples and cultural practices—it is also rendered potentially movable."[18] Mufti's concept of *minoritization* usefully marks the distinction between "minority" as a political status produced by majoritarian nationalism and actual groups of people, who can understand their relationship to and within nation in a multitude of ways.

In developing the concept of internal frontier, this book follows Mufti's insistence that the relationship between nation and diaspora is not predetermined by demography, but is the product of an ongoing process that generates *both* the majority and minority as interlacing political identities. In its modern form, the phenomenon of diaspora resides at the intersection of the global distribution of certain ethnic or cultural identities—such as Jew or Indian—and an international system based on the territorialization of identity in the form of the nation-state. (It is notable that comparisons between Indians and Jews were a fixture of both popular discourse and the postwar iconography of Indian political struggles in South Africa.) As many scholars have observed, this territorialization is always, necessarily incomplete.[19] Political projects of assimilation or ethnic cleansing might asymptotically approach the classic ideal of European nationalism ("one people, one territory"), but the complexity of existing populations and the transnational movement of migrants render its ultimate realization impossible.[20] Because homogeneity remains elusive, diaspora functions as a shifting boundary—an interior limit to the project of majoritarian democracy—that destabilizes territorial nationalism and forces the continuous elaboration of a bounded national subject. This dialectic of interruption and reassertion changes, however subtly, the dominant identity over time. As Paul Gilroy argues, the effects of diaspora on a cultural landscape make it impossible to theorize without developing a new perspective on national culture as a whole.[21] At the same time, *Internal Frontiers* extends—and to a degree departs from—Mufti's argument by raising the possibility of subverting the majoritarian logic of nationalism. Because Mufti accepts that the trajectory of postcolonial politics necessarily recapitulates the Romantic ideal of peoplehood, his critique assumes a tragic structure. In his account, diaspora only ever becomes territorialized through the legal-juridical category of minority. Is it possible to invert this movement and rethink the nature of national community through its essential permeability? What would it mean to leave the internal frontier open?

PHILOSOPHICAL IDEALISM

Both a neighbor and an outsider, unmistakably South African and cosmopolitan, "the Indian" displaced the problem space of postwar

African nationalism from within. If the liberation struggle necessitated a unified people, then what was the place of the also-colonized other in the nationalist project? What type of unity could allow for an irreducible plurality of cultural and political subjects? In his enormously influential *Provincializing Europe*, Dipesh Chakrabarty argues that imperialism and Third World nationalism, by equating modernity with a highly ideological construction of the "West," universalized a particular subject of history, the sovereign subject of the nation-state.[22] Echoing the Indian psychologist Ashis Nandy (and through him Frantz Fanon), this argument suggests that anticolonial struggles emulated the subjectivities, political forms, and normative conceptions of their ostensible enemy, the European colonizer.[23] Along similar lines, Mahmood Mamdani claims that African nationalism limited its goals to the deracialization of civil society and therefore left the distinction between the citizen and native (embodied in the institutions of indirect rule) intact.[24] In contrast, *Internal Frontiers* argues that an important group of African intellectuals explicitly questioned the foundation of nation in settler civil society and, in the aftermaths of Partition and the 1949 Durban Riots, sought to reconceptualize the subject of anticolonial nationalism by privileging the question of difference. Articulated most fully in the writings of a group of Natal intellectuals centered on ANC president Albert Luthuli, this position upheld the central agency of Africans in their own liberation—and the broadly African character of postapartheid national culture—while rejecting a racial or majoritarian basis for a future political community. Drawing on precolonial practices of social inclusion and a Christian critique of materialism, these thinkers argued that a common set of values would provide the foundation for the liberation struggle and a historically dynamic nation-building project. Their conception was self-consciously idealist in a philosophical sense. The most powerful force binding the nation was the idea of the nation itself. Unlike the categories of race or civilization, idealism could incorporate the also-colonized other without postulating the existence of a national majority or threatening assimilation: it provided a basis of unity that did not presuppose homogeneity within the realm of the social.

The idealist critique of philosophical and economic materialism represented a major strand within twentieth-century thought.[25] As Michael Adas argues, the profound crisis generated by the First World

War challenged a central precept of colonial ideology: that the tech-noscientific strength of Europe embodied its civilizational superiority over the colonized world.[26] In the wake of the horrors of industrialized warfare, an increasing number of European and colonized intellectu-als rejected the identification of moral progress with material power. According to Adas, the resulting debate over the future of European civilization, and its putative basis in secular progress, was the first truly global intellectual conversation.[27] Eventually, this exchange would encompass thinkers as diverse as the philosopher Henri Bergson, the Nobel Prize–winning poet Rabindranath Tagore, the Catholic theo-logian Jacques Maritain, the Muslim-Indian thinker Mohammed Iqbal, and the theorists of negritude, Paulette Nardal, Aimé Césaire, and Léopold Senghor. Pankaj Mishra explains: "Often drawing upon philosophical and spiritual traditions in Islam, Hinduism and Confu-cianism they developed a refined suspicion of the 'brave new world' of science and reason, insisting on the non-rational, non-utilitarian aspects of human existence."[28] While many proponents of idealism op-posed foreign rule, they nevertheless understood the crime of colonial-ism in philosophical rather than political terms. They believed that the West's overreliance on technology and its one-sided emphasis on an abstract form of rationality denied the very things that give human life value: the moral and spiritual dimensions of being. This critique displaced European nationalism's fixation on primordial or substantive attributes—a homogenous culture or a unified political economy, a racial identity or a shared territory—and instead emphasized the col-lective project of building new societies founded on shared ideals and an expanded vision of humanity. To quote the philosopher Achille Mbembe, the struggle against colonialism created the space in which to articulate a "volunté active de communauté," an active will to share in community.[29]

AFRO-ASIAN SOLIDARITY AND ETHICAL NATIONALISM

In recent scholarship, Afro-Asian solidarity—symbolized most power-fully by the 1955 Bandung Conference—has elicited two conflicting interpretations. Among one group of scholars, the "Bandung moment" represented the most powerful expression of the anticolonial will-to-community, the highpoint of the revolutionary movement to build societies free of empire and racism. Recovering the radical aspirations of Bandung (often against the actual policies pursued by postcolonial elites), Vijay Prashad argues that the Third World was not a place, but a political project that sought to reimagine the international order against the bipolar system of the Cold War. Although this project ultimately collapsed through a combination of external sabotage and its own internal contradictions (including structures of class and neotraditional patriarchy), it nevertheless pointed to unrealized trajectories of liberation and new forms of political subjectivity.[30] By shifting the focus from high diplomacy to grassroots activism and imaginations of Afro-Asianism, other scholars underscore the internationalist character of anticolonial politics. Not only did nationalist movements incorporate diasporic communities and transnational practices of solidarity, they reimagined self-determination and liberation by envisioning decolonization as a global revolutionary process.[31] In a significant body of writings, the novelist Amitov Ghosh connects the expansive ethos of Afro-Asian solidarity with deeper histories of cosmopolitanism, exchange, and travel throughout the Indian Ocean. With their limited resources, Ghosh argues, resistance movements strove to articulate a universalism based on older conversations between entangled and intimately connected worlds: "Those of us who grew up in that period will recall how powerfully we were animated by an emotion that is rarely named: this is xenophilia, the love of the other, the affinity for strangers."[32] Employing a strategy of "nostalgic futurism," Ghosh and others read the unrealized visions of Bandung as an archive and resource for creating a postnationalist politics in the era of neoliberal empire.[33]

In contrast, historians of southern and eastern Africa generally express skepticism regarding the reach of Afro-Asianism while raising questions about the ways that anticolonial nationalism presupposed a majoritarian political subject that racialized postcolonial citizenship.[34] In a trenchant discussion of mid-century Tanzania, James Brennan argues that the country's Indian community functioned as the primary other for the development of a dominant, racialized African nationalism. However inclusive its official rhetoric, the Tanganyika African Union (TANU) embraced and reinforced popular discourses of racial purity—grounded in patrilineal modes of reckoning descent—by defining nation in terms of Swahili civilization and common (African) economic suffering.[35] Though individuals of South Asian descent

participated in anticolonial struggles such as Kenya's Mau Mau uprising, such solidarity coexisted with—and in certain ways drew its
strength in opposition to—a forbidding backdrop of colonial segregation, ideas of Indian racial and civilizational superiority, and equally
racialized African resentments.[36] In her wide-ranging *Africa in the
Indian Imagination*, Antoinette Burton describes the ways in which
heroic narratives of Afro-Asianism inscribe "brown" over "black" while
lionizing the masculine subject of anticolonial nationalism.[37] These
accounts resonate with an important critique of solidarity—as both
concept and practice—that warns about the ways that progressive alliances serve to disavow white (and other kinds of) privilege while disciplining more radical black political aspirations in the name of unity
and respectability.[38]

Rather than celebrating or critiquing the project of Afro-Asian unity,
Internal Frontiers describes how an important group of intellectuals
attempted to overcome the limitations of solidarity by reconceiving
the nation in ethical terms. Because nationalism was a narrative of the
African people's participation within (a particular conception of) history, later historiographical debates were anticipated within the antiapartheid movement as disputes over basic principles. A breakthrough
occurred in the process of organizing the 1952 Defiance Campaign
against unjust laws. Following this first mobilization of Africans and
Indians together in nonviolent civil disobedience, Luthuli and other
ANC leaders linked the possibility of Black-Indian solidarity to a re-
formulation of the African nation-building project. The foundation of
this compact was Indian recognition of the ANC's leadership. If Indians (and later others) endorsed the African liberation struggle through
personal risk and genuine material sacrifice, the ANC would welcome
these communities *as distinct communities* within a broad project of
African nationalism. This act of welcoming, which was deeply resonant with the importance of hospitality in precolonial African cultures,
represented the inclusive moment of the ANC's idea of an "inclusive
African nationalism."

Unlike liberal conceptions of solidarity or multiracialism, this alliance did not presuppose the equivalency of its members.[39] Rather, reciprocity was both asymmetrical and particularized: African acceptance
of the other's claim to indigeneity presupposed Indians' prior recognition of the country's fundamentally African character. In two important

senses, this reimagining of solidarity articulated the nation as an ethical relationship between distinct yet entangled communities.[40] In the first instance, this relationship was ethical because the form of reciprocity it demanded was based on the individuality of each group rather than the general obligations of citizenship. Indeed, every demarcation of *ethnic* boundaries requires the negotiation or disavowal of an *ethical* disposition toward others.[41] More profoundly, this relationship was ethical because it incorporated an open-ended negotiation with the other within the historical process of creating a South African identity. This openness was possible because the ultimate basis of inclusive nationalism was a shared commitment to transcendent ideals.

This understanding had significant repercussions for the meaning of liberation. As philosopher Gillian Rose warns in a different context, recognition entails the discovery of "the self-relation of the other as the challenge of one's own self-relation."[42] If national identity is inseparable from the other's ideas and practices of community, freedom can no longer be expressed in terms of asserting independence, but instead requires a deepening of entanglement.[43] Consequently, self-determination becomes a set of relationships that required continual elaboration both within and beyond the borders of the national state: it possessed an external and internal dimension.[44] This form of belonging also created vulnerability and, therefore, the possibility of particularly brutal and wounding forms of violence.[45] Of the many problems that this vision posed, one stands out. Could this understanding of nation expand to include the white settler population, which was committed to defending its apartheid—the Afrikaans word for "separation"—by force? In the context of the protracted fight against white supremacy, this question became entangled within a second debate: Was it possible to achieve democracy without civil war?

THE NATAL CRUCIBLE

Located on the southwestern rim of the Indian Ocean, the province of Natal was a world composed of multiple worlds. Not only did each of these social universes, in turn, contain other milieus (nested inside one another much like a series of fitted Russian dolls), the worlds abutted and overlapped, creating a complex pattern that changed forms depending on the viewer's perspective. In the first instance, it was conquest and settler society that bound these realities together. Beginning in the late 1830s, Afrikaner and then English incursion established a white presence in the region that slowly expanded over the course of the next two decades. As anthropologist Patrick Wolfe argues, colonial invasion was "a structure not an event": the violence of settlement continues to exist as an ongoing process embodied and reproduced by the institutions of colonial civil society.[46] In the case of Natal, these institutions developed through the gradual incorporation of the region into broader international networks: the administrative structures and political institutions that linked the colony to the British Empire (Natal was later the most English of South Africa's four provinces); the port that opened Natal to the currents of the Indian Ocean and the global capitalist economy; and the schools and mission stations that made Christianity a central presence, including (by the end of the nineteenth century) African American missionaries who would form a vital connection to the Black Atlantic.[47]

While such forces drew the colony together, they failed to destroy and fully assimilate the region's preexisting societies, most importantly the powerful Zulu Kingdom, which defended its independence until 1879. Even as significant numbers of Africans came to live on mission stations or in reserves (Natal was also a pioneer of indirect rule), converted to Christianity, and entered into the colony's economy as migrant workers, the continued existence of an autonomous Zulu way of life—symbolized by the monarchy and the royal house—contributed to a profound consciousness of belonging and indigenousness across an increasingly differentiated African population.[48] Furthermore, the continual violence of conquest may have integrated settlers and Africans into a range of hierarchal formations, but the settler state was not yet strong enough to restructure social relations according to a single, overarching racial order. A binary discourse of race burnished the increasing heterogeneity of both white and African society. Among Natal's Africans, new social categories proliferated and combined: urban and rural, Christian and traditional, aspirant middle class and migrant worker—each generating different versions of a common Zulu identity.[49]

Into this chaotic and inchoate universe, the SS *Truro* (sailing from the southern Indian port of Madras) brought 342 workers of South Asian origin on 16 November 1860.[50] The ship's list tells its own story of distinct and interwoven worlds. The passengers included men, women, and children whose "castes" were identified variously as Christian, Muslim, Rajput, Gentoo, Pariah, Malabar, Myset, and unknown. Ten days later, a second ship (whose voyage started over a thousand miles north in Calcutta) arrived bearing a cargo of people from an equally diffuse range of backgrounds. Because most Africans still retained access to land (and therefore a measure of independence from the colonial economy), Natal's coastal planters turned to the indenture system—developed in the Caribbean after the abolition of slavery in 1834—to support the colony's struggling sugar industry. By the time that the colony terminated the system in 1911, 152,184 indentured workers had come to Natal. In their powerful account, Ashwin Desai and Goolam Vahed capture the motivations that drove people into contracted servitude: fathers chasing means to support families in the midst of imperialism's economic ravages; "untouchables" hoping to escape caste oppression; young men thirsting for adventure or elusive fortune; widows and single women escaping forms of patriarchal constraint; and unfortunates simply defrauded by recruiters.[51] After the conclusion of their contracts, a significant number remained in Natal despite the hardships of poverty and colonial racism. Others signed new contracts after returning to India or traveled back to South Africa on their own tickets.

These migrants largely originated in two different regions of the subcontinent (the Tamil- and Telugu-speaking south and the Bhojpuri-speaking plane of the Ganges River), spoke at least seven distinct Indian languages, and carried (willingly or not) numerous religious, village, familial, and occupational identities.[52] Nonetheless, the momentous act of boarding a ship together began a long process of discarding, reconfiguring, and expanding notions of self and community that would eventually produce a common sense of Indianness across persistent ethnic, class, and religious divides. As Desai and Vahed underscore, Indian immigrants to Natal resisted the colonial labor system, in part, by struggling to create new homes: the construction of a shared India through places of worship, festivals, new family traditions, plays, songs, and dress.[53] The relationship with an Indian past was not automatic, but complex, selective, and contested. The formation of the Colonial Born Indian Association in 1911 reflected the growing sense, at least among a literate stratum of former indentured workers, of common political interests among a population that planned to stay. At the same time, the establishment of regional, language, and religious associations—which became the central focus of community outside the family—and the influence of Hindu missionaries encouraged an inward-looking social life that assumed some caste-like elements and further insulated Indians from interaction with Africans.[54]

Following the indentured population, a second group of South Asian migrants, sometimes traveling through Mauritius or East Africa, began to arrive during the 1870s. Generally described as "passengers" (since they paid their own fares) and identified with the male figure of the Gujarati merchant, this group—as Uma Dhupelia-Mesthrie shows—was considerably more diverse in gender, origin, and occupation.[55] Involved in almost every aspect of Natal's economy (from agriculture to blacksmithing), many passengers retained close ties to India, returning home to visit or marry, and they soon began to establish institutions in South Africa on the basis of religion, language, and (more rarely) caste. In the late nineteenth century, this group stressed its distinction from "coolies" (a derogatory term for unskilled labor that was also used as a slur against Indians) on religious or racial grounds. In an effort to differentiate their legal status from the formerly indentured, for example, some Indian Muslims asserted an "Arab" identity. As newer migrants followed opportunities across South Africa, they established communities in the Transvaal and the Western Cape (with Indian populations of 9,979 and 10,242 in 1909, respectively) of significantly different ethno-religious compositions and demographic weight than in Natal.[56] This layer created a new hierarchy among South African Indians, which overlapped partially with the division between Muslims and Hindus/Christians, while interspersing Indians within the sociopolitical landscape of the country as a whole. Because many passengers made their living through activities such as running stores or working in service professions, they frequently resided in urban centers catering to shoppers of all races or in the neighborhoods where their customers lived. Driven by the backlash among whites over perceived economic competition, the provinces attempted to restrict Indians to specific locations starting the 1880s or, in the case of the Orange Free State, banned Indian residents altogether. Nevertheless, Indians became the group most likely to live near or among other racial groups. The 1950 Group Areas Act, the apartheid legislation that established segregated residential and business zones in cities, resulted in the displacement of Indians at a higher rate than any other section of the population.[57]

GANDHI IN SOUTH AFRICA

No figure looms larger in the history of Indians in South Africa than Mohandas Gandhi. As a substantial literature attests,[58] Gandhi's South African years were the most important period of his adult intellectual formation. The man who arrived as a prim, suit-wearing lawyer—a quirky Anglophile who believed in the promises of liberal empire—would eventually leave after he had renounced the materialistic philosophy of Western civilization and devised a series of new ideas that he would employ to historic effect in India. Born on 2 October 1869 in Porbandar, Gujarat, Gandhi qualified as a lawyer in England where he became interested in vegetarianism and theosophy. In 1893 he traveled to the Transvaal in order to translate in a legal dispute between two Gujarati businessmen. Gandhi then remained in South Africa for the better part of the next twenty-one years. In 1894 he plunged into local politics by organizing opposition to a bill introduced by the Natal legislature that would have disenfranchised Indians on the basis of race. Initially, Gandhi's political agitation centered on the defense of Indian rights as British imperial subjects. He adopted the legalistic methods of elite nationalist politics. However, his experience living in South Africa (he was a firsthand witness to the industrial revolution emanating from Johannesburg) slowly propelled him toward different forms of spiritual and communal experimentation. In 1903, he established the journal *Indian Opinion*, which—as Isabel Hofmeyr argues—served as a space for nurturing different modes of community and subjectivity through "slow" practices of reading. Slowness, for Gandhi, functioned as an ethical counter to the acceleration of modern capitalist society.[59] In 1904, he established the first of a series of famous retreats or ashrams, the Phoenix Settlement outside of Durban, where he practiced collective forms of work, prayer, and service with family and followers. After the tabling of the Asiatic Registration Act in 1906, Gandhi again assumed leadership of the opposition, but this time he departed from his earlier legalistic methods by refusing to comply with the measure. The resulting struggle, which ebbed and flowed until Gandhi's departure in 1914, witnessed definitive moments in his biography and South African history: Gandhi's first imprisonment, the public burning of the hated registration cards, the entrance of women into the struggle in opposition to the Supreme Court's invalidation of Indian marriages, the famous march from New Castle to the Transvaal in defiance of provincial travel bans, and the 1913 strikes of Natal's coal and cane workers.[60]

The great philosophical breakthrough of Gandhi's South African years was the development of satyagraha. Adapted from a suggestion sent in by a reader of *Indian Opinion*, this term was used by Gandhi to differentiate the strategy of his campaign from the more circumscribed (and English-language) concept of passive resistance.[61] Satyagraha combines the Sanskrit words for "truth" and "endurance." Gandhi also glossed the concept as "truth force." (Martin Luther King Jr. would later speak of "soul force."[62]) In contrast to passive resistance, satyagraha is less a specific political tactic than a set of guiding principles that define the success of struggle: persistence in the face of suffering, absolute nonviolence, and the transformation—rather than the coercion—of the oppressor. Requiring inner discipline and intense spiritual preparation, satyagraha could assume varying forms in practice, including refusal to submit to unjust laws, fasting, economic boycotts, mass political mobilization, and creating alternative communities and institutions. The unifying thread of these different actions was the active subordination of self to the pursuit of justice and divine truth. Sidestepping the assumed community of deliberative reason, satyagraha insists on the recognition of common humanity by placing the suffering and vulnerable life of the satyagrahi in the hands of his or her opponent. Whether the object of protest accepts this responsibility or (generally) not, the opponent becomes a custodian of the other's wellbeing. Consequently, there exists an enormous potential for violence in satyagraha, but it is a violence shouldered by the satyagrahi in the service of a higher purpose. Most radically, satyagraha entails a conception of struggle as the deepening of the ethical relationship between the two contending parties.[63] These ideas—especially Gandhi's emphasis on sacrifice, his critique of materialism, and the idea of struggle as spiritual conversion—would later interact and combine with the Christian traditions that nourished the intellectual life of the ANC.

Gandhi's South African career remains engulfed in controversy. These debates center on two related questions. First, during his time in South Africa, Gandhi remained loyal to Britain and repeatedly defined his political goals in terms of the achievement of equal rights for

South African Indians. To prove Indian fidelity, he mobilized a volunteer ambulance core to care for British soldiers during the 1899–1902 war between the Crown and the Afrikaner republics. When a section of the Zulu people rebelled against a colonial poll tax in 1906 under the leadership of Chief Bambatha kaMancinza, Gandhi once again offered his services by mobilizing an ambulance contingent. (In this case, he found himself caring for Africans who had been left to die after British troops butchered villages. He described these events as "No war but a man hunt."[64]) Given his later status as the most globally recognized icon of anticolonialism, his early career invites accusations of hypocrisy. Desai and Vahed subtitle their searching exploration of these years "Stretcher-Bearer of Empire."[65]

Second, not only do Gandhi's South African writings describe Africans in racialized and pejorative terms (especially by utilizing the epithet kaffir), they also stress the danger of Indians sinking to the levels of "Natives." Describing his first stint in prison, Gandhi writes: "We were then marched off to prison intended for Kaffirs. . . . We could understand not being classed with the whites, but to be placed at the same level of the Natives seemed too much to be put up with. It is indubitably right that the Indians should have separate cells. Kaffirs are as a rule uncivilized—the convicts even more so. They are troublesome, very dirty and live almost like animals."[66] Statements like this were not simply expressions of common prejudice. Because Gandhi rejected an alliance with Africans, his struggle to obtain rights for Indians as British subjects endorsed the colonial racial order: the "uncivilized" Native served as a common boundary that aligned Indianness with empire.[67] It is also true that Gandhi moderated and, after he returned to India and embraced a more radical anticolonial position, eventually discarded these views. At moments in his South African writings, he praised individual Africans, most notably his neighbor John Dube, and imagined a far distant future when a new nation would arise from blacks, Indians, and whites.[68] By the end of his life, he lent his considerable authority to a younger faction in South African Indian politics that sought a strategic rapprochement with the ANC. Nor were such racial views unique to Gandhi or his Indian peers. As Franco Barchiesi demonstrates, the early leaders of the ANC expressed similar sentiments about the "ruck of the native," reflecting their embrace of liberal empire and a politics of inclusion within settler civil society.[69] Be that as it may, Gandhi's outlook helped to cement a conservative tradition in diasporic politics and a rhetoric of Indian civilizational superiority that long survived his departure.

Following Gandhi's return to India in 1914, the Natal Indian Congress persisted as a small organization, composed mostly of passengers and their descendants, and dedicated to advocacy regarding issues that affected the Indian middle class. When a younger generation won control of the Indian Congress in the early 1940s, these activists seized on Gandhi's time in South Africa—which since had been invested with the prestige of the Indian independence struggle—as a legacy to be appropriated and reinvented.[70] Known as the "Radicals," this group consisted of South African–born professionals and working-class militants, many of whom were drawn into politics by the Communist Party. It eventually included the dashing Communist and proudly Muslim physician Yusuf Dadoo, the avowed Gandhian "Monty" Naicker, the trade union stalwart and socialist H. A. Naidoo, the courageous medical student Zainab Asvat, and the intellectual firebrand Fatima Meer, among many others. Some of these activists possessed childhood memories of Gandhi's campaigns or grew up listening to their parents' stories about the Mahatma. Nevertheless, they appropriated and reworked his legacy for a politics inspired by Nehru, the Indian independence struggle, and (in some cases) the party. Under Nehru's influence and the pressure of events, this group drew the far-reaching conclusion that the struggle of South African Indians could only succeed as part of a broad alliance led by the ANC. This stance required surmounting the fears, racial prejudices, and structural insecurity of their immediate families and broader communities. Especially after the 1949 Durban Riots, they faced significant opposition from other organizations as well as many working-class and poorer Indians.[71] Although they are not the focus of this book, the Radicals appear frequently in its pages. They played an irreplaceable part in the developments that it charts.

POSTCOLONIAL INTELLECTUAL HISTORY

As a history of ideas and intellectuals, *Internal Frontiers* contributes to the broader project of decolonizing and globalizing political theory. Its main goal is to explore new modes of thought that emerged from the struggle against colonialism and apartheid. In this respect, this book is part of a growing literature of postcolonial intellectual history that has begun to elaborate the implications of Third World nationalism and decolonization—central experiences of the twentieth century by any account—for our understandings of foundational philosophical concepts such as sovereignty, nation, citizenship, ethics, civil society, and alterity. Drawing on the pioneering efforts of Edward Said and Sylvia Wynter (among others), this scholarship insists that the long, many-faceted battle to assert the dignity and equality of the "darker nations"—the majority of the human race—could not fail to transform our understanding of the political in far-reaching ways.[72] At the same time, *Internal Frontiers* adopts a different approach from some recent studies of intellectuals such as Gandhi, Fanon, and B. R. Ambedkar. Grounded in a close reading of texts, these accounts reconstruct the normative arguments of anticolonial figures to demonstrate that they were not only political actors, but important thinkers in their own right. As Hamid Dabashi argues in a key programmatic statement, a powerful set of discourses continues to deny the existence of meaningful philosophical production beyond the West. The "non-European" remains the perpetual object of historical, biographical, or ethnographic analysis—never the universal subject of a truly revolutionary mode of thought.[73] While postcolonial intellectual history challenges this positioning in significant fashions, it frequently replicates the mode of "high theory" that remains dominant within the Euro-American university. By reducing intellectual production to a written corpus, the historian can distill a series of arguments that mimic the form of Western political philosophy: disembodied, textually based, and universalizing. At its worse, intellectual history adopts a practice of cultural brokering. After rendering the anticolonial intellectual a "theorist," the historian then validates the figure's standing (and by implication his or her own) through a critical dialogue with pillars of the Western canon, whether John Locke or Michel Foucault.[74]

Individual thinkers populate this book. Nevertheless, *Internal Frontiers* returns to the grounds of their thinking: their families and others that they loved; their circles of collaborators; the branches and committees of their political organizations; the cities where they lived, traveled, and worked; the structures of race, class, and gender that generated the social field of their everyday experiences; and the institutional and ideological frameworks of white supremacy that they fought. The purpose of this reconstruction is not the saturation of thought with biographical or empirical context. Far more than is often realized, intellectuals such as Lembede and Luthuli drew on Western political theory to articulate universalizing claims even as they critiqued the form of abstract reason that characterized secular politics. Rather, this attentiveness to personal and social terrains reflects the fact that the work of thinking always remains open to and interwoven with its outside.[75] At another level, this approach attends to the specific character of philosophical practice that developed within the antiapartheid struggle of the 1950s. The intellectual and aesthetic labors of African thinkers—and a central argument of this book is that these modes are indissociably linked— were instruments for sustaining a resistance movement and building a new form of national community. This living community, rather than a master text or a new articulation of universalism, was the true medium of African nationalist thought.[76]

The most important space for the elaboration of this project was the commercial African press of the 1950s. These publications, written in English and African languages, play a central part in this book. They are both significant protagonists and the stage on which much of the drama takes place.[77] As Ntongela Masilela observes: "The real intellectual history of South Africa is predominantly traceable through newspapers."[78] Although the ANC lacked a national paper during this period, three major African publications—*Bantu World*, *Ilanga lase Natal*, and *Inkundla ya Bantu*—were edited by influential members of the ANC. Two of these editors were members of the Natal ANC Youth League: Ngubane ran *Inkundla* and H. I. E. Dhlomo oversaw *Ilanga* with his brother Ralph.[79] If editorial lines generally followed their personal convictions, these individuals were proud professional newsmen and opened their pages to articles about (and by) the major factions in black politics. The press not only provided a forum for intellectual debates, it allowed grassroots followers of the ANC, Unity Movement, the Communist Party, and Indian Congress to evaluate and publically respond to the policies of their own and other organizations. This openness also reflected a particular understanding of the newspaper's function. In the absence of institutions controlled by black South Africans, newspapers served as something like makeshift governments: they stood in for missing schools, national representative institutions, even health departments.[80] As this book argues, the ANC became increasingly media conscious during the 1952 Defiance

Campaign and its depiction by the black press—especially the legendary lifestyle magazine *Drum*—contributed to the development of a new aesthetic of political struggle that celebrated the cosmopolitanism of urban South Africa, especially Johannesburg. Once intellectuals such as H. I. E. Dhlomo and Luthuli became aware of local reworkings of this aesthetic, they drew a significant conclusion: a shared symbolism could help unite an otherwise heterogeneous people if it created space for different groups to write *themselves* into an unfolding national narrative.

AFRICAN NATIONALISM AND NONRACIALISM

Internal Frontiers reconstructs the debates over two questions—the place of the Indian diaspora in South Africa and the postwar reconfiguration of African nationalism—and describes when their intersection became central to the development of the ANC. This book is therefore neither a linear narrative of the liberation struggle nor a comprehensive treatment of the diverse (and very different) contributions of Indian South Africans. Occasionally, canonical people and events are passed over lightly. "Minor" figures sometimes take center stage. Through telling the story of how the "Indian question" became central to the organizational structure of antiapartheid politics and the broader culture of resistance, *Internal Frontiers* argues that the problem of the also-colonized other drove the ANC's formulation of an inclusive, *African* nationalism. This understanding of nation, articulated by Luthuli on his election to the ANC presidency in 1952, became a major intellectual current within the organization and, perhaps as importantly, reinforced the emergence of a political culture organized around a powerful symbolic politics, which I call "symbolic constitutionalism." Based on participation "from below" and affective communities nurtured in struggle, this culture generated a new aesthetic of nationhood: the struggle itself provided the image of a multiracial African nation that affirmed the claims of each group to belonging. In direct opposition to apartheid's discourse of "separateness" and its fantasy of coherent racial subjects, this imagery located heterogeneity, entanglement, and an asymmetrical form of reciprocity at the center of a shared identity. Luthuli and his co-thinkers, the Natal Group, developed their interpretation of African nationalism through their defense of the African-Indian alliance of the early 1950s and the experience of solidarity during the 1952 Defiance Campaign. They subsequently generalized from the relationship with the also-colonized other to an ethics of nationhood that presupposed recognition and negotiation across multiple forms of difference. In other words, they attempted to leave the internal frontier open by enfolding alterity within the conceptualization of the nation form.

Most accounts of the antiapartheid struggle during the 1950s focus on one of two developments. The first involves Mandela and the Communist Party. After recognizing the strategic importance of African nationalism, party members within the ANC and Indian Congress played a major role in championing non-European cooperation as well as the alliance between the ANC and left-wing whites organized in the Congress of Democrats.[81] Perhaps the only organization in South Africa where whites and blacks could meet on equal terms, the party attracted a key group of younger African nationalists, including Walter Sisulu and Mandela, and helped break this group from an exclusionary Africanist ideology. During this same period, the party codified an understanding of the national democratic revolution that projected the overthrow of white supremacy by the African majority leading other oppressed groups and progressive whites. This position understood South Africa as composed of one nation, the African majority, and several national minority groups.[82]

The second event was the emergence of the Africanist opposition within the ANC and its split in 1958 to form the Pan Africanist Congress (PAC).[83] Originating as a loose-knit opposition to collaboration with Indians and Communists, the Africanists became a major force in black politics and (in some areas) channeled popular disillusionment with the ANC. The leadership of the PAC, especially the brilliant Robert Mangiliso Sobukwe, believed that the revolutionary struggle of the African oppressed could create a nonracial, Pan-African identity by abolishing the system of white supremacy and replacing it with a democratic government founded on equal rights for individual citizens. This program, however, required mobilizing the explosive anger of the PAC's grassroots supporters—a rage which often expressed itself as explicitly anti-Indian and antiwhite—in the service of a revolution that would somehow transform their collective racial consciousness.[84]

These stories intersect *Internal Frontiers*'s narrative at several turns. However, they concern people and events that were centered in the

Transvaal and, when juxtaposed, frame this period in terms of the opposition between the Communist Party's "nonracialism" and the PAC's Africanism. In contrast, this book moves back and forth between Johannesburg and Durban and includes a wider cast of characters. Its focus is a group of African intellectuals in Natal who simultaneously remained outside of the Communist Party and opposed the strategy of the Africanists. Originating in Durban student circles during the early 1940s, this group included Lembede (the Philosopher), H. I. E. Dhlomo (the Poet), Jordan Ngubane (the News Man and Publicist), and M. B. Yengwa (the Organizer). Known among themselves as *ibandla* (the historical term for the council of the Zulu king's advisiors), they were instrumental in the election of Luthuli (the Liberation Theologian) to the Natal ANC presidency in 1951.[85] At some point in their careers, the writings or statements of each of these individuals reflected anti-Indian resentments and stereotypes. They also struggled against this form of racialism: in their communities, inside the ANC, and personally. In arguing for the centrality of the Natal Group to the intellectual evolution of the ANC, *Internal Frontiers* suggests that the most significant debates of this period occurred *within* the ANC between different interpretations of African nationalism.

The reassertion that the ANC was first and foremost an African nationalist organization represents a departure from another current of scholarship: the narration of the antiapartheid struggle in terms of the development of nonracialism.[86] A major focus of postapartheid debates over South African identity, nonracialism is an unstable and much contested term. Dependent on the protean concept of "race," it has been claimed for multiple agendas, including the liberal project of race-neutral laws and institutions, a radical vision of transcending race through nation building, and the Marxist program of working-class solidarity.[87] An important tradition describes the ANC's ideological evolution in terms of the development and then gradual extension of nonracialism, first through its collaboration with white organizations (most importantly the Communist Party) and later through its admission of non-African members at the 1969 Morogoro conference. In another context, I argue that this narrative is anachronistic.[88] In the early 1960s, some ANC leaders, including Luthuli and Mandela, adopted the phrase "non-racial democracy" to express their support for the constitutional principles of equal protection and individual (rather than group) rights. However, it was only later—especially during the Mass Democratic Movement of the 1980s—that the idea of nonracialism became virtually synonymous with the ANC's vision of nation.[89] At the time of its banning in April 1960, the ANC possessed several competing philosophies of nationalism: the Natal Group's ethical vision of a multiracial African nation, the Transvaal Leadership's majoritarian nationalism based on an African-led struggle for power, the liberalism of an older generation of intellectuals such as Z. K. Mathews, the Federation of South African Women's appeal to shared women's experiences, as well as more racialist forms of Africanism. The postapartheid focus on the origins of nonracialism, however it is defined, not only compresses this series of complex (and largely unresolved) discussions into an evolutionary narrative, it obscures the central question debated by the ANC during the 1940s and '50s: What understanding of the *African* political subject could escape the racial logic of a classic, majoritarian nationalism?

BOOK STRUCTURE AND CHAPTER SUMMARIES

This book is divided into three sections composed of two chapters each. The first section explores the ramifications of the Second World War and Indian independence on African politics at local and international levels. Accelerated by wartime industrialization, the large-scale migration of Africans to urban areas propelled growing political militancy and working-class resistance that contributed to the revitalization of organized African politics. While these developments encouraged the proliferation of popular nationalisms and millenarian aspirations throughout South Africa, Durban witnessed a distinctive pattern of urbanization: most Africans entered the city illegally and survived through an ad hoc infrastructure of housing, transport, and stores provided by (generally poor) Indians. Prejudice and local conflicts between Indians and Africans certainly preexisted these developments. However, this pattern of African migration—and the resulting organization of urban space—created the conditions for the generalization of local racial dynamics and the emergence of populist resentment against the alleged domination of "Indian over African." In contrast to other South African cities, where African-Indian conflict generally remained confined to specific neighborhoods, anti-Indian populism developed into a powerful force on a city-wide and provincial scale. Chapter 1 explores the consolidation of this binary "African-Indian" racial discourse and the methodological problems of writing about race in contexts where a variety of social relationships either traverse or simply ignore the racial scripts that dominate popular imagination.

Coinciding with these developments, the foundation of the United Nations and Indian independence created a global context for the reimagination of South Africa after the end of empire. Chapter 2 describes how intellectuals within the ANC, represented by Xuma and Lembede, began to reorient African nationalism within the newly emerging international order. These efforts were informed, directly and indirectly, by a new generation of South African Indian activists, the Radicals, who seized control of the Indian Congress in the mid-1940s. In 1946, the Radicals launched a mass campaign of nonviolent civil disobedience. Invoking the Indian independence struggle (they carried the flag of the Indian National Congress on demonstrations), the Radicals sought to utilize India's growing influence in world affairs to pressure the South African government. At the campaign's height—which saw tens of thousands join protests and vigilante retaliation by racist whites—India brought a case against the Smuts government in the United Nation's general assembly, internationalizing the debate over South Africa's racial policies. Simultaneously, the Radicals pursued an alliance with African political organizations, especially the ANC and black trade unions. Their entry into the political field transformed the ANC's relationship with the Indian Congress—and the ANC's position on the status of Indians in South Africa—into a matter of national and international political significance. The election of the Nationalist Party in 1948, which slandered Indians as "alien" and considered their expulsion, further underscored the urgency of a common front.

This series of rapid developments intersected a parallel set of discussions. In the early 1940s, the founding of the Cape Town–based Non-European Unity Movement (NEUM) forced a debate over the relationship between the existing African, Indian, and Coloured political organizations. In response to the NEUM's proposals for "unity," Xuma (who was supported by the Communist Party) advocated a more limited conception of cooperation between racially defined parties. In turn, ANC Youth League intellectuals, particularly Lembede, rejected all but the most limited collaboration with Indians, arguing that "they" were "foreign exploiters" who sought to manipulate Africans for their own ends. Acutely sensitive to popular resentments, the Natal ANC leadership echoed Lembede's position and argued that the strained relationship between the two groups rendered an alliance impracticable. The ensuing controversy raised fundamental questions about the nature of the struggle. Did the separate political parties imply that non-European groups were distinct nations and therefore possessed unique claims to group representation within a democratic state? What was the relationship between party structure and the political subject of the liberation struggle? Did national boundaries correspond with the "common sense" racial categories of South African society, or were the ideas of race and nation irreconcilable in principle? After 1948, the significance of these questions was underscored by the fact that the apartheid regime legitimated its segregationist ambitions on the basis of an ethno-nationalist appeal to white self-determination. The Afrikaner Nationalist rhetoric of "separation" saturated the discursive space of politics and provoked competing (and sometimes conflicting) rejoinders of South African unity. In this context, the Indian became the focal point for a reconsideration of the idea of nation. Were Indians foreigners, immigrants, or South Africans—and, if they were South African, what was the basis for their inclusion within this entity? In translating diaspora into the categories of the nation-state, these responses invoked different criteria of nationhood (racial, cultural, political, and legal-juridical) and generated competing visions of political community.

The second section focuses on two events that interrupted these debates and challenged the majoritarian basis of anticolonial nationalism: the Partition of India and Pakistan and the 1949 Durban Riots. Partition severely damaged the credibility of the Indian National Congress, especially Nehru, and prompted some African intellectuals to begin reflecting on the dangers of the claim to popular sovereignty based on majority rule. Situated across the newsprint page from the postwar refugee crisis in Europe, the creation of Israel, and the victory of the National Party, Partition was as much a global moment as a singular event: it revealed the dangers inherent to the demand for national self-determination within multiracial or multinational territories. Less than a year after Gandhi's murder in the midst of ongoing communal violence, Partition was followed by another rupture: the 1949 Durban Riots. Prompted by a clash between a shopkeeper and boy in Durban's

Grey Street area, a melee among Indian and African men escalated into two days of attacks directed against Indians and their property. Chapter 3 explores the ways that this violence polarized African public opinion and generated an unprecedented crisis in the ANC, leading to the downfalls of both Xuma and Natal president A. W. G. Champion. In the Riots' aftermath, a diverse group of intellectuals within the ANC—including Luthuli, Ngubane, and Youth League leader A. P. Mda—experienced a genuine crisis of conscience and began to rethink the relationship between African nationalism and a broader South African identity. Although they differed considerably in outlook, these thinkers rejected a racial definition of national community (Mda denounced what he called African "fascism") and created a space for the conceptualization of the national subject as simultaneously singular and multiple. In the following decade, these arguments would inform a larger set of discussions about the constitutional structure of a postapartheid government, the character of a future national culture, and the relationship between the Union of South Africa and the African continent.

Chapter 4 uses the Riots to explore the role of gender and interracial sex in structuring Natal's African-Indian dynamics. As Philip Bonner observes, the dominant culture within the ANC understood the national as a masculine domain and located women within the terrain of local politics.[90] This national public was also constructed around the use of English, while provincial political life largely transpired in vernacular languages. (This fact allowed Indians and whites, who rarely spoke vernacular languages, to participate in national African politics without necessarily transforming their relationship to African cultural and social life.) As a result, gender, the vernacular, and the "local"—which sometimes occupied the same physical space as the "national"—each became associated with the disruptive effects of African-Indian racial dynamics on the ANC's construction of the nation. A frequent complaint raised by African men in Durban during this period (particularly in the isiZulu-language pages of black newspapers) was the "Indian peril": purported sexual predation against African women. This allegation underscored the gendered character of urban space and the perceived absence of social reciprocity. According to this discourse, Indian men mixed freely with Africans in buses, movie theaters, and jazz concerts—where they "seduced" African women, often urbanized professionals—while Indian women remained isolated within the temple, mosque, or home. Simultaneously, the Indian woman became the central icon of a cultural discourse that circulated between colonial sources, diasporic versions of Indian nationalism, liberal social science, and African stereotypes. These "citings/sitings" (to use Burton's evocative coinage) of gender and race both underwrote and troubled the ideas of nation that are the focus of this book.[91]

The third section explores the transformation of the ANC following the 1949 Riots. Chapter 5 focuses on a pivotal event: the 1952 Defiance Campaign, the first mass mobilization of Indians and Africans together. Near the end of the campaign, ANC leaders called for the creation of a white organization (the Congress of Democrats) to work with the other two groups, generalizing the form of its partnership with the Indian Congress and laying the foundations for a new political formation, the Congress Alliance. Drawing on the earlier symbols, slogans, and iconography of the ANC, the Defiance Campaign generated—to invoke the philosopher Jacques Rancière—an aesthetic of struggle: a "redistribution of the sensible" that made visible new political possibilities and therefore facilitated the emergence of unanticipated identifications.[92] The Congress Alliance provided the image of a single, united South Africa in which each "section" (alliance leaders generally avoided the terms "majority" and "minority") possessed a claim to belonging. In other words, the principles of national unity and racial multiplicity were reconciled at the level of political symbolism. While this imagery developed organically, ANC leaders, especially Luthuli, soon began to reflect on this process and strategize the aesthetic dimensions of the antiapartheid struggle. On the basis of these experiences, Luthuli (now the president of the ANC) formulated a philosophy of African nationalism that rejected a materialist foundation of politics, especially the liberal claim that democracy presupposed social homogeneity based in a common civil society. Reworking earlier contributions by Lembede, Ngubane, and H. I. E. Dhlomo, Luthuli's ideas developed in active collaboration with a group within the Natal ANC (including Ngubane and Dhlomo) and represented a distinct Natal synthesis of African nationalist thought.

Chapter 6 reconstructs the Natal synthesis and Luthuli's struggles to defend it against other currents within the ANC, namely an insurrectionist African nationalism associated with the Transvaal-based leadership and the Cold War anticommunism of Luthuli's erstwhile friend and collaborator, Ngubane. The Natal synthesis envisioned nation as a plural political subject that would emerge through the struggle for universal values. The result was a layered conception of nationalism. African nation building, embodied in the ANC, could exist side-by-side with the struggles of other peoples. Together, they could fold into a broader South African identity. Because African nationalism was already a pluralistic identity, incorporating multiple groups in the pursuit of a greater ideal, it could open itself to others without endangering its essential unity. In isiZulu, Luthuli expressed this idea in terms of a nation composed of many nations: "kulelizwe siyizizwe eziningi." At several points, he stated that it represented Africa's most significant contribution to human culture. Luthuli's ideas, and his promotion of symbolism as an instrument of articulating unity in heterogeneity, had a significant impact on the ANC's broader political culture, especially through the celebration of 26 June ("Freedom Day") and the campaign for the 1955 Congress of the People. By the mid-1950s, however, Luthuli found himself defending his philosophy on two fronts. On the one hand, he led a factional battle against proposals, embodied in the so-called Tambo constitution, to centralize the ANC and to adopt the Freedom Charter as the basis for cooperation with other groups. On the other hand, he conducted a public fight against Ngubane over the role of the Communist Party within the ANC. In both cases, the debate over the African political subject—and its relationship to the also-colonized other—became entangled with the global imaginary of the Cold War.

Internal Frontiers concludes with an epilogue that considers the long-term influence of Luthuli's ideas within the ANC. Despite its popularization through Luthuli's presidency, the Natal synthesis was only one of several competing formulations of African nationalism. At the same time, Luthuli either introduced or reworked ideas that would become more widely influential: the centrality of ideals to nation building, the importance of symbolic politics and popular participation in rituals of nation, and (most importantly) the constructive role of African nationalism in creating a broader South African identity. Although they rejected many of his philosophical assumptions, both the Pan-Africanism of Sobukwe and the Communist Party's concept of the "national democratic revolution" incorporated elements of the Natal synthesis, especially the production of a common identity through the African liberation struggle. The ANC's launch of sabotage in 1961, and the Communist Party's growing influence within the ANC in exile, resulted in the eclipse of the Natal synthesis by a more traditional, majoritarian conception of nationalism. Despite this fact, the ANC incorporated Luthuli into a narrative of its history organized around major figures (especially presidents) and "stages" of struggle. Even if represented as surpassed, earlier leaders functioned as symbols of tactics and values that remained part of a living Congress tradition. At key moments during the Mass Democratic Movement of the 1980s and early 1990s transition, ANC leaders drew on the political aesthetic of the Congress Alliance and revivified elements of the Natal synthesis.

~

In his memoir, the antiapartheid activist Ismail Meer recalls a day he spent with Lembede shortly before the philosopher unexpectedly died at the age of thirty-three. After walking through Johannesburg, Meer took Lembede to see the library at Wits University. Lembede, who had earned two advanced degrees by correspondence, physically trembled at the site of the books. "This is what the bastards have kept from me," he exhaled.[93] The two young men proceeded to Orient House, where they shared a lunch of curry cooked by the charming Amina Pahad, whose imprisonment in the 1946 Passive Resistance Campaign helped shatter Mandela's belief that Indians were incapable of struggle.[94] Lembede later wrote a letter thanking Meer: "The day was full of wonders, but what moved me most was to see all of you eating with your fingers." He then claimed this experience as his own: "Unless we respect our own culture we will never be able to respect ourselves and we will never be free."[95]

The individuals discussed in this book are often described as elite. In some respects, they merit this designation. Their education, literacy, facility with Western languages, urban status, and social position differentiated them from most other black South Africans. The main figures of this book also enjoyed the privileges of masculinity in a decidedly patriarchal world. But an adequate treatment of their careers must also capture the insecurity, poverty, family worries, confrontations with subtle and brute racism, and genuine vulnerability to violence that permeated each day of their lives. Despite many advantages, they lived in black working-class and rural communities, participated in their struggles, and suffered their strangulation by the apartheid regime. They saw their most important work as the distillation of these experiences into a new philosophy of nation. Ultimately, it is the dialectic between a group of extraordinary, if flawed, thinkers and the lives of their complex, multiracial, and deeply divided communities that this book strives to recover.

PART ONE

1 ⤳ The Racial Crucible

Economy, Stereotype, and Urban Space in Durban

In Durban itself Indian women are distinctive in vivid saris; mosques and temples break the line of colonial architecture with minarets and domes adorned with statues of the Hindu pantheon; shops are stocked with silk, brassware and spices; in the 'Indian markets', which are among Durban's main tourist attractions, stalls are crammed with oriental jewelry and trinketry, with a variety of lentils, rice, beans and oils, with betel leaf and areca nut, lime, camphor, incense sticks, with currie powders, masala, all kinds of fruits and herbs, as well as with more familiar goods which themselves become unfamiliar in the excited atmosphere of oriental bargaining.[1]

—Hilda Kuper

Now Indians, as you are aware, were the shop keepers of the time, they provided transport, they provided land so Africans were literally helpless. Now this brought about a situation that when an African wrongly boarded a bus and wanted to jump off, invariably he was assaulted and murdered and the Africans couldn't do anything about it: the shops belonged to the Indians, the very land on which they lived belonged to the Indians.[2]

—C. C. Majola

IN THE years following the First World War, the rapid and large-scale urbanization of Africans and Indians permanently transformed the social landscape of Durban and other cities in Natal. The expansion of secondary industry created new prospects for employment, especially for former indentured laborers who left the countryside in ever-growing numbers. The same period witnessed a protracted crisis in the "Native Reserves" — the desultory fragments of the Zulu kingdom maintained by the colonial state as labor reservoirs. Land shortages, population growth, overstocking of cattle, intermittent years of severe drought, and taxes imposed by the colonial state encouraged an exodus of Africans. These were (mostly) young men who lived in the backyards of white and Indian households or government-controlled hostels, or found rooms in the shack lands that began to surround Durban and other cities. The social and political consequences of the "African industrial revolution" dominated the first half of the twentieth century: the rise of Indian and African labor unions, the emergence and radicalization of mass-based nationalist organizations, and the new system of racial governance implemented by the Afrikaner Nationalist regime under the slogan "apartheid." Yet historians have generally analyzed the urbanization of Indians and Africans in parallel—as largely distinct stories of racial groups, occasionally intersecting in the form of political cooperation or social conflict.[3] These two processes were interwoven in the details and patterns of urban life, conditioning and transforming the other on multiple levels. To paraphrase E. P. Thompson's famous discussion of class, relationships precede identities.[4] In order to understand Natal's racial politics, we must analyze the concrete social conditions that integrated Zulu-speaking migrants and Indians of differing class, linguistic, and religious backgrounds into a common urban landscape.

The image of the apartheid city continues to exercise considerable power over the imagination of South Africa's historians. Since most of the writing on urban history concerns the origins of racial segregation and institutionalized white supremacy, historians have often neglected those aspects of the pre-1948 city (or, more accurately, the city before the forced removals of the late 1950s and early 1960s) that succumbed to later developments.[5] At its height, the apartheid city boasted large-scale, systematically planned, and clearly demarcated residential segregation between white, African, Indian, and Coloured areas. Although significant regional variations existed, the apartheid regime succeeded in enforcing a strong correlation between race and class, particularly in the larger cities. Most of the industrial working class was African; Indians made up a "middle group" of businessmen, professionals, and skilled workers situated between white and black. The apartheid regime sought to secure the correspondence of race and space (in terms of both social and geographical segregation), although the economy's dependence on African labor ultimately made this goal unrealizable.[6]

Little of this picture held true for Durban before the forced removals of late 1950s. Although a clear pattern of segregation had emerged between white and Indian areas by the close of the nineteenth century, the growth of African and Indian neighborhoods in later decades followed a different logic. The city of Durban established municipal housing for workers at locations like Lamontville and Magazine Barracks, but these provisions were inadequate for the scale of urban migration. By the 1930s, the Durban Commission reported the growth of a "black belt" around the city: a network of racially mixed shack settlements and sprawling, working-class neighborhoods.[7] In areas largely outside of municipal control, the poor of all races (including a small number of whites) utilized buses, stores, and housing in large part established or owned by Indians.[8] When Africans complained bitterly about the "color bar" in these areas, they were referring to their treatment in local stores and exclusion from Indian community institutions. Indians and Africans of all classes lived among and adjacent to one another, shopped at the same stores, and rode on the same buses. To the extent that segregation existed in the black belt, it was imposed and policed through institutions erected by the inhabitants themselves.

This chapter has two principle goals. First, it provides the background necessary to understand how Durban's racial dynamics came to play a decisive role in the reorientation of African politics during the late 1940s and early 1950s. Indeed, the city itself functioned as a central protagonist in the larger story of African nationalism during this period. Other South African cities, including Johannesburg and Cape Town, possessed economically and politically significant Indian communities. Durban was distinctive, however, in both the size of its Indian population—people of South Asian descent were still the single largest group in 1951—and the nature of the spatial regime that developed during the interwar years. As new African migrants rapidly outstripped the housing and other amenities provided by the municipal government, they turned to the informal sector, especially stores, transport, and land owned and operated by Indian families. This ersatz infrastructure not only supported most of the new population, it integrated the two groups into a hierarchical relationship of "Indian" over "African" that transcended neighborhood dynamics and operated on the scale of the city. Symbolized by the picturesque and centrally located Grey Street complex, this hierarchy provided the basis for a powerful discourse of

"Indian domination" that connected the antagonisms of multiple, and sometimes very different, sites around the image of the merchant. If stereotypes regarding Indians were common across southern and eastern Africa, they usually represented one element of a complex and motile urban reality whose predominant feature was white domination. In Durban, things worked differently. By the mid-1940s, the polarization between the two colonized and disenfranchised populations was a defining, if not the definitive, fact of social life.

Second, this chapter suggests a way of analyzing Durban's racial polarization that resists, however paradoxical it might seem at first, endowing the categories of "Indian" and "African" with political or sociological coherence. Whatever its basis in a specific urban geography, the antagonism between Indian and African became generalized through the work of discourse. Outside of structures of representation, racial groups do not exist as collective agents: individuals and factions *claim* to embody racial or national totalities as a strategy for mobilizing sections of populations. Consequently, racial conflict can coexist—indeed, it always coexists—with social formations and relationships organized according to other categories and logics. If an Indian-owned infrastructure instantiated the hierarchy of "brown over black," this hierarchy was haphazard and rested on local foundations whose dynamics varied considerably.[9] Alongside depersonalized (and depersonalizing) interactions in buses and shops, more familiar and sometimes intimate relationships developed: between doctors and patients, landlords and tenants, friends, neighbors, coworkers, and lovers. When younger activists from the ANC and Indian Congress began to grapple with the question of African-Indian political cooperation in the mid-1940s, they confronted a polarized terrain of distinct organizations and identities, which they knew from their own lives did not express the complexity of race in Natal. As later chapters will show, this dilemma would lead them to rethink the relationship between race, political organization, and African nationalism—but only after considerable suffering and loss.

STEREOTYPES, DISCOURSES, AND DESCRIPTIONS

In sources relating to the question of African-Indian social dynamics (newspapers, memoirs, interviews, and government reports), three distinct forms of racial language appear: stereotypes, generalizing discourses, and specific descriptions. All three of these modes are grounded in a racial consciousness that, however much it might incorporate an individual or group's lived experiences, translates social relations into idealized images and, in turn, shapes the field of personal interactions in racial terms. Because these types of language presuppose the existence of coherent groups ("the Indian" and "the African"), they should not be used as direct evidence of an underlying reality: racial language organizes and shapes social life in ways that require historical analysis and explanation. As Sander Gilman argues, stereotypes operate at the level of fantasy.[10] They are images that have broken free from their original context through assimilation into collective identities.[11] Because they are a means of self-definition in terms of an "outsider," they can function in contexts where there is no empirical correspondence between the stereotype and its putative object. A stereotype generally takes the form of a core association—for example, "white South Africans are racist"—accompanied by a cluster of related attributes that are invoked selectively and shift overtime. In most cases, multiple stereotypes exist regarding the same group, allowing racial fantasies to shift between differing, and often contradictory, characterizations without any underlying logic. For a historian, stereotypes serve largely as evidence of the imaginations, desires, and resentments of the individual or group deploying the image, rather than the actual content of racialized interactions.[12]

In contrast, racial discourses are the product of specific socioeconomic contexts. They incorporate stereotypes into narratives that correspond, in however partial and distorted a fashion, with existing social realities. Racial discourses are common stories told about the relationship between groups, although one protagonist (usually the group of the narrator) can remain implicit and therefore invisible in the account. Such stories often relate to specific kinds of spaces—the everyday theaters where the drama of interaction unfolds—or geographic areas. They provide relatively fixed scripts that influence the expectations and behavior of individuals within these sites while molding broader perceptions through their circulation as rumors, jokes, and urban legends.[13] Since racial discourses are organized around the existence of an imagined binary, their basic structure assumes one of two forms: cooperation or conflict, friendship or war. In a very real sense, they form part of the material infrastructure that reproduces social interactions in a racialized form. In turn, the authors of specific descriptions seek to confirm or contest an established racial discourse. These sources recount events (an unusual or exemplary encounter, for instance) in the concrete language of personal experience. Descriptions often contain elements or details that subvert the generalizing terms of racial discourse while employing the same stereotypes. In such cases, specific descriptions do not necessarily provide evidence of a competing discourse. Nor should they serve as the basis for alternative sociological generalization regarding "race relations." They relate events, relationships, or interactions that confirm or disrupt a standard script even as the author continues to perceive the participants and overall context in racial terms.

The most striking aspect of stereotypes regarding Indians was their uniformity. The same basic image appears across much of southern and eastern Africa, despite the varying character of the colonial policies and racial dynamics of different states, regions, and cities. Moreover, the core attributes of this image remained generally stable even as concrete social relationships and their underlying political economies transformed significantly. The "Indian" was synonymous with the "merchant." The principle traits of this figure expressed popular resentments over the reputed practices of shop owners: "dishonest," "crafty," and "exploitative" were common epithets. Correspondingly, this language presupposed an undifferentiated victim of the Indian's machinations, the African, who assumed the opposite characteristics. These were the common, even universal, terms of struggle between moral economies based on different forms of wealth: the honor-based ethos of an agrarian society and a mercantile diaspora's profit-driven reckoning of value.[14] The Indian was not just ethnically foreign, but embodied the increasing power of an alien mode of calculating and distributing wealth.[15] One informant told Leo Kuper in the 1950s: "We cannot compete with Indians in business. Far from it. I don't think we'll ever pitch up to their understanding. Where merchants work it out for us, it's alright."[16] As a figure, the merchant gave phenomenological immediacy to market forces that were capricious and otherwise invisible.

Whatever its origins, once this association was fixed as a stereotype, an enormous range of human behavior—from the thrift of working-class housewives to the international diplomacy of Krishna Menon and Nehru—became legible in terms of a common racial essence. The resulting image lent itself to paranoid and conspiratorial readings of social relationships. If Indians pursued their economic interests through duplicitous means, then acts of friendship, altruism, or solidarity (the distinction scarcely registered) masked their true intentions and therefore, paradoxically, were the most "Indian" forms of deception. Later, the same logic would transform the Indian into a highly visible embodiment of postcolonial (and postapartheid) corruption.[17] By projecting threatening qualities onto the other, the merchant stereotype neutralized the internal conflicts and heterogeneities of urbanizing African society, and therefore provided an alibi for the divisions that troubled political, religious, or cultural nationalist claims to represent a coherent moral community. If we somehow resemble the corruption of the outsider, according to this argument, it is due to the outsider's corrupting influence among us. Even proximity (spatial as well as social) could be recast as a form of infiltration, and therefore served as a confirmation of the Indian's devious nature. This reiteration of distance reflected the most important attribute of the merchant stereotype. No matter how long his or her family had lived in South Africa, the Indian would always remain a foreigner. In popular culture, this image often appeared alongside signifiers of cultural difference: the smell of curry, the sari of the woman shopkeeper, and the intonations of South African Indian English. Several observers of mid-century Durban noted that these associations echoed core tropes of anti-Semitism. The Indian was, according to a common saying, the Jew of Africa.[18]

Because of its near ubiquitous presence in interviews and sources written by Africans, the merchant stereotype produces something of a false surface. Circulating between editorials and racist jokes, between political speeches and township gossip, this image encouraged many contemporaries (and some later accounts) to postulate a general hostility to Indians and a bifurcated social landscape.[19] Underneath this surface, the reality was considerably more complex. It is important to remember that racial language is, after all, a form of language: a contextually specific act of speech or writing directed toward an audience. The same words could mask opposed attitudes and intentions. In the years following the Durban Riots, H. I. E. Dhlomo and Ngubane wrote a series of articles analyzing the complexity of African-Indian relations and urging closer political cooperation. Nevertheless, these same articles generalized about the Indian in ways that reflected the power of the trader stereotype.[20] In different contexts, this image could express an almost bewildering range of emotions: resentment, fear, jealousy, anger, and humiliation as well as admiration, gratitude, and—of course—desire. The very ambiguity of the stereotype facilitated inversion. Stigmatized characteristics could double as valued traits. Cunning, for example, sometimes transmuted into resourcefulness. Moreover, stereotypes are always inadequate to the complexities of social interactions. Individuals frequently upheld the validity of anti-Indian generalizations while making exceptions in practice.[21] The abstract idea of "amaKula" (the isiZulu calque of "coolie") was not necessarily the same thing as one's neighbor, friend, or coworker. Many Africans employed a Manichean language of enmity. At the same time, they lived in a world composed of complex relationships and subtle negotiations involving multiple groups—racial and otherwise. In some cases, these relationships elude the historian precisely because they were considered unremarkable: they do not appear in sources because they were not translated into the idealized languages of conflict or racial friendship.

More than anything else, the merchant stereotype was a transplant. This language may have originated in the confrontation between the farmer and shopkeeper, but only a minority of Durban Indians were traders of any sort. The majority were former indentured workers who migrated to the areas surrounding the city in the late nineteenth century or early twentieth century. Most were desperately poor and lived near or below substance level.[22] The single largest occupation among Indians was semi-skilled and unskilled industrial labor.[23] Even in later decades, visitors were struck by the size and poverty of the Indian working class. In his memoir *Coolie Location*, Jay Naidoo recalls his first trip to Durban: "I also saw something I had never seen in Pretoria: Indian petrol attendants, Indian refuse collectors, Indian street sweepers—Indians, in sum, doing all the menial tasks which in Pretoria were reserved for Africans."[24] In both popular discussions and the African press, however, the significant class divisions among Indians were generally invisible. On the rare occasions when *Ilanga* and *Inkundla* mentioned poorer Indians, these references served to buttress the overall case against the merchant.[25]

To a considerable degree, this absence reflected the consolidation of a new racial discourse beginning in the late 1930s and early 1940s. Despite ongoing attempts to clearly demarcate white and Indian areas, the Natal state lacked an overall legal or political framework for incorporating the different groups—however they might be defined— into a larger, segregationist order. Settler power and white supremacy were, of course, the bedrocks of social and economic life. However, urban racial hierarchies, especially among non-European populations, developed on a local basis and possessed a makeshift and informal character. The large-scale movement of Africans to Natal's cities began to alter this situation. Crucially, a new racial structure emerged not through the direct actions of the state, but in areas outside of government control created in large part by the decision to relax pass law enforcement during the war. As African migrants arrived in the city, they largely relied on Indian-owned stores, buses, and land to meet basic needs, especially during times of rationing and food shortages. At the same time, the majority of Africans found themselves either excluded from community institutions coded as Indian (like tea rooms, social centers, and most cinemas) or incorporated into common spaces in subordinated roles, for example as domestic workers in Indian households.

In this context, a powerful discourse emerged that stressed the control of the Indian over virtually every aspect of the African's existence. "Now Indians, as you are aware," recalled Kwa-Mashu resident C. C. Majola in 1979, "were the shop keepers of the time, they provided transport, they provided land so Africans were literally helpless."[26] This language fused two scales of phenomena: resentments grounded in the micropolitics of multiple urban sites and a broader image of Indian domination symbolized by Grey Street, the iconic shopping district located at the heart of Durban. As a result, the Indian came to exemplify the dependent position of the African within a series of spaces that governed core aspects of daily life: habitation, transport, work, and consumption. The fact that this discourse integrated experiences that traversed the city's geography resulted in the generalization of local conflicts and facilitated the development of a widespread anti-Indian populism that assumed directly political forms.

PATTERNS OF URBANIZATION

Beginning in the late nineteenth century, a significant Indian presence developed in Natal's cities and the surrounding peri-urban areas.[27] After their contracts had expired, most indentured workers sought to stay in Natal and some managed to lease and acquire land. On the outskirts of the official Durban borough limits, Indian households could participate in the growing economy of the city (through market gardening, fishing, hawking, and various crafts), while remaining largely beyond the reaches of the government. Forty percent of South Africa's Indian population eventually settled in the Durban region and smaller communities grew along the "main line" towns connected by the Durban-Rand railway and near the northern Natal coalfields.[28] As a market developed among indentured and former-indentured workers, a second migration of "passenger" Indians, largely composed of Gujarati merchants and their poorer kin, began to arrive in Natal and the Transvaal in the mid-1870s. Goolam Vahed explains: "The special circumstances of merchants enabled them to keep their social distance from other Indians and identify with India as their home country. The main distinction in Natal was between Gujarati speaking Muslim and higher caste Hindu traders from northern India and Telugu and Tamil speaking indentured Indians from south India."[29] By the 1880s, sections of the Gujarati community had become an outsized power in Indian business and, especially, politics.[30] This layer accumulated a considerable amount of wealth. In Durban and Pietermaritzburg, Indians collectively held property valued at £40,000, including sixty retail shops in Durban and two Indian-owned shipping lines.[31]

The increasing visibility of an urban Indian population coincided with a series of racist campaigns by white South Africans and the implementation of laws directed at controlling Indian movement and economic activity. In 1885 the Transvaal introduced formal segregation for Indian residential areas and the Orange Free State prohibited Indians from owning and occupying land in 1891. At the end of the decade, the mayors of Durban, Pietermaritzburg, and Newcastle petitioned the colonial secretary for a ban on the purchase of land by Indians—although the secretary refused to comply with their request.[32] As Maynard Swanson and others have argued, the Natal ruling class's reaction to the perceived economic, cultural, and demographic threat posed by the Indian resulted in some of the first attempts to segregate urban space. By the late nineteenth century, a combination of legislation (particularly the regulation of trading licenses) and informal coercion had produced "bipolar, spatially juxtaposed European and Indian business districts" in Durban and the creation of Indian residential enclaves throughout Natal.[33] These enclaves, in turn, were often internally organized around close-knit networks of Indian families or linguistic communities.[34]

This early stage of Indian urbanization contrasted with the migration of Africans in two important respects. First, a significant number of Indians managed to purchase land.[35] Along with the growth of Indian business and residential districts, this fact encouraged Indian elites to finance the creation of local community institutions, many of which were organized along linguistic or religious lines: temples, mosques, schools, and social centers.[36] In contrast, the social lives of African migrants centered on municipal beer halls, hostels, dancehalls, and illegal shebeens. Second, Indian areas developed around networks of intimately connected family homes.[37] As Hilda Kuper observes: "A house in an Indian area is never an isolated dwelling; it is integrated into the street, neighborhood, and community. Kinsmen often live near each other, affairs of the neighborhood arouse the gossip that controls the moral standards of the whole area."[38] Although a small number of African women established themselves in Durban as sex workers, brewers, and "shebeen queens," the overwhelming majority of migrants were single men, many of whom maintained close ties with rural society and frequently returned to homesteads in the countryside. Zulu working-class culture developed largely through associations comprised of male migrants. For example, domestic servants organized *amalaita* gangs around stick fighting, crime, defending territories, and distinctive modes of dress. An adaptation of rural youth organizations, these gangs drew on both rural solidarities and an urban criminal subculture.[39] Other important groups included Zionist religious movements and African "buying clubs" and cooperatives.

In Durban and other Natal cities, the division between European and non-European areas developed on the basis of a pattern established by early Indian enclaves.[40] Critically, the legislation that existed before the Group Areas Act (1950) prevented Africans from residing within European residential areas, but generally overlooked the residential penetration of other groups. As the urbanization of both Africans and Indians accelerated, the provisions made by the local government for housing proved inadequate and shack settlements began to encircle the city. The scale and pace of this influx was extraordinary. By 1951, two thirds of Natal's Indian population had either moved to the cities or been born in urban areas.[41] During the same period, the percentage of Africans present in Durban increased threefold.[42] The population of Cato Manor—the famous concentration of shack settlements two miles from the center of Durban—expanded from about 2,500 Africans in 1936 to an estimated 50,000 at the end of 1950.[43] Although census figures from 1951 show that Indians still constituted the largest population in Durban, Africans appeared as a very close second.[44]

Poverty often threw those newly arriving from the countryside together. Africans, Indians, Coloureds, and even some whites lived "cheek-by-jowl"—an ubiquitous term in accounts of this period.[45] Letters to African newspapers occasionally celebrated the fact that urbanization was erasing racial distinctions. In certain areas, there was some truth to this claim. According to a 1952 housing survey by the University of Durban, African residences were relatively evenly distributed throughout Durban (reflecting employment in European households) with the highest concentration in Cato Manor.[46] Although the maps of residential distribution published with the survey show areas of predominantly African habitation (the Chesterville and Lamontville locations), heavy interpenetration of the two groups occurred in several neighborhoods: Cato Manor, Sydenham, Central Durban (the Grey Street area), the South Coast Junction, and to a lesser extent Clairwood. Durban's small Coloured population mostly lived interspersed with Indian families, although a significant number lived in Cato Manor as well.[47] Describing similar conditions faced by Afrikaners in the townships surrounding Ladysmith, Ngubane recalls:

> They [Afrikaners] did not have the money with which to pay for expensive accommodation. As a result they often settled in the cheaper parts of Ladysmith where their neighbours were often either the Africans or the Coloureds or the Indians. . . . The poor Whites discovered that only the poor Blacks were their real allies; they could borrow salt or sugar or food or money from them in the hour of need and did not laugh at them when they saw them sew pieces of hessian inside white calico flour bags to make blankets. The poor Africans, Coloureds and Indians did these things too.[48]

The character of social relations differed between city center and outlying shack settlements, from urban location to urban location, and sometimes from street to street. Each area possessed its own mood and racial texture. The Johannesburg location of Vrederdorp ("Fietas"), although predominantly Indian, included a significant number of Malay, Chinese, and African families, all of whom lived together in rows of tiny houses stretched along narrow lanes. Perceived as an Indian area by most outsiders, the social distinctions between Tamils, poorer Gujaratis, and the Gujarati middle class insured that these groups maintained separate identities within Fietas, undercutting an internal sense of domination by a single race. In this context, individual streets developed the solidarities of an extended family: households shared toilets, women spent their days talking as they worked on adjacent porches, and children grew up together under the neighborhood's watchful eyes. The main social division was between the poor of all races and the largely Gujarati landlords and storeowners of nearby 14th Street, although families ties, shared religious affiliations, sports teams, and patronage bound these two worlds together.[49] Neighborhoods like Cape Town's District Six, Johannesburg's Sophiatown, and (to a lesser extent) the Macabise district of Edendale contained a significant degree of residential integration. The presence of property owners and petit-bourgeois professionals from different groups promoted class tensions within as well as solidarity across racial lines. Beginning in the 1950s, African newspapers and magazines, most notably *Drum*, would develop a popular image of South African cosmopolitanism by celebrating these communities. Idealized by musicians, artists, and writers, spaces such as Sophiatown would provide the imagery and language for a discourse that playfully subverted racial binaries by celebrating a shared style of living within the modern city.[50]

Several Durban neighborhoods, including sections of the Grey Street complex, developed along similar lines. However, Durban differed from other South African cities not only in the size of its Indian population, but in the overall structure of its urban geography. In important respects, the massive shack lands of Cato Manor helped set the overall tone of the city's racial politics. According to one former resident, "Cato Manor was a lifestyle."[51] On the weekends, Africans traveled from across Durban to visit its shebeens, dance, buy dagga, trade in stolen goods, and hire prostitutes. By the 1940s, Cato Manor had developed predominantly African and Indian neighborhoods, with substantial sections of mixed residency interspersed with the more homogenous sections. Largely peopled by migrants and others living illegally in the city, the African section possessed a powerful sense of collective identity articulated, to a considerable degree, against absentee Indian landlords and local traders. In a fashion similar to the Johannesburg township of Alexandra, a bitter rivalry developed between established Indian storeowners and aspirant African merchants, a rivalry intensified by the sentiment among Africans that Mkhumbane (the isiZulu name for Cato Manor) was theirs by right.[52] When journalists or racial populists sought to illustrate a narrative of antagonism between Africans and Indians, they invoked the social conflicts in these or similar areas. (*Bantu World*, for example, published articles on the rivalry between Indian and African traders in Alexandra during the early 1950s as part of its campaign against cooperation with the Indian Congress.) In the Transvaal, such rivalries sometimes simmered for years, occasionally erupting in violence and the looting of stores, but they nevertheless remained confined to specific neighborhoods.[53] Durban, however, was a smaller and more centralized city. If Cato Manor's size, location, and cultural importance insured its broader influence on Durban African politics, the Grey Street complex provided a unifying center that connected—both symbolically and physically—local dynamics that may have otherwise remained discrete.

GREY STREET AND THE INDIAN MERCHANT

The Grey Street complex was located at Durban's center, adjoining the white-owned commercial district and the City Market. Similar, if less spectacular, areas existed in other Natal and Transvaal cities. Visitors to this area were struck by the minarets and colonnades of the buildings, the art deco facades sprinkled with Eastern motifs, the reverberating tones of Indian languages, the saris of women working in shops, and the smells of curries and spices. The area around Grey Street included factories, apartment blocks, and hotels—many owned by Indians. A liberal anthropologist like Hilda Kuper could wax romantic about the excited atmosphere of "oriental" bargaining and the timeless seductions of the marketplace. However, as Omar Badsha underlines, Grey Street was never a purely Indian district.[54] The neighborhood also included the Native Meat Market, the city council–run African "Macheni" beer hall and small stalls, the Native Women's Hostel, several African churches, the Bantu Social Centre (a major site of political and trade union activity), and numerous small eating rooms catering to either (or sometimes both) groups. Because the city's major transport hub was located on Victoria Street next to four major markets, thousands of Africans and Indians passed through the area each day to catch connecting buses. Additionally, many Indian-owned stores employed African men to work as "boys"; that is, as menial laborers. In some descriptions of Grey Street, the sensory mélange of the market place and the blunt give-and-take of urban bustle embodied the spirit of the city.[55] But Grey Street's "Indian" character produced enormous bitterness. For many Africans, its mosques, colonnades, and colorful storefronts became symbols of a foreign people settling in their land and achieving a prosperity denied to them. During the 1949 Riots, for example, a rumor circulated that the severed head of an African boy hung from the dome of the Juma Masjid, the most visible building in the neighborhood.[56]

In fact, Grey Street did serve as a central space where sections of Durban's Indian population monumentalized and celebrated their presence in the city. Religious communities constructed impressive places of worship (the Juma Masjid was the largest mosque in the southern hemisphere), businessmen sponsored community centers and language schools that advertised the importance of their groups (Parsis, a tiny section of the Indian population, owed much of their considerable visibility to building projects such as the Gandhi Memorial Library), and a wide range of cultural and religious associations used its streets for processions. Alongside these performances, Grey Street also provided a venue for conspicuous consumption and highly visible modes of leisure. A self-styled, urbane middle class made Saturday night appearances at legendary jazz clubs such as the Goodwill Lounge, sat ringside at widely hyped boxing matches, or took their "Coloured girlfriends" to exclusive clubs (public displays of romance, especially when combined with "race mixing," were signs of modernity).[57]

The district was also the epicenter of one of Durban's most popular and accessible forms of entertainment: the cinema. Major cultural landmarks that sometimes doubled as meeting halls, Grey Street's six theaters were venues within which a range of people—including Indian women and African youth—nurtured class aspirations and new forms of international awareness. These "bioscopes" were seen as distinctly Indian spaces.[58] The Grey Street complex arose out of efforts to build institutions that manifested the claims of particular groups — religious and linguistic, "traditional" and "modern" — to form part of a larger Indian community. The success of this strategy generated an ironic result: the popular association of the Indian with the wealth of Grey Street and the deliberately cultivated image of an elite.

This image obfuscated enormous disparities of wealth, security, and prestige. After a new generation of Indian activists emerged in the 1940s, several of whom were members of the Communist Party, the term "merchant class" came into increasingly widespread use to describe the most economically successful layer. By clearly demarcating the trader from the proletarian, the concept suggested that political conservatism, racial prejudices, and exploitative practices were the attributes of a small minority, which possessed little in common with the overwhelming majority of Indians. The idea of the "merchant class" functioned as a moral category: it reproduced the content of the trader stereotype while circumscribing its applicability to a small group, characterized in sociological rather than racial terms, and located outside the authentic (that is, working-class) Indian community.

In reality, only a few hundred Indian professionals and businessmen had obtained levels of wealth comparable to their white counterparts by the beginning of the 1960s. C. A. Woods warns: "To the casual onlooker the obvious wealth of some Indian traders with well-established premises and first class fittings and stock is apt to give the wrong idea. The other side of the picture, however, shows many small back street traders whose turnover is probably very low."[59] Most Indian shops in Durban, which were often little more than stalls, operated with rudimentary stock and survived by mobilizing unpaid family labor, especially that of women and children.[60] Although some Africans may have frequented higher-end establishments, the majority interacted with a far poorer, more dependent, and insecure layer of retailers. In the Grey Street area, the stores that specialized in "African goods" (that is, daily provisions for the working class) were concentrated on Queen Street. Many of these traders cultivated good relationships with their African customers, offering them credit and selling special meals at an affordable price.[61] In outlying areas, the Indian-owned shop sometimes functioned as a meeting point where groups of men exchanged stories, read newspapers aloud, and ate meals together.

Beginning in the mid- to late 1930s, the influx of African migrants began to transform Durban's demographics. Shortly afterward, wartime shortages gave birth to rationing and a black market developed for many items. Hoarding became common and shop owners, white and Indian, often refused to sell to Africans or charged inflated prices.[62] These crosshatching trends would have enormous repercussions for the city's racial politics. Even as migrants negotiated an urban landscape in many respects defined by Indian institutions, their steadily increasing numbers altered the composition of existing communities and expanded areas of predominantly African settlement. In most cases, these migrants lacked the ties to Indian storeowners, co-workers, and neighbors that sometimes developed in Durban's older, more mixed areas. At the same time, most of these new arrivals depended on Indian-owned shops for their survival, including within the more homogenous enclaves that some perceived as refuges from "Indian domination." Already a deeply ambiguous figure in the urban imagination, the merchant now became the focal point of widespread frustration and anger. In letters to *Ilanga* and other papers, African customers complained bitterly about dishonest business practices, contemptuous treatment by storeowners (which they often compared to segregation and the "colour bar"), and their own powerlessness in the face of abuse.[63]

The persistence of these conditions after the war, especially black marketing, reinforced the popular association between the shopkeeper's dishonesty and racial arrogance. "In almost all of their dealings with Africans they show marked colour bar segregation," wrote G. R. Moya in 1947. "In some of their shops they single out Africans for contemptuous treatment. 'No bread', 'no tea', 'no sugar' applies only to Africans."[64] A repertoire of stock complaints became standardized through multiple retellings and generalized to Indian shops and then Indians as a whole. Store owners tried to segregate Africans from other customers.[65] They insulted Africans by calling them "boy." They spoke to them in "Kitchen Kaffir" (Fanagalo) rather than English or isiZulu. They overcharged Africans and manipulated the weight of bulk goods. They gave incorrect change and threatened to call the police if the customer protested.[66] As Tunya Dlamini later recalled, many Africans attributed the origins of the 1949 Riots to the actions of Indian store owners: "One [reason] was that the Indians were ripping them off, the other was they put glass in their sugar."[67] *Ilanga* called these traders "sharks" and published the addresses of stores fined for overcharging Africans.[68] Most Africans, however, stressed their helplessness: "We can't quarrel with our shop; it is the only place where our people can buy food."[69] On some occasions, individuals petitioned white employers to intercede on their behalf.

Even in these circumstances, some depictions of the merchant expressed envy, ironic appreciation of their cunning, and—more rarely—gratitude.[70] This ambivalence was particularly marked in writings and statements by members of the African middle class. Almost every aspect of their economic and social lives interpenetrated in some fashion with the world of the Indian petite bourgeoisie. Individuals like Luthuli, Champion, Ngubane, Yengwa, and the Dhlomo brothers negotiated with Indian creditors, established (sometimes clandestine) businesses with Indian partners, used the services of Indian printers, consulted Indian medical specialists and lawyers, held events at Indian-owned theaters and conference halls, paid rent to the Indian landlords willing to provide them with office space, and developed close relationships with Indian social peers through liberal organizations like the International Club and the Joint Council Movement. Unsurprisingly, their statements regarding the Indian often reflected a complicated—and frequently convoluted—synthesis of respect, their own class aspirations, and tempered mordancy.

In a 1946 column, "Rolling Stone" (*Ilanga* editor R. R. R. Dhlomo) lauded the proliferation of Indian-owned stores and taxis boasting isiZulu names throughout Durban. After celebrating the acumen of Indian entrepreneurs, Dhlomo suggested reversing this gimmick—a thought experiment designed to indict the double standard of the Indian merchant. "We think that is business enterprise and there is nothing wrong with it," Rolling Stone pontificated, "although we still have to meet an enterprising Zulu store owner who would dare to name his shop or tea-room 'KwaMaharaj' or 'Isitolo sakwaNaidoo' and expect the people from the East to flock to it."[71] If an Indian-owned store could sell medicinal herbs to Africans, perhaps Africans could utilize these same marketing practices? Dhlomo exclaimed: "Why, he might live to see that rarest of occurrences. Indian customers in an African store!" Begrudging admiration bled together with jealousy. Both sentiments coexisted with frustration toward Africans drawn to such ploys. At the end of the day, Dhlomo's irony in this article only worked because some Africans embraced devices like the patronizing signs outside Indian tearooms. Nor would this marketing have been effective unless the storeowners in question knew enough about the local market—including Zulu medicinal practices—to satisfy African customers.[72] Ultimately, Dhlomo implied, Africans participated in their own humiliation by flocking to these places. Perhaps, he intimated, the Zulu should strive to be a bit more like the Indian.

LANDLORDS AND HOUSING

The rapid, and largely unregulated, growth of Durban's African population resulted in an acute housing shortage. In previous decades, the majority of migrant workers found accommodation in the backyards of European and Indian households.[73] Their options, however, were restricted by the 1923 Native (Urban Areas) Act, which prohibited Africans from living in white-designated areas unless housed in hostels, government locations, or servant quarters.[74] As a result, Africans began to lease shacks from Indian landowners or build their own informal housing on Indian-owned land in areas like Cato Manor, Happy Valley (the location of the Wentworth oil refinery), and north of the Umgeni River in the Newlands area. Given the relatively high rents charged by landlords, several individuals typically crowded into a single room. In 1952, the Natal University Department of Economics estimated that half of Durban's African population of 132,000 lived in illegal slums.[75] According to one estimate, Indians owned 80 percent of the land rented by African shack dwellers.[76]

As in the case of the "Indian merchant class," the category of landlord must be disaggregated. Some notorious slumlords like Omar Sayed owned blocks of flats and vast tracks of land in Cato Manor, which they exploited by allowing Africans, Coloureds, and poor Indian families to erect dwellings.[77] Indian business men also let flats to Indian and Coloured families, charging exhorbitant sums of "goodwill" for security.[78] But Africans also lived on land provided by Tamil- and Telugu-speaking market gardeners, who had purchased plots on what was once the urban periphery and later abandoned farming in favor of subletting their land. During the 1940s, *Ilanga* alleged that Indian landlords charged immorally high rents—"sheer extortion"—based simply on the reality that Africans had no alternative.[79] These landlords, however, were not necessarily elite.

As with the complaints regarding traders, a mood of powerlessness, even futility, pervaded statements about landlords. In addition to the economic insecurity of the war years, many African renters were in the city without authorization, living illegally on Indian-owned land. Not only did few other housing options exist, tenants had no legal recourse to challenge the dictates of landlords since their own presence broke the law. This intersection of illegality and precariousness generated a specific zone of social interaction: economic relationships that were outside of state regulation and characterized by asymmetrical vulnerability. (African domestic workers in Indian households occupied a similar position.) At the same time, this zone opened the space for an independent African urban existence, and sometimes small-scale capital accumulation, beyond the reach of segregationist institutions and state control. The hierarchies that solidified in this context were frequently personalized (many tenants knew their landlords), proximate (the material advantages of many landlords were small), and unstable (the situation possessed no direct legal sanction). The fact that some landlords faced similar forms of insecurity only intensified bitterness: different layers of the poor struggled against each other for increasingly scarce resources.

During the 1940s, the city council directed owners of over 1,800 shacks to provide basic services like water and sanitation to their tenants. In the majority of cases, the landlords refused to comply, petitioned for the authority to evict the squatters on their premises, and eventually paid fines rather than improve their sites. Only two of more than seven hundred landowners made any modifications.[80] Such resistance did not necessarily reflect callousness or profiteering. Given the insecurity of their property rights, owners—even when they had the resources to improve lots—often refrained from investing in the land on which they themselves lived. The threat to their titles had been further underscored by the hysteria among whites over "Indian penetration" into European areas during the early 1940s. Nevertheless, the refusal to provide basic amenities reinforced the perception among African tenants that the Indian profited from their hardships.

In parallel to this system, a set of more complex relationships also emerged. Barred from owning property in most urban areas, some Africans utilized the space created by Indian landownership to establish themselves as landlords. Since many landowners provided vacant lots, Africans would construct multiroom dwellings and sublet these accommodations. By the late 1940s, rack renting by both Indians and Africans had developed in Cato Manor on a vast scale.[81] In the Grey Street area, central Johannesburg, and other city centers, African businessmen, trade unionists, and professionals rented office space in Indian-owned buildings.[82] In his autobiography, Mandela recalls: "'Mandela and Tambo' read the brass plate on our office door in Chancellor House, a small building just across the street from the marble statues of Justice standing in front of the Magistrate's court in central Johannesburg. Our building, owned by Indians, was one of the few places where Africans could rent offices in the city."[83] Champion, who occupied premises in a Grey Street building owned by Dawood Jeeva, praised the role of Indian landlords: "The Indian Landlord acted as a Saviour when he gave them a piece of ground to live. While other Indian Landlords are bad we have a number of Indian gentlemen whose good memories will remain honourable in our minds!"[84] By the early 1950s, *Ilanga*'s rhetorical posture in describing Durban's housing crisis had shifted, perhaps in response to the emergence of a new layer of African landlords after the 1949 Durban Riots.[85] Now the newspaper overwhelmingly blamed official neglect for the emergence of Durban's slums. The editor wrote: "The African and Indian landlords who now are being blamed for creating a slum area and exploiting poor workers were in fact meeting a great social need and doing work that should have been done by the authorities."[86] As later chapters will discuss, this argument echoed the defense of the merchant by Indian newspapers in 1949. From the perspective of landlords and shopkeepers, their actions provided for the poor by stepping into a breach created by the indifference of the state.

SITES MOVING THROUGH SPACE: BUSES

By linking African residential areas to the Grey Street complex, buses helped to integrate a largely haphazard urban landscape into a system characterized by the subordination of "African" to "Indian." Although a small number of African operators maintained routes between Durban and outlying districts like Port Shepstone and Inanda, Africans only owned four buses in Durban during the late 1940s.[87] In the years immediately preceding the 1949 Riots, there was an increase in applications for motor carrier certificates by African operators. These efforts became an important focus of local politics (the Lamontville Native Advisory Board attempted to ban Indian buses in 1939) and the Zulu royal house took an active part in supporting African petitions for licenses. A memorandum to the Riots Commission describes the scene at one motor certificates hearing: "In the Port Shepstone Court House the decision of the Board to award the above Certificates was received with mighty shouts of "BAYETE" from the chiefs and their Indunas—this was the Royal Salute presented to the Government as represented by the Board. There were seven Chiefs present including members of the Zulu Royal Family."[88]

However, such efforts were actively resisted by the Bus Owners Association, a body established in 1930 by Indian drivers. In many districts, Indian-owned buses provided the only transport and when Indians applied for new or extended routes, these petitions sometimes found support among Africans desperate for improved service. Initially, most of these vehicles were wide-bed trucks converted to resemble city buses. Although some companies began to expand and hire full-time drivers by the late 1940s, most of these ventures were shoestring affairs, owned and operated by individuals who parked their vehicle outside the family home at night.[89] These drivers charged roughly a third of the fare of the municipal buses that operated on some of the same routes. Nevertheless, many Africans still could not afford to travel on them every day.[90] A substantial number of people walked or took pushbikes from African locations to the city center.

As with Indian-owned stores, a stock set of complaints cohered around the space of the bus, which then solidified into a racialized script through multiple reiterations. This narrative began with waiting for the bus itself. Drivers frequently ran behind their schedules and made impromptu stops to grab passengers walking from African areas into the cities. As riders fretted about the consequences of arriving late to work, the indifference of drivers seemed calculated. Complaints over service might lead to ejection. Z. A. Ngcobo remembers: "You would be anxiously looking at your watch, realizing that now you would be really late for work. . . . They were only too ready to take your fare, and if you opened your mouth in protest at the delay they would say to you 'If you are in a hurry why don't you walk?'"[91] In the center of Durban, the situation was even worse. A report by the Durban Transport Commission captures the daily gauntlet of the Victoria Street taxi rank:

All the Non-European bus services in Durban have one starting point—the Victoria Street Extension Bus Rank—from where 116 operators are expected to operate 177 certificated vehicles to various termini. This bus rank is an uneven patch of ground without any facilities for passengers or buses. There are, in fact, periods during the day when there is nothing like sufficient standing room for either buses or passengers, and the crowds of waiting passengers are forced to surge into adjacent streets, where buses also have to stand owing to lack of room or order.

There are no loading platforms where buses could be ranged along-side according to their various routes. There is no shelter whatsoever provided for the passengers. . . . These passengers often, during the rainy season, have to stand in pouring rain for 30 minutes and more. There are no public conveniences and the lighting is extremely poor.[92]

After riders endured this ordeal, the driver would generally board Indian passengers first. "Ladies first" meant Indian women—conductors would push Africans of both genders back.[93] Then a new stage of this ritual would commence: passengers and driver would debate over fares. Adding insult to this injury, conductors regularly gave passengers incorrect change. Some drivers ripped off poorer Indians as well.[94] If passengers pressed the issue, they were cursed, struck, and sometimes tossed out. *Ilanga* describes "the prevalence of the assaults on Africans in some buses by some conductors and the insolent language used whenever Africans complain to some of these drivers: 'This is not your father's bus.'"[95] This exchange occurred so frequently, and impressed itself so profoundly in popular memory, that housekeeper Josephine Hadebe repeated virtually the same words thirty years later in an isiZulu interview: "the Indians (*amakula*) were insolent, and on the buses they used to say, 'No, this is my father's bus, not yours,' and push a black man so that he would be injured for the sake of a ticket."[96] Notably these anecdotes drew together a set of classic themes associated with migration and the city: the anonymity of the crowd, the negation of individual dignity, and new forms of right conferred through the ownership of private property. The repeated accusations of abusive behavior were not only an indictment of the Indian. They also served as a commentary on the African's situation within the city as a social form. In effect, they protested a loss of social status so great that it could not be protested: the denial of any position from which to speak. This is not *your* father's bus, the statement suggested, so *you* have no standing. This experience of voicelessness would later connect anti-Indian sentiment to broader opposition against foreign domination, especially colonialism's denial of African capacity for self-representation.

AFFECT, CLASS, AND SPACE

The hierarchy that developed in shops, neighborhoods, and buses was both haphazard and brittle. As Ashwin Desai observes, "Middlemen minorities are visible, vulnerable, and accessible."[97] This combination of racialized inequality with relative legal and economic parity would produce significant consequences. For most Africans, the authority exercised by traders, landlords, and drivers lacked any justification beyond the simple fact of the hierarchy itself. In his editorial on the 1949 Riots, H. I. E. Dhlomo summarizes this sentiment: "Africans would be less than human not to feel humiliated, frustrated and outraged to find what to some of them are 'foreigners' and 'people who did not conquer us and who came here as slaves,' lording it over them in the land of their birth."[98] Witnesses before the Riots Commission voiced these same views: "The Indian was introduced into this country as a labourer. Now we find we have to serve two masters. Our ancestors fought the Europeans and lost. We accepted the European as our master—we will not tolerate this other black master."[99] Not only did Indians and Africans live (in many cases) side-by-side, but Indians had suffered the indignities of conquest, plantation labor, and poverty. They lacked the de facto legitimacy of a conqueror. Africans frequently articulated this resentment through a discourse of affect: two of the most common words used to describe Indians were "insolent" and "arrogant." A common term in racialized discourses, "arrogance" generally designates the refusal of individuals or groups to abide by the terms of a dominant script: the arrogance of the subaltern, for example, is frequently invoked as a justification for violence designed to enforce the terms of an established racial order.[100] In mid-century Durban, the term functioned somewhat differently. The idea of Indian arrogance reflected the assumption of authority in the absence of shared social norms; that is, illegitimate (or, more precisely, unlegitimated) forms of privilege and agency. In this context, when Africans complained about "the arrogant Indian," they were describing the unjustified refusal of individual respect, fair treatment, and reciprocity. These are the core entailments of social recognition based on a shared sense of community.[101]

Particularly in the writings of younger, educated African men, this thwarted recognition was simultaneously desired and feared, particularly when associated with "modern" spaces like dance halls, clubs, and cinemas. At one level, acceptance would provide entry into a cosmopolitan world of equality, urban sophistication, and middle-class pleasures. At the same time, the presence of a small minority of Africans within these spaces, especially political leaders, raised the specter of their material and moral corruption. In psychoanalytical terms, the Indian was an ambivalent figure par excellence. Letters in *Ilanga* and other papers claimed that African politicians "sell the African people to foreign nations" (*udayisa ezizweni*)—the language always invoked the subversive role of money—to win acceptance and the financial privileges gained from socializing with the Indian.[102] This accusation combined popular anxieties about the relationship between class and political leadership with an acute sense of economic vulnerability. Under the sway of Indian wealth, it claimed, African leaders were "losing touch" with the desperate situation of their followers, who faced exploitation and abuse by the Indian at every turn. The fear of abandonment and political powerlessness was assonant with the general precarity of urban life. Letters and newspaper articles also linked these anxieties with the question of language. Since only a minority of Africans spoke English, the lingua franca in middle-class Indian spaces, many Africans felt that the "white language" excluded them from significant aspects of modern social life and, increasingly, the national arena of African politics. During the 1950s, the frequency with which ANC leaders delivered important speeches in English and published in Indian-owned newspapers elicited similar concerns.[103]

Because of their popularity and public visibility, movie theaters were an important focus for middle-class aspirations and resentments. In Durban, six cinemas operated in the Grey Street area (including the Raj, the Royal, the Shah Jehan, the Albert, and the Avalon), one in Mansfield Road, one in Bellair Road, and three or four in the Jacobs area.[104] Theaters were centers of social life for the black middle classes: going to a movie publicly exhibited a set of values associated with leisure and modern life. Younger Africans voiced frustration over their exclusion from Indian-owned theaters and, more subtly, used these complaints to mark their distance from the uneducated of both races.[105] A letter to *Ilanga* complains: "Indians look upon us Africans as inferiors. There are some places where—no matter how decent you are they won't allow you in; such places as restaurants and cinemas with the exception of the Avalon."[106] The writer asserts that Indian owners made exceptions for prominent Africans and thereby purchased their complacency. "We non-leaders and small fry," he continues, "will always be on the 'Not yet fit' for such privileges list." His choice of English underscores the substance of his allegation: the Indian continued to sneer at the African even when they had obtained the accouterments of modernity and Western civilization. Rolling Stone expresses identical sentiments: "There are many, many places here in Durban where yours truly Rolling Stone cannot dare put his foot with all his qualifications and Degrees and Civilizations because he is an African, but in which he has seen Indians not worth his salt allowed because they are Indians."[107] Those theaters that admitted Africans generally enforced a policy of segregated seating. Writing for *Drum* magazine, the novelist Peter Abrahams relates a story about a manager's refusal to seat a young African intellectual next to his Coloured girlfriend.[108] Here again, ideas of civilization, interracial sex, and modernity were closely adjoined. By refusing to recognize these markers of achievement, the Indian cinema owner evinced the same hypocrisy as the apartheid government. In his eyes, no African would ever be civilized enough.

While the dominant discourse related to the intersection between the circulation of consumer goods and services and the racialization of space, there were also important instances of class antagonism between African labor and Indian employers. Africans frequently asserted that they would rather work for Europeans than Indians. A common stereotype was "the Indian exploiter who treats his employee poorly, overworks and underfeeds him."[109] An African who worked for a Grey Street shop owner during the 1940s recalls waiting two weeks for wages already past due, waking at three a.m. to start work at four, laboring throughout the day with only a cup of tea and piece of bread, and never receiving overtime. The mindlessness of the work inspired bitterness: "You would do the work without knowing much about its purpose or implications."[110] Some members of the Indian elite expressed horror at the treatment of African workers. In a *Drum* exposé on working conditions in the sugar industry, A. P. Naidoo (a leading merchant from Stanger) publicly denounced the practices of many plantation owners: "I honestly feel that in many instances Indian farmers treat their labour worse than do many whites."[111] The harshness of Indian employers had an economic impetus. Possessing substantially less capital then their white counterparts, and often forced to work in their own business or fields, many Indian employers doubtless struggled to cover baseline expenses. But economic pressures also intermixed with chauvinism. Indian market gardeners generally paid African labor half the amount that an Indian would receive.[112] Wage discrimination occurred against workers from the Tamil community as well. Mr. Drum (the pen name of investigative journalist Henry Nxumalo) describes a Hindi speaking plantation owner who paid laborers from his own linguistic group more than Tamils.[113]

Yet even in these circumstances, relationships developed that were more complicated and sometimes mutually benificial. Market gardeners demanded that Africans perform strenuous labor from dawn to noon for substantially less pay than the Indian standing across the same field, but they also allowed some of their African employees to cultivate their plots. If many Africans strongly resented the failure of Indian firms to hire qualified Africans for skilled positions, they also greatly respected those individuals and businesses that defied the norm.[114] The Daughters of Africa, an uplift organization active in Durban and Pinetown, petitioned Indian store owners to employ Africans in order to ameliorate tensions.[115] Africans also used these relationships to pursue their own ends. In some cases, Africans served an informal "apprenticeship" with Indian craftsmen so as to accumulate the experience necessary to set off on their own. ANC Women's League leader Bertha Mkhize and her brother, for example, worked for a tailor on Field Street during the late 1940s before leaving and setting up a successful business at the Native Market.[116]

CONCLUSION

By the early 1940s, Durban had become a fractured and bitterly divided city, although the severity of these developments—despite repeated warnings in *Ilanga* and *Inkundla*—would only become apparent to most observers later. Unlike the qualitative social and economic differentiation later engineered by apartheid, however, this hierarchy of

Indian over African was local, unstable, and relatively fragile. The centrality and visibility of the Grey Street area ensured that the mosques, stores, and movie theaters of central Durban would come to symbolize Indian power and privilege. But on an everyday basis, the drama of race transpired between Africans and a poorer layer of former indentured laborers who drove buses, worked in small stores, and lived in tightly knit communities among and adjacent to African areas. The powerful discourse of "Indian domination"—an all-encompassing narrative that linked together different sites, social dynamics, and resentments—reflected the centrality of Indian-owned spaces and infrastructure to the lives of most Africans. It could not have been further from the lived realities of working-class Indians.

The prose of everyday life—the complicated, protean, and often-incoherent realm that Ranajit Guha has called *historicality*—was far more diverse and varied than the polarization of racial discourse suggests.[117] Africans and Indians were friends, drinking partners, criminal coconspirators, comrades, and lovers. Individuals shopped at the same stores, rode buses together, worked in the same factories, and played football together at lunch. They joined Christian communities such as the church of the Zulu prophet Isaiah Shembe.[118] A privileged lawyer attended the same university classes, negotiated the same professional and political milieus, and visited each other on social occasions.[119] Interviews mention a street named after an Indian who lived in a community of *iqenge* and *isikhesana*—"husbands" and "wives" who built a vibrant subculture around rituals of dating and marriage between men.[120] Photographs show African participants joining in the celebration of the annual Muharram festival as it wound through the Grey Street area.[121] Yet in representations of Durban from the 1940s and '50s, these relationships mostly appear in the form of anecdotes, marginal details of the city's social fabric, or individual exceptions.[122] They are found in descriptions of remarkable events or unexpected interactions. It is not simply that an African nurse dating an Indian doctor, or a close bond of affection between a worker and the family of a market gardener, were uncommon. As individual relationships, they managed to navigate—or, briefly and on a personal terrain, overcome—barriers of community structure, language, legal status, and social prejudice. In their motivations, affections, and social circumstance, they were often singular, contingent, accidental. They took place in the interstices of the city.

Beginning in early 1940s, a new generation of activists and intellectuals—both African and Indian—began to debate the relationship between the two groups. Propelled by the Indian anticolonial struggle and new arguments for non-European unity developed in the Western Cape, this discussion initially focused on the question of nationalist formations: what was the proper relationship between the historic organizations that claimed to represent the different groups? Everywhere, this question was divisive. It demanded a general reconsideration of the nature of black politics. Would an alliance between African, Indian, and Coloured organizations imperil each party's capacity to represent the distinctive interests of its own constituency? Given the relative privilege enjoyed by Coloureds and Indians, were their interests ultimately reconcilable with those of the African majority? What would be the political and philosophical basis for an alliance? Liberal, Marxist, or nationalist? And if nationalist, what kind of nationalism could encompass peoples of different historical origins, cultures, and identities? In Durban, such questions of principle and ideology, important as they were, came face-to-face with the growing anger of isiZulu-speaking migrants, the prejudices and fears of many Indians, and the enormous complexities of race as it was lived. The Indian question was not, as it was for African intellectuals outside of the province, one issue of many. With Indian independence on the horizon, and South Africa's future increasingly in question, it would come to dominate both popular politics and the calculations of the African leadership.

2 ～ Beyond the "Native Question"

*Xuma, Lembede, and the Event of Indian
Independence*

And then—UN! The whole of South Africa has been shaken by the deci-
sions of that Assembly. The decisions have had international repercussions.
The main source of the upheaval which is revolutionizing race relations
in this country is—Durban! The centre of the Indian problem is Durban.
And but for Durban there would have been no reverse for this country
at the UN. . . . In Durban, the Indians (like the uprooted, war torn new
European settlers) are experiencing rebirth. What of the African? May not
Durban be the spring—or at least a chief actor in the story—of African
Regeneration?[1]

—X. [H. I. E. Dhlomo]

THE MID-1940S witnessed a series of watershed moments: the revitalization of the Indian Congress under a younger, more dynamic leadership,
their launch of a campaign of passive resistance against the Asiatic Land
Tenure Act in 1946, and the first censure of South Africa's treatment
of Indians by the UN later the same year. Occurring in break-neck
succession, these events had an enormous influence on the thinking
of African intellectuals, especially a new generation of activists associated with the ANC Youth League. At the same time, the ANC was
divided over the proper response. The emergence of a new left-wing
party based in the Cape, the Non-European Unity Movement, posed
a direct challenge to the older organization and forced it to clarify its
position on a series of questions, most significantly cooperation with
other non-European groups. At the same time, the new leadership of
the Indian Congress, the Radicals, pursued a closer working relationship with the ANC. The ensuing debate over cooperation versus unity

between the ANC and other groups revived an older discussion about the place of the Indian in Africa and contributed to a broader reflection on the racial basis of African nationalism. In effect, it raised the question of the nation's internal and external boundaries.

After the Indian government invited ANC president Dr. A. B. Xuma to travel to the UN, it became evident to the ANC leadership that their relationship with the Indian Congress (and their attitude toward Indians) was a matter with international ramifications. On 9 March 1947, the presidents of the ANC, Transvaal Indian Congress, and Natal Indian Congress—Xuma, Dr. Yusuf Dadoo, and Dr. Monty Naicker— released a statement of common interests following a meeting in Johannesburg. The Doctors' Pact, as it came to be known, announced that "a Joint Declaration of co-operation is imperative for the working out of a practical basis of co-operation between the National Organizations of the non-European peoples."[2] An important breakthrough, the pact reflected the competition between political organizations (especially the Unity Movement, the ANC, and the Communist Party) and the rivalry between different factions within the ANC itself. Shortly after it was signed, the Natal ANC leadership refused to implement it.

These rapid changes occurred against the background of two transformative events: the establishment of the UN in October 1945 and the 1947 independence of India and Pakistan. Far reaching in their geopolitical implications, these developments were also philosophical ruptures in the form that Susan Buck-Morss attributes to the Haitian Revolution of the late eighteenth century.[3] By creating a new global context for anticolonial politics (and the discourse of politics in general), they generated an intellectual space for the reconceptualization of "universal history": the extension of the Enlightenment project of modernity beyond the limiting boundary of colonial racism.[4] Although dominated by Anglo-American interests (as reflected by South African Prime Minister Jan Smuts' role in drafting the preamble to its charter), the UN suggested the possibility of a world after empire for many African thinkers.[5] Conceptualized in the aftermath of the Second World War and the Nazi genocide of Europeans Jews, this new order presupposed two founding principles: the sovereign nation-state and the international legal framework of universal human rights. In asserting the capacity of a heterogeneous people for democracy, Indian independence represented a realization of this vision which, simultaneously, challenged the normative Western ideal of the homogenous nation. Although the partition of Indian and Pakistan underscored the limitations of this achievement, India nevertheless provided African nationalists with a new model for thinking about sovereignty and nationhood.

This chapter begins by surveying the early history of the ANC, its attitudes toward the Indian diaspora, and its complex relationship with empire and colonial liberalism. It then focusses on two individuals, Lembede and Xuma, who sought to reorient the ANC in the 1940s and—in very different ways—articulated a vision of African nationalism beyond the framework of liberal empire and settler civil society. After discussing the impact of the 1946 Passive Resistance Campaign on the ANC, this chapter reconstructs the debate regarding "non-European unity" and the fallout over the Doctors' Pact. In the process, it introduces individuals and organizations that will play important roles in the remainder of the book, including the Indian Congress Radicals, the Unity Movement, the Communist Party, Lembede's co-thinker Mda, the Natal ANC president Champion, H. Selby Msimang, and (most importantly) Ngubane and H. I. E. Dhlomo. If the postwar moment created a new problem space for African nationalism, the question of the also-colonized other interrupted this opening and forced a reflection on the internal frontier of the nationalist project.

THE EARLY ANC, EMPIRE, AND THE NATIVE QUESTION

From its founding on 8 January 1912, the ANC's vision of the future was characterized by a fundamental tension between an inclusive idea of a civilized South Africa and the belief in African unity.[6] At the level of political strategy, the early ANC sought to secure the access of literate, property-owning African men to the rights of citizenship promised (or so they believed) by the British Empire. Explicitly rejecting the settler discourse of a "white South Africa," ANC leaders fought for a common society based on a number of grounds, including British imperial citizenship, Christianity, a shared concept of civilization, and the contributions of African labor to building the country.[7] Although imperial citizenship did not suggest social integration (and it certainly did not entail the assimilation of racial groups), it implied a political identity based on Western civilization and democratic institutions: white and black would share South Africa together. At the same time, the formation of the ANC reflected the conviction that only independent African activity could secure this outcome. Following the 1910 Union of South Africa, the government's tabling of the 1912 Native Lands Act promised the dramatic curtailment of African rights. Little remained of the liberal pretense of African progress under white tutelage. Rejecting the framework of trusteeship, the founders of the ANC concluded that only African unity could secure their people's access to civilization and modernity.[8] African nationalism and the embrace of a broader South African identity were thus interdependent, rather than distinct, strands of thought within the early ANC: a national organization was the necessary instrument for achieving a democratic South Africa. This vision was possible because the horizon of early African nationalist thinking was not a South African nation-state, but the multiracial British empire that incorporated numerous nations and peoples in complex political and legal-juridical configurations.[9] The early ANC aspired to a radical renegotiation of the relationship between black and white *within* the context of liberal empire.[10]

During first half of the twentieth century, the most widely accepted framework for describing this relationship was the "Native Question."[11] Articulated in nineteenth-century debates over the responsibilities of empire, the Native Question cohered into an administrative paradigm during the 1920s. Premesh Lalu explains: "Caught between a discourse on vanishing cultures and the story of progress, academic disciplines performed the role of trusteeship over the category of the native, which appeared resolutely bound to administrative decree and capitalist demand."[12] In other words, the Native Question defined the problem of colonial governance as the disciplining and management of populations no longer located in the idealized realm of African tradition, but not yet fully incorporated as modern subjects within liberal capitalism. In this paradigm, the Native occupied a (perpetually) liminal space: colonial modernity had disrupted or destroyed precolonial African societies without fully assimilating Africans into the political, economic, and cultural institutions of Western civilization.[13] Because Africans allegedly lacked the discipline formed by participation within settler civil society, they had not yet developed democratic capacity; that is, the ability to rationally and responsibly exercise the rights of citizenship. The cornerstone of this discourse was the identification of historical progress—the assumed form of a people's participation within universal history—with the development and spread of Western civilization.[14]

Early leaders of the ANC rejected the Native Question's means of bringing Africans into modernity—the settler population's commitment to white supremacy vitiated the framework of trusteeship—while generally accepting the larger vision that associated progress and historicity with Western civilization. At its founding, the ANC consisted of a relatively elite and entirely male group of intellectuals, professionals, and chiefs. Its activities focused on appeals and delegations to the South African and British governments. ANC leaders argued that racial citizenship violated the universality of the law and therefore threatened to undermine empire's foundation on the principle of justice. At the same time, they challenged a narrow determination of democratic capacity by invoking other criteria such as universal male suffrage in England or the existence of democratic institutions within African societies.[15] If a later generation of African intellectuals saw this strategy as insufficiently radical, many contemporaries understood the subversive character of the ANC's claim: these delegations and petitions performed the African's right to approach the Crown without intermediary. Such assertions of modern political subjectivity—"the right to have rights" in Hannah Arendt's well-known formulation—produced full-throated outrage among white settlers.[16] Nevertheless, these activities failed to arrest the implementation of racist legislation and the expropriation of African land. In 1919, the ANC leadership expelled its founding president, the Natal educationalist and newspaperman John Dube, on the grounds that he endorsed working within the framework of segregation. This schism resulted in the secession of the Natal congress from the national organization.[17] After a brief period of greater militancy, the ANC stagnated during the 1920s. Both the International Commercial Union (ICU), a rural trade union movement influenced by Garveyism, and the Communist Party surpassed the organization in membership and influence. Anthony Butler concludes, "The ANC could easily have died in the 1930s."[18] When the Natal ANC reunited with the national body following Dube's death in February 1946, the new president was a former leader of the ICU, the formidable operator Champion.

Alongside Ethiopia, Liberia, and (most importantly) the United States, references to India occurred regularly in the writings of early

ANC figures. The famous opening line of Sol Plaatje's 1916 *Native Life in South Africa* includes a citation, consciously or not, of untouchability: "Awakening on Friday morning, June 20, 1913, the South African Native found himself, not actually a slave, but a pariah in the land of his birth."[19] Across multiple iterations, India served both as a reference point within a common imperial geography and an emblem of the global struggle against colonialism that flared following the end of the First World War. In *Abantu-Batho* (the ANC's newspaper of the 1920s), the Amritsar massacre was invoked to show that "there is no moral code among nations" while India's revolt for national recognition appeared alongside Abyssinia and the Caribbean labor revolts as a warning to empire.[20] Other articles invoked Gandhi as the Indian version of Marcus Garvey.[21] Attitudes toward South African Indians were, predictably, more varied. Even as writers such as Plaatje celebrated the courage of Gandhi's 1913 campaign, anxieties regarding Indian migration were a regular theme of African newspaper articles. In Natal, broadsides against Indian exploitation were a staple of ANC articles and speeches, including in statements by individuals who praised the industry of Indians and cultivated personal alliances with Indian leaders.[22] In general, a consensus existed that the different political situations of Africans and South African Indians rendered an alliance between the two groups impractical. Writing about Native policy and racial reconciliation in 1930, a young Xuma captured this outlook: "The Indian in South Africa does not fall within the purview of our discussion, because . . . the Indian cannot make common cause with the African without alienating the right of intervention on their behalf on the part of the Government of India." [23] According to this view, the "Asiatic Question" and the "Native Question" represented distinct problems within the overarching framework of liberal empire.[24]

XUMA, THE REVITALIZATION OF THE ANC, AND THE POSTWAR WORLD

During the Second World War, the ANC experienced the beginnings of a revival. Tom Lodge has aptly described the 1940s as "a watershed moment."[25] In the year following the armistice, three explosive social struggles shook the country: a national anti-pass campaign coordinated by the Communist Party; the eighty-thousand-strong African mineworkers strike on the Rand gold mines; and the initiation of passive resistance by the Indian Congress for the first time since 1913. As the ANC began to reorient strategically and intellectually, two figures exemplified its search for a new direction: the prim, studious, and determined physician A. B. Xuma and the brilliant president of the ANC Youth League, Anton Lembede. Mandela's autobiography suggests that the conflict between Xuma, representing the older generation's gradualism, and the Youth League dominated the ANC during the 1940s. Militant African nationalism, according to this account, confronted and triumphed over the delegation-and-petition school of black leadership.[26] However compelling, this narrative obscures the ways in which Xuma, who entered politics some fifteen years after the founding of the ANC, embraced the idea of national liberation and charted an ambitious new direction for the ANC in the context of a rapidly changing international order. Despite their intellectual, strategic, and temperamental differences, Xuma and the Youth League sought to conceptualize the project of African nationalism outside the framework of the Native Question. In different fashions, they drew on the experiences the Indian anticolonial struggle and the event of Indian independence in their efforts to articulate a basis for the claim to nationhood beyond empire and settler civil society.

Born in the Transkei to devout Methodist parents, Xuma's childhood—like that of many African figures in this book—spanned two distinct worlds: the village life of rural African society and the discipline of the mission school. After training as a teacher, Xuma traveled to the United States where he studied at Booker T. Washington's famed Tuskegee Institute in Atlanta and the University of Minnesota. Xuma's American years were marked by periods of financial hardship and efforts to remedy the limits of his earlier education through night school. But he also benefited from the generosity of Christian networks, connections developed through the YMCA, and personal benefactors, including the chair of zoology at Minnesota. Working his way through medical school as a waiter on the Northern Pacific Railway, he passed his exams at Northwestern University in 1925 before proceeding to Hungary and Budapest to specialize gynecology and surgery. In 1927, he returned to South Africa and established his practice in Sophiatown. He named his surgery "Empilweni" (place of healing).[27]

Xuma entered politics in response to the Herzog government's 1935 segregationist legislation. Elected to the vice presidency of an organization founded to coordinate black opposition, the All African Convention, Xuma achieved national prominence and became an advocate for independent African political organization. Although he worked closely with liberal whites at points in his long career, he fiercely resented paternalistic efforts at European "guidance."[28] Notably, he convinced the convention to reject an early proposal for unity with the liberal South African Institute of Race Relations. He also declined to stand for the Native Representative Council, an advisory board to the government created by the Hertzog legislation. If US black politics remained a touchstone for Xuma, he followed developments in India closely and concluded that the end of the war would create unprecedented opportunities for the colonized to participate in the crafting of peace.[29] As early as 1935, he began weighing the consequences of employing "passive resistance" to gain African rights.[30] His papers at the University of the Witwatersrand contain a complete press run of an *Indian Opinion* supplement on the Indian independence struggle from the mid-1940s.[31]

In 1937 Xuma returned to the United States to fundraise and consult with the National Association for the Advacement of Coloured People (NAACP), among others. He also met Maddie Beatrice Hall, who married Xuma in 1940. The following year, he studied public health in London, where he cultivated connections with Pan-Africanist circles. After he returned to South Africa, the Reverend James Calata asked Xuma to run for the presidency of the ANC, which he assumed in 1940. As the ANC's seventh president, Xuma overhauled a collapsing, provincially fragmented, and clique-ridden apparatus. He passed a new constitution, fought to professionalize finances, and worked to create a functioning branch structure. Through these efforts, membership increased from around 1,000 in the 1930s to 5,517 in 1947.[32] Xuma explicitly invoked the Indian Congress as a model for his effort to reconstruct the ANC.[33] In a fateful move, he supported the unification of the Natal ANC under the presidency of Champion, who brought the province back into the national organization for the first time since 1919. Xuma defended the trailblazing efforts of his wife to revitalize the ANC Women's League.[34] He also embraced equal membership rights for women and sought to build stronger ties between the ANC and black trade unions.[35]

A younger generation of ANC leaders, such as Mandela, remembered Xuma as an elitist who, despite his important achievements, was caught in a gentleman's politics ill-suited to a mass movement.[36] It might be fairer to suggest that Xuma promoted an NAACP-style politics of racial uplift, respectability, and aggressive legal activism whose South African moment—if it ever existed—was shuttered by apartheid. In Xuma's eyes, India's independence under the leadership of a cultivated middle-class intellectual such as Nehru, and its self-appointed role as the diplomatic champion of the Third World, may well have represented the possibility that world politics was in the process of becoming more "American."[37] It was in this postwar opening that he saw the greatest opportunity to advance the African's cause.

Whatever its continuities with earlier ANC traditions, Xuma's approach departed from his predecessors by articulating the national aspirations of Africans within an internationalist framework of human rights and the nation-state. After the publication of the Allied war aims, the 1941 *Atlantic Charter* signed by Churchill and Roosevelt, Xuma began to strategize ways to interject the ANC's voice into the coming negotiations over the contours of the postwar world.[38] He also recognized that the foundation of the UN created the possibility for Africans to circumvent their disenfranchisement and utilize the body to indict South Africa's racial policies. The consequences of this strategic reorientation were far reaching. Removing African politics from the geography of the British Empire, Xuma located the project of African nationalism within a problem space defined by the globalization of the nation-state and a new understanding of legitimate sovereignty. As independent India demonstrated, membership in the community of nations was no longer based on liberal conceptions of homogenous political community and democratic capacity derived from Western civilization. In this emerging world order, the nation-state derived its authority from the promotion of a globally binding framework of international law based on universal human rights.[39]

The signal statement of Xuma's presidency was the 1943 *Africans' Claims in South Africa*. Conscious of the consequences of the war for the future of empire, Xuma established a committee to draft a document intended for presentation at a peace conference after the conflict. Z. K. Mathews, a member of the Native Representative Council and a respected academic who taught anthropology and native administration at Fort Hare, assisted in coordinating the committee.[40] *Africans' Claims* called for the abolition of racial discrimination and universal adult citizenship rights. Following a preface written by Xuma, the first section provided a point-by-point interpretation of the *Atlantic Charter*. The second section was composed of a far-reaching African Bill of Rights, which included demands for equality before the law, the abolition of racial discrimination in industry, a fair redistribution of land, free compulsory primary education, and adequate medical and health facilities for the entire population. Steven Gish observes that "the charter represented a break with the past tradition of African nationalist leaders who accepted trusteeship and hoped for British intervention in South Africa."[41] Earlier ANC leaders may have raised the demand for universal adult suffrage, but *Africans' Claims* codified this position as ANC policy.[42]

The most radical aspect of *Africans' Claims* was the structure of its political appeal. After noting ambiguities in the use of the terms "nation" and "peoples" in the *Atlantic Charter*, the document asserted that Africans possessed equal standing with other nations to claim rights and privileges under international law.[43] When confronted with arguments for African rights, liberal colonial politicians such as Smuts invoked the discourse of the Native Question: they upheld the universality of democratic principles while insisting on the exceptional situation of South Africa. Because Africans supposedly lacked the discipline acquired from participation in civil society, the extension of rights would disrupt their process of development, imperiling the future of black and white equally. Segregation did not violate the principle of equal rights because—excepting a few rare individuals—Africans lacked the capacity to exercise such rights.[44] In contrast, *Africans' Claims* asserted the standing of Africans as a national subject within the legal framework of the emerging international order. Writing in the late 1940s, Xuma encapsulated this strategy by describing the UN as the African's "Court of Appeal."[45] At the same time, Xuma was aware of the irony contained in this approach. *Africans' Claims* sought to circumvent the Native Question by appealing to a higher legal principle and forum. However, the principle that *Africans' Claims* invoked—the foundation of the international system on the right of nations to self-determination—limited full standing in the UN General Assembly to recognized nation-states while enshrining their autonomy in domestic affairs.[46] Consequently, Africans found themselves in a situation parallel to war refugees and other stateless peoples. Because it lacked direct access to the "court of appeal," the ANC needed a strategic ally to present its case. India stepped forward to play the part.

LEMBEDE, PHILOSOPHICAL IDEALISM, AND BIOPOLITICAL CRISIS

Born in January 1914 on a white-owned farm in the Natal midlands, Lembede would come to embody—more than any other intellectual of his generation—African nationalism as a political philosophy. His educational accomplishments impressed even his more brilliant contemporaries. Mandela remembers Lembede as "a magnetic personality who thought in original and often startling ways."[47] The son of a farm laborer and a school teacher who tutored him devotedly as a child, Lembede worked as a "kitchen boy" in Indian households around Pietermaritzburg and eventually won a scholarship to study at Adams Mission College, where his teachers included future ANC leaders Z. K. Mathews and Albert Luthuli. [48] (At the time of Lembede's premature death in 1947, Luthuli told the newspaper *Inkundla ya Bantu* that he was attempting to establish a scholarship in the name of his former pupil.) His classmate and friend at Adams, the future Natal Youth League leader and journalist Ngubane, remembered Lembede's threadbare pants and secondhand jackets. His obvious poverty embarrassed the other students.[49] A strong sense of austerity, which Lembede associated with childhood among the Natal peasantry, later characterized his personal, political, and intellectual style.[50]

After graduating from Adams, he held a series of teaching posts while earning a Bachelor of Law degree (1942) and a Master of Arts in Philosophy (1945) by correspondence. In a period when professionals achieved local fame in the society pages of black newspapers, Lembede's advanced degree in philosophy—a first for a black South African—won him renown. In 1943, he moved to Johannesburg to article in the law firm of the aging Pixley ka Seme, a founding member of the ANC and president of the organization from 1930 to 1937. Lembede became increasingly active in ANC circles. Although he was not present at its founding meeting in April 1944 (which included Sisulu, Mandela, and Ngubane), the ANC Youth League elected Lembede as its president, a position that he held until his unexpected death in 1947. Working closely with Ngubane and his close friend Mda, Lembede wrote some of the Youth League's early documents, including

its founding manifesto. Through speeches and scathing polemics published in the African press, he became the authoritative voice of the
Youth League's revolt against the ANC "old guard." [51] This identification of philosophic principles with individual figures represented a
deliberate strategy. The 1944 Youth League Manifesto declared that
leaders should personify and symbolize national ideals. [52]

In Lembede's writings, African nationalism was not just an ideological doctrine. It was an historical force capable of giving unity and
self-awareness to an African political subject. For this reason, the philosophical, political, and organizational dimensions of nation building
were inextricably connected. "The African Natives," he wrote in 1945,
"then live and move and have their being in the spirit of Africa, in
short, they are one with Africa. It is then this spirit of Africa which is the
common factor of cooperation and the basis of unity among African
tribes." [53] Explicitly rejecting race, language, geography, custom, and
common origins as the basis for national unity, Lembede nevertheless
restricted this unifying sprit to black Africans: it was a philosophy embodied in a particular mode of life that "foreigners" could never fully
understand. This nativism reflected his larger historical-theological
worldview. According to Lembede, white supremacy and colonial
domination reflected the triumph of a mechanistic weltanschauung
that falsely reduced human beings to one aspect—either the economic
or biological—of their complex and multifaceted nature. He explained:
"Man [sic] is body, mind and spirit with needs, desires and aspirations
in all three elements of his nature. History is a record of humanity's
striving for complete self-realization." [54] The struggle against colonial
domination was therefore part of a larger battle to reassert the spiritual
dimensions of humanity and create a society based on a holistic conception of the human.

In developing this argument, Lembede combined the redemptionist
strand of black Christian thought—exemplified by the young W. E. B.
Dubois's argument that each race possessed a unique world-historical
mission—with the critique of materialism contained in the writings of
figures such as Gandhi and the exponents of negritude, especially Senghor. [55] At several points, his arguments also bear a striking resemblance
to the French Catholic intellectual Jacques Maritain, who developed
the concept of "integral humanism" in opposition to the split between
secular and religious conceptions of human life. [56] Lembede's most

original contribution was that he synthesized these different critiques of modernity in order to reconceptualize the foundational category of secular modernity, the nation. Identifying materialism with the West and spiritualism with the East, he argued that each nation had a divinely inspired contribution to make to human progress. African nationalism's historic mission was the reconciliation of these competing principles into an organic, truly human whole.[57] This political theology functioned as a critique of colonial liberalism and the Native Question's identification of nationhood, and therefore democratic capacity, with social homogeneity and the institutions of Western civilization. Despite their fragmentation, linguistic heterogeneity, and exclusion from citizenship within settler civil society, Africans possessed the essential prerequisite for national self-determination: a unifying spiritual mission.

The Indian anticolonial struggle exemplified Lembede's vision of nation. Writing in *Inkundla ya Bantu* in February 1947, Lembede began a defense of African nationalism with a lengthy quote from Nehru's semi-autobiographical *Discovery of India*. Describing Nehru as one of the greatest men of modern times, Lembede chose a quote that emphasized both the profound force of nationalism and its inevitability among colonized people: "Nationalism was and is inevitable in the India of my day; it is a natural and healthy growth. For any subject country national freedom must be the first and dominant urger." Rather than fading away before a new spirit of internationalism, Nehru averred, global events demonstrated that nationalism remained the dominant force in world affairs.[58] (The following paragraph of Nehru's text, which Lembede does not cite, warns that the sway of nationalism should be limited to a narrow sphere.[59]) Ultimately, Nehru's account of the fundamental unity of the India nation rested on his *experience* of its oneness: India was a millennia-old spirit that had bound together the vast religious, linguistic, racial, and sociological diversity of the subcontinent across catastrophe, invasions, and eventually colonial domination.[60] It was Nehru's epistemology that seems to have most impressed Lembede. He followed the Indian leader in defining the knowledge of nation as fundamentally emotional. By connecting individuals to the people's divine mission, the affective power of nationalism could overcome the inferiority complex that colonialism had instilled within Africans. The resulting power, he prophesized, would outstrip atomic energy.[61]

At the same time, Lembede saw both the Indian diaspora and the Communist Party (which included several highly visible Indian leaders, such as Dadoo) as genuine threats to African nationalism. Crucially, Lembede's philosophical idealism developed in the context of a biopolitical vision of catastrophe. In this respect, his theorization of African nationalism remained influenced by the framing of the Native Question. Because colonialism had undermined "tribal society" without fully assimilating Africans into modernity, Africans persisted in a developmental limbo that threatened their very existence. This manifested in poverty, crime, social pathology, venereal disease, female promiscuity, and cultural breakdown. Unless they won freedom, Africans faced moral degeneration and physical extermination.[62] This fear of an African genocide was genuine and widespread. It appeared in the writings of H. I. E. Dhlomo, Luthuli, and—as late as 1993—Mandela.[63] In this context, national spirit, embodied in an African political organization, was the essential resource of a people robbed of all other resources. When Lembede coined the slogan "freedom in our lifetime" (apparently during a period of debilitating personal illness), he was not only declaring that Africans were prepared for freedom "now." He was also expressing the urgency of a bio-existential crisis.[64]

While African unity provided the means to confront this crisis, the political and economic activities of "foreign" groups endangered both the consciousness of historic mission and self-reliance that animated nationalism. "Africans are fighting for Africa," Lembede wrote in 1945, "but other sections are fighting only for their right to trade and extract as much wealth as possible from Africa."[65] Lembede conceded that cooperation between Africans and other non-European groups was necessary on individual questions. He also, on a personal level, developed friendships with Indian activists such as Ismail Meer. Nonetheless, he urged Africans to denounce efforts by "foreigners" to lead the African people. Not only would Indian leadership replicate trusteeship's denial of the African's capacity for self-representation, any dilution of African identity would undermine the project of nation building, threatening spiritual and physical death. Non-European unity, he insisted, was a "fantastic dream which has no foundation in reality."[66] Ultimately, this exclusion revealed a contradiction within his philosophy. Despite the fact that he envisioned nationalism as a synthetic force capable of uniting a diverse people on spiritual grounds, he stipulated an a priori limit—an internal frontier—to this process. In effect, he assumed that the historical form of nation, based on the Western identification of democratic community with a homogenous racial identity, could not itself be transformed.

"THE RADICALS"

In many respects, the prewar Indian leadership shared the political outlook and social character of its African counterpart, although its situation was compounded by the much smaller size of the Indian population and its own accretion of material advantage. Except for a brief period following the 1913 Passive Resistance Campaign led by Gandhi, the Indian Congress largely ignored issues confronted by poorer Indians or addressed them through charity organizations. Its political activities centered on the recognition of Indian rights as British imperial subjects and the protection of trader interests.[67] Nor did the prewar Indian Congress champion the cause of the country's dispossessed majority. The Indian elite generally held attitudes of paternalism or veiled anxiety toward the political aspirations of Africans. Indian newspapers published human interest stories about white assaults and humiliations of "natives." Leading politicians, like P. R. Pather and A. I. Kajee, maintained cordial relationships with ANC leaders and donated money to African charities. But such gestures of "friendship" could also serve to mark and reinforce social distance. In an article following the suppression of the 1946 African mine workers' strike, *Indian Opinion* expressed the remote and sometimes condescending attitude of this stratum: "The Indian community has all these years given its moral and material support to the uplift of the natives whenever required and that we should still continue to do." The columnist then proceeded to warn: "But there is a long way yet to go before the natives can be expected to resort to methods commonly used by Europeans and Indians for the redress of their grievances excepting at their peril."[68] More often than not, the writings and speeches of the Indian leadership passed over Africans in silence.

In 1945–46, a group of younger Indian activists captured the leadership of the Natal and Transvaal Indian congresses with overwhelming working-class support. They immediately undertook to rebuild the congresses as mass-based organizations, develop closer working relations with the ANC, and mobilize Indians in a campaign of passive resistance against the Smuts government.[69] The Radicals, as they subsequently came to be known, drew on two political traditions. In many of their homes, Indian nationalism was a virtual birthright. These activists cherished family connections with the subcontinent and personal memories of Gandhi and Sarojini Naidu. They followed the progression of the Indian anticolonial struggle in the pages of newspapers like *Indian Views* and *Indian Opinion*. Several of them, including Dadoo and Dr. Kesaveloo Goonam, were exposed to Indian nationalist politics while attending school abroad or traveled in India during the height of the Quit India Movement. While prominent leaders such as Dadoo and Monty Naicker frequently spoke of Gandhi in reverential terms, their views were closer to those of Nehru. Beginning in the late 1920s, Nehru had consistently argued that overseas Indians must identify their interests with the indigenous majority and abandon their colonial-derived privileges in favor of African rule.[70]

The other source of the Radical's political education was provided by the Communist Party of South Africa (CPSA) and the Natal trade union movement. In the mid-1930s, a small layer of Indians began to join the Communist Party in Durban, which at the time was mainly older and white. A few years later, prominent Indians in the Transvaal, such as Dadoo, also began to join the party. The party provided its members an unparalleled experience of camaraderie. Despite some internal tensions, it was perhaps the one organization in South Africa where members of all races could meet, interact, and debate on equal terms.[71] Party activists, including H. A. Naidoo, Pauline Podbrey, and George Ponen, played a central role in the revival of the Natal labor movement, organizing unions in industries such as sugar, textiles, laundry, and dairy. Beginning with a wildcat strike at the Falkirk industrial plant on 3 May 1937, a wave of working-class militancy inspired the formation of unregistered, nonracial unions that included African and Indian sections. These unions provided significant spaces for activism, although the employment of designated "African" organizers and the de facto use of English created some bitterness among Africans over a two-tier leadership structure.[72] This generation of struggles served as a crucial precedent for radical labor organizing in the 1950s and 1970s–80s.[73] By the early 1940s, however, employers responded by appealing to the government to ban strikes under wartime laws and establishing company unions to undercut organizing efforts.[74] At the end of the

Dunlap strike of 1942–43, the company fired over four hundred workers and replaced Indian as well as African trade unionists with quickly trained scab African labor. This and other defeats resulted in lasting bitterness—hundreds of Indian workers were blacklisted from future employment—and appear to have strengthened the wariness regarding common struggle that already existed among sections of the Durban Indian community.[75]

The Radicals' dual emphasis on Indian racial identity and non-European solidarity necessitated a complex and sometimes fraught strategy of political negotiation. On the one hand, the Indian Congress played a prominent role in supporting and sometimes leading African struggles. Beginning in 1938, the Non-European United Front (NEUF, headed by Dadoo in the Transvaal and H. A. Naidoo in Natal) organized antiwar protests in African townships and produced both English and isiZulu leaflets defending arrested leaders. According to Indian Congress activist Ismail Meer, "the membership of the NEUF increased and exceeded that of the ANC."[76] During the war, the Radicals in both Johannesburg and Durban confiscated black-market staples from Indian shops and then sold these goods to poor Africans and Indians at cost. Indian activists assisted in the anti-pass campaign in 1944, supported the Alexandra bus boycott, and carried out relief work during the 1946 African mine workers strike.[77] On the other hand, the agitation of the Radicals within the Indian community helped reinforce a sense of Indian racial pride and self-confidence that appears to have grown stronger in anticipation of Indian independence.[78] As Goolam Vahed observes, "Only 'Indian' issues successfully mobilized the Indian masses who failed to embrace the broad non-racial and class alliances that were taking shape."[79]

"COOPERATION" VERSUS "UNITY"

When the Hertzog government tabled a new package of segregationist legislation in 1935, no viable organization existed to coordinate opposition. In response, black leaders from across the country came together to establish the All African Convention (AAC).[80] The ANC later withdrew and a group of leftist intellectuals based in the Cape, some of whom were members of the Workers Party of South Africa (affiliated with the Trotskyist Fourth International), gained increasing influence. In 1943 the Cape activists used the convention as a platform to launch the NEUM and adopted a ten-point program of democratic demands. The Unity Movement focused on two main axes: noncollaboration with state institutions and non-European unity.[81] Although smaller than the ANC, the Unity Movement's militant rhetoric and denunciation of the moderate ANC leadership won a hearing among younger Africans.[82] Lengthy exchanges between ANC leaders and the Unity Movement filled the English-language pages of African newspapers throughout the 1940s. These debates forced Youth League members to clarify their own ideas. On certain questions (such as nonparticipation in government institutions), the Youth League adopted the smaller group's position. The Unity Movement pushed for the immediate formation of a federated organization of all non-European groups. The ANC leadership, the Communist Party, and the Youth League—each for different reasons—saw this proposal as a threat.

Earlier black leaders had supported some form of closer cooperation among the non-European organizations. In 1924, the Indian politician and poet Sarojini Naidu conducted a speaking tour across South Africa that galvanized many activists, including young women such as the Cape radical Cissie Gool. Although she spoke as Gandhi's emissary, Naidu stressed the common interests of the oppressed and argued that overseas Indians were first and foremost South African, directly challenging the ideas of "greater India" and imperial citizenship.[83] In response to her visit, the esteemed Cape politician Dr. Abdullah Abdurahman organized the first of four Non-European Conferences which took place between 1927 and 1934.[84] Co-convened with Fort Hare professor D. D. T. Jabavu, the first gathering attracted delegates from the ANC, International Commercial Workers Union, African People's Organization (an historically Coloured organization led by Abdurahman), the Indian Congress, and other smaller groups. Significantly, the Indian Congress abstained from voting on most of the motions because domestic political involvement would contradict its claim to representation by the government of India.[85] At the fractious 1934 conference, Abdurahman argued for the creation of a permanent, cohesive organization. The rejection of his proposal marked the end of an era. Significantly, Abdurahman's death in 1940 left a hole in Cape politics and propelled the disarray of the African People's Organization. As the Unity Movement gained followers within the Coloured community (as well as among Indians in northern Natal), the

ANC was left without an obvious partner that could claim a significant Coloured following.[86]

The challenge posed by the Unity Movement forced Xuma to renew these earlier discussions. In May 1945, the Unity Movement contacted Xuma, requesting that he attend a meeting of its central executive committee to discuss the prospects for African politics following the end of the war.[87] After he failed to attend, the NEUM wrote him immediately, requesting an audience in Johannesburg. In reaction to these overtures, Xuma sent letters to the Indian Congress and African People's Organization that motivated a meeting among the leaders of the three parties. His overriding concern, stressed repeatedly in a half page missive, was to preserve the integrity of the existing organizations. Xuma wrote:

> I am suggesting this as a precaution against disruption within our respective groups through individuals and local organizations trying to form unity.
>
> There could be only two or three leaders from each as the case may be, to explore ways and means whereby leaders of the three organisations could co-operate on points of common suffering without trying to force artificial unity of the groups. . . .
>
> There is no other reasonable and logical approach to co-operation of the "Big Three" on behalf of the three groups without causing divisions among the respective communities.[88]

By August 1945, Xuma was preoccupied with the conditions for greater cooperation and the dangers posed by a polarization over unity within the ANC. His writings of this period show considerable insight regarding the impediments to sustained collaboration. [89] They also express the outlook of a moderate, insistent on the subordination of mass struggle and working-class organizations to a "responsible" leadership, and committed to political mobilization along racial lines. The watchword of this perspective was "cooperation at an organizational level" — in other words, between the established leadership of racial groups — rather than a "fusion of groups" that would dilute their identity.[90]

Xuma's stance received support from the Communist Party, which also sought to reverse the growing influence of the Unity Movement. In a 14 November letter to Xuma, Moses Kotane wrote: "You will also doubtless agree that unless this co-operation is established soon the people who are at present fiddling with the wonderful ideal of unity of the non-European people will create further confusion in the minds of our people and we are likely to be regarded as being against unity."[91] Following the Seventh Congress of the Comintern in 1935, the South African party moved away from its earlier "Black Republic" slogan and adopted the perspective of the "anti-fascist popular front." As a result, the party downplayed the questions of class struggle and African majority rule, instead centering its agitation on democratic demands directed against the Smuts government.[92] When Germany invaded the Soviet Union, the Communist Party shifted its attention from union activity to "mobilizing support for the war effort" and correspondingly opposed actions that might interfere with transport or war-related production.[93] In the early 1940s, the party leadership mandated the NEUF's liquidation and ordered its members to strengthen the existing "national" political organizations.[94] By the mid-1940s, the Communist Party had begun to advocate the alliance of the Indian Congress, African People's Organization, and ANC in opposition to the Unity Movement's proposal of amalgamation through a federated body. Dadoo was a key spokesperson for this position. In a 1945 article published in *Freedom*, he attacked the Unity Movement for ignoring the ANC, which he defended as the representative of the African people despite its organizational weakness, and stressed that unity could only be achieved through the "existing national liberatory organizations."[95]

PASSIVE RESISTANCE AND THE UNITED NATIONS

After the Radicals assumed leadership, they launched a campaign of passive resistance against the Asiatic Land Tenure and Indian Representation Act of 1946. Christened the "Ghetto Act" by the Indian Congress, this bill made permanent the earlier restriction of Indian landownership to scheduled areas and provided a limited form of group franchise. The term "ghetto" directly cited the persecution of European Jews and the Holocaust. In June 1946, the Nuremburg Trials of prominent Nazi leaders were ongoing. A pamphlet published during the campaign included a cover image of a family standing behind barbed wire, echoing photographs of the death camps.[96] Because of the identification of the Indian as the Jew of Africa, the Nazi genocide served as a powerful point of comparison and rendered the situation of the Indian diaspora legible in terms of international discussions over human rights, minorities, and the causes of the Second World War. In equating Smuts's policies with Nazi racial ideology, the comparison also suggested that the persecution of Indians was a genuine threat to world peace.[97]

The two-year campaign of passive resistance—which saw crowds of Indians assaulted by racist whites and Indian men and women sentenced to hard labor in prison—galvanized African politics. Some Natal ANC leaders warned that Africans could fall behind the other two races. But the response of most African political activists was ebullient. On its front page, the first bulletin of the ANC Youth League declared that: "it is time we emulated the excellent example of the freedom-loving Indian people in rejecting segregation. Our answer to the inevitable UNO condemnation of the Union's policy of racial oppression should be a full scale mobilization of the African people."[98] Numerous articles, some written by Indian activists, debated the meaning of these events in the African press.[99] Significantly, the African press began to report that Gandhi—following the lead of Nehru and Muhammad Ali Jinnah—had changed his longstanding position and accepted joint political action with Africans.[100]

Significantly, African politicians cited the prominence of Indian women in the Passive Resistance Campaign to urge the greater political participation of African women. The leading role of a small group of female professionals galvanized the Indian community, especially younger women, and the physical attacks against passive resisters inspired a new layer of recruits. Goonam remarks: "We learnt later that we had unwittingly set the pace for a woman's libratory movement and there were wives who had defied their husbands and recruited."[101] At Sastri Indian College, women students risked expulsion by reaching out to the male class (Fatima Meer remarks: "The very idea of coeducation was taboo.") and inviting them to form a student support council for the campaign.[102] The participation of women in the campaign, many of whom faced beatings by white thugs and voluntarily went to jail, jolted the ANC into self-examination. A 1946 *Ilanga* editorial concluded on the following note: "Just one word to our womenfolk. Indian women who are regarded as 'stay-at-homes' and only interested in the kitchen and the nursery are today in the spearhead of the attack for Indian freedom in this Country. In their remarkable faith in the righteousness of their Cause they are daily going to prison."[103] Writing in *Ilanga*, Champion saluted Dr. Goonam's leadership and heaped praise on the impassioned speeches of the teenage Fatima Meer. At the same time, he voiced concern that Africans might fall behind the level of progress achieved by other non-Europeans.[104] A call for African women to attend the 1947 provincial conference likewise warned: "All races are fast moving forward in this country and yet the African is left behind. The Indian women have participated in the Passive Resistance struggle and are to be congratulated."[105] Indian women had ostensibly managed what Africans had not yet attempted: they transcended the constraints of tradition in pursuit of national liberation.[106]

At the height of the Passive Resistance Campaign, the Indian government brought the treatment of South African Indians before the UN General Assembly. As the first question moved by India, the petition stoked enormous international attention.[107] Seizing an opportunity to augment pressure on South Africa, the Indian Congress financed a delegation of H. A. Naidoo, Sorabjee Rustomjee, and Xuma to travel to New York and advise the Indian effort. Vijayalakshmi Pandit (Nehru's sister) presented the Indian case before the assembled countries and the media of the world. The resolution, which passed in December 1946, was limited to the treatment of Indians and the strained relationship between South Africa and India. Nevertheless, the Indian delegation utilized the opportunity to launch an attack on the overall racial policies of the Union, especially its treatment of Africans. Given Smuts's renown, the mere fact that the case appeared before this body represented a humiliating defeat. As Mark Mazower argues, the architecture of the UN sought to preserve international stability and state cooperation in a postwar "world of empires and great powers."[108] The Indian delegation's victory challenged this framework for the first time.

The African press reported these events with undisguised glee. According to one account, Smuts and Xuma both attended a cocktail party as honored guests and Smuts—unaware of the ANC president's presence in New York—rushed over to ask: "Xuma are you here? What are you doing here?" In the style of high apocrypha, Xuma replied: "I, on behalf of the African National Congress, have for many years been trying to get near you without success and I have had to come to New York to meet my Prime Minister for the first time."[109] Other press reports reveled in Pandit's rhetorical humiliations of an inept and racist South African delegation, particularly the Durban politician and sugar grower G. Heaton Nichols.[110] While in New York, Pandit and Xuma spoke together at a November 17 demonstration commemorating African mine workers shot during the strike the previous August.[111] In his capacity as acting president general of the ANC, Champion gave a widely circulated speech calling for Africans to "view the Indian cause as their cause" and promoting greater cooperation. *Inkundla* ran the headline "India Triumphant!" and *Ilanga* immediately translated the speech into isiZulu.[112] After returning from the United States, Xuma traveled to Natal and spoke to thousands of Africans and Indians at a rally organized by the Indian Congress. Introducing Xuma, NIC president Monty Naicker declared that "this meeting proved there was unity between the Africans and the Indians." Xuma defended the contributions of Indians to South Africa and argued that they deserved full citizenship rights. "If India comes of age," he added, "there is hope for world peace."[113]

Despite the euphoria that greeted the UN decision, the outcome of the Passive Resistance Campaign was anticlimactic and ultimately represented a defeat for the new leaders of the Indian Congress. The two-year campaign failed to achieve concessions from the government and resulted in widespread disillusionment. The membership of the organization initially swelled. But from the beginning, the Indian Congress struggled to mobilize the working class, which was less affected by the new restrictions than middle-class property owners.[114] A thoughtful article in *Inkundla* (almost certainly written by H. I. E. Dhlomo) argued that a white boycott of Indian businesses—which resulted in the cancellation of important contracts and rising Indian unemployment—produced greater support for the Indian opponents of Passive Resistance, particularly among merchants and in the districts of northern Natal. In addition, Partition and communal violence damaged the authority of Nehru and the new Indian government, which had strongly supported the movement.[115] According to a police report, the formation of the conservative Natal Indian Organization in May 1947 undermined the campaign and a number of prominent Indians, particularly wealthy Muslims, soon joined the "moderate" and anticommunist organization.[116] The struggle between the two factions culminated during a visit by the British royal family to Natal. Despite the Passive Resistance committee's call for a boycott, a celebration organized by the Natal Indian Organization brought out tens of thousands at Curries

Fountain.[117] A giant streamer across from the Indian Congress's Grey Street office declared: "The Indian community Welcomes the Royal Family."[118] The Transvaal Indian Congress launched a new phase of the campaign in January 1948. However, the effort soon dissipated and attendance at Indian Congress meetings faded to a "handful."[119]

Around this time, *Ilanga* began to voice concerns regarding Xuma's actions in Natal. In a generally positive commentary, the paper observed that Xuma had broken ranks with the Natal ANC by openly announcing his indebtedness to the Indian Congress and addressing an Indian political gathering. "In other words," *Ilanga* sermonized, "Dr. Xuma rode roughshod over the taboos, tactics and feelings of some local schools of political thought and did and said things that are simply not done in Durban, things for which a local man would be chastised, branded, ostracized."[120] While the author noted the approval that these actions generated in some circles, he observed that they also produced much concern. Was Xuma aware of the hostility to his course? Did he fully understand the dangers of the rift developing between him and Champion? The article's message was clear: the national ANC leadership should work to strengthen elements that shared its viewpoint and act far more deliberately. Otherwise, the writer intimated, Xuma was headed for disaster.

THE XUMA-DADOO-NAICKER PACT

The ANC debated its attitude toward the Passive Resistance Campaign and relationship with the Indian Congress at a special meeting of the national executive in Bloemfontein, early February 1947. The question emerged when the working committee proposed a motion "pledging full active support to the struggle of the Indians." In response, the Natal ANC secretary H. Selby Msimang—seconded by R. G. Baloyi, the ANC's treasurer—moved to defer a motion on the UN resolution and the Passive Resistance Campaign until after "a decision had been arrived on the question of co-operation with the other non-European national organisations."[121] While Msimang recognized the "gallant men and women" of the Indian community, his maneuver likely antagonized some present, especially Xuma, who had just returned from the UN. The discussion continued under a separate point on "Co-operation with other non-European national groups." After the reading of a letter from the Passive Resistance Council, a lengthy debate erupted between those who stressed economic competition between Indians and Africans and others emphasizing the urgency of finding common ground in the struggle for full citizenship rights. In the course of the exchange, Lembede and Mda supported the reservations of Natal, which insisted that it should play a central role in any negotiations.[122] The executive empowered the working committee to arrange a meeting "of the three national groups for exploration of the basis for co-operation." Although most present voiced some degree of reservation, Xuma and other Transvaal-based leaders effectively marginalized these concerns by encompassing the question of Indian-African relations within the broader issue of non-European cooperation — a far less charged rubric than unity.

The meeting took place on 9 March 1947 in Johannesburg and produced a declaration signed by Xuma, Dadoo, and Naicker, which soon became known as the Doctors' Pact. It read:

> This Joint Meeting between the representatives of the African National Congress and the Natal and Transvaal Indian Congresses, having fully realized the urgency of co-operation between non-European peoples and other democratic forces for the attainment of basic democratic rights and full citizenship for all sections of the South African people, has resolved that a Joint Declaration of co-operation is imperative for the working out of a practical basis of co-operation between the National Organizations of the non-European peoples.[123]

The pact included a program of democratic demands: the achievement of universal franchise, state recognition of trade unions, the removal of land restrictions and the provision of adequate housing, free compulsory education, abolition of laws restricting movement, and the elimination of discriminatory legislation. Regarding strategy, it called for a campaign that would compel the government to implement the UN resolution and adhere to the principles of the UN Charter. However, the text provided no concrete guidance for the proposed action. The organizational measures proposed were decidedly limited. The three signatories would meet "from time to time" to take steps advancing this perspective.

Different motivations guided the hands of the signatories. For the Communist Party and Indian Congress, the pact represented a first step toward a formal alliance between the "national" organizations. It was, perhaps more than anything else, Dadoo's victory: he had pursued a closer relationship between the Indian Congress and the ANC since the late 1930s.[124] But other considerations were also involved. Dismissing the UN resolution, the Smuts government showed no signs of granting the demands of the Passive Resistance Campaign, which faced increasingly harsh repression. As Unity Movement polemics noted, Nehru continued to pressure South Africa's Indian population to work with African organizations and Dadoo wanted tangible evidence of progress before visiting India later that year.[125] On Xuma's part, the pact was based on the idea of collaboration between established leaderships. In public interviews, Xuma was quick to emphasize that it did not entail fusion: "Co-operation is a working together of two bodies in which the organizations or bodies retain their identities, whereas in unity the groups or bodies are merged into one."[126] Xuma's goals were twofold: maintaining the unity of the ANC and preserving the ANC's alliance with the Indian government. Other ANC leaders stressed the limited character of the pact. "Isharina" (a pseudonym used by Mda) enthusiastically promoted the agreement to readers of *Inkundla*, while making clear that its terms differed fundamentally from the earlier position espoused by the Communist Party: "Therefore talk of an amorphous 'unity' of a type that Dr. Dadoo and his African satellites once preached in Johannesburg in their non-European United Front, is nothing but glib nonsense."[127]

At one level, the pact represented a significant development. Articulating the aspirations of both groups in the universalizing language of human rights, the agreement broke decisively from the understanding that differentiated African and Indian struggles in terms of each group's relationship to imperial citizenship. In this respect, it built on the political vision articulated in *Africans' Claims* and implicitly denied that there were separate "Native" and "Asiatic" questions.[128] Among younger Indian activists, the agreement possessed great emotional importance: the alliance with the ANC reinforced a growing commitment to the idea that Indians were, beyond anything else, South Africans.[129]

In practice, however, the pact was stillborn. The fact that it was announced in Johannesburg—and without the approval of the Natal executive—insured that it would face resolute opposition. Xuma soon acknowledged that implementation of the agreement had been prevented by "constitutional difficulties" and ruled out launching a campaign in sympathy with the Passive Resistance Campaign.[130] In August 1948, a Unity Movement spokesperson observed that the agreement was dead.[131] The Youth League, particularly Ngubane and Mda, shared this assessment. Evaluating Xuma's tenure in June 1949, an *Inkundla* editorial concluded: "On the question of non-European unity, the Durban riots are the best commentary on his [Xuma's] success."[132] Indian Congress stalwart Ismail Meer later acknowledged the deficiency of the agreement: "Time alone would tell if there was any reality to the Pact. In retrospect, the Pact may be deemed as having been premature."[133] Within the ANC, its impact was largely negative: it provoked a backlash among the Natal leadership, jeopardized the Natal Youth League's efforts at cooperation, and reinforced the nascent Africanist current's stance against African-Indian unity.

BACKLASH IN THE NATAL ANC

The initial drive against the pact was spearheaded by the established leadership of the Natal ANC, especially Champion and Msimang. After news of the Doctors' Pact appeared in the press, the executive committee of the Natal ANC protested. There were also reports of dissatisfaction throughout the branches. Several letters to *Ilanga* testified to the reaction: "I say it with full confidence that public opinion especially in Natal, a people who know something about the psychology of the Indian, is much aversed [*sic*] to cooperation in any form."[134] While the record is vague, Xuma appears to have first written Champion regarding the question on 14 April 1947, over a month after the document was signed.[135] Caught off guard, Champion and Msimang, rivals throughout much of the forties, closed ranks and attempted to overturn the decision. The Natal ANC leadership justified its opposition by pointing to the outrage of African public opinion. With characteristic bravado, Champion challenged the national working committee to travel to Natal and see the reaction for themselves.[136] Msimang emphasized "the very strained relationship between Indians and Africans in this province." When Xuma suggested a public meeting on the topic of non-European cooperation—largely to clear up misrepresentations of the ANC's position in the Natal press—Champion blocked him by claiming organizational difficulties.[137] Champion could ill-afford close public association with the pact's African signatory. Xuma dug in.

Other ANC leaders adopted a more conciliatory posture toward the Natal executive and admitted that the pact was, in fact, an error. In a letter to Msimang dated 17 June 1947, Reverend Calata wrote:

> Please allow me to plead with your Congress not to kick too hard so as to give UNO the impression that we are divided. The Indians helped us at the UNO last year and we still need their help even this year. By that I do not mean that no mistake has been made. I just want you to be careful of the manner in which you handle this matter for it concerns two of the most important provinces of the INDIAN NATIONAL CONGRESS. Transvaal to my knowledge is not complaining and I want to ask Natal also to put their case tactfully.[138]

Msimang responded that the pact violated Xuma's mandate. The Transvaal and Natal Indian Congresses were provincial organizations. The purview of negotiating any arrangement with them thus belonged to the respective ANC provincial congresses—and only Natal, in his view, was competent to negotiate an agreement with the Indian organizations. While his letter reflected longstanding tensions between the Natal and Transvaal leaderships, Msimang's fundamental point was twofold: the Doctors' Pact constituted an end run around the local ANC leadership and was concluded at the expense of Natal's Africans. Msimang wrote: "Before an agreement could be reached with the Indians therefore, very important and vital issues involving political, economic and social differences would have to be examined and determined in the light of the very strained relations between Indians and Africans in this province."[139] First and foremost, any statement of cooperation must "guarantee the Africans a measure of protection from the Indians." Absent such promises, he concluded, the Natal Congress could not lend its support to the pact, but would refrain from voicing public opposition for the sake of unity.[140] The message was unambiguous: the agreement would not be implemented in Natal.

THE ANC YOUTH LEAGUE

Despite the focus of most accounts on the Transvaal, the ANC Youth League operated from three intellectual centers by the mid-1940s.[141] The founding branch was in Johannesburg. After an abortive attempt to establish a youth wing in 1940, several activists, most of whom were teachers or students, approached Xuma to launch a new effort. This group included William Nkomo, Mda, Mandela, Ngubane, and Lembede. With Gandhi and the Quit India Movement on his mind, Xuma somewhat caustically observed that these eager young men were prepared "to march barefoot."[142] If Lembede set the intellectual direction, there was nonetheless considerable debate from the start. According to Peter Walshe, incipient tensions existed between the "Africanists," who stressed the perils of collaborating with Indians and Communists, and the "Nationalists," who worried about the dangers of inward-looking racialism.[143] The Youth League also included a small number of Marxists.

In May 1944, the Natal ANC Youth League was established and both Ngubane and H. I .E. Dhlomo were elected to its executive branch (Dhlomo soon took over as acting president).[144] Ngubane, who had returned to Natal to assume editorship of *Inkundla*, was shortly afterward elected president.[145] Under the leadership of Ngubane and Yengwa, the league grew quickly while facing fierce opposition from Champion, who had reversed course to oppose its existence.[146] The Natal Youth League's greatest assets were the editorships of Ngubane and Dhlomo.

The third intellectual center was Fort Hare, the Eastern Cape university dedicated to African higher education. Although an official branch was only established in 1948, Youth League members had been active at Fort Hare since the organization's beginning.[147] According to Sobukwe, debates with supporters of the Unity Movement influenced the thinking of early Youth League members during their studies.[148] The renowned ANC intellectual Z. K. Mathews was another significant presence. Although Youth League members rebelled against his gradualism, Mathews introduced students to a tradition of thinking about liberalism, nationalism, and the Native Question by assigning the work of the philosopher R. F. A. Hoernlé, among others.[149] Notably, Mathews earlier taught both Lembede and Ngubane when they were students at Adams College.

The two most influential figures in the intellectual life of the Natal Youth League were Ngubane and H. I. E. Dhlomo. Born in 1917 at Nkwebebe (outside of Ladysmith), Ngubane studied journalism by correspondence and then worked on *Ilanga*—Dube himself suggested that the paper hire the young writer—until he departed for

Johannesburg in 1943.[150] Although he authored early Youth League documents with Lembede, Ngubane did not fully embrace his friend's philosophical idealism.[151] In writings from the 1940s, he argues the case of a modernizing nationalist committed to liberal ideals (he was a rare Zulu republican) while endorsing a pragmatic approach to politics and nation building. Like many of his contemporaries, Ngubane wore multiple hats: historian, fiction writer, authority on Zulu poetry, Natal Youth League president, newspaper editor, factional publicist, journalist, and (during the 1950s) proud chicken farmer. His greatest influence, however, was exercised through his hard-hitting and frequently truculent political journalism, which purported to give "the inside story" of ANC affairs. A synthesizing thinker with a penchant for dichotomy, Ngubane's articles helped shape (and often simplified) the contours of ideological debate by encapsulating the positions of different ANC factions. Mda described him as "simple, modest, natural and intelligent. He makes friendships easily and has a limitless capacity for keeping them."[152] Significantly, Mda underlined Ngubane's pragmatism by describing him as a thinker in search of an ideal that could survive "in an environment of grim and ugly reality."[153] Keenly interested in international relations, Ngubane wrote extensively on Indian independence, Partition, and their implications for Natal's African-Indian racial politics.[154]

In contrast, H. I. E. Dhlomo was widely known as "the poet." He was older than the other Natal Youth League members. Born in 1903 to a family of early Christian converts, Dhlomo trained as a teacher at Adams College and subsequently held a series of positions in the Transvaal during the 1920s. In 1935, he left teaching to write as a journalist for *Bantu World* and (in 1937) he became the librarian for the Carnegie Non-European Library.[155] Before returning to Natal in 1940, he wrote a famous sequence of English-language plays on Zulu history known as the "Black Bulls." Dhlomo was a more subtle and complex thinker than Ngubane. Committed to a modernizing vision of African nationalism (he opposed the institution of chieftainship, for example), he was also influenced by English Romanticism and a Christian rejection of philosophical materialism. European modernity, Dhlomo believed, was inevitable, progressive, and nonetheless intrinsically flawed. There was an ambivalent and tragic dimension to Dhlomo's understanding of progress, expressed most powerfully in his plays about the African past.[156] As Masilela suggests, his driving concern was the synthesis of Western civilization and African culture.[157] Dhlomo initially shared Xuma's optimism regarding the possibilities opened by the UN and postwar transformation of the international system.[158] He also wrote regularly about Indian politics in Natal and African-Indian racial tensions (sometimes as *Inkunda's* anonymous "Indian expert").[159] Despite his angry and caustic commentary on the relationship between the groups (which frequently employed the merchant stereotype), Indian activists such as Ismail Meer considered him a pioneer of mutual understanding. At the beginning of the 1946 Passive Resistance Campaign, Dhlomo spoke at a mass meeting organized by the Indian Congress and supported the movement on behalf of "young Africans." Remembered years later in Durban, this endorsement represented a significant turning point.[160]

THE YOUTH LEAGUE AND THE DOCTORS' PACT

According to Elinor Sisulu, Lembede surprised his Youth League colleagues by enthusiastically supporting the Doctors' Pact.[161] However, his unexpected death in July left it unclear how he would have interpreted the agreement's implementation. Mda's letter to *Inkundla* almost certainly reflected conversations with Lembede and likely expressed his evaluation. After describing the pact as a political advance, Mda stressed that the agreement could either be extended indefinitely or cancelled the next day. His main point was that the pact was not prefatory to unity. Indeed, Mda stressed that it represented a defeat for the Unity Movement's ideas. At the same time, he lambasted elements in "Johannesburg and Orlando"—probably other members of the Youth League—who claimed that the Doctors' Pact transformed the ANC into an "appendage" of the Communist Party. Like other Youth League statements from this period, his letter included a strained and self-negating attempt to challenge popular anti-Indian sentiments:

> It is to be hoped that many of our avaricious, money-grabbing, black-marketing and parasitic Indian brethren, will be led to see a new light and end their career of merciless exploitation of our people; whilst on the other side our people should sink their strong but sometimes stupid personal prejudice against the Indians in the face of a common enemy—the dragon of white domination![162]

Mda concluded by warning the Indian Congress to settle accounts with the "quislings" (the pro-regime collaborators) who divided the Indian masses. This emphasis on racial unity reflected a core assumption of Mda's thinking. The Youth League believed that a meaningful rapprochement required a clear understanding between the African and Indian peoples as united groups. At the same time, Africans were entitled to leadership within any coalition based on their numbers and claim to indigeneity. Moreover, African leadership of black political movements was required was needed to break the masses from a colonial mindset of dependence on other races. If this logic was not anti-Indian per se, Mda's language revealed that he continued to reduce all Indians to the figure of the exploitative merchant. This equation rendered anything but the most circumscribed forms of collaboration dangerous: either Indians participated in African politics to further their economic interests or Indian organizations diluted African nationalism to protect their minority privileges. Ostensibly, in Mda's reading, the pact would protect Africans from these threats.

The Doctors' Pact placed the Natal Youth League in some difficulty. Given the outrage over the agreement in Natal, a strong defense of the pact was likely to undermine more long-term efforts at cooperation. In general, the Transvaal Youth League's debates over unity reflected competing interpretations of African nationalism. In contrast, the Natal youth leadership's approach to this problem was more strategic and less explicitly ideological. After the 1946 Passive Resistance Campaign, Dhlomo and Ngubane began to advertise the importance of common struggle with the Indian Congress in their newspapers. Writing in 1947, Ngubane argued that "the Indian's battle is ours" and "there is a dangerous tendency among sections of our people to fall in for the propaganda from white circles to the effect that the Indian is the African's worse exploiter."[163] Well in advance of the Transvaal Youth League or the national ANC, the Natal Youth League concluded that Indians and Africans faced the same enemy and therefore needed to develop a permanent alliance of some form. "The Indian's battle is ours" was a powerful statement of identity.

However, Ngubane and Dhlomo placed two significant preconditions on any agreement. First, Africans needed to build unity among themselves. Only a united African movement would allow the ANC to pursue collaboration from a position of strength. Second, the Indian had to make significant economic concessions to resolve the conflicts produced by the exploitation of Africans. However great their admiration of India and sympathy for Indians, Ngubane and Dhlomo invoked the merchant stereotype and their newspapers regularly sounded the themes of anti-Indian populism. Both men, for example, advocated for the boycott of Indian stores in the 1940s.[164] Given their location in Natal, Ngubane and Dhlomo doubtlessly recognized that a permanent understanding between the ANC and Indian Congress was not only strategically necessary, but desirable given the Indian elite's financial resources and international connections. At the same time, they believed that the intense prejudices of many Africans mitigated against a formal pact without major conciliatory gestures by Indian leaders. In their view, anti-Indian prejudice was too strong to impose cooperation from above.

A significant group within the Transvaal Youth League, including Mandela and Tambo, continued to oppose African-Indian collaboration in all forms. In a 1948 resolution later published in the *Rand Daily Mail*, the New Clare Youth League called on the minister of the interior to impose segregation between Indians and Africans. After Xuma publicly repudiated the report's accuracy, the New Clare branch wrote him: "The committee feels that the president is working hand in glove with the Indians in imposing these economic difficulties on Africans. We have also felt that the president has forsaken our cause by going to the press without calling the League, for information."[165] During this period, anti-Indianism increasingly coalesced with anticommunism. In March 1950, the executive of the Transvaal Youth League issued a leaflet entitled "Our Fight."[166] Denouncing the Free Speech Campaign to defend Indian Congress leaders against government banning orders, the authors proclaimed that Africans would no longer be a football for political parties (the Communist Party) or racial groups (Indians) striving for self-preservation. They demanded:

> What is the basis of this pact? What are the terms of this pact? Africans offer their sweated labor and the strength their numbers give. What is the whole Indian community represented by the T.I.C., prepared to and indeed pffer [sic]. What are the details? Your prophets cannot answer this question. The answer for them is given by us. There are no terms; there are no details. What

they say, is: "ride on the devil if you can't cross the river, and kick him back to the river when you reach the other bank." This is both fascinating and thoroughly misleading. But our contention is, it is the African who has become now, as in the past, the Devil of the Prophets. The African is not riding. He is ridden on.

The possibility of Indians speaking for Africans inspired the leaflet's polemical rage. The authors believed that Indian leadership of African campaigns could only reinforce and replicate colonial disenfranchisement by robbing Africans of their voice. During the early 1950s, Youth League members, including Mandela and Tambo, physically disrupted integrated meetings in the Traansvaal, including once dragging Dadoo off a platform in New Clare.[167] In the township of Alexandra, Youth League members campaigned for the expulsion of Indian traders—a demand popular among many African residents.[168] Within a few years, members of this current would claim the mantle of "Africanist" and draw on Lembede's arguments against non-European unity to assert that the ANC had abandoned African nationalism.[169] Yet even as this critique was being formulated, Youth League intellectuals confronted an unexpected and devastating event: the explosion of anti-Indian violence in Durban on 13 January 1949.

PART TWO

3 ᔒ "That Lightning That Struck"

The 1949 Durban Riots and the Crisis of African Nationalism

> I had been shaken profoundly by the error into which we had fallen when
> we saw reality from perspectives rendered fashionable by the race oppres-
> sor. The riots were proof to me that the old humanity [which privileged the
> group over the individual] had dangers for us. African Nationalism, I began
> to realize, had committed the blunder of seeing events and the relations
> between Black and White through borrowed eyes. To correct this error I
> had to work as much for the widening up [of] the area of identification as
> for the emancipation of the African. This was the lesson of the riots.[1]
>
> —Jordan Ngubane

On 13 January 1949, an argument between a shopkeeper and a
fourteen-year-old boy escalated into a melee between crowds of men,
many returning from work, near the Grey Street taxi rank. After word
of the battle spread overnight, workers from local hostels organized to
retaliate, leading to large-scale racial violence directed against Indians
throughout Durban and outlying areas. At the height of the assaults,
groups of African men humiliated, beat, and killed people identified
as Indians and raped Indian women. The attackers also defaced and
burned Indian-owned stores. The rioters focused their anger on those
nearest at hand. As the violence spread from the city center, they targeted poorer Indians who lived near and among Africans in the city's
slums. Many Africans who worked for Indians fled, afraid for their own
safety. Others shielded Indian friends and neighbors from the mobs. Indian men, sometimes armed with guns, retaliated when they found opportunity. After two days, South African police and navy forces began
to suppress the rioters with heavy weapons fire, killing dozens more.

These events resulted in the death of over 140 people, the temporary displacement of nearly half of Durban's Indian population, and the destruction of the Indian presence in large parts of the city, including the racially mixed shantytown of Cato Manor.[2]

The Durban Riots remain a charged part of Natal's living memory. The year itself has become iconic. In 1976, members of the Kwa-Zulu Natal legislature made threatening references to 1949 after Fatima Meer suggested that the true leaders of black South Africans were imprisoned on Robben Island, not running the Bantustans.[3] When the Soweto uprising erupted the same year, a large number of Indians—especially of the older generation—feared the possibility of anti-Indian violence and directly referred to 1949.[4] These associations have continued in the postapartheid period.[5] One apocryphal narrative, frequently reiterated in memoirs and novels, depicts Indians as victims of a state-orchestrated plot to disrupt non-European unity.[6] This account suggests that the Riots interrupted a long history of friendship between Indians and Africans. Another version (which became central to an ideology of Zulu plebeian nationalism during the 1950s) describes the Riots as a battle to liberate the city from the foreign and exploitative Indian.[7] According to this narrative, the war between the Indian and the Zulu not only retaliated against Indian arrogance, it also facilitated the emergence of African self-assertion through business.[8] Despite their diametrically opposed valence, both discourses situate the Riots within a vision of history whose protagonists are coherent racial formations. Both accounts also lay claim to an experience of collective victimization.

As Jonathon Glassman observes, writing about racialized violence raises fundamental, and ultimately intractable, questions regarding language.[9] The Riots generated new social configurations and divisions—novel ways of articulating the relationship between "Indian" and "African"—even as contemporaries understood both the causes and aftermath through established racial categories. By selecting an entire group as its object (an object that can only exist at the level of fantasy), the attacks produced a powerful consciousness of collectively embodied difference. Every person identified as an Indian became a potential target of actions through which rioters asserted themselves *as* Africans. At the same time, the violence fractured local communities in ways that cut across race, split the leaderships of both the ANC and

Indian political organizations, and resulted in the emergence of unprecedented relationships and alliances. Even the unity suggested by the designation "Riots" is potentially deceptive. As this chapter argues, the nature of violence changed over time and assumed diverse, localized forms. Generic terms like "attackers" and "rioters"—necessitated by the anonymity of the crowds and the vagueness of the sources—not only obscure the different (and evolving) motivations behind the attacks, they also imply a continuity of agents across time and space. This was not necessarily the case. The Riots produced a discourse of African-Indian racial difference centered on the imagery of "African attacker" and "Indian victim." But the stories of what transpired differed from neighborhood to neighborhood, from street to street, and from hour to hour.

The election of the National Party government in 1948 reinforced a growing sense of despair among many Africans in Natal. The postwar optimism regarding the *Atlantic Charter*, the UN Charter of Rights and Freedoms, and a coming "New Africa" had begun to fray. The victory of India at the UN in 1946 and Indian independence the following year raised expectations of rapid, profound change in South Africa. Even relatively sober observers felt a sense of possibility. Less than two years later, *Inkundla* described a widespread view "among African people today that they are facing the grave threat of physical extermination."[10] This chapter begins with a discussion of the coverage of Indian independence and Gandhi's assassination in the Natal press. If India's decolonization served as a model that allowed African intellectuals to imagine possible futures, Partition illustrated the failings of the Indian National Congress and the dangers of majoritarian nationalism. In the context of the postwar universalization of the nation-state, the sundering of India and Pakistan—followed soon afterward by the UN's passing of the Partition Plan for Palestine in November 1947 and the election of the Nationalist Party on a platform of apartheid or separation in May 1948—exemplified the schismatic logic of national self-determination. As Mufti observes, "Nationalism has historically been a great disrupter of social and cultural relations."[11] Alongside the emergence of both revanchist and new modes of nationalism, the dismantling of empire precipitated a global moment of partition.

Arguing that African intellectuals understood the Riots in terms of this moment, this chapter then provides an account of the Durban violence and the discussions that followed in African- and Indian-owned newspapers, especially *Ilanga lase Natal* and *Indian Opinion*. In his editorial on the Riots, H. I. E. Dhlomo denounced the violence. At the same time, he attempted to refute the depiction of the rioters as "African savages" through an economic analysis of African-Indian race relations that ultimately conflated Indian victims with the figure of the merchant. In response, Manilal Gandhi (Mohandas Gandhi's son and the editor of *Indian Opinion*) predicated his defense of the Indian's place in South Africa on a celebration of the merchant's generosity toward Africans. The final section of this chapter will explore the crisis in the ANC precipitated by the violence. In the aftermath of the Riots, the ANC's leadership was divided over cooperation with the Indian Congress and many of their supporters openly rejected this course. After Xuma visited Natal and signed a statement that ignored the resentments of many Africans, the Youth League publically challenged Xuma, declaring that his leadership had become "outmoded." This breach would soon prove irreparable. At the same time, Youth League intellectuals such as Ngubane, Tambo, Sisulu, and Mda were shaken by the Riots and began to question the racial foundations of Lembede's Africanism. The events of January 1949 represented a major organizational and ideological turning point. By revealing the devastating potential of a racialized African nationalism, the Riots forced sections of the ANC to rethink the form of the liberation struggle and the very idea of self-determination.

INDIA ON THE WORLD'S STAGE

The Second World War, as Iain Edwards observes, magnified the interest of working-class Africans in the "outside world."[12] In Durban, demobilized service men and foreign sailors—including Indian and Black American seamen—found audiences hungry for information, however anecdotal. The experience of food rationing and blackouts made the events transpiring on other continents tangible in the rhythms of daily life.[13] African newspapers published articles in English and isiZulu on antisemitism, the Greek Civil War, and the foundation of Israel that invited readers to draw parallels and appreciate differences between developments transpiring in South Africa and elsewhere. These stories self-consciously promoted the emergence of nationalist consciousness by encouraging readers to conceive of themselves as potential members of an emerging international order, a community of sovereign nations in part defined by its collective interest in the shared arena of world affairs.[14] In other words, African nationalism encouraged an international awareness, particularly concerning political changes elsewhere in Africa and throughout the colonial world.[15]

In the pages of African newspapers, the independence of India in August 1947 possessed a monumental significance. Columnists enthusiastically speculated on the impact that an independent India—a country of 347 million and the oft-celebrated "jewel" of the British Empire—would have on the Commonwealth of Nations and the colonial system in general. Not only did the adoption of universal franchise establish the capacity of the non-European ("civilized" or "uncivilized") for self-government, black intellectuals also hoped that an Indian democracy would provide a powerful counterweight to Western imperialism in the UN and elsewhere.[16] In the weeks before the momentous date, Natal was gripped with anticipation. The topic preoccupied both Indians and Africans. Festive decorations covered buildings across the province, and thousands of men, women, and children attended political meetings and celebrations at which the new Indian flag was unfurled.[17] In Johannesburg, Xuma publicly thanked Nehru for his messages to Africans and predicted: "the light of the East will naturally spread to Africa and help the African people's struggle for freedom."[18]

Covering these developments, African journalists employed India as a device that allowed them to reflect on South Africa's colonial experience and future prospects. This genre of reportage sometimes approached allegory: journalists used India to reframe the particularities of Africa's history within a universal narrative of colonial oppression and (implicitly) postcolonial deliverance.[19] At the same time, African newspapers—especially in Natal—anxiously questioned the significance of India's independence. *Ilanga* ruminated darkly: "Must both the Indian and the European be the supreme masters in the land of his [the African's] birth, whilst he remains a hewer of wood and drawer of water? Must he be crushed economically between the European and Indian 'grinders'? Must he politically and socially remain their underdog?"[20] Many Africans worried that a sovereign India would strengthen the position of South Africa's Indians to their increasing detriment.

On 30 January 1948, an assassin shot Mohandas Gandhi in Bombay. Most coverage in the Natal African press did not, strikingly, mention Gandhi's years in South Africa.[21] Perhaps the editors of *Ilanga* and

Inkundla, sincere in their expression of grief, judged that such a discussion would raise uncomfortable questions regarding Gandhi's attitude toward Africans. In any case, their outrage and sorrow was undeniable. Writing in *Inkundla*, Ngubane sermonizes: "By murdering the greatest advocate of peace, the advocates of violence have only exposed the poverty of their own human worth."[22] His editorial focused on defending India itself from cynical accusations of national failure leveled by the pro-colonial newspapers. The true friends of India, he argues, would not turn their backs on the "non-European democracy." Africans should see in India's staggering sacrifices the path of struggle yet ahead. Gandhi died at India's hands, Ngubane implies, and this tragedy was India's trial to endure and overcome. In effect, the article was a defense of the principle of Indian nationhood (and hence the general possibility of non-Western sovereignty) in the face of Partition, communalist strife, and Gandhi's murder by a right-wing Hindu nationalist.

The article on Gandhi's death in *Ilanga*, written by H. I. E. Dholmo, expresses a more complex and uncertain set of attitudes. Dhlomo begins by meditating on Gandhi's exemplification of the human soul's universal and constant dignity, a magnitude of personhood that transcended "race and colour, creed and class, clime and time."[23] Greatness, the writer eulogizes, knows no tribe and is respected everywhere. This appropriation of Gandhi for the entirety of the human race, ironically, served to contest his status as a specifically Indian symbol. Admiration for the fallen leader, he soon made clear, did not entail respect for the political and economic doings of Indians—even if, the article conceded, some Africans believed that "we can profitably learn from them." Dhlomo prophesizes:

> Naturally, most of us will think about the practical and political implications of the matter not only in connection with India, but as it affects South Africa and other parts of Africa where the presence of the Indians is creating complex problems. There were some who think that Mahatma Gandhi was a steadying and sublimating influence in this direction; that he was against nascent Indian imperialism and Indian exploitation of the peoples of Africa. Now that he is gone they fear that Indian economic greed and exploitation, Indian adolescent political assertiveness and Indian expansionist tendencies will have a new lease on life.

They doubt if free and ambitious India and Indians care for the freedom and aspirations of Africans.

The tone of the Natal African press had shifted considerably since the first victory of India at the UN.[24] Now, two themes achieved prominence. First, *Ilanga* and *Inkundla* worried about the increasing diplomatic assertiveness of India and began to depict the Indian diaspora as the potential instrument of a new empire. Articles in *Inkundla* first sounded this note in the mid-1940s, but this concern intensified considerably after Nehru began to assert India's interest in East African affairs.[25] In 1946, Nehru argued that India, along with Britain, should oversee a UN trusteeship over Tanganyika.[26] *Ilanga* and *Inkundla* greeted this proposal with alarm. *Inkundla* warned: "It is not impossible that certain Asiatics might support our own cause so that they should have our people's support for their expansionist ambitions."[27] Second, the Indian National Congress's role in Partition severely damaged the moral authority of Nehru and the new Indian state. The scale of the displacement and communal violence outstripped anything that African leaders had previously contemplated. *Ilanga* cautioned African leaders to learn from India's failures: "Events in India show how deep, dangerous and crippling cultural, language and religious differences can be among people supposedly of one nation. . . .African leaders should heed this warning and lesson."[28] Dhlomo and Ngubane continued to insist that India's fate would have far reaching consequences for South Africa as a whole. But the postwar optimism regarding Indian independence had faded. In the columns of African newspapers, India increasingly appeared as a warning.

If Gandhi's murder and Partition soon passed from the headlines, they remained a significant reference point for African intellectuals throughout the 1950s. In a 1959 manifesto released after breaking away from the ANC, the Pan Africanist Congress declared that it "den[ies] the foreigners any right to Balkanize or Pakistanize their country."[29] The following year, Albert Luthuli (then president of the ANC) wrote these words in the margin of a notebook containing material for his autobiography: "India and Pakistan partition not parallel."[30] These and similar invocations demonstrate the way in which Partition functioned as a limit scenario in African nationalist thought: it encapsulated the dangers of ethno-nationalism for a country composed of multiple, historically interconnected groups. Even when it was not explicitly invoked, the threat of territorial division often haunted discussions regarding the meaning of self-determination during the 1950s.

This anxiety was reinforced by a terminological development: the introduction of "Bantustan" to describe the apartheid policy of semiautonomous, "tribal homelands." A reference to the creation of Pakistan, the term surfaced at a Dutch Reform Church Conference in 1949 and was originally used by liberal opponents of apartheid as well as international newspaper correspondents based in the country. Over the next decade, the term "Bantustan" passed into common usage, including by spokesmen for the government. As a result, an implicit (and frequently explicit) comparison between South Africa and India/Pakistan entered everyday political vocabulary.[31] In May 1959, Mandela published an article in the leftist journal *Liberation* warning against the confusion of Bantustans and Partition: the government's plan promised the intensification of white supremacy, not the creation of separate and truly autonomous states.[32] This confusion posed a real danger. There was genuine concern among ANC leaders that Africans would endorse Bantustans under the illusion that they would provide a return to the self-sufficiency of precolonial African societies (an aspiration that was, in Natal, frequently expressed in the language of Zulu nationalism) and therefore freedom from Indians and whites.[33]

THE 1949 ANTI-INDIAN RIOTS

Early in the evening of Thursday, 13 January, a shop owner named Harilal Basanth struck a fourteen-year-old African youth named George Madondo, knocking him through a window and cutting his head.[34] Physical conflict between Africans and Indians occurred regularly in Durban, particularly in stores and on buses.[35] But this altercation, as Tim Nuttall describes, took place in particularly explosive circumstances: "It happened at the end of the day amidst the crowds of Victoria Street, near the central bus depot where thousands of Africans and Indians queued for a bus home. This was the heartland of the Indian commercial centre, and the site of Durban's largest 'Native' beer hall and market stalls."[36] Outraged bystanders attacked the shopkeeper and Indians rallied to his defense. With lightning speed, rumors circulated through the market that a crowd of Indians had beaten or killed the boy. Indian men and women hurled brickbats and bottles from the balconies onto the heads of those below.[37] African men rushed to the scene.[38] According to *Inkundla*, "within an hour it had spread to every part of the Indian quarter of [central] Durban. Groups of Indians all over engaged in free fights with Africans. Stones and sticks were freely used."[39] As the number of combatants swelled, an African crowd set out from the scene of the initial fracas—chanting "Usuthu!"[40] (the battle cry of the Zulu royal family)—and began to attack individual Indians, stone vehicles not driven by Africans, and vandalize Indian stores. *Ilanga* claimed "Indians were as much responsible and fought as wildly and behaved as recklessly as Africans at the beginning until superior strength told and Indians retired. Innocent people suffered on both sides."[41] Sporadic looting continued late into the night.

However spontaneous the initial melee, evidence suggests that the next day groups of Africans, organized through workers hostels and other social networks (perhaps *ingoma* dancing troops and boxing clubs), sought to take advantage of the situation.[42] Doubtlessly encouraged by the laxity of police intervention (numerous reports also indicate whites cheered on the African assailants and joined in raiding stores), crowds of African workers sought out confrontations on Friday and open skirmishes occurred whenever groups of Indians were in a position to retaliate. The epicenter remained in Grey Street. By the early evening, government troops blockaded the center of the city. Organized gangs then moved from central Durban to outlying districts, including Cato Manor. News of these clashes spread throughout the city, resulting in outbreaks of violence among residents of mixed areas.

As the violence moved into the shantytowns and shack lands, its character changed. Crowds burnt houses and stores, raped Indian women and girls, and attacked Indians of all ages, sexes, and social classes. These mobs assailed the poor and working class—the only target readily available. The goal was clear: to drive Indians out. An article in *Indian Opinion* captures the devastation: "Huddled under the flames of one of the burning shops were four Indian women and a dozen weeping children. The male owner was in a grotesque attitude on the front path, knifed in several places and dying. A younger son staggered in the road with his head split open. This was one of the hundreds of pathetic sites that were witnessed in Cato and other districts of Durban."[43]

Friday night saw the apogee of the violence. Attackers hurled paraffin tins into Indian-owned buildings, families burned alive, homeowners retaliated with weapons fire, desperate individuals offered money for their lives and the lives of their families, individuals who worked for Indians fled for their safety, women hid in their homes and begged their husbands to stay with them while bullets flew overhead.[44] State repression also intensified. According to Nuttall: "For a local news reporter it seemed the clock had turned back to battles he had observed during the Second World War. Machine guns were set up, and sometimes fired 'for five minutes at a time' in the direction of groups looting and burning buildings."[45] The military and police established order by Saturday, despite scattered acts of revenge by gunmen.[46] A more limited outbreak of looting occurred a few days later in Pietermaritzburg.[47]

The official commission of inquiry set the following casualty and damage figures: 87 Africans, 50 Indians, 4 unidentified, and 1 European killed; 1,087 people injured; 40,000 Indian refugees; over 300 buildings destroyed; and more than 2,000 structures damaged. Articles in both the African and Indian press insisted that the number injured and killed was higher.[48] After the Riots, newspapers like *Natal Mercury* reiterated these (or similar statistics) in the context of coverage that presented a racialized image of African savagery and Indian victimhood, implying that all African casualties were perpetrators killed by police gunfire. The reality was significantly more complicated. Multiple reports of Africans killed while helping their neighbors, as well as the use of firearms by Indian men, suggest that the aggregate statistics obscure very different kinds of violence, each embedded in a specific set of social relationships. In other words, the figuration of the Riots as a single event was the epistemological precondition for their depiction as a race war.[49]

Drawing a parallel with American "race riots," the white press immediately dubbed these events "The Durban Riots." The South African Institute of Race Relations soon developed the comparison explicitly.[50] In the US context, this term provided a thin euphemism for "a tidal wave of homicides, arson, mayhem, and organized racial combat" that swept the country in response to growing African American political assertiveness, particularly following the First World War.[51] The term "Riots" reduced the precipitating causes to antagonisms between coherent groups, disappeared the structuring role of social hierarchies grounded in state racism, and—perhaps most disturbingly—abstracted acts of violence from both perpetrators and victims. As a result, the word "Riots" elided separate, if overlapping, dynamics operating on different scales. Several firsthand reports, including *Ilanga's* major isi-Zulu article, commented not only on the phases and escalation of the Riots, but also on the violence's divergent character in different sections of the city.[52] After the Thursday brawls throughout Grey Street, the next day's assaults focused on Indian men in the downtown area. These were premeditated acts of retaliation designed to teach the Indian a lesson. Significantly, these attacks took place in the literal and symbolic center of the city, its "Indian district." According to *Ilanga*, criminal elements and white "bystanders" carried out the looting at this point—not the organized groups of hostel dwellers.[53] The eruption of violence in outlying locations assumed a different character. In some cases, groups marched from central Durban into surrounding districts, entering neighborhoods as outsiders. In other cases, the attacks were initiated by residents returning home from work.[54] In shantytowns like Cato Manor, where the hierarchy of "Indian over African" was local and proximate, the Riots developed into a pogrom. In these spaces, a mobilization that began as a collective rebellion against "Indian arrogance" fused with acts of retaliation against people who lived within the same community: landlords, storekeepers, and neighbors.

Several African intellectuals immediately contested the appellation "Riots." In its editorial the following week, *Ilanga* avoided using the word, in large part because it implied that the participants were "mad, blind and unreasoning impis."[55] While deploring the all-sided suffering, *Ilanga* and *Inkundla* argued that African participants—however misguided, tragic, and destructive their actions—were redressing collective humiliation and fighting to assert their rights as human beings. Numerous articles in the African press also observed that far more Africans had been killed (some by Indians) and harshly criticized accounts that represented Indians as the only victims.[56] In isiZulu, these events were frequently called an *impi*: a war. Both participants and letters to the press described the outcome as a military victory over a foreign opponent.[57] This rhetoric legitimated the Riots by invoking martial traditions identified with the Zulu kingdom: "We beat them up. We 'burnt them.' Even though I did not join that company, I can say 'we did it' because it was done by Zulus."[58] In this discourse, conquest entailed a right over peoples and territory.

Why did individual Africans take part in the attacks? Testimony at the Riots Commission and later interviews contained multiple justifications, including economic desperation and fear of retaliation for siding with the Indian. When reflecting on the Riots in the third person (that is, as an event that transcended individual motivations), participants generally describe the motivations for the attacks as revenge for Indian "arrogance."[59] As one participant boasted almost thirty years later: "They learned a great lesson, and to this day you will not hear an Indian say to an African, 'Voetsak' ['fuck off']. No matter where he is working, if you say 'Hey!' there is perfect silence to this day."[60] Many of the rioters' actions appear to have been specifically aimed at humiliating victims. One Cato Manor resident explained: "When the men returned and told us about it all, they said tins of oil had been poured out on the floor of Indian stores, making it so slippery that people fell and hurt themselves. They looted whatever they could from the shops whenever they saw an Indian they hit him, and that would be that."[61] As the next chapter will discuss, sexual violence directed at Indian women and girls was sometimes described as retaliation against Indian men, who (many Africans believed) used their wealth and superior position to "seduce" African women.

No contemporary source provides a reliable estimate as to how many people participated in the attacks. This vagueness strengthened the image of racial conflict between two seamless entities. Among Durban Africans, the Riots found broad support, although many people also expressed shock, horror, and disgust over the violence. *Inkundla* reported: "Almost every African this correspondent asked about the riot had a measure of sympathy with the Indian's attackers. This does not mean that they approved of the methods used."[62] The same article claims that Africans were almost evenly divided over the use of force. Resentment and anger at the Indian were ubiquitous; the complete depersonalization of Indians was not. Additionally, many Africans—especially middle-class Christians—expressed a deep sense of shame over the fact that their racial compatriots had acted like "savages." Reflecting the way that relationships structured the course of the violence, some rioters made efforts to protect familiar individuals even while they lashed out against the property and lives of others.[63]

Many Africans opposed the attacks. The followers of the Christian prophet Isaiah Shembe stationed guards outside the houses of Indian church members.[64] Goonam recalls: "All Africans did not attack Indians. Many, in fact, in Cato Manor, Mayville, Second River, Briardene, Sea Cow Lake, and Springfield protected their Indian neighbors and sheltered them in their home against attacks by Africans."[65] Significantly, Goonam's list includes neighborhoods in which the violence escalated into a pogrom. In response to press coverage that demonized all Africans, *Inkundla* celebrated the "Heroes of the Riots": men and women who risked their own personal safety to shelter Indians in their homes and nurses who cared for the wounded, regardless of their race. According to the newspaper, many of those who shielded Indians lost their homes and escaped only with their lives. "There are hundreds of instances," Ngubane claimed, "where Africans were beaten up by their own people for giving sanctuary to Indians."[66] One editorial focused on the sacrifice of an unnamed man in Cato Manor, who died attempting to rescue two Indian children from the flames of a burning house. Comparing this individual to Gandhi and Abraham Lincoln (great leaders also murdered by members of their own race), *Inkundla* eulogized that he "was the true representative of the Africa that will endure. When friends and foes heap insults on the whole African race, the Unknown Man of Africa stands out as a silent rebuke to their smallness of mind."[67]

POLITICAL RESPONSES

In the preceding years, *Ilanga* had pointedly warned the ANC that the failure to defend African trading rights "might lead to organised and patriotic gangsterism when impatient Africans will raid and damage or burn Indian buses and stores in African areas."[68] Few Durban Africans expressed surprise over the events.[69] In striking contrast, the Riots caught the Transvaal leadership of the ANC and the Indian Congress off guard.[70] In the immediate aftermath, Naicker and Champion toured the city with loudspeakers, both men appealing for calm in isiZulu and English. The ANC and Indian Congress cooperated in providing relief to those displaced.[71] The Communist Party sent a team of Moses Kotane and H. A. Naidoo to assist.[72] On 6 February, the ANC and Indian Congress released a joint statement, signed by African and Indian leaders from across the country, expressing "deep and heartfelt sympathy to the relatives of all the victims." Sidestepping the grievances voiced by Africans, the statement indicted the policies of segregation: "The fundamental and basic causes of the disturbance are traceable to the political, economic, and social structure of the country, based on differential and discriminatory treatment of the various racial groups and the preaching of racial hatred and intolerance."[73] When the government commission of inquiry refused to allow the cross-examination of witnesses by African and Indian organizations, the ANC and Indian Congress protested and then boycotted the proceedings.

Ngubane was profoundly shaken after witnessing the pogrom first hand. He began to question significant aspects of the Youth League's understanding of African nationalism, particularly its racial exclusiveness. According to Ngubane, Mda (who had taken over the Youth League presidency following Lembede's death) reacted strongly to the violence, blaming the poor quality of leadership on both sides. After traveling to Natal, Mda warned against the possible development of an African fascism, a concept that linked the danger of emulating the racialized subject of Afrikaner nationalism (which was widely compared to Nazism in the black press) with the problem of difference as figured by the diasporic Indian ("the Jew of Africa"). Ngubane remembers:

> After the riot, Mda came out clearly with his insistence on the quality of our ideals in the League being above reproach. He had been a very close friend and admirer of Lembede, who had attempted to popularize Africanism. Mda did not say Africanism should be scrapped. He produced a new phrase. African Nationalism was the force for which he stood. For him, Africanism had racial connotations he found dangerous.
>
> At the Bloemfontein Conference toward the end of 1949, he delivered a long speech in which he warned that the African's fight for freedom would be in vain if it was waged merely to ensure that the African debased the human personality in the way the white man did. Fascism, he said, like race oppression, was evil from the White side as it was from the African. He warned that there could be fascists also right within the League itself who had in mind the idea of establishing a closed racial state precisely in the way Afrikaner Nationalism wanted to do. These were the most dangerous enemies of African nationalism. . . . Uttered against the background of the riots, these were brave words.[74]

Other Youth League intellectuals shared Mda's trepidations. In effect, the Riots strengthened the idealist conception of African nationalism at the expense of a racial biopolitics.[75] Tambo's first national responsibility for the ANC was to visit Durban following the Riots. Luli Callinicos explains that he was greatly disturbed by his encounter with the anti-Indian racialism common among Durban's Africans. He began to develop "a new outlook on the complexity of race relations, identity, and struggle in South Africa."[76] Sisulu, who would beome ANC Secretary General at the end of 1949, also rushed to Durban. Appalled by the violence, he became an important champion of the need for African-Indian collaboration and reached out to the Indian Congress shortly after assuming office.[77]

In October, Sobukwe delivered the annual address on behalf of the graduating class at Fort Hare. In an audacious speech that surveyed epochs and continents, Sobukwe defended African nationalism by asserting its role in the development of a truly global civilization. The question of "minorities" and the dangers of racialism featured centrally. He rejected a negative understanding of nationalism and asserted the willingness of "the whole of young Africa" to work with any individual willing to fight for liberation. Because of Africa's world historic role, love for the continent was identical with love for the human race: "We breathe, we dream, we live Africa: because Africa and humanity are inseparable."[78] He then invited the "minorities in this land, European, Coloured, and Indian" to find mental and spiritual freedom through participating in this shared, affective commitment.[79] More secular-minded ANC statements stressed that the struggle against apartheid was a philosophical battle between irreconcilable concepts of humanity: one narrow, the other universal. When the ANC adopted the Programme of Action at the end of 1949, it stressed opposition to "the conception of segregation" and the "idea of white domination."[80] An ideology—not a people—was the true enemy.

The Indian Congress declared that the hand of a third party was behind the Riots. Speaking at a press conference in England on 27 January, Dadoo (who employed the terms "pogrom" and "massacre" rather than "Riots") alleged the existence of a government conspiracy to disrupt the emerging forces of opposition to apartheid. Dadoo cited the race policies of the "fascist" regime and the enormous utility of the Riots for the state:

One cannot escape the conclusion that the outbreak here has the resemblance of an organized attack, that it was premeditated, although something went wrong with the timing, that a hidden hand of instigators lurks behind the events, that such events eminently suited the Government in order to weaken the growing opposition to the Government's policy, and that it may be used as a weapon to impose further repression on both Indian and African people.[81]

As many Indians struggled with the trauma of the events, the leaders of the Indian Congress remained silent regarding the grievances voiced by Africans. Among intellectuals and activists, considerations of strategy (that is, attributing primary blame to the unjust system rather than its foremost victims), a powerful sense of community pride, and personal denial all contributed to embracing a narrative of white instigation. Fatima Meer later summarized this position: "Direct blame was apportioned to the Government, the white public, and the local authority in Durban, which had for years waged a vendetta of unrestrained malignancy against the Indian people."[82] Activists pointed to circumstantial evidence that suggested a state-orchestrated conspiracy: anti-Indian statements by the government, the intensified campaign of vilification by the white press during the Passive Resistance Campaign, the failure of police to protect Indian property and lives, the participation of whites in looting, the undisguised glee of white Natal at Indian suffering, and the cynical manner in which the white press circulated African complaints. A paternalist undertone sometimes accompanied this explanation. It implied that white propaganda had misled credulous and unsophisticated Africans: Indians were a convenient and accessible scapegoat for their real frustrations over poverty, urban overcrowding, and segregation.

This position, however, did not reflect the rage, despair, and horror of most Indians. *Indian Opinion* followed the NIC in blaming the government, but it also voiced outrage at the attackers, who were generalized to represent all Africans: "The murders committed, the ravages on our women and girls, the burning of our homes and our business premises, make us wonder whether there is human feeling in some human breasts. The hatred shown and the fury with which our people have been attacked, makes one shudder."[83] In Indian press accounts, the strident denial that Africans were ultimately responsible for the violence went hand in hand with images of Zulu barbarism, primitiveness, and savagery: Shaka reborn and unleashed during the evening rush hour. *Indian Opinion* praised the "good work" of the navy and police who suppressed the rioters. *Indian Views* printed ominous reports of African drilling squads preparing for war in central Durban and nurses in an unnamed hospital attempting to poison Indian patients.[84] Multiple sources indicate that some Indians threatened retaliation and Indian vigilantes attacked Africans in the days afterward.[85]

The ANC faced significant pressure to prevent another conflagration and develop stronger ties with Indian organizations. Representatives of the Indian government warned ANC leaders that African anti-Indian sentiments compromised India's efforts to isolate the apartheid regime internationally.[86] They also challenged both the outpouring of anti-African racism and the willful indifference of Indian leaders (both conservative and radical) to the grievances articulated by Africans. Addressing a forum in Pietermaritzburg, Secretary to the High Commissioner for India in South Africa R. T. Chari demanded that relief funds sent by India be used to assist all sufferers, Indian *and* African. He strongly criticized a speaker who had argued that political unity was impossible because Africans were savages. "Because people are illiterate and do not conform to Western standards of life," he pointedly declared, "it does not mean they are savages." In villages across India, he cuttingly observed, thousands of such "savages" now possessed full franchise rights. Chari went on to argue that Indians must stop ignoring Africans and find a way to come to their aid. If Africans had not felt truly aggrieved, the Riots would not have been so widespread.[87] Having witnessed the riots in Clairwood, Chari spoke with a degree of authority and an edited version of his remarks appeared in *Inkundla* and *Indian Opinion*.[88] But as the thousands of displaced sought new homes and families interred their dead, the equanimity of his stance found little popular resonance.

THE DEBATE BETWEEN *ILANGA LASE NATAL* AND *INDIAN OPINION*

The outpouring of accusations by Africans provoked swift and impassioned denials from Indian newspapers. "It is an irony of fate," the small journal *Pravasi* lamented, "that of all people the Indian should have suffered for no fault of their own."[89] None of the charges were new: they included blackmarketing and overcharging in shops, exploitative rents charged by landlords, the alleged arrogance that Indians displayed toward Africans, the seduction of African women, and the abuse of legal and social privileges created by the policy of segregation. African newspapers had regularly voiced these complaints in the past. But the Riots compelled the Indian press to respond to these grievances in print, particularly after white newspapers such as *Natal Mercury* began to publicize African statements in lurid and sensationalized detail.[90] The result was a rare debate over the relationship between the two communities that centered on the figure of the Indian merchant.

In his editorial on the Riots, H. I. E. Dhlomo places the violence of recent days within the broader context of South Africa's system of discrimination. At the same time, he trenchantly criticizes the attitudes and actions of many Indians. In contrast to press reports that invoked stereotypes of Zulu primitiveness, the editorial emphasizes the objective basis of long-simmering African resentments and the extent of the violence directed against both Indians and Africans. The stunning first paragraphs of his article survey the misery and devastation unleashed by these events without so much as mentioning race. While insisting that the "conflict" was perfectly foreseeable (and therefore preventable), Dhlomo also attempts to capture a human dimension to the all-sided suffering that transcended any group:

> The inevitable has happened. The flood has burst out. Much damage has been done. Many places lie waste and desolate. Some people mourn and will not be comforted. There is fear, shock and confusion. There is hate, the nursing of wounds and a fatal desire for revenge. Although the main current of the storm has passed, there are rumblings of discontent, uncertainty and a savage desire to hurt. People continue to be assaulted and killed indiscriminately.
>
> If what has taken place is tragic, sudden and regrettable, it is not surprising nor was it unexpected by unprejudiced, honest and well informed observers of our racially corrupted society. The whole grim business was logical, simple, and inevitable.[91]

Despite the painstaking evenhandedness of the above passage, Dhlomo's article proceeded to reiterate a series of racial stereotypes based on the image of the Indian merchant. In many respects, this process of generalization was the product of a deterministic analysis that derived racial antagonisms directly from the legal-economic system. The repetition of the word "inevitable" conveyed that Africans, however brutally, were responding to a situation that they neither created nor had any recourse to change. The ambiguity of agency in the above description implies that Africans and Indians were both victims in a tragedy that neither had scripted.

After the initial paragraphs, Dhlomo enumerates a comprehensive list of complaints against Indians. The first and most virulent charge was directed against the practices of shop owners and merchants: "It is a well known if unpalatable fact that many Indian business men use unfair and immoral business methods. Haggling and downright fleecing of Africans is the order of the day, and has been going on for decades." Underscoring the questions of space, land, and property at the heart of African resentments, Dhlomo particularly objects to Indian efforts to defend their monopoly position in "the Reserves and exclusively or predominantly African areas." Dhlomo assailed not only the deliberate sabotage of African business, but also the quotidian humiliations suffered by Africans in spaces coded as Indian: "the very Indians who oppose to the bitter end those Africans who desire to run their own buses, stores and cinema houses, behave with nauseating, adolescent arrogance, superiority, patronage and even brutal insult to African customers and patrons." It was, he implied, simply too much to endure.[92]

In effect, Dhlomo's editorial contends that each racial group responded rationally to an unjust system that gave Indians legal and economic advantage: Indians, by exploiting these avenues for profit and advancement; and Africans, by striking out against Indians. However inadvertently, he shifts in the course of his argument from an empirically qualified assessment of "many" Indians to an evaluation of a racial group based on actions and prejudices that he himself recognized were prevalent, but not universal.

This generalization served his defense of the rationality of those Africans that participated in the violence. Although he uses words like "tragic" and "regrettable," Dhlomo rejects the term "Riots" and condemns the exclusive emphasis on Indian victims. He describes the pogrom as a battle that the Indians lost: "Indians were as much respon-sible and fought as wildly and behaved as recklessly as Africans at the beginning until superior strength told, and the Indians retired. Inno-cent people suffered on both sides."[93] He also defends the rationality of the African combatants in their choice of targets (particularly their decision not to attack whites) and ultimate objectives:

> The so-called mad, blind and unreasoning impis were angry groups of Africans who sedulously attacked Indians only, were most careful even at the height of the storm not to have clashes with Europeans. . . .
> To paint the whole affair as the work of wild, blood thirsty savages doing they knew not what, is not true. . . . as if the fight-ing taking place in Greece, Palestine, etc., is the work of wild savages and not men prepared to die for their rights.[94]

Dhlomo's bitterness throughout is extraordinary. "It should be remem-bered," he asserts, "that in normal times Indians assault Africans daily." Once Africans reversed the terms of oppression and retaliated against decades of abuse, they immediately became unreasoning barbarians — a racial slander whose intent in the post-war international order was pellucid: Africans were incapable of self-government. Already, the Na-tionalist Party and European press had begun to argue that the Riots illustrated the necessity for apartheid. In his response, Dhlomo predi-cated a defense of the African capacity for political reason, and there-fore the very possibility of national self-determination, on the equation of the Indian merchant with the Indian victim. Behind this argument rested a vicious irony. If white liberals and Indian nationalists could rationalize that the behavior of merchants did not represent a racial group, but instead reflected a natural response of individuals to the structural conditions created by an unjust system, the same could be said of their African assailants.

It is easy to imagine Manilal Gandhi's shock and disbelief while reading Dhlomo's article. Even if these accusations were true—which Gandhi did not concede—how could Dhlomo possibly justify the rape of young girls or the immolation of entire families, atrocities the *Ilanga* editorial passed over in silence? The editor of *Indian Opinion* felt compelled to reply in the next issue of his journal. Gandhi ominously concludes that *Ilanga* "is believed to be a Bantu paper, but here too there seems to be a hidden hand doing mischief."[95] His own article the previous week had already endeavored to refute the allegation that African resentments ultimately precipitated the violence.

The contrast between the two accounts could scarcely have been more dramatic. "Our people being non-violent by nature," Gandhi sermonizes, "do not arm themselves with any lethal weapons and, fully armed, as they were, the Africans found a defenseless people, an easy prey."[96] Dhlomo's attempts to qualify his racial generalizations, however partial, did not find a parallel in *Indian Opinion*'s columns. Refusing to countenance any suggestion of Indian culpability, Gandhi presented the tenents of the Mahatma's philosophy, particularly nonviolence and personal sacrifice, in the form of shared Indian racial attributes. He questioned the humanity of African rioters and pointedly expressed sympathy for the Indians who had lost their homes and members of their families.

Echoing the position taken by the Indian Congress, Gandhi alleged that the Riots were orchestrated by an unknown mastermind, most likely the apartheid state. Africans, oblivious to the government's strategy of *divide et impera*, had been duped: "The Africans have no hatred against the Indian people but their pent-up feelings resultant of the repression by the Whites, have had to be directed against the innocent and defenseless people." In the same issue of *Indian Opinion*, Gandhi reprinted articles from the more liberal European newspapers and statements by Indian leaders that broadly supported his claims. Many of these pieces also contained the imagery that informed Gandhi's own paternalism. "We must try to tolerate the African," he warned Indians, "because it was their savage instinct that prompted them to do what they did." Employing a logic perfectly symmetrical to *Ilanga*, Gandhi's insistence on the irrationality and primitiveness of the rioters coincided with a defense of the Indian merchant. Crucially, Gandhi employed an alternate spatial language to describe their role. Against the accusation of exploitation and undermining African control in their own areas, he claimed that the merchant—here also standing in for the entire racial group—had served the economic needs of Africans despite the barriers erected by the state:

> One word to the Africans. Both the Indians and Africans are repressed by the same law. The Indian suffers from discrimination

just as much as the African. It grieves us to learn that Africans are attributing economic causes for these disturbances. Nothing could be more absurd. It was the Indian who ventured into the wilds to serve the wants of the Africans. It was the Indian who had pioneered in the Transport business and carried the African to their remote homes. It was the Indian who, as the vegetable gardener, had been supplying the Africans at prices which are within their reach.[97]

Several crosscurrents are at work in this passage. In asserting that Indians suffered "just as much as the African," Gandhi expresses the enormous pride within the Indian community over efforts to create livelihoods in the face of government hostility and often crushing material destitution. White racists, especially in Natal, had long decried these same economic successes in the hysterical language of Asian peril. In response, a generation of Indian leaders had inverted this rhetoric and predicated their demand for citizenship rights on their contributions to the country's prosperity.[98] Gandhi perceived *Ilanga's* criticisms of Indian business practices in this light. They seemed to challenge the very basis on which leaders of the community (or at least its more elite elements) had defended the place of Indians in South Africa. His reaction was visceral. The fact that these accusations appeared in the mouths of Africans, who lived and suffered alongside Indians, felt like an act of betrayal. In his eyes, only white manipulation could possibly explain this siding with the forces of oppression.

Gandhi's article, like much of the writing on the Riots in Indian-owned newspapers, voiced a profound feeling of political isolation. Victims of discrimination from above and unforeseen violence from below, Indians—South Africa's smallest racial group—had no reliable allies and no obvious place to turn. Under threat from all sides, their future seemed genuinely desperate. Yet this sense of betrayal was also inflected by Gandhi's community pride, a profound and genuine commitment that shaded into an unconscious sense of superiority. In the face of the Riots, he flinched when confronted by the question of privilege and refused to acknowledge any of the issues raised in Dhlomo's article. In this context, his continued use of the term "Bantu" only underscored his ignorance of African public opinion. What did it mean to claim equal suffering and then demand that Africans show Indian traders gratitude? The implication was that Indians had provided what Africans could not. The Indian had ventured into the "wilds" of Natal, "pioneered" transport, and tilled the land—the merchant had, to borrow a phrase, "made the desert bloom." In chastising African ingratitude, Gandhi employed the stock tropes of settler colonialism.

There was an important coda to this exchange. Ngubane responded sharply to Gandhi's article in *Inkundla ya Bantu*, pointing out that Africans were divided over the Riots and wealthier Indians had behaved provocatively toward Africans.[99] *Indian Opinion* refrained from issuing a public response. Perhaps Gandhi worried that the sensitivities of his readers would not bear any intimation of responsibility. Whatever his motivations, Gandhi answered in a personal letter, apologizing and then inviting Ngubane to visit the Phoenix Settlement. The Mahatma's son chose to reach out to his critic in a way that directly echoed the great acts of reconciliation pursued by his father. This correspondence inaugurated a close friendship and political alliance. Propelled by their anticommunism, both men later joined the Natal Liberal Party and became outspoken critics of the ANC.[100] Beginning in 1952, Ngubane became a regular contributor to *Indian Opinion* and, after Gandhi's death, assumed editorial responsibility. This friendship was a rare, although by no means unique, example of individuals and groups reaching out to form new alliances following the Riots.

THE CRISIS IN THE NATAL ANC

The political rapprochement between the ANC and Indian Congress was built on precarious foundations. The Natal ANC was fragmenting under the strain of events. *Inkundla's* diagnosis was clear: "African leadership has never been so divided."[101] Without consulting the Natal executive, Xuma initially organized a joint meeting with the Indian Congress in Kimberley. We do not know exactly what Champion said to the ANC's president, but his and Msimang's protests forced Xuma to change his plans and move the venue to Durban.[102] After arriving with a group of advisors, Xuma then hastened to convene a joint meeting with Indian and African leaders without first consulting with the Natal ANC or holding a public rally to speak to Durban's Africans. Rumors of a deep rift between Xuma and Champion circulated throughout the province.[103] According to the writer Mary Benson, Champion, Msimang, and Luthuli initially opposed cooperation with the Indian

Congress, but eventually acquiesced to Xuma's arguments.[104] In an act of startling indifference to local opinion, Xuma apparently left Durban immediately after the joint statement's release.

The 6 February statement soon generated its own share of controversy. Writing in *Ilanga*, H. I. E. Dhlomo openly declared that Xuma had become outmoded: "The statement itself was a futile and puerile attempt to avoid the facts and difficulties of the situation." Lambasting Xuma's maneuvers, the newspaper declared: "All along the line, it seems the African leaders have been made pawns of the Indians." [105] Without descending to the same depths of naked race-baiting, Ngubane's response in *Inkundla* likewise condemned "the cowardly and not convincingly sincere effort."[106] Neither paper denied that the policies of segregation bore ultimate responsibility for the explosion. But in their eyes, this truth hardly accounted for the depth of antagonism between the two parties, which they attributed to the complicity of Indian merchants in blocking African economic development and the complacency of African leadership.[107] Additionally, *Inkundla* argued that the Doctors' Pact had misled Indian leaders by minimizing the intensity and significance of African resentments: "In so far as these African leaders misled the Indians and did not advise them to mend their ways, they are guilty of the Durban massacres."[108] Shortly afterward, the Transvaal ANC Youth League raised almost identical criticisms.[109] In effect, the Youth League broke publically with Xuma's handling of the crisis and the ad hoc policy embodied by the Doctors' Pact.

African figures soon began to distance themselves from the joint statement. In an interview with *Ilanga*, S. B. Ngcobo (secretary of the Combined Locations Advisory Board) denied that he had wished to sign the declaration and protested that "he had nothing to do with the statement . . . he attended the meeting as an observer, was not allowed to speak, and was not even present when the resolution was made." Another alleged signatory, D. W. Moshe, also claimed that his name had been falsely appended.[110]

In the midst of such recriminations, Champion clearly sensed that the Natal ANC leadership had lost control of a volatile situation. Acting on their authority as members of the Native Advisory board, Champion and Ngcobo organized a public meeting at the Bantu Social Centre "with the people of Durban in order to enable them to express themselves on the Riots."[111] According to the press report in *Ilanga*, the meeting teetered on the brink of chaos as different factions made impassioned speeches—"impossible to report verbatim"—from both the platform and the floor of the house.[112] Aware of the widespread dissatisfaction with the ANC's response to the Riots, Champion launched into a lengthy and emotionally charged apologia that defended his actions and violently berated the "mushroom leaders" who had begun to spring up around the city. After strongly denying that "he was under the influence of certain Indians," Champion insisted that the issues dividing Africans and Indians were "not political but economic," invoked Nehru's warnings to South Africa's Indians, attacked the Indians for "things they had done," and lambasted all the South African governments for their crimes against the Africans. Despite its longstanding disagreements with Champion, *Ilanga* characterized the performance as brilliant. Nevertheless, a series of "rank-and-file" speakers rose to challenge the stance taken by Champion and other African leaders. *Ilanga* reported:

> From this point, there came fiery after fiery speech from the floor of the house. It was clear even to a child that the cleavage that had been caused by the riots would be most difficult to repair. Leader or no leader, trouble or no trouble, the people are grimly determined to have their way. . . . What the people demand is separate land and residential areas for each group. They demand not to be mixed up either in the Reserves or in the city. They want Africans to run their own buses and stores. Many attacked the European bitterly for giving Indians better rights and treatment.

This public revolt against Champion and the ANC's right to speak on behalf of Natal's Africans was the culmination of mounting distrust and frustration by the Durban African working class in the postwar years. Previously, *tsotsis* had disrupted ballroom dance classes and musical recitals at the Bantu Social Centre and intimidated "educated Africans" to such an extent that they stopped attending Joint Council meetings.[113] Following the Riots, this diffuse, plebeian assertiveness expressed itself in the form of a direct challenge to Champion's personal leadership, the ANC's style of politics, and "non-European cooperation." As one critic from outside the province argued: "The Riots show, too, that no African leader enjoys the confidence of the people. The people are ripe for political organization; the leadership, at any rate the present leadership, is out of touch with them."[114] A contributor to *Ilanga* similarly observed: "We have now come to a point where people in Durban are out touch with their leaders on the question of the riots. They prefer now to place more reliance on the authority than on their leaders."[115] Increasingly frustrated with the paralysis of the Natal ANC, some Africans turned directly to the government. *Ilanga* and *Inkundla* published several letters calling on the state to intervene and impose segregation between the two groups.[116]

A mass boycott of Indian stores and buses began immediately after the end of the repression. At the same time, African small traders seized the opportunity to displace Indian businesses in areas like Cato Manor.[117] In the eyes of many observers, these actions dramatized the gulf between the ANC's declarations on the Riots—particularly the 6 February statement—and the attitudes of most Africans. The reality was even more convoluted. Working through African newspapers and the Native Location Advisory Boards, Natal ANC leaders supported the campaign against Indian businesses and attempted to co-opt it for their own purposes—even while they worked with Indian leaders to calm the city, negotiated with the Indian Congress, provided relief to the displaced, and signed the joint statement.

The boycott was apparently "spontaneous" (a characterization denoting that the action was organized outside the formal channels of the ANC's authority). Nevertheless, it was immediately defended by the Advisory Boards, which included leading members of the Natal ANC. By 16 January, the boards had already petitioned the Durban City Council to provide de facto legal sanction of the displacement of Indian traders. Their demands included the banning of buses operated by non-Africans, new premises for African traders in predominantly African areas, the exclusion of non-African hawkers from African locations, and the reclassification of the areas of Cato Manor "which are at present predominantly occupied by natives."[118] According to *Inkundla*, unnamed ANC leaders drafted this program.[119]

A month later, the advisory boards organized a mass meeting at the Bantu Social Centre, nominally to endorse the ANC's boycott of the Riots Commission. Yet far from echoing the position of the national

ANC leadership, the motions proposed at the rally called on its conveners to give every possible support to the boycott.[120] They continued:

> This mass meeting of Durban Africans instructs the African National Congress of Natal and the Durban Locations Advisory boards either jointly or separately to set up machinary [sic] to, (a) stop malicious and anti-African propaganda in sections of the Indian press; to stop Indian attacks on isolated Africans; to stop the eviction of African tenants by Indian landlords; and these things are regarded as evidence of lack of goodwill towards the Africans; (b) impress on the Indians that African development is such that African economic progress can no longer be delayed or obstructed; (c) ensure that whenever the African expresses willingness to take over the services at present in Indian hands in predominantly African areas the Indian should give proof of his goodwill by disposing of these to the African at a reasonable price and that the African be given every facility to trade and to run buses to and from African areas.[121]

Although the boycott movement began to atrophy by February, Indian businesses in African areas still suffered in early March, a month and a half after the Riots. Educated African leaders helped hundreds, perhaps thousands, apply for trading licenses in areas that were previously almost the exclusive preserve of Indians.[122] The boycott also received extensive and positive coverage from the Natal African press, although *Inkundla* warned that it might veer out of control without proper leadership.[123] The government and Durban Corporation directly condoned many of these efforts, for example by expropriating Indian traders in areas of Cato Manor and allocating their shops to Africans.[124] Uniquely, the Communist Party opposed the boycott and distributed leaflets warning "African workers . . . that their problems will not be overcome with the granting of licenses to African businessmen."[125]

THE VICISSITUDES OF A. W. G. CHAMPION

The Natal ANC had been significantly compromised by the contradictions between the national policy and the actions of its leaders. Champion's opportunism and prevarications were largely responsible for this outcome. Nevertheless, the statements and actions of his harshest critics—Ngubane, H. I. E. Dhlomo, and Yengwa—evinced similar inconsistencies: they rejected the violence of the pogrom, but endorsed many of its goals; they argued for collaboration with the Indian Congress and simultaneously embraced the boycott; they denounced anti-Indian racialism while perpetuating its stereotypes. Both Champion and Yengwa utilized the Riots and subsequent boycott to advance their own business interests, for example by investing in the Zulu Hlanganani trading cooperative that established its dominance in Cato Manor.[126] In later years, Champion would become an intensely bitter racialist. But it is impossible to make sense of his actions in January–February 1949 solely in those terms. According to Edwards, Champion openly expressed joy on multiple occasions regarding the Riots.[127] But he never removed his name from the 6 February statement and, despite widespread criticism of this stance, honored the commitment not to testify at the Riots Commission. Not only did he publicly defend the ANC's actions, Champion took cautious steps to implement the new understanding with the Indian Congress. In May 1949, Champion launched a joint conciliation board with the Indian Congress—a decision that was deeply unpopular with "the rank and file of his followers."[128] Within the ANC, however, he opposed moves, especially by the Youth League, to give this alliance greater political substance.[129]

As a younger generation of activists understood, Champion's gyrations represented the failure of a style of Durban African politics based on state patronage through advisory boards, the authority of the chiefs, personal enrichment in the name of race progress, provincial insularity, and Zulu nationalism.[130] His conflicted actions stemmed from conflicting imperatives. He struggled to maintain the position of the Natal ANC in the national organization, fulfill his official responsibilities as a member of the advisory board, and safeguard his personal alliances with key Indian political and business figures. At the same time, he moved to reinforce his rapidly collapsing authority among urban migrants and utilized the Riots—and the possibility of future violence—to negotiate personal business deals behind closed doors.[131] He also tried to silence his critics within the ANC, especially the Youth League. As the Youth League pushed for the adoption of a militant program of action, Champion's position—particularly his continued reliance on the Native Representative Councils—led him to oppose this course. Consequently, he attempted to cut Youth League members out of Congress activities and bar new members sympathetic to their views.[132] At the ANC's annual conference in Bloemfontein, Champion denied that the Youth League existed in his province, leading to a shouting match with delegates on the conference floor.[133] In the Youth League's eyes, Champion's presidency imperiled the very future of the league, and therefore the ANC, in Natal.

In this context, Xuma miscalculated and supported Champion's leadership in the name of maintaining the ANC's unity.[134] As a result, a number of distinct questions became linked through the dynamics of factional struggle: the Youth League's public claim that the ANC leadership bore responsibility for the Riots; the fight between Champion and the Youth League over its right to exist; and the broader debate within the ANC over the relationship between African and Indian political organizations. Ironically, Xuma's alliance with the Natal ANC president further alienated the Youth League while undermining his own position in favor of Afro-Indian cooperation in the province. At war on multiple fronts, Natal Youth League leaders—supported by Mda—concluded that both men would have to go.[135]

UNFORESEEN CONSEQUENCES

After opposing Xuma over his response to the Riots, the Youth League immediately clashed with him over the boycott of government institutions and the timing of mass protest. At the Cape and Transvaal provincial conferences, the Youth League argued that the time for action had come and convinced the assembled delegates to pass strongly worded motions boycotting the next Native Representative Council elections.[136] The conferences also endorsed drafts of a Program of Action that committed the ANC to civil disobedience guided by the philosophy of African Nationalism. Established ANC leaders, including the widely respected Z. K. Mathews, acceded to this course. The Durban Riots had reinforced broader anxieties among the African intelligentsia regarding the potential dangers of spontaneous rebellion and outright racial warfare.[137] In turn, Xuma saw the Youth League's efforts as an insurgency. He balked at the Program of Action and resisted the Youth League's attempts to use the executive to assert greater control over his office.[138]

At the national conference in Bloemfontein, the Youth League campaigned against Xuma by promoting an outsider by the name of

Dr. James Maroka. Xuma was defeated. While the African press generally depicted this outcome as the victory of an insurgent nationalism, the tone of the Youth League's speeches, especially Mda's, was far from triumphalist. His somber warnings against the dangers of African "fascists" would become a signal reference point in future debates. At the moment of the Youth League's first major political victory, Mda drew a line in the sand: true nationalism would not be built on the foundation of racial exclusiveness.

In Cato Manor, African politics followed a different course. After the repression of the rioters, the Durban police carried out mass arrests and expelled nearly four thousand Africans from the city. An anti-Indian political group called the Bantu National Congress attempted to capitalize on the Riots and presented itself in opposition to the ANC. Despite support from the government, its efforts met with only scattered success. African politics reverted to local struggles over trade and housing. In the period following the Riots, the Durban city administration actively supported efforts by traders to displace Indian-owned businesses in locations reserved for Africans.[139] Capitalizing on this policy, traders organized buying clubs and cooperatives that fought to secure licenses in urban locations. Mobilizing a rhetoric of Zulu nationalism and racial uplift, these organizations became the strongest political force in many shack settlements.[140] The two most powerful clubs in Cato Manor, the Zondizitha (Destroy our enemies) Buying Club and Zulu Hlanganani (Zulus unite), directly linked economic empowerment with anti-Indianism.[141] "Our enemies" were, unmistakably, Indians and the call to "unite" served as a repost to the ANC's policy of cooperation (expressed as *ukuhlangana* in isiZulu). By the early 1950s, Zulu Hlanganani obtained economic and political dominance in Cato Manor and held an annual celebration of the Riots.[142] Some ANC members participated in its activities or maintained close ties with its leadership. Born from the redistribution of Indian property to Africans, these forces were hostile to collaboration with the Indian Congress.

Writing in the early 1960s, Fatima Meer denied that the Riots had produced lasting resentments among the Indian community. "The outburst against the Indians," she claimed, "was a freak occurrence, a deviation from the common rule, which—due to some rare chance causes—lost its target and became confounded in a mood of violent human imbalance."[143] This statement represented the projection of an activist's perspective onto the community as a whole. For many people, these events were profoundly traumatic. When Luthuli won the Nobel Peace Prize in 1960, Indian Congress activist Phyllis Naidoo asked students at the Durban Indian High School if they had read about the award: "A deathlike silence greeted me. Then a shy student said, 'You were not in Cato Manor when we hid in our ceilings and they burnt our homes in 1949.'"[144] The Riots became a central reference point in Durban Indian culture, the cornerstone of an entrenched mythology demarcating "Indian" from "African."[145] In the year following the Riots, the NIC nearly collapsed. Only two branches remained active. Sections of the Indian elite made explicit gestures of reconciliation. Indian businessmen, and perhaps the Indian government, increased their financial support for the ANC during this period. When the Congress Alliance called for days of action during the 1950s, most Indian-owned businesses closed in hartal. These acts of solidarity, however, also reflected genuine and pervasive fear. Large segments of Durban's Indian population, wary of Africans and uncertain of the future, retreated into stunned quietude.

In his autobiography, Ismail Meer argues that "the riots unwittingly had positive results, in that they provided a basis for Afro-Indian cooperation."[146] This sentiment is echoed in the recollections of other activists, including Goonam, Nbugane, and Yengwa. Among a layer of politically conscious Indians, the Riots discredited the idea of a parallel Indian political struggle that would be somehow allied with the African cause.[147] After the Riots, the symbols of Indian nationalism and the invocation of a collective identity remained central to the politics of the Indian Congress. However, this rhetoric shifted in a subtle, but nonetheless important, fashion. By emphasizing the place of Indians within a unified movement for freedom, the Indian Congress not only rejected a political course separate from Africans, they also made an implicit claim regarding the nature of the struggle and the society that it would produce. If the fate of Indians could no longer be disentangled from the self-determination of Africans, the reverse was also true: Indians would be an essential part of both the fight for national liberation and a future South Africa.

For the leaders of the ANC Youth League, the Riots illuminated the failures of three powerful currents within African politics: Xuma's policy of non-European cooperation, Lembede's racial nationalism, and

Champion's mode of authoritarian populism. As the ANC turned toward direct confrontation with the regime, the Durban violence served as a harrowing reminder of the dangers involved in mass action along racially exclusive lines. Aware that the government sought to manipulate tensions, sections of the ANC leadership worried about the possibility of an anti-Indian alliance between reactionary African groups and the state. Ngubane remembers: "We began to examine more critically our relationship with the Indian community and endeavored to find a formula which would enable both sides to work effectively for the prevention of the recurrence of the riots."[148] As whole districts of Durban lay in ruins, and bodies continued to be pulled from the charcoaled remnants of shacks, intellectuals within the ANC—especially in the Youth League—concluded that the nature of the struggle would have to change. The ANC Youth League was already committed to a militant course heavily influenced by the Indian independence struggle and the Passive Resistance Campaign. Some of these same intellectuals understood that an alliance with the Indian Congresses was a strategic necessity. The obstacles were formidable. The ANC was divided over collaboration, most Durban Africans openly rejected this policy, and many people within the Indian community—including some politically conscious activists—genuinely feared the prospect of any large-scale African mobilization. The first moves toward a permanent alliance were halting and driven by the force of circumstance. Nevertheless, they represented a momentous step.

4 ↬ The Racial Politics of Home

Sex, Feminine Virtue, and the Boundaries of the Nation

A wealthy merchant in East Africa answered his door one evening to find two young Africans. Upon enquiring the purpose of their visit, it turned out that one of them had come to ask for the hand of the merchant's daughter in marriage. With due decorum, and considered coolness, the merchant called the visitors into the living room, offered them a drink, and called in his daughter. The proposition was put to her. Respectfully she replied that she had nothing against it if the gentlemen would take care of her and if she were to have her parents' permission. The merchant then told the young men that, in accordance with tradition, it would only be correct for them to bring their parents to formally approach him. That night, after the guests had left, the family packed its belongings and fled the country for India.[1]

> —Apocryphal story frequently told by South African Indians during the apartheid years

You came to their country when they were ruling themselves and you took away all their rights in their country of origin, you took away their cattle from them and their lands and placed on them the burden of passes together with harsh laws that cause them to fill goals without any cause, and they are persecuted by your laws that bring about sin.[2]

> —Jeremiah Sithole, a Zulu prophet

ON THE first evening of the 1949 Durban Riots, a crowd of African men gathered outside the Grey Street Women's Hostel, demanding the delivery of women who associated with Indians.[3] This harrowing moment is only a passing detail in a submission to the government commission following the Riots. There is no further information regarding the people involved, or what happened next. Nonetheless, it says a great deal about the centrality of gender, sex, and violence to the racial dynamics of mid-century Natal. At the inquiry into the Riots, the liberal senator E. H. Brookes observed that interracial sex was the second most common complaint raised by Africans in the period before January 1949.[4] Numerous articles and letters in *Ilanga* accused "certain Indian men" of seducing or preying on African women.[5] Sexual violence against Indian women also played a central role in the Durban events. In her autobiography, Dr. Goonam recalls: "I treated girls of 14 and 15 who had been raped in Clairwood, Jacobs and Merebank."[6] In later testimony, some participants boasted of targeting women rather than the possessions of Indian men.[7] In turn, these assaults against Indian women and girls further enflamed the stereotype of the violent, savage, and (now) sexually threatening Zulu.

This chapter explores some of the complex intersections between race, the constitution of public and private spaces, and gender in mid-century Durban. As urbanization accelerated during the interwar period, debates intensified within both groups over the meaning of nation, tradition, and the status of women. Many Africans and Indians understood the proper boundaries between the races—boundaries that were in continuous dispute during the 1940s and '50s—in terms of the relationship between gender and social space. In this context, questions such as public interactions between African women and Indian men, African domestic workers in Indian households, and interracial sex became lightning rods for conflicts over the external and internal boundaries of nation and community. Both the ANC's and Indian Congress's politics necessitated the development of new public spaces within colonial and apartheid society—a process often contested precisely because it created (or reproduced) forms of hierarchy and exclusion among the subjugated. In the eyes of many Africans, institutions of Indian diasporic culture—marriage, religion, domestic space, dress, even music and food—became signifiers of social hierarchy and racial exclusion. In mid-century Durban, the separation between public life and the private sphere did not occur solely, or even primarily, in terms of the state. Whatever the explicit content of nationalist discourse, the domestic realm was in the first instance demarcated in relationship to the also-colonized other.

This chapter begins by describing parallel attempts by African and Indian intellectuals to construct a program of modernizing nationalism on the basis of women's dual role as agents of progress and bearers of "tradition." In different but ultimately related fashions, these discourses constructed interracial sexual intimacy as corrosive to the foundations of national identity. Reacting to the place of women in the Native Question's construction of "tribe," *Ilanga* championed equal rights for African women and a modern vision of femininity even as the newspaper encouraged greater control over female sexuality in the name of moral reform and racial uplift. These contradictory commitments rendered sex between Africans and Indians dangerous: Indian "seduction" of African women figured the loss of patriarchal control and a deeper crisis of African masculinity. Among many Indian politicians, social scientists, and community leaders, a singular idea of Indian tradition — sometimes identified with "racial purity" — underwrote both Indian national aspirations in the subcontinent and the unity of the diaspora. Accordingly, the Indian's rejection of interracial sex, frequently conflated with procreation and the racialized body of the Coloured, testified to the power and endurance of diasporic identity. This chapter proceeds to juxtapose these discourses with more subaltern articulations of the relationship between race, gender, and sexuality: the gospel of moral redemption promoted by African hristian churches, the assertion of urban independence and sexual right by African domestic workers, and the fear among Indians of the sexually threatening Zulu following the 1949 Durban Riots. The contrast between these representations not only illustrates the depths of hardened racial divisions, it also reveals the frictions between popular and more elite versions of African nationalism. As later chapters discuss, these conflicts would become a major faultline in Natal ANC politics during the mid-1950s.[8]

AFRICAN NATIONALISM, GENDER, AND URBANIZATION

Since the late nineteenth century, the Durban government's attempts to establish and control a dependable supply of migrant labor centered on preventing the movement of African women to the city. David Hemson explains: "The influx of African women, although posed in terms of prostitution, venereal disease, and public morality, threatened the drive to force all African workers into barracks by posing the alternative of working-class households in the towns."[9] The increasing urbanization of Africans and Indians following the First World War — and especially the development of racially mixed working-class neighbor-hoods—produced a growing panic among missionaries and some local politicians over the "degeneration" of the African and the dangers of interracial sex.[10] Expulsions of African women from Durban occurred during the 1920s and 1930s, and in 1935 the Durban council passed a resolution banning African women from entering the city without permission. Town councilors called for the organized medical exami-nation of African women.[11] In addition to the ubiquitous threats of po-lice harassment, deportation to the reserves, and political repression, African residents of Durban increasingly confronted another aspect of state power: intrusive biomedical surveillance that not only displaced and "humiliated" Zulu patriarchal authority, but transformed the Afri-can woman's body into an object of symbolic and political struggle.[12]

Two other agencies contributed to the politicization of women's sexuality: the influence of the mission-educated petite bourgeoisie and the authority of Natal's "traditional" leaders, the Zulu chiefs.[13] As Shula Marks argues, the social dislocations caused by the Mineral Revolution and the intensification of migrant labor precipitated the alliance of these forces in the late 1920s. A formidable bloc developed between the Natal Christian elite, the Zulu royal house, and elements within the government based on ethnic nationalism and a neotraditional cult of the monarchy.[14] "It was," Marks argues, "in the position of African women that the forces of conservatism found a natural focus."[15] On the part of the Natal state and the chiefs, the continuing subordination of women in the reserves played an economic function. The labor of African women subsidized the system of low-paid migrant labor; their near complete legal disenfranchisement—and the need for young men to pay lobolo to marry—enabled chiefs to assert control over migrant workers and their earnings.[16] The Christian middle class had been deeply worried over the disruption of authority within the African fam-ily, premarital pregnancy, and the spread of venereal disease since at least the first decade of the twentieth century.[17] Such concerns reached new heights in the 1930s, and many intellectuals believed that a mod-ernized Zulu culture, grounded in respect for male elders and the dis-cipline of the home, could counteract these scourges.[18] For the next two decades and beyond, the status of women was at the heart of de-bates over Zulu tradition and modernization. Lobolo, female initiation rites, social etiquette for women, and witchcraft continued to provoke vigorous exchanges in *Inkundla* and *Ilanga* during the 1940s and early '50s, especially in the isiZulu pages.[19]

By the mid-1940s, several additional factors had combined to accentuate the political importance of the African woman. Not only had migration to cities accelerated during the war, but women began to enter new spheres of employment, including factory work and professions that potentially afforded some measure of financial independence.[20] African women also started to displace men in the role of domestic servants or "kitchen boys."[21] The response to these developments among African intellectuals was decidedly complex. Given the strangulating impact of the "colour bar" legislation on the employment prospects of most men, African newspapers and politicians saluted the growing number of women in distinctly modern professions like nursing, factory work, and teaching: "Today African women are winning major battles by themselves as nurses and factory operatives—many of these receiving better wages than men."[22] In numerous articles in *Ilanga* during the late 1940s and '50s, H. I. E. Dhlomo extolled the virtues of cultural transformation and scientific progress, imprecating those who would intern the contemporary African within the mockery of unchanging "tradition." "Tribalism," he prophesized, "is doomed."[23] A frequent target of his critique was the legal status of African women: they were considered perpetual minors under Natal's Native Code. In the middle of the growing disillusionment of the late 1940s, the success stories of nurses, teachers, and women factory workers were one of the few clear signs of race progress. Profiles of attractive, smartly dressed young nurses soon became a fixture of *Ilanga*, foreshadowing the celebration of the sleek, cosmopolitan—and sometimes bathing suit-clad—woman emblematic of *Drum* magazine.[24]

The greater financial and personal independence of women also generated fear over the loss of patriarchal control. *Ilanga* published a regular satirical column by Rolling Stone, which sometimes featured a nurse named Jane Maplank. A misogynist caricature directed at the "wrong kind" of women in the professions, nurse Jane used her uniform to set up "dates" around town—scandalously blurring the distinction between profession and prostitution—and could be bought (lobolo) for a single car ride. Rolling Stone (*Ilanga* editor R. R. R. Dhlomo) directly associated these attitudes with promiscuity: "She is a progressive nurse with modern outlook she does not see why she shouldn't love to be inside the car of anybody even if he is not an African."[25] While the new African woman may have embodied modernity and racial advancement, she also revealed the dangers to male authority posed by urbanization, novel forms of mobility, and the "perversion" of African institutions (in this case, the transposition of bride price with purchasing sex).[26] Moreover, most African women in Durban were not relatively well-paid professionals. They often lived in fetid hostels or cohabitated with boyfriends, and many women survived through brewing sorghum beer or prostitution. Drawing on Victorian conceptions of propriety and eugenics, articles in the Zulu press directly linked socioeconomic progress and the question of female promiscuity.[27]

The panic over the sexual foundations of African nationhood was closely related to a second question: the crisis of the African family. An increasing body of social scientific research, much of it organized and funded by the South African Institute of Race Relations, catalogued the social impact of migrant labor, pass laws, and slum existence on new urban households. Columns in *Ilanga* praised the efforts of the Race Relations Institute and often reiterated its claims, particularly in denouncing pass laws: "One of the strongest things that can be said against them [the pass laws] is that they have helped to break African family life. And since the family is the fundamental unit of society, it would be superfluous to mention the evils and misery caused by a system that breaks down family life."[28] *Ilanga* argued that the absence of housing produced overcrowding and the abrogation of familial privacy. Low wages necessitated that mothers work, leaving children subject to pernicious influences. In addition, *Ilanga* asserted that the prohibition of alcohol resulted in the transformation of private homes into public shebeens, while pass and liquor laws allowed police to enter the African's home with impunity.[29] The result of this abeyance could only be national degeneration. "Children see their parents' nakedness," H. I. E. Dhlomo lamented. "There is no privacy between sexes. It is a slow process of debasement, torture, and death—both physical and spiritual." The next sentence proceeded to finger an accomplice to this process: "Meanwhile Indian and other landlords are reaping a huge and rich harvest fleecing the people who have no alternative."[30]

Ilanga and *Inkundla* employed the same language in discussing the status of women that informed the rhetoric of anti-Indian populism: the discourse of economic self-help and race progress. The African woman simultaneously provided an index and vehicle of such progress, but the dominant position of the Indian merchant and landlord—or, at least, so it seemed to many Africans—directly interfered with the African's national aspirations. These articles also reflected the growing influence of American consumer culture—and the capitalist mythology of "fast cars" and "clean bodies"—on urban African ideas of femininity.[31] In the mid-1940s, *Ilanga* began publishing a family and children's supplement and, by 1947, a "Women's Corner" appeared that mixed domestic and fashion advice with nationalist platitude: "In the world of to-day, civilization is making great strides and it is our duty as mothers of the race to move forward with the rest."[32] Proliferating advertisements for skin cream, hair products, and beauty pageants articulated a self-consciously modern ideal of womanhood mediated by commodity consumption. For many middle-class Africans, nationalism was impossible without a new femininity.[33] This modern femininity, however, was located and performed in the same contested spaces—cinemas, buses, hospitals, and shops—where the Indian stood as a figure for African alienation. In the case of Ngubane and H. I. E. Dhlomo, this intersection revealed a contradictory set of commitments: a vision of African culture that included "the modern girl" and sexual equality, African nationalism as vehicle for the redemption of black masculinity, and a secular program of moral reform that reflected their belief in racial uplift. In different ways, each of these commitments informed their newspaper's depictions of female sexuality and rendered interracial intimacy perilous.

AFRICANIST CHRISTIANITY AND SUBALTERN PATRIARCHY

By the 1950s, African newspapers had managed to create a sophisticated and wide-reaching public sphere despite political persecution, economic insecurity, and the white ownership of most African press (*Inkundla* was the notable exception). At the same time, the discourse of literate nationalists coexisted, competed, and sometime blended together with other powerful cultural formations, especially Natal's independent African churches. With the hypertrophy of Natal's shantytowns during the interwar period, millenarian churches spread rapidly, and their messianic gospel contributed to the development of a new, subaltern Zulu nationalism.[34] The disruption of patriarchal authority and the proliferation of "sin" (venereal disease, premarital intercourse, and interracial sex) were significant motifs in the liturgy of these groups.[35] Their cosmology drew heavily on ancestor veneration, healing practices, and the traditions of the Zulu monarchy.[36] It also employed a melancholic narrative of collective loss that generalized a vision of Zulu national redemption from the shattered moral economy of the individual homestead. Part of millenarianism's power was that it promised the moral regeneration of the Zulu nation, while simultaneously upholding older forms of patriarchal authority. If articles in *Ilanga* and *Inkundla* generally expressed the worldview of modernizing nationalists, millenarian preachers voiced similar anxieties regarding gender and the crisis of the African family in a more subaltern idiom.

On 26 August 1933, Isaiah Shembe (the founder of the Nazareth Baptist Church and arguably the most influential African Christian leader in Natal) delivered his first sermon at Rosboom, a small town near Pietermaritzburg. Shembe began the Rosboom advice by warning the house of Senzangakhona (the Zulu nation) not to worship its enemies: the people from the ends of the earth who had annihilated their livestock and left them without maize. After castigating his audience with quotations from scripture, Shembe then proceeded to declare that the black man's name had become a term of derision in his own land. Rather than returning home "to milk the cattle of his father" after his education, the son of the black man went to another nation and labored for men who were not his father and women who were not his mother.[37] But the most searing humiliation that Shembe invoked was the inability of Zulus to protect their daughters from seduction—a visceral image of the nation prostrate, biologically disrupted:

> And so the word of Jehovah, who does not lie, was fulfilled: that you will bear sons and daughters but they will bring you no joy because you will be oppressed (Deuteronomy 28 v 41). Today, your young girl is made pregnant by an Indian and then flung aside like snot because she is a prisoner's girl. Today, your young girl is made pregnant by a white and then flung aside like snot because she's a prisoner's girl.[38]

Shembe described foreign domination in terms of a collective loss of control over the labor of young men, female sexuality, and ultimately the entire process of social reproduction. Incorporating the promise of messianic redemption into his narrative, Shembe understood this crisis of moral economy in terms of a profound disruption of the Zulu's relationship with God. The Rosboom advice concluded with a parable-like story of an educated son who left home to become a minister in the European church, giving his parents' savings to foreign schools and women, and thus leaving his father destitute and his mother naked. The son's actions synthesized the spiritual, economic, and sexual betrayal of the Zulu nation: worshiping Christ in the conqueror's church (breaking the Zulu nation's pact with Jehovah), giving labor and money to the European economy (sabotaging the collective accumulation of wealth), and pursuing an affair with a foreign woman (dishonoring his mother's sacrifices by failing to return home and lift her from poverty and pre-Christian barbarism).

These themes, particularly the identification of national deliverance with the restoration of masculine authority and female virtue, circulated widely. Eighteen years after the Rosboom advice, a prophet named Jeremiah Sithole—who lived in the Durban location of Baumannville—wrote a letter addressed to the manager of the Native Administration Department.[39] Although it did not discuss interracial sex, Sithole's tract (which seems to have been dictated to a professional notary) followed Shembe in emphasizing both colonialism's sexual dimensions and the perturbation of Zulu gender norms. The letter began by announcing that God had sent him to this earth to wipe away the tears of Senzangakhona's children, for the sufferings of the Zulu people had come before the eyes of God. "Did you create these people whom you are troubling," he demanded, "or are they God's creation?" Sithole caustically enumerated the agonies inflected by the conquering nation: the dispossession of rights, land, and cattle; the imposition of passes and causeless imprisonment; the creation of persecutory laws that bring about "sin." In Sithole's language, foreign domination, urbanization, and the daily humiliations of settler colonialism ("You cause them to go to the pass offices to be in the hot sun suffering") fused into a state of moral degradation that simultaneously crippled the Zulu and exposed the satanic nature of the colonizer. The Europeans had illegitimately disrupted both Zulu patriarchal authority and divine sovereignty, violently inserting themselves into the Zulu's place.

In this context, Sithole invoked the European woman's body—or rather its concealment—to exemplify the perversity of the new order.

Although Western-styled clothing initially symbolized moral probity and the evangelical rationale for conquest, Sithole proclaimed that the actual conduct of Europeans had denuded their women under the divine gaze:

> In the land of their origin you have caused them [the Zulu] to suffer through hard and bad tasks and you refuse them licenses to do work that would improve them because you are a bad nation that came under religion into this country when your woman folk were wearing long cloths, to-day they go about naked in the eyes of God—you are a bad nation that is jealous and with hardened hearts, and God—God has sent me to ask where you have placed Dinizulu and Cetshwayo—bring them back to-day or . . . you will be sorry for some time.

The visual force of these words was intended to strip the European, replicating the moment of self-awareness in the Garden of Eden and humiliating the colonizer. This image also invoked the function of clothing and sexual inaccessibility in distinguishing civilization from savagery. By appealing to the divine's transcendental vision, Sithole inverted the relationship between the appearance of the colonial order and its underlying reality. If the European woman served to embody rectitude in the midst of native sinfulness, the judgment of heaven had determined that the jealously and cruelty of the foreigners had driven the African people to this current depraved state. This image was one of several symbolic reversals that culminated in the demand for the return of the vanquished Zulu kings. Sithole concluded the letter by swearing that he would overthrow Europeans with soldiers from heaven, employing water and fire against guns, unless the government set his people free: "I who is the truth, the Faithful of God, I have now come to Durban, a city of sins. I was born amongst you but you cannot see me during 1951, I live on the space above. I am not seen. I rise with the sun and set with the sun—look at the sun with telescopes." The figure of the sun embodied the cyclic inevitability of restoration, while revealing the intrinsic limitation of the colonizer's vision and strength: the impotence of European technology when confronting the raw power of the cosmos's natural order.

By the early 1950s, two thirds of Natal's Indian population lived in urban or peri-urban areas.[40] In contrast to African migrants, Indians moved to the city not as individuals, but as families: a substantial minority succeeded in purchasing land and building a local community infrastructure of temples and mosques, movie theaters, and homes.[41] Several areas in Grey Street contained a dense mixture of people from different religious, linguistic, and class backgrounds. But most Indians—over 80 percent—lived in outlying regions where neighborhoods usually formed around ethnolinguistic communities: Telugu speakers in Puntans Hill and Stella Hill, Hindi speakers in Newlands, and Tamil speakers in Springfield and along the South Coast.[42] Hilda Kuper and Fatima Meer provide rich descriptions of these areas. In the average Indian suburb, the better houses—sometimes owned by quite wealthy individuals—lined the few good roads; behind them, rows of wood-and-iron shacks lacked kitchens or bathrooms and relied on communal taps.[43] Most households were large, averaging seven people. Two or three families often rented the same piece of land. As a result, strong communities developed around extended families or groups of neighbors informally incorporated into an enlarged kinship group.[44] As Kuper wrote in the late 1950s:

> A house in an Indian area is never an isolated dwelling; it is integrated into the street, neighbourhood and community. Kinsmen often live near each other, affairs of neighbours arouse the gossip that controls the moral standards of the whole area; temples and schools are subscribed by local donations and become local and public meeting places; shops give credit to the families in the area; the local community develops an in-group awareness expressed in a number of local associations.[45]

Although some evidence suggests that joint families were a minority by the mid-1950s, the ideal of the extended family (*kutum* in Gujurati and Urdu; *kudumbom* in Tamil) continued to inform aspects of social life ranging from business decisions to marriage negotiations.[46] Although a small elite had begun to rebel against such norms by the early 1950s, most Indians, of all classes and religions, continued to live in a world tightly circumscribed by family life.

As Bill Freund observes, many Indian men actively participated in two worlds: a public universe of gambling, sport, horse racing, and bars, *and* a self-consciously traditional universe of temples (or mosques), cultural associations, language schools, and family life.[47] With the exception of a small number of professionals, the social activities of Indian women largely remained confined within the extended family: collectively raising children, performing rituals, preparing food, and adding their energies to family economic activities like shopkeeping, market gardening, or craft production.[48] When women participated in cultural or recreational activities outside the home (for example, attending cinema), they often did so accompanied by a male relative or a significant part of the household.[49] Reflecting the outlook of her informants, Kuper argues that women—through "their enforced attachment to the home, their constant influence over the children, and their adherence to traditional rituals"—bound separate households together within the extended family and thereby preserved the *kudumbom* as the basis for urban Indian life.[50]

Within and between these communities, ideas of caste possessed significant, if highly uneven, force. In her work on the history of caste in South Asia, Susan Bayly writes "caste was and is, to a considerable extent, what people think of it, and how they act on these perceptions."[51] In most usages, the Portuguese-derived term "caste" stands in for one of two words: *varna* (the four ritual categories of Hinduism) or *jati* (an endogamous, occupationally specialized group claiming common descent). Both phenomena evince considerable local and regional variation; the relationship between the two has changed over time. Although innumerous representations of India convey the image of an ancient caste system, Bayly and others argue that a pan-Indian system of caste relations organized around Brahaminical values and embracing the majority of the subcontinent's population is relatively modern, particularly in southern India.[52] Rather than postulate a single definition of "caste," it is necessary to examine the reconfiguration of concepts and practices of caste hierarchy in different political and economic circumstances. Most of the literature on caste in South Africa postulates a unified system in India that then underwent a dual process of disintegration and selective retention.[53]As Sidney Mintz and Richard Price argue regarding Afro-Caribbean culture, this approach both homogenizes the societies of origin and misrecognizes the process of creative reinvention necessitated by radically differing material circumstances.[54] It also overstates the general autonomy of caste from its articulation with related forms of class and gender dominance.[55] For a number of reasons, the experiences of plantation labor and urban community life resulted in significant transformations of the ideas about caste that were brought to South Africa.[56] Many practices were just abandoned. But this distillation and reconfiguration also facilitated the synthesis of caste with other discourses and forms of organizing community.

Among the relatively small populations of Gujarati Hindus, Hindi-speaking Brahmans, and Telugu Naidu, families continued to adhere to caste endogamy, some prohibitions on commensality, and ritual exclusiveness until at least the 1960s.[57] In the case of Gujarati Hindus (who came to South Africa as passengers), their class position and continued ongoing ties with their communities in India facilitated a degree of continuity in practice.[58] A significant number of Telugu indentured laborers migrated from the same castes and districts of Andhra, allowing them to recreate aspects of their former community structures after they had fulfilled their contracts.[59]

The majority of South African Hindus, however, incorporated particular elements of caste into a more diffuse idea of Indian tradition. By the 1950s, restrictions on commensality and diet, caste terminology, and many aspects of the pollution barrier had disappeared except among some more conservative members of the older generation. But a general awareness of caste status and its accompanying prohibitions remained widespread, particularly among Indian elites, and the middle class often attributed lower caste status to working-class professions.[60] The available evidence suggests that distinct communities consolidated around religious and language-based institutions: a form of linguistic identity heavily conditioned by class or general social status, and further modified by the differentiation between families who continued to employ some caste criteria in arranging marriages (and who generally identified themselves as high caste) and those who did not.[61] These linguistic identities remained powerful even after, as Rajend Mestrie shows, the majority of South African Indians adopted English as their main language of communication.[62] The principal mechanism for reproducing these communities was control over marriage: women assumed the material and symbolic responsibility for maintaining the integrity of the community.

PROGRESS, TRADITION, AND
THE "INDIAN WOMAN"

With the crucial exception of the imprisonment of female passive resisters, the question of the Indian woman rarely entered into the public discourse of the Indian Congress during the 1940s and '50s.[63] Indian nationalist discussions of gender and the family—which were heavily influenced by the Race Relations Institute, liberal social science, and the discourse of the Indian anticolonial struggle—generally abstracted "Indian culture" from the South African political context. This reification enacted a characteristic gesture of secular nationalism: literate, nationalist Indians and white liberals debated social practices like marriage, education of girls, and purdah within an idealized schema of progress and modernization, while ultimately locating the problem of culture in the private spheres of community, temple (or mosque), and home.[64] As a result, the distinctive practices of Indian social groups were displaced (at least in theory) from the political sphere and then subsumed under the unifying rubric of "Indian tradition." In many respects, this conception of unity had its origins in the alliances among different ethnolinguistic and religious factions brokered by Gandhi in the early twentieth century.[65] By the mid-1940s, both moderate and conservative leaders employed a social scientific idiom of progress alongside an overarching conception of a single Indian tradition. Their statements generally approached the future of the Indian in terms of an irreducible dualism: either the preservation of Indian culture or assimilation to Western social norms.

Following the Second World War, relatively little had changed in the situation of most Indian women. The first girls' high school opened in 1936. Fewer than seven thousand women held formal employment in 1951 (7.3 percent of the Indian workforce). In 1956, girls constituted 15.6 percent of Standard 9 and 10 pupils.[66] Although some degree of education had become a marriage criterion among the elite, the small number of women doctors, lawyers, and teachers continued to encounter wide-spread disapprobation.[67] The female Indian Congress members who assumed public positions of leadership—women such as Fatima Meer, Dr. Goonam, and Zainab Asvat—were self-conscious trailblazers who used the struggle to create new identities and roles for women. Importantly, some of these activists (along with ANC leaders such as Mkhize) also worked with the multiracial Durban and District's

Women's League, which agitated for women's rights and carried out social work in Cato Manor after 1952.[68]

Despite the limited numbers involved, many observers suggested that these limited developments reflected a general process of Westernization. The education of girls and the adoption of Western dress by younger Indian women drew special attention. Writing in the *Race Relations* journal, S. Coopan and B. A. Naidoo argued: "In urban areas the Indian is subject to the dual influence of urban conditions of living and of a Western pattern of culture. This may be observed in the changing dress habits of working and adolescent girls. Western frocks have found favour amongst them, and response to variations in fashion has become sensitive."[69] Significantly, these celebrations of Indian progress directly assimilated the social dynamics of Natal to similar processes underway in India itself. In a 1955 dissertation on the education of Indian women, Birbal Rambiritch treated social change in both countries as a single phenomenon.[70]

This construct of the Indian woman—which appeared in newspaper articles, scholarly journals, and speeches to the Rotary Club—performed three functions. First, it unified the various segments of the diaspora into a single historical agent by abstracting an idea of "Indian culture" from different practices: the decisive question became the collective dynamic of reform. The very notion of a generic Indian woman negated the continuing salience of religious, ethnolinguistic, and caste differences as well as the persistence of endogamy within all three categories.[71] Second, it generalized a linear trajectory based on the experiences of a small section of the middle class. Indian women from working-class families primarily lived within contexts shaped by family. However, their activities could include assisting in stores, hawking produce, working in market gardens, and shopping; that is, labor outside the space of the home. Although a widely shared ideal of the Indian wife stressed delicacy and seclusion, only the elite practiced: most women's experiences defied both poles of the expected transition from a normative "traditional" to a singular "modern."[72] Third, this construct removed the issue of cultural identity from the context of South Africa. At one level, this gesture undercut a form of racial essentialism (the equation of India with a set of cultural traits) by emphasizing a shared project of modernization throughout the colonial and postcolonial world. It also ensured that a "Western" modernity was the sole axis of comparison. African women appeared in these discussions rarely, if ever.

By the 1940s, deep misgivings about the impact of Westernization began to appear. Drawing on the anthropological model of "cultural contact" and the ideas of colonial ethnopsychiatry, the first South African Indian social scientists warned that the new generation of urbanized youth faced a crisis of identity: "The younger generation, educated in English only, and absorbing the superficial characteristics of western civilization, in the absence of more intimate contacts with European culture . . . are in danger of being deprived of moral and spiritual purpose in life."[73] Religious and social organizations voiced these fears more forthrightly. In 1944, an Indian Youth Cultural Conference organized by the journalist P. S. Joshi declared: "This conference calls upon Indians of Greater India in general and of South Africa in particular to respect, to follow, and to maintain Indian culture in place of the indiscriminate imitation of the Western one." Emphasizing the essential unity of India and its diaspora, both the conference greetings and subsequent motions strongly endorsed national unity across caste, provincial, and "communal" (that is, religious) lines, and repeatedly referred to culture in an all-embracing singular. The motions called on educational institutions to impart "Indian culture, community, and mother tongue," and urged "the Indian people to use their mother tongue at all times and on all occasions — except where it is inevitably necessary — in order to maintain the dignity of Indian nationhood."[74]

What did the globalizing term "Indian culture" signify in these conflicting discourses? In an influential critique of secular nationalism, Marxist scholars have argued "the period when an anti-colonial national identity was being forged was also the period when the Indian national polity was being communalized, and the congress-led National Movement cannot escape most of the responsibility for this."[75] According to this argument, Gandhi and the Indian National Congress relied heavily on religious leaders and cultural organizations for mass mobilization, conciliated caste and religious divisions, and — in the final analysis — constructed a "national" movement on the basis of vertically organized and mutually exclusive communitarian blocs. Despite its secular and universalizing ideology, the Indian National Congress further politicized religious identity and created the structural conditions for the identification of the nation and Indian culture with the Hindu majority.[76]

In South Africa, a similar construction of the Indian nation—also underpinned by a bloc between several religious and ethnic communities—served a different function. Although the idea of Indian culture lacked unifying content, it reinforced a distinctive identity by constructing a common origin in an (ultimately imaginary) historical past. National progress and the maintenance of cultural integrity demanded a politics grounded in racial difference. The Indian Youth Cultural Conference discussed above sharply denounced the "mixed marriages taking place in this country, and in order to protect the purity of the Indian race, [entreated its] countrymen to take pride in their own culture and marry within [their] religious communities." The education of girls, communal harmony, and cultural education would serve these ends. As Sir Maharaj Singh, former agent general for India in South Africa, stated in his greetings to this same gathering: "The Indian race in South Africa should be kept pure and unsullied. For this purpose an ardent love for India, her wisdom, her language and her ideals must be maintained."

THE PROBLEM OF SEX

The question of African-Indian sexual intimacy was therefore located at the intersection of several debates over modernity, tradition, and nationhood. For many Africans, it represented the usurpation of sexual access to women by a race whose relative achievements not only illuminated a profound crisis of African society, but supposedly came at their immediate expense. The idea of Indian men seducing African women exemplified the nation's powerlessness, humiliation, and collective loss of patriarchal right. Sometimes intellectuals also alleged that a certain kind of African women—modern, professional, and outside proper channels of familial control—sought out these attentions, in the process compromising their own people. In most circumstances, Indian nationalists rejected that sex between Africans and Indians happened on any significant scale.[77] The possibility of interracial sex, and especially "mixed race" children, threatened a powerful construction of diasporic identity.

Indian and African sources diverge sharply regarding sexual intimacy. With few exceptions, Indian political leaders and social scientists rejected the idea that relationships between Indians and other racial groups occurred with any frequency. In a pamphlet assembled for the Race Relations institute, M. Sirkari Naidoo (a researcher at the University of Natal) wrote: "Pride of race and culture has, in large measure, preserved the purity of the [Indian] race and prevented miscegenation with the other two races."[78] Monty Naicker employed almost identical language in order to deny that legal equality would lead to marriages between Indian men and European women: "Those who have lived amongst Indians will bear testimony to the fact it [intermarriage] is a false alarm; in fact, their civilization has instinctively instilled into them the ideals to preserve intact the purity of their race." Naicker then proceeded to cite statistics demonstrating that marriages between whites and other non-Europeans vastly outnumbered those between Indians and Europeans.[79] The submission of the Natal Indian Organization to the Durban Riots Commission played the same chords:

> The Indian people deny most emphatically that promiscuity between Indian males and African females is common. There might be a few cases here and there and this is understandable in a multi-racial country. If this occurrence were as common as it is made out to be, the attention of the Indian people would have been drawn to it long ago. This is an allegation we submit has no substance. Indians have been in South Africa for nearly 90 years, and it is to their credit that they have not created a community of Indian-African origin by promiscuous relations. On the contrary, extremely conscious of their race pride, they have maintained the purity of their race.[80]

Significantly, the repeated invocation of race pride and Indian cultural values was not, at least in the first instance, meant to demarcate Indians from Africans. Rather, the disavowal of interracial sex served to indict the mores of whites and the moral pretenses of South Africa's Western civilization. Few readers would have missed the implication that the existence of a Coloured population betrayed white society's true level of restraint or that the values of Indian culture had prevented sexual unions across racial lines without resorting to the statutes brandished by the South African state. The invocation of the Coloured as a sign of racial breakdown both echoed and inverted the figure of the "Coloured girlfriend," which represented the urbanity of Indian (and sometimes African) men in other sources from this period. Whether viewed as corroding or liberating, interracial sex was persistently conflated with procreation and then figured in the racialized and eroticized body of the Coloured.[81]

The African press conveyed a different reality. The accusation that Indian men seduced, mixed with, or dated African women was ubiquitous during the 1940s and 1950s. It appeared in African newspapers, religious sermons, testimony in front of government commissions, short stories, and right-wing African propaganda produced with the support of the apartheid state. This claim often took a specific form: the denunciation of unequal control over women and unequal access to social space more broadly. A letter to *Ilanga* from the mid-1950s typified this duality: "What's funny is that you will never find Indian girls at the Y.M.C.A. They only come when the function is strictly theirs. I hate this business of Indians mixing with us in our concerts. Now they take advantage and go so far as to date African girls."[82] Following the 1949 Riots, a full-page editorial of *Ilanga* explicated this lack of reciprocity at greater length:

> The moral attitude of some Indian men towards African women is shocking to say the least. (It would be unfair and inflammatory to refer to Katherine Mayo's "Mother Indian" although one cannot help recalling its contents.) They associate with African women openly! This incenses the most humble and even some of the most advanced "I-know-it-is-the-system-and-not-the-Indian-as-such" Africans.[83]

Coyly citing Mayo's notorious tract of pro-imperialist feminism (which reduced Indian civilization to a sensationalist depiction of patriarchal lechery), Dhlomo mobilized anti-Indian stereotypes even as he warned Indians against the consequences of certain actions: they risked validating the oppressor's racial discourse through their unconscious disregard of male African sensibilities.[84]

These rumors depicted Indian men taking advantage of superior wealth and status and—implicitly—the vulnerability of recently "de-tribalized" women. Their focus was often on specific urban spaces. In addition to the dances mentioned above, stories about interracial sex often took place in or around cinemas, hospitals, urban streets, stores, and (especially) buses. Interrupting a diatribe against the behavior of Coloureds at Indian-owned cinemas, Rolling Stone sardonically alleged: "we even have Indians who really want to be near African women—as near as makes no difference—if you get our meaning."[85] One African witness at the Riots Commission opined that Indians sought bus licenses as "just another avenue, which they explored to get a hold of our womenfolk."[86] Rumors circulated that certain Indians traded goods for "services" behind the closed doors of their shops, and people gossiped about relationships between African nurses and Indian doctors.[87] Not only did each of these sites create the possibility for a promiscuous mingling of the races and sexes, they also represented the institutionalization of Indian social privilege based on both economic and legal advantage. Even the Durban streets—the quintessential locus of movement, intermixing, and social collectivity—necessitated that African men, unlike both Indian men and African women before the mid 1950s, carry passes.

This representation of Indian male sexuality embodied a profound ambivalence regarding the impact of urban modernity on African culture. In psychoanalytic terms, the Indian became a "screen" on to which African intellectuals could project conflicts among their own political and cultural commitments. In other words, this device located the frictions between celebrating modern and independent womanhood, affirming nationalist virility, and reasserting patriarchal authority outside the project of African nationalism. In 1948, *Ilanga* carried an article titled "Stopping the Bus," a paean to the modernizing powers of new public spaces. In almost breathless ecstasy, H. I. E. Dhlomo hails the fact that buses mixed all classes of people, upsetting the regimental etiquette of both missionary schools and rural Zulu society.[88] Buses, Dhlomo eulogizes, provided a theater where Africans could develop a new psychology: the collective outlook of an urban, democratic society. However, Dhlomo also warns about certain dangers associated with the dramatic transformations the bus introduced:

> In parts of this country buses are ethical questions. An Indian
> bus is introduced into a self-contained, quiet rural or mis-
> sion with high standards of morality. In no time, pop goes the
> self-sufficiency, quietness and morality and ethical codes of the

place. An enterprising African ousts the Indian, and morality like the coy and slow-moving maiden she is, returns slowly and diffidently through the back doors—but the village returns not to quietness and self-sufficiency. The habits and outlook of the people are changed forever.[89]

Dhlomo proceeds to celebrate the life of the bus, the dramas of waiting at the stop, the raucous conversations between men and women who could sit together and talk freely. The expulsion of the Indian resolves the peril threatened by the disruption of rural self-sufficiency—a peril clearly tied to the Indian's economic role and symbolized by the (implied) violation of maidenhood. Later in the same essay, Dhlomo praised the sexual conquests of African men, drawing a parallel between the African's awakening to modern forms of consciousness (such as democracy, theater, and nationhood) and the loss of innocence. "A wolfish man sits next to a beautiful but obviously uninitiated woman—a newcomer in town," he narrates. "In no time, in no whispers, he is making love to her. . . .Give me drunkards, bootleggers, pads, murderers and other bad characters! Of such is the kingdom of literature!" Comparing the "dashing" traveler to Don Juan and Romeo, Dhlomo endows his act of backseat seduction with mythic significance—a foundational act in the literature of modern nationhood. But when the Indian appears again, he poses a sexual threat. An African woman exclaims: "Hang this Indian who pesters me about where I am going and tries to be familiar."

How often did African-Indian liaisons take place? The pervasiveness of African accusations suggests that interracial sex had a much greater impact on Durban's race politics than indicated by the virtual silence surrounding the question.[90] Nevertheless, evidence concerning actual frequency is necessarily anecdotal. In small town Natal, African-Indian marriages did take place. Sometimes African women converted in order to be married under Indian religious law. These unions took place often enough that one could be reported in *Indian Opinion* in 1935 without any additional comment.[91] A survey of Indian households in the peri-urban settlement of Edendale reported one mixed couple in 1947–48, a Hindu man married to a Christian African woman.[92] Marriages between Indian men and Coloured women were more common, a fact that *Ilanga*—mobilizing the image of the Coloured as a "play" or aspiring white—cited to demonstrate that Indians had chosen to assimilate into Western culture and the framework of white supremacy: "Some [Indians] use the official languages as their home language, others intermarry with Coloureds. Thus it is difficult to know where they owe their allegiance and where they stand politically."[93] Sex poses an even more intractable question.[94] Indian men growing up in Durban during the 1950s and '60s often had their first sexual experiences with African or Coloured domestic servants ("Zim" as it was called), either in weekend trips to small-town Natal or sometimes in servant quarters and bucket toilets.[95] Rape and sexual abuse of servants working in Indian homes certainly occurred. But few sources discuss this question.[96] The averment of sex did not generally take the form of naming specific instances, but circulated as rumor. These accusations were anonymous, embedded in the experiences of everyday life, and centered on powerful symbols resonant within the codes of several competing discourses (the changing moral economy of the country side, African nationalism, black Christianity).[97] Perhaps most importantly, this rumor condensed an intricate web of social conflicts, economic relations, and political actors into a single, tangible object. It created a materiality.[98]

This allegation against Indian men remained common during the years following the Riots. In the early 1950s, the "Indian peril" was a staple in the propaganda of the Bantu National Congress, the pro-apartheid political organization allied to Zulu Hlanganani in Cato Manor.[99] In a social distance survey conducted a few years later in the Durban location of Baummannville, most residents disapproved of interracial contact with Indians, although only 8 percent complained about sex. Significantly, while most people surveyed rejected interracial marriage, an inverse relationship emerged between education and willingness to associate with other races: "Better educated respondents appear to be more intolerant than less educated; for instance, about one fifth of those educated to standard II or less favor intermarriage, while only one-tenth of those who have passed a higher standard do so."[100] Given the racial divisions of mid-century Durban, the fact that some twenty percent of less educated Africans interviewed in the survey—who were, moreover, a larger proportion of the location's residents—favored intermarriage was remarkable.

Ilanga continued to print letters that complained about the "growing practice" of seduction and the hypocrisy of Indian men throughout the 1950s.[101] Many of these pieces berated the adoption of Western fashion by women, expressing horror at the *Drum*-inspired culture of beauty pageants, cosmetics, and "vices" that had spread among urban Africans in the 1950s. Conflating social independence with prostitution, one contributor alleged that uncritically adopting the gender norms of "more civilized" races led directly to interracial sex: "They paint their lips, straiten their hair, and to complete the outfit most favorable for attracting races who are more civilized than we are, walk about the streets in the evening puffing cigarettes. At this stage they can then be able to respond to invitations to cocktail parties specifically arranged for them in the backyards of a Mr. Smith or most commonly a Naidoo."[102] Not surprisingly, the reader soon learns that some of these women were nurses. Mocking the camouflage of lasciviousness under a sophisticate's veneer ("cocktail parties specifically arranged for them"), the author established the familiar connection between women, moral turpitude, and new forms of social mobility and interaction created by urban life. While his animosity is directed at those who mimic European aesthetics of beauty, the sexuality of the Indian man remains the foremost emblem of this debauched modernity.

DOMESTIC SPACE: EXCLUSIONS AND INCLUSIONS

Some African men, especially intellectuals and activists, also voiced bitterness regarding their exclusion from Indian social, cultural, and domestic spaces: "In their residential quarters, social and public institutions they do not want the African, but they gate crush African institutions and locations."[103] A regular target of these complaints was the sequestering of Indian women from social interactions with Africans. In a 1953 article, H. I. E. Dhlomo argued that no sane person could deny that gender relations represented one of the most explosive issues in Durban's complicated fabric of racial politics. He did not, however, proceed to discuss sex. Instead, he focused on how Indian cultural norms shaped quotidian interactions between groups, particularly within social spaces associated with the outlook of modernization and nationalist politics:

> Indian custom and tradition keep a jealous and 'regimental' eye on THEIR women folk. There is purdah and the keeping away of Indian women from public contacts. Even 'liberal' advanced, modern-minded Congress and Unity Movement Indians are

not untainted. In the Defiance Campaign and University and other functions where Indians mingle with their African and Coloured equals and have no excuse for it, it is often seen that their women are left behind while they frequently with startling forwardness approach other women. [104]

This emphasis on the hypocrisy of sexual attitudes—Indians guarding "THEIR" women from contact with Africans while ignoring the patriarchal sensibilities of African men—was meant to illustrate an engrained sense of social superiority. But the actual protagonist of this passage is a personified "Indian custom and tradition," whose watch enforces a form of gender apartheid. Even supposedly liberal Indians, who in other respects interact with Africans on equal terms, ostensibly could not erase this polluting intersection of premodern custom and contemporary socioeconomic privilege. As Shalini Puri observes in another context, this type of rhetoric deploys the same ideal of the woman as Indian cultural nationalism: the secluded, sexually modest bearer of Indian tradition.[105] In the course of daily social interactions, Dhlomo and others interpreted the general isolation of Indian women in terms of a particular practice characteristic of the economic elite. "Purdah" became a generalized marker of cultural distinctiveness and Indian exclusiveness.[106] Other representations (including some written by South African Indians) employed caste in a similar fashion. It served as a trope that explained Indian behavior in terms of an unchanging, cultural essence.

The postwar period saw the increased employment of African women in Indian homes. According to Kogila Moodley, the shift from male to female domestics reflected the fear of African violence: Indians believed that women would be more "controllable" than men in the aftermath of the 1949 Riots.[107] In some cases, African domestic workers stayed with the same family for decades and learned Indian languages.[108] But many faced harsh conditions: lower wages than in white households, demanding work, and sometimes abuse. The presence of Africans within Indian domestic space posed the problem of their symbolic exclusion (from the home itself despite their continual presence) and subordinate incorporation (in the form of labor).

The mechanism for this dual process was frequently a series of prohibitions concerning food. Z. A. Ngcobo worked for an Indian family in Durban before the Riots. In a 1980 interview, he described the bitter irony of physical proximity without meaningful personal or social exchange. The issues of domestic space and dietary prohibitions dominated Ngcobo's recollections. While Africans bought from Indian storekeepers, they in turn faced exclusion from Indian residences: "They would tell you to stand over there, at a distance. Others would say 'You are a beast eater! How can you come in here?'" When employed working for an Indian family, he and his coworkers either slept each night in the vehicle outside his boss's house or in the basement. Ngcobo recalled meals with acrimony: "Furthermore the eating utensil you are given to eat from when working for them is issued separately. It is kept over yonder below the house where it is taken when your food is dished up. It goes to emphasize the discrimination, the colour bar. You are served your food like a dog."[109]

The same elements recur in the testimony of both Indians and Africans. In many homes, Africans were served with separate utensils. They were not allowed to eat at the family table or from the same plates as their employers (even when they washed these dishes). They did not use the same toilet.[110] The reasons offered for this treatment related to hygiene and diet. Africans were "dirty": they did not adhere to the Hindu prohibition against eating beef or keep halal in the case of Muslim households. These practices and rationalizations strongly resembled caste restrictions or—for example—the form of "untouchability" practiced by Hindus toward Muslims in parts of South Asia.[111] But such prohibitions were not a direct transposition of caste. Rather, the social grammar of caste or religious hygiene was reconfigured to institutionalize racial difference within the home. The organizing category of these new relationships was not purity or auspiciousness (religious values justifying caste restrictions), but the concept of tradition integral to diasporic identity.

After the implementation of the Group Areas Act, Africans who worked in Indian areas did so illegally and were subject to frequent police raids. In these neighborhoods, stories of break-ins by Africans were part of an everyday racial discourse concerning "African violence."[112] In interviews conducted in a Durban slum during the mid-1960s, Fatima Meer found that although they had almost no contact with Africans, Indian women nonetheless had strong impressions: "The house wife remembers the Riots. She remembers too one evening when she was accosted by two African men at the bus stop. The girl who works at the factory offers an opinion. '*Crooked hair and crooked brain*.'"[113] Concerns over the "Indian peril" also persisted. In 1965, the Natal Native Affairs Commissioner issued an order banning the husbands and boyfriends of domestic workers from cohabitating in backyard quarters. In several Zulu-language letters, domestic workers vehemently protested this edict. These letters complained that the intervention of the state into conjugal arrangements involved an illegitimate usurpation of patriarchal responsibility. At the same time, they made clear that the banning of husbands would increase the sexual access of employers to domestic servants. One letter threatened to ensnare white and Indian men with sorcery in order to undermine apartheid racial divisions:

> We received your notices, separating us from our husbands, which is going to cause us to sleep with our bosses. When you wrote this notice did you realize what the outcome shall be? Since we are so many, do you think that we can all sleep with you and be satisfied? Europeans stay with their wives night and day. Do not force European customs on us.
>
> What are you aiming at? Is it not through this reason that we have Coloured children by Indian and European fathers? We are now going to sleep with them as they are also fond of sleeping with us. We are going to attract them by using love charms then you shall realize that by separating us from our husbands and wives you are causing interracial mating.
>
> That is a stiff question we have asked you, so come out with it. We are challenging you for sexual intercourse with all of us.[114]

Another letter (written by a man) questioned why the Native Commissioner should concern himself with someone else's visitors and warned that the unwarranted intrusion into African relationships threatened the sexual boundary between races: "Allow us to sleep with your female folks and our female folks to sleep with European males."[115] These letters captured a fraught dynamic. The authors clearly believed that Indian and European men regularly sought sex with African women.[116] The presence of their husbands would have shielded women from such molestations. Notably, these letters also articulated a powerful sense of domestic and sexual right. They rejected European customs, demanded that the Native Commissioner personally fulfill the sexual role of the displaced husbands (since the state had usurped their masculine prerogative), and threatened to undermine the racial order of apartheid by actively reciprocating the attentions of European and Indian men. The figure of the Coloured appeared once again to represent the danger of racial breakdown. The above invocation of witchcraft was a powerful threat. In response to the violation of her perceived domestic rights, the author promised to exploit the structural ambiguity of her position within the Indian or white household to attack the biological separation of races themselves.

⤳

If these letters were closer to the idiom of Shembe than H. I. E. Dhlomo, the vision of African womanhood that they asserted was incompatible with either man's understanding of nation. In Dhlomo's case, his comments about the behavior of Indian men in political circles reflected (among other things) the tensions and bitterness that accompanied the early experience of Africans and Indians working together after the 1949 Riots. Others sounded similar themes. When the novelist Peter Abrahams (who dedicated his first collection of poems to the Indian Congress activist Cassim Amra) returned to South Africa from abroad in 1952, he wrote an article in *Drum* complaining about the condescension of Indian activists toward Africans. "There is then," he observed, "platform unity between the two Congresses and a degree of social apartheid in personal relations."[117] Given differences in life experiences, class backgrounds, and the strength of prejudices, some degree of resentment, suspicion, and genuine misunderstanding was inevitable. What Dhlomo's remarks about Indian purdah capture, however, is the extent to which "national" political milieus, despite the increasing importance of women activists in the 1950s, were still imagined as male spaces. Ultimately, Dhlomo was lamenting the lack of social reciprocity (and perhaps the sexual competition) between men.

In contrast, Meer's anecdotes about the Indian housewife and the letters of the domestic workers belong to far more quotidian worlds of working-class experience. They were, however, as distant from each other as they were from Dhlomo's attempts to envision the public spaces of modern nationhood. In the case of many African women (as well a significant number of men), they reflected the humiliations of incorporation into the other's household, the ongoing battle to create and maintain families amid the displacements of urbanization, and the hard-won concept of right embraced by African women who had fought to establish their urban independence. These struggles expressed themselves through ideas of feminine virtue, discourses of subaltern Zulu nationalism, and vernacular political idioms such as witchcraft. After 1956, these ideological currents would pervade a massive revolt of African women against the extension of the pass system in Natal: this wave of protests would challenge both the largely male leadership of the ANC and the policy of collaboration with the Indian Congress. In the context of the early years of apartheid and the aftermath of the 1949 Riots, the Indian housewife's remarks capture pervasive feelings of fear, insecurity of livelihood, and collective isolation that were, frequently, projected onto the figure of the "violent" Zulu male. When the ANC and Indian Congress drew together following the Riots, they had to find ways of motivating the alliance in the face of distrust informed and infused by these (and other) resentments. As the following chapter explores, they responded by nurturing an image of multiracial unity built (to a considerable degree) around the public friendship of African and Indian men. Viewed through the nexus of class, gendered labor, and the racial politics of home, these performances of friendship could, in reverse, underscore the distance between political leaders and their often bitterly divided supporters.

PART THREE

5 ↬ The Cosmopolitan Moment

Chief Albert Luthuli, the Defiance Campaign,
and a New Aesthetics of Nation

At one moment this doctor is the implacable Marxist and the next he is
a passive resister—a mystic—the fervent Gandhi disciple he has always
been.... One might even say Yusuf Dadoo has a Marxist head, a Hindu
heart, Mohammedan nails, and an African blood system. No more a
nationalist, he believes in the unity of all democrats and even has White
friends.... And for your dessert, Dr. Dadoo is an excellent cook who puts
everything in one pot.

—Ezekiel Mphahlele, *Drum*, October 1956

Today it is the people who dictate the course along which they want to
march to freedom. It is they who set the pace, the leader is only their
servant.

—Jordan Ngubane, *Drum*, March 1953

AFTER THE Nationalist Party consolidated its parliamentary majority in
the 1950 election, the government enacted a series of racist laws that
would create the architecture of apartheid, including the Suppression
of Communism Act (1950), the Population Registration Act (1950),
the Group Areas Act (1950), and the so-called Immorality Act (1950).
Although the idea of apartheid remained ambiguous and (at a certain
level) internally contradictory, the Nationalist Party's legislative agenda
made certain ambitions clear: the division of the population according
to racial categories, the destruction of mixed residential areas, the elimination of the few remaining black political rights, the strengthening

of chiefly power, and the resolution of the "Native Question" through forced retribalization. As much of the world was still recovering from a war marked by the Holocaust and systematic racial violence on an almost unimaginable scale, the Nationalist Party proclaimed its defense of a white South Africa and promised to restructure society according to this quixotic ideal. Their slogan, *separation*, now dominated the public space of South African politics. In response, the African National Congress and the Indian Congress (supported locally by smaller Coloured organizations) initiated the Defiance Campaign in 1952. For the first time in South African history, thousands of Africans, Indians, and Coloureds came together in a campaign of nonviolent civil disobedience. The Defiance Campaign answered the concept of apartheid with a display of unity in action.

In the lead up to the campaign, a remarkable exchange appeared between two ANC supporters in the pages of *Bantu World*. Part of a larger debate in the black press, their dispute concerned the role of Indians in the Defiance Campaign and South African society more broadly. In its 1948 election manifesto, the National Party declared that Indians were "a foreign and outlandish element which is inassimilable."[1] While the apartheid minister of interior floated the possibility of an Indian Bantustan, the preferred solution of the government was largescale repatriation. (The regime only recognized South African Indian citizenship in 1961 — the same year Indians were officially recognized as a racial group).[2] When parliament passed the Group Areas Act, many observers initially concluded that its primary aim was the destruction of Indian business and the economic devastation of the Indian community.[3] In Natal, the Bantu National Congress supported apartheid on the grounds of protecting Africans from Indian exploitation. While the ANC's Nationalist Bloc (the small opposition group headed by Transvaal ANC treasurer R. G. Baloyi and Selope Thema, then editor of *Bantu World*) did not endorse apartheid, its statements echoed the Nationalist Party's anti-Indian rhetoric. During this period, India continued to table resolutions on South Africa's racial policies at the UN, a symbolic act that internationalized the debate over the regime's policies. On multiple levels, the first years of apartheid increased the urgency of the "Indian Question."

Writing to *Bantu World* in May 1952, the journalist Walter N. B. Nhlapo ridiculed the Nationalist Bloc for turning to cheap anti-Indianism. Nhlapo sneered: "Such soap-box sound and fury is in a greater or less degree the mind of defeated men who, to win the unreasoning masses, are forced to think with blood than with brawn. Hitler did it."[4] Elaborating this comparison with fascism, Nhlapo suggested that the bloc was appealing to "primitive emotions"; that is, dark and uncontrollable forces that threatened to undermine the work of nation building. In a subsequent article, Nhlapo equated anti-Indian demagoguery with Jew hatred by citing the nineteenth-century German poet Heinrich Heine's essay on antisemitism and Shakespeare's *The Merchant of Venice*.[5] The implications of these comparisons were clear. If apartheid resurrected the spirit of fascism on the southern edge of Africa, a chauvinist African nationalism mirrored the philosophy of the oppressor. The Defiance Campaign, he stated proudly, was a sign of the growing maturity of non-Europeans.[6]

The response to Nhlapo came from Josiah Madzunya. In a cogent and contemptuous letter, Madzunya denied that the Nationalist Bloc advocated the hatred of any racial group even as he insisted that Indians could not "run away" from their exploitation of Africans. In order to secure the "rightful recognition by other nations of the world," Africans needed to unite and rise by their own efforts. "No race can get freedom and independence from another," he observed. If Nhlapo thought that he could win liberation through a foreign country or leadership, he was—alleged Madzunya—"fast asleep."[7]

It would be hard to imagine two figures who cut more sharply contrasting profiles. An activist in the Africanist opposition that would soon develop inside the ANC, Madzunya was a fiery rabble-rouser who boasted a massive beard and wore a long black coat during the heat of summer. Infamous for advocating "God's apartheid" (Africa for the Africans, Europe for the Europeans, and Asia for the Asians), he became the prophet-cum-spokesperson for a layer of Africans on the Rand who felt abandoned by the ANC's policy of cooperation. He resided in a single room in the Alexandra township, along with his wife, and made his living selling boxes on the corner of Troye and President Streets.[8] An ANC polemic once described him as a "semi-articulate wildman."[9] He channeled the rage of Johannesburg.

Precious little is known about Nhlapo's biography. Since the 1930s, he had written regular articles about culture for the Johannesburg black press, especially on the development of jazz. Widely cited in academic scholarship on township music, he was one of the pioneers of South African musicology.[10] At some point, he lived in Orlando (the famed residential area of Soweto where the Mandelas and other professional black families lived) and could claim, like many Africans, Coloured relatives. He was close friends with H.I.E. Dhlomo. If Nhlapo's references to Christian civilization reflected the prewar ethos of the ANC, his razor-sharp wit, literary internationalism, and unabashed love of urban life made him the pioneer of a new urban sensibility.

In the 1950s, a younger generation of writers—many of them working for the legendary *Drum* magazine—would incorporate his style and subject matter into a highly successful literary movement that celebrated the modern and cosmopolitan character of the South African city. Mythologizing neighborhoods such as Sophiatown, Vrederdorp, and Cape Town's District Six, these writers openly celebrated the place of Indians within the urban landscape. When Can Themba extolled the freedoms of Sophiatown, he waxed lyrical about eating Rhugubar's curry with bare fingers. Neither this indulgence, nor listening to jazz at a Chinese-owned record shop, nor taking a "Coloured girl" to the cinema entailed the least "heresy."[11] They were rights bestowed by the city. Eulogizing Vrederdorp's Fourteenth Street, Nat Nakasa marvelled at Indian storeowners who ran global businesses and young Muslims dressed like Mods. In its "slummy" way, he boasted, Fourteenth Street was Johannesburg's exotic and colorful Fifth Avenue.[12] In a 1955 article in *Bantu World* on African anti-Indian sentiment, the silver-tongued Lewis Nkosi declared that "racialism is an evil that must be fought."[13] These writers gave voice to a new popular mood through a reading of Johannesburg's promise.

In a very real sense, these two currents would transform the relatively staid culture of organized African politics. The growing desperation and anger of the Africanist's base fuelled a factional division over the alliance with the Indian Congress and the Congress of Democrats that produced the ANC's first major schism.[14] The relationship between the cosmopolitan moment and African nationalism was more complex and nuanced. Urban, racially mixed, and (in many respects) autonomous spaces provided a setting and sensibility that influenced both younger activists and the ANC's political imagery. At the same time, the new cosmopolitanism transformed the landscape of black media. This revolution not only changed how the ANC appeared in black newspapers, it also influenced the ANC's political culture (as activists and leaders alike followed national campaigns through newspapers such as *Drum, Ilanga,* and *Bantu World*) and the organization's public self-presentation.

The figure who came to exemplify the cosmopolitan moment was Chief Albert Luthuli. This unlikely outcome is the focus of this chapter. Elected to the presidency of the Natal ANC in 1951, Luthuli became the organization's national leader the following year with the backing of the Natal Youth League. Luthuli was a product of rural Zulu politics and missionary education. He was also a devout Christian and widely known as a moderate with close ties to white liberals, Indian philanthropy, and the middle-class African establishment. By the end of the decade, Luthuli's name had become synonymous with the freedom struggle. He appeared in *Drum* as a bold and militant leader, protestors across the country justified their actions by invoking his leadership, and his portrait had become a fixture of political households. One resonant story tells of two African burglars breaking into an Indian home in Johannesburg, seeing Luthuli's picture, and then apologizing before they left.[15]

In tracing how he came to occupy this position, this chapter begins by situating Luthuli within the racial landscape of rural Natal and discussing his trip to southern Indian and Ceylon in 1938. Following the 1949 Riots and the crisis in the Natal ANC, Luthuli went through a lengthy period of personal crisis and intellectual reflection. Confronted with the question of the also-colonized other, he rejected the liberal postulate that nationhood and democracy presuppose racial homogeneity. This rupture helped create a new problem space for African nationalism: what force could unite a racially heterogeneous people? At the same time, the government's plans forced the ANC and Indian Congress into action. After a period of reorientation, the two organizations launched the Defiance Campaign. Initially opposed to the campaign, Luthuli led the movement in Natal despite considerable opposition, both within the ANC and outside. When the Native Affairs Department demanded that he resign either his chieftainship or his ANC presidency, Luthuli refused to comply. His subsequent dismissal cemented his national identification with the campaign and the cosmopolitan moment.

This chapter argues that the Defiance Campaign generated a new aesthetic of African nationalism. Not only did the campaign break from the ANC's legalistic mode of politics, it began to elaborate an iconography and vocabulary of struggle centered on the African-Indian alliance. In confronting the strategic dilemmas of building a unified movement composed of historically distinct groups, the campaign and the resulting Congress Alliance (formed in 1953) created a new *image* of the nation. Constructed around figures such as Dadoo and Luthuli, this image drew on the earlier history of the ANC, the terminology of the Communist Party, and the rhetoric of the Indian anticolonial struggle. Platforms at political meetings that included representatives of the Congress's component organizations, the four-spoke wheel representing the "sections" of the alliance, and the coverage of the different "national" groups in pro-Congress newspapers came to symbolize an inclusive South African nation in which each racial group possessed a full claim to belonging. In confronting apartheid's project of racial separatism and white supremacy, the Defiance Campaign produced a new "distribution of the sensible."[16] In other words, it made visible (and therefore possible) new political subjectivities that were fundamentally incompatible with apartheid. Crucially, the role of the Indian Congress in the campaign placed the also-colonized other—and therefore the question of the nation's internal frontier—at the center of the debates over this new aesthetic.

LUTHULI, STANGER, AND THE 1949 RIOTS

Born in 1898 near Bulawayo in Southern Rhodesia, Luthuli belonged to a distinguished *amakholwa* family (*amakholwa* is isiZulu for "the believers" and referred to Natal's landowning Christian class). His uncle, Martin Luthuli, functioned as the president of the Natal Native Congress during its first three years and was the first democratically elected chief of the Umvoti (Groutville) Reserve in 1908.[17] After his education at the Edendale and Adams mission schools, Albert became one of the first two Africans to receive academic appointments at Adams in 1921 (the other was his lifelong friend and collaborator, Z. K. Mathews). Elected president of the African Teachers Association in 1933, Luthuli rose to prominence in Natal society. He was not only a "first" in the sphere of education (and therefore an incarnation of race progress in the eyes of his contemporaries), but a leader responsible for training a new generation of black teachers: pioneers of African self-advancement and civilization. In 1935, the Umvoti community elected Luthuli to the vacant post of chief and Luthuli resigned his position at Adams. Supporting his family as a farmer, Luthuli championed modern methods of agricultural production, revived the Groutville Cane Growers Association, and built ties with white and Indian associations dedicated to "native uplift." The concrete, practical struggle to create a livelihood from inadequate land and the day-to-day challenges of living as neighbors in a rural community would inform Luthuli's approach to politics for the remainder of his life. Among the personae that he would nurture and deploy during his long political career (teacher, elder, Christian pastor, chief, and militant), the farmer remained one of Luthuli's favorites. At the height of his national popularity as the ANC's president, he appeared in *Drum* magazine proudly displaying a rooster.[18]

Luthuli was one of a small number of African political leaders with firsthand knowledge of South Asia. In 1938, he attended the Conference of the International Missionary Council in Tambaram, Tamil Nadu, and then traveled to Ceylon. Convened at the Madras Christian College, this gathering of ecumenical Christians became the occasion for an important debate over the relationship between Christianity and other religions. Given that nationalist leaders such as Gandhi perceived conversion (especially of Dalits) as a British effort to undermine Hindu unity, the nature of the church in India came under intense scrutiny. A significant group of attendees criticized the existing institution as "western, hierarchical, colonial, and a stumbling bloc to Christian converts."[19] Describing this trip in his 1962 autobiography, Luthuli emphasized the contrast between the "aggressive" church in India, which launched programs to confront poverty and other social evils, and South African Christianity's complacency.[20]

This presentation reflected his intended audience. Edited by the Anglican priest Charles Hooper and published after Luthuli won the Nobel Peace Prize in 1960, *Let My People Go* portrayed Luthuli as an avuncular pacifist to appeal to an international Christian readership. Speaking before black South African audiences in the 1940s, Luthuli's emphasis was different: he championed the Indian anticolonial struggle.[21] This topic would remain a favorite theme. In a 1967 statement written for the Mahatma Gandhi Memorial Society at Howard University, Luthuli praised Gandhi as an "Indian saint" and expressed pride over the fact that Gandhi began his struggle in South Africa. "I have no doubt," he postulated, "that his efforts for his people inspired . . .

Dr. J. L. Dube and others to concern themselves with seeking human rights for their people, the Africans, in South Africa, their Native land."[22] Incorporating Gandhi into the ANC's political genealogy, Luthuli celebrated personal sacrifice, the pursuit of liberation through nonviolence, and the struggle for a "spiritually integrated" society. In other words, Luthuli invoked Gandhi as a predecessor and model for his own philosophy of African nationalism.

If travel to India left Luthuli with "wider sympathies and wider horizons," his approach to African-Indian racial politics reflected his formative experiences in rural Natal.[23] The area surrounding the Umvoti Reserve, and the Natal countryside more generally, was not immune to tensions. During the period of indenture, planters encouraged hostility between Indians and Africans by hiring Zulus to work as watchmen and "whipping boys," who often meted out brutal punishment to workers.[24] In an important article on race in nineteenth-century Natal, Heather Hughes shows that competition over land between Africans and former indentured laborers, differentiated laws and rent structures, and missionary anti-Indianism all encouraged African resentments.[25] Such antagonisms survived well into the twentieth century. Luthuli's notebooks contain minutes from a 1951 meeting of chiefs from the Lower Tugela region during which one participant complained bitterly about the conditions of African workers on Indian-owned farms and asserted that the use of child labor had undermined the establishment of a school in his district. "He does not want Indians in his area," Luthuli recorded.[26] When Luthuli dined with an Indian family in the nearby town of Stanger, the event scandalized neighbors.[27]

Nonetheless, rural Natal was less polarized than Durban: a greater range of relationships transversed or simply ignored racial boundaries. The pace of life (Luthuli's younger collaborators were continuously frustrated by his—quite deliberate—slowness in thought and action), the different spatial organization of social relationships, and even the conservatism of communities contributed to a more relaxed atmosphere. Both reflecting and enabling the greater depth of interaction, it was significantly more common for Indians in rural Natal to speak isiZulu than in Durban.[28]

Few accounts capture this world better than Goolam Suleman's reminiscences of working with Luthuli. Suleman grew up alongside the children of Africans who worked on nearby sugar estates. His

second language was isiZulu (after Gujarati) and he remembers African friends—who, he observes, worshiped the same true God—gathering outside his home to pray when his brother fell ill. His father told
him stories about the British repression of the 1906 Bambatha rebellion and he was aware of the difference in life opportunities between
himself and his playmates from an early age. When migrant workers
wanted to send letters in isiZulu to their families, they would go to the
Suleman family store to ask for assistance writing the letters.[29]

In 1945 Luthuli spoke at the Stanger debating club about the Indian independence struggle. Suleman listened in awe of his eloquence:
"This was the first time that I heard someone talk about our common
struggle, as opposed to the oppression of Indian people alone."[30] After
joining the Indian Congress, Suleman met E. V. Mahomed, another
Indian Congress member and Luthuli's accountant. Since Luthuli did
not own a car, Mahomed and Suleman began to serve as Luthuli's
drivers, covered the costs of Luthuli's political work in Stanger, and
Luthuli began to use Suleman's store as his office. They became the
unofficial treasurer and secretary of the Stanger ANC branch.[31] After
Luthuli's election to the presidency in 1952, Suleman and Mahomed
used their homes and businesses to provide a cover for Luthuli's activism while he was under constant police surveillance and government banning orders. Suleman's memoirs describe the mobilization
of networks in the Stanger Indian community, including the family
of Krish Naidoo (a local tough), to distribute correspondence, arrange
clandestine meetings in the backs of stores, and board ANC members
traveling illegally.[32]

Luthuli first entered public political life in 1946 when he ran for
the Native Representative Council and the provincial executive of the
Natal ANC. At this point, Luthuli's views were (in the language of the
Youth League) "realist": he supported a qualified franchise, the gradual
self-improvement of Africans through work and education, and reasoned
dialogue between the races. According to an unpublished account by
Jordan Ngubane (who, along with his wife Eleanor, organized Luthuli's
election campaign for the NRC), two events shattered this worldview.
The first was the onset of apartheid. The election of the National Party
severely undermined Luthuli's faith in the prospect of obtaining greater
rights for Africans through negotiation and public debate. Although
Luthuli had initially aligned himself with Z. K. Mathews and other

moderates on the council, the Malan government's refusal to hear their grievances provoked both his moral conscience and deeply engrained sense of decency. Unsure of what to do, Luthuli was dismayed. He began to contemplate the prospects of accepting a leadership role in the ANC and direct opposition to the new government.[33]

The second event was the 1949 Durban Riots. According to Ngubane, Luthuli was greatly disturbed by the Durban violence: "By 1950 Luthuli was caught in a major spiritual and political crisis. The riots had created challenges which no man with a moral conscience could evade." In the factional confusion that followed, Luthuli found himself isolated and adrift. As he moved away from the ANC's earlier politics of legalism and uplift, he was unable to support any of the competing alternatives: Champion's erratic and largely self-serving leadership; the Africanist biopolitics of Lembede; the Communist Party's Marxism (as Ngubane observes, "God stood in the way"); or the quietist stance of the Natal chiefs and much of the *amakholwa* elite.[34] Luthuli's impasse coincided with a new awareness of the strategic—as well as the human and moral—dangers represented by Natal's racial divisions. Suleman recalls: "The Riots dismayed the Chief. . . . At all subsequent rallies, he strove to unite the opposing groups and promote solidarity for the African cause."[35] During the 1959 ANC-organized boycott of potato farms, a Stanger activist and shebeen owner named Esther Mkwananzi decided to burn down the shop of a grocer who refused to participate in the campaign. When Luthuli learned of this plan, he was furious. He stormed into Suleman's office and demanded an immediate meeting with the organizers, despite the fact that he was under a banning order and the meeting was therefore illegal. Afterward he explained that targeting one shop would unleash criminal elements and escalate into a general "free for all."[36] This story conveys Luthuli's fear regarding the possibility of renewed African-Indian violence: the Natal ANC leadership believed that the conditions for another 1949 remained ever present.

Luthuli's writings during the late 1940s were preoccupied with the problem of racial difference and its consequences—both practical and theoretical. Influenced by the philosopher R. F. A. Hoernlé's reflections on liberalism in multiracial societies, Luthuli understood that existing Western models of democracy assumed the existence of a homogenous community. Democracy required a shared national loyalty grounded in common institutions, political economy, culture, and sense of heritage (which Hoernlé collectively assimilated to the category of race).[37] By late 1949, Luthuli began to question this normative presumption and ask how democracy could develop in the context of social plurality. He formulated this problem explicitly in an unpublished text contained in his notebooks, "How to Develop a Unified South Africa." After denouncing forms of segregation that undermined interracial cooperation, Luthuli approvingly cited Booker T. Washington's speech at the 1895 Atlantic Convention: "In all things which are purely social we can be as separate as the fingers, yet one as the hand in all things essential to material progress."[38] (Interestingly, he replaced Washington's "mutual progress" with "material progress."[39]) Luthuli's hostility to white supremacy was unmistakable. At the same time, he concluded that multiple social identities, and therefore some forms of parallel institutional and cultural life, were an unavoidable fact. South African society, he asserted, was characterized by the "simple, normal" separation of the races—a reality that was "accepted by all sections of our community as necessary and correct."[40] Rather than question the distinct character of the races, Luthuli's concern was with the second half of the African American leader's famous sentence. In the absence of either social homogeneity or racial domination, what force could bind the different fingers together?

Writing two decades before the emergence of liberal multiculturalism in Canada, Australia, and Western Europe, Luthuli developed his thinking without reference to ideas such as value pluralism or constitutional patriotism.[41] Even if he had read Isaiah Berlin, John Rawls, or Jürgen Habermas, attempts to ground political community in a common (or at least overlapping) set of loyalties to citizenship, public ideals, or democratic institutions would not have answered his fundamental question. Because of the colonized's exclusion from the domain of the political, Luthuli could not presuppose settler civil society as the *means* for reconciling different identities. Luthuli needed a basis of coexistence that could bring historically antagonistic groups *into* a shared social life while preserving their self-conscious sense of collective political interests.

At one level, this approach reflected a tension present within the ANC's political thinking from its founding. Early leaders of the ANC advocated for the (more or sometimes less) gradual entry of Africans into the institutions of civil society created by settler colonialism. They believed that a common political life presupposed a common civilization. At the same time, they rejected colonial liberalism's mechanism for creating the conditions for African admission: trusteeship. Following the erosion of the Cape franchise and the introduction of the 1913 Native Land Act, the founders of the ANC concluded that both independent political organization and the building of black institutions (such as schools, newspapers, and the ANC itself) were the necessary instruments for obtaining citizenship. This perspective contained a latent tension. If Africans could only gain full entrance into civilization through their efforts at self-emancipation, then a common society would be divided from its inception by the identity necessary for its achievement. In such a context, unity could not develop out of pre-existing social cohesion. At least initially, it would have to incorporate difference: a plurality of cultural and political subjects.

At another level, the timing of Luthuli's notes—the "spiritual and political crisis" of 1949–50—suggests that the Durban Riots weighed heavily on his reflections. While the ANC remained committed to the achievement of freedom through African unity (in this sense, all factions of the ANC were nationalists), the relationship with the Natal Indian population had become strategic to African politics. Luthuli possessed a methodical and deeply spiritual bent of mind. He faced this moment by returning to basic principles. Initially, he proposed solutions that were drawn from the repertoires of liberal race relations and the church: interracial contact, the cultivation of Christian virtues, respect for the distinct personality of other racial groups, education, and acceptance of a shared, God-given destiny.[42] While he would recast these ideas in his later thinking, it was the question itself that was ultimately more important. Washington's "fingers" helped articulate the problem space within which Luthuli would elaborate his new understanding of African nationalism.

REAPPRAISALS AND REALIGNMENTS

With the Natal ANC riven by open political warfare between Champion and the Youth League, Indian activists focused on developing ties with African leaders in Johannesburg. In early 1950, the Transvaal Indian Congress and the Communist Party launched a "Free Speech Convention" in defense of several banned leaders, including Kotane, Marks, and Dadoo. Without consulting the national executive, Moroka (the ANC president elected in 1949) agreed to chair the convention, which called for a one-day general strike on the first of May. The Youth League rejected the initiative, arguing that it represented a diversion from the Program of Action.[43] The rally attracted close to ten thousand protestors and between half and two thirds of Johannesburg's African workers joined the May Day strike.[44] The police responded by breaking up gatherings of workers and firing into crowds, killing eighteen and injuring more than thirty.[45] For those who opposed non-European cooperation, the May Day deaths became a major example of Indians and Communists recklessly sacrificing African lives for their own political purposes.[46] In the immediate aftermath, however, the Transvaal Youth League (albeit suspiciously and reluctantly) agreed to the formation of a coordinating committee with the Indian Congress and jointly organized the first national work stoppage for 26 June. According to Mary Benson, the response among Indians in both Johannesburg and Durban — shops and factories closed, students stayed home from school, and waiters disappeared from Durban restaurants — challenged suspicions that Indians were "simply opportunists."[47]

Increasingly, a diffuse opposition to political collaboration with the Indian Congress became linked with concern over Communist influence in both organizations. When party member J. B. Marks ran for provincial president of the Transvaal ANC in November 1951, his campaign further galvanized opposition from both the younger generation and elements of the old guard, especially Baloyi and Selope Thema, editor of *Bantu World*. As a result, the newspapers' reporting on questions of Afro-Indian relations became directly tied to factional struggles in African politics. Yet during this same period, many younger ANC members were also impressed by the militancy and antiracism of both Indian and white Communist party members. Even Sobukwe — no friend of the Party — later recalled: "We knew that if someone was a communist it meant he had no colour prejudice. He accepted you as a human being, this you just knew."[48] Not only did they watch Indians of all ages go to prison during the Passive Resistance Campaign, Youth League activists also became increasingly aware of the personal sacrifices made by Indian Communists in the service of African working-class causes.

Especially in Johannesburg, a smaller number of activists interacted with Indian peers as students or younger professionals. Mandela began to develop friendships with activists Ismail Meer, J. N. Singh, and Ahmed Bhoola during his legal studies in the early 1940s. In his autobiography, he fondly recalls time spent with this group at Meer's flat: "There we studied, talked, and even danced until the early hours of the morning, and it became a kind of headquarters for young freedom fighters. I sometimes slept there when it was too late to catch the last train back to Orlando."[49] According to Mandela, discussions with Meer—whose fluency in isiZulu impressed the young nationalist— challenged his belief that all Indians were "rich shopkeepers." They also spent long hours analyzing the parallels between the Indian and South African national liberation struggles, including discussions of Nehru, the militant Indian leader Subash Chandra Bose, and Gandhi's place in South African history.[50]

These friendships, which developed in situations defined by student camaraderie and the intimacies of home, helped break down his preconceptions and internationalize Mandela's understanding of the South African liberation struggle.[51] It is also possible that these relationships prepared Mandela's later entrance into the Communist Party by eroding his anticosmopolitanism and introducing him to left-wing circles (Singh and Meer, at the time, were party cadre). In turn, Mandela's example influenced other Youth League members, including leftists Joe Mathews (Z. K.'s son) and Diliza Mji.[52] Despite these personal affections, Mandela remained steadfast in his opposition to working with Indian organizations until December 1951, when the ANC national conference endorsed preparations for the Defiance Campaign.[53] His prejudice still ran deep, as did his fear that ordinary Africans would reject an alliance with the Indian.[54] It was his close friend Sisulu who first broke ranks with the Transvaal Youth League leadership and began to argue for joint action following the 1949 Riots.[55]

In July 1951, a Johannesburg conference of the ANC and Indian Congress established a coordinating committee of J. B. Marks, Sisulu, Dadoo, Moroka, and Y. A. Cachalia to develop a political response to the new battery of racial legislation adopted by the Malan government. The committee proposed a campaign centered on defying unjust laws through noncooperation. They chose the three hundredth anniversary of Jan van Riebeeck's first landing to inaugurate the movement.[56] Their proposal envisioned disciplined volunteer units divided according to racial groups with exceptions made in cases "where a law or regulation to be defied [applied] commonly to all groups."[57] Luthuli, who defeated Champion for the Natal ANC presidency by a small margin earlier in the year, first heard about the plan en route to the December 1951 national conference.[58] In the midst of Natal's struggles, Champion had concealed the plans for the campaign from the provincial executive.

At the conference, Luthuli spoke strongly against the campaign and warned against precipitous action. In all likelihood, he under-lined that the provincial ANC was in a state of disarray and warned against trying to mobilize Indians and Africans together in the af-termath of the Riots. According to one report, the Natal delegation objected to the establishment of a permanent joint committee of Af-ricans and Indians.[59] It seems possible that these frictions between Natal and the Transvaal ANC, a historic dynamic in the organization, reflected genuine misunderstanding as much as political differences. Having only just seen the proposal for the most ambitious action in the ANC's history, the Natal delegation pleaded for time to consider the campaign, which they knew would be deeply unpopular in their province.[60] The leadership of Transvaal ANC attributed this request to Natal's conservatism and—among Transvaal Youth League mem-bers—the cowardice of the old guard. Further complicating the situa-tion, the prominence of Communist Party members, and the reading of numerous statements of support by Eastern bloc countries, appears to have alarmed members of the Natal delegation. *Ilanga's* coverage of the conference (almost certainly written by Dhlomo) emphasized an atmosphere of lurking controversy, backroom maneuvering, and high emotion. Amid widespread rumors that it might exempt itself, the Natal executive waited more than two months to publicly an-nounce its participation.[61]

GANDHI AND THE QUESTION
OF INDIAN INFLUENCE

At the end of May 1952, the executives of the ANC and Indian Con-gress met in the Eastern Cape city of Port Elizabeth to announce the campaign and establish a national coordinating committee. In the lead up to the meeting, Manilal Gandhi warned against Communist infiltration of the ANC and implied that Africans had not yet devel-oped the "spiritual discipline" necessary for passive resistance. There should be "no drinking or gambling," he lectured "The soul should be perfect. Passive resistance should be truly spiritual."[62] His immense sincerity ill masked the condescension. T. N. Naidoo, vice president of the Transvaal Indian Congress and an adopted son of the Mahatma, issued a stinging rebuke.[63] At the Port Elizabeth meeting, the assembled delegates debated whether nonviolence was a matter of tactics or an inviolable principle. Some Indian Congress delegates urged that the campaign adopt the philosophy of satyagraha along Gandhi's lines. The majority, endorsing arguments made by Mandela, supported nonviolence as long as it was "effective."[64] During these discussions, members of the Transvaal Youth League rejected the language of passive resistance and insisted on the term "defiance" in order to underscore the militancy of the campaign.[65] They contrasted the reliance on "the aggressive pressure of the masses" to Gandhi's attempts to awaken the moral conscience of the oppressor.[66] The name choice also guarded against suggestions that the Indian Congresses had inspired the movement. In their published statements, ANC leaders carefully avoided any intimation that Gandhi or the 1946 Passive Resistance struggle had informed their strategy.[67]

Behind the scenes, however, it was a different matter. Moroka studied Gandhi's writings while crisscrossing the country on an organizing tour.[68] Writing to his father, Z. K., the decidedly left-wing Joe Mathews mused: "I am quite sure in the long run Natal will beat everybody in the response they get. I only hope it will be possible to keep down the spirit of Chaka and infuse the spirit of Gandhi among the Zulu masses."[69] In notebooks from the period of the campaign, Luthuli consistently referred to "passive resistance"—making the connection with 1946 explicit—and he invoked Gandhi during speeches.[70] ANC leaders may not have accepted every aspect of his philosophy, but Gandhi served as a lodestar for their strategic thinking. They used the Passive Resistance Campaign and Indian anticolonial struggle as both a precedent and an archive. If accounts that suggest Gandhi directly inspired early ANC leaders such as Dube are largely mythological, it is nonetheless true that later ANC leaders assimilated Gandhi into their organization's intellectual lineage.[71]

What explains the reticence to acknowledge this debt? First and likely foremost, ANC leaders had concluded that Gandhi's strategy of satyagraha was inapplicable. While older intellectuals such as Luthuli and Mathews did not necessarily share the Transvaal Youth League's contempt for his renunciation of violence (Tambo derided "self-pitying, arms-folding, and passive reaction to oppressive policies"[72]), their later statements suggest that they too concluded that Gandhi-like appeals to white moral conscience were futile. Luthuli himself came to believe that the majority of white South Africans supported apartheid and would only change course as the result of enormous domestic and international pressure. If he warned that Africans must sacrifice for freedom, he did not believe that this suffering would lead to the white minority's inner conversion. It is also possible that African leaders were reacting against the implication that Gandhi's earlier campaigns had inaugurated the South African freedom struggle. Certainly, a popular narrative emerged later, especially among some Indian activists, which depicted the antiapartheid movement in just these terms (for example, by suggesting the ANC was founded in emulation of the Indian Congress). While this account served to write Indians into South African history through a foundational role, the idea of a foreign provenance for African nationalism must have sounded like another version of missionary arrogance.[73] Last but hardly least, popular mistrust of Indians necessitated that the ANC insist on the African origination and leadership of the campaign.[74]

In addition, Congress leaders soon had to contend with propaganda that depicted the campaign as the marionette of the Indian government. On 15 October, Prime Minister Malan launched a broadside against India for interfering in South Africa's affairs by exploiting the country's Indian minority. Railing against India's annual vote at the UN, Malan warned that the unchecked meddling of foreign powers in other countries' internal matters threatened the global order. Malan then cited discrimination against India's Muslim population as well as Nehru's belligerence in the face of outside suggestions that India should withdraw its troops from Kashmir. Every country, he propounded, faced difficult questions regarding ethnic minorities. In domesticating South Africa's racial politics, Malan equated India's intervention in South Africa and the "technique" of global Communism, an association proven—he alleged—by the fact that the SA Indian Congress president (the unnamed Dadoo) was a self-confessed Communist. This Cold War rhetoric, which was already finding an echo in the pages of *Bantu World* and *Ilanga*, reworked earlier tropes of "Indian imperialism" and the deracinated (Jewish) Communist. The Indian cosmopolitan, fused with the Marxist internationalist, became a general figure for forces hostile to the territorial sovereignty of the ethno-nationalist state.[75]

A NEW AESTHETIC OF STRUGGLE

On the first day of the Defiance Campaign, volunteers gathered at the Anderson Street Hall in Johannesburg. After an orientation, they marched past crowds of relatives and supporters (who "sang majestically") before driving to the Boksburg location, which they planned to enter without permits.[76] In the campaign's early stages, reports emphasized the diversity of the protestors and crowds (underlining not only their racial composition, but also the mixture of ages and sexes), the repeated use of specific songs and symbols, and the mood of events. Evoking the atmosphere of the opening day, *Bantu World* described a young Coloured volunteer bursting into tears as he walked past a racially mixed crowd of supporters. A Coloured woman then stepped out of the crowd to "grasp the weeping volunteer."[77]

Such anecdotes conveyed the unprecedented feeling of unity among the protestors, the symbiotic relationship between volunteers and the crowd, and the sense of moment. When the protestors arrived at the location, they discovered that police had barricaded the entrance. Led by Sisulu and Nana Sita (who participated in Gandhi's campaigns), the volunteers stood in formation before the gates, singing and shouting "Afrika." The police demanded that the Africans produce passes and then detained them. Several Indian resisters slipped into the location, followed by police and a large crowd, which cheered and gave the "thumbs-up" salute when the protestors were arrested.[78] After their release from custody, the volunteers filed into the Johannesburg Trades Hall where they received a standing ovation and the thumbs-up salute representing the African continent (the extended digit symbolized the Horn). A thousand men, women, and youth greeted them by singing the African national anthem, "Nkosi Sikelel' iAfrika." After impassioned speeches by Indian and African volunteers, the evening concluded with the chant of "Africa is proud of you" and another singing of the anthem.[79]

These scenes reoccurred across the country and became a weekly feature in the black press. No account conveys this spirit better than

Benson's *Struggle for a Birthright.*[80] To some degree, younger activists seized the limelight. But it was thousands of working-class, church-going Africans who sustained the campaign. While only a small number of women defied laws in the first stages, their significance was immediately visible (as was the importance of women in the crowds and directing song) and their numbers increased. Groups of women prayed for their husbands before they "went to action," organized support for the campaign, and then—after their husbands were arrested—stepped into leadership roles or went to prison themselves.[81] As the ANC shifted from its earlier legalism and became a vehicle for mass struggle, a new space emerged for women, especially working-class women, within local and national African politics. Many of these activists went on to play roles in the founding of the Federation of South African Women and the national anti-pass campaign of the 1950s.

From the beginning, the leadership gave considerable attention to the appearance, tone, and—almost certainly reflecting Gandhi's influence—the emotional dimension of the protests. Volunteers received instructions regarding their dress and hygiene, their bodily comportment, and the subjective disposition underlying their public political performance ("Volunteers . . . are required to salute in an appropriate manner as a mark of love, respect, and discipline").[82] As the campaign gained momentum, the state inadvertently contributed to its multiracial imagery (as it would on an even larger scale with the 1956 Treason Trial) by arraigning African, Indian, and Coloured protestors together. The courts themselves became sites of demonstrations and press coverage. While in prison, activists composed new freedom songs by setting lyrics to church hymns and popular radio tunes.[83] The mood was "exultant."[84]

This new style of politics combined the historic symbols of the ANC—especially Congress flag and colors—with the experience of solidarity in mass struggle. While the alliance between the ANC and Indian Congress provided the campaign's main axis, the participation of Coloured and (at the very end of the campaign) white volunteers contributed to the emerging sense of a new type of unity. Especially for younger activists, the campaign created a world of constant, and frequently unprecedented, interactions across racial lines: multiracial rallies addressed by African, Coloured, and Indian leaders, organizing meetings, door-to-door canvassing, and parties where jazz, alcohol, and the ever subversive experience of dancing symbolized a collective transgression of South Africa's racial mores.[85] The sheer pace of activism contributed to breaking down barriers.[86] (As the previous chapter noted, this atmosphere of permissiveness also spurred bitterness over relationships between Indian men and Africa women.[87]) In Johannesburg, the collaboration between the ANC and Indian Congress Youth groups was constant. Rumors circulated that Ahmed Kathrada, the young Communist firebrand, had joined the ANC Youth League.[88] In Durban, the ANC and Indian Congress, which both had offices at the Lahkani Chambers building in the Grey Street area, issued a common bulletin entitled *Flash* throughout the campaign.[89] After having endorsed the ideology of African nationalism in the 1949 Programme of Action, the ANC was leading a multiracial protest movement under its own banner.

This development was strongly marked at the level of rhetoric. Before the protests, ANC leaders motivated cooperation with Indian organizations in cautious terminology taken from the Doctors' Pact and the liberal framework of race relations.[90] From early in the campaign, organizers placed a new emphasis on the common struggle of the oppressed. Speaking to the November 1952 conference of the Natal ANC, provincial leader Dr. J. L. Z. Njongwe observed: "the greatest achievement of our defiance campaign has been the welding of a . . . singleness of purpose and the development of a common South African outlook between Indians and Africans."[91] Mandela also noted this transformation at the time.[92] Although the language of cooperation did not disappear, it was incorporated within a new lexicon that drew on the rhetoric of African nationalism, the precedent of the Indian anticolonial struggle, and antifascist slogans drawn from the Communist Party's 1930s "Popular Front" period. Reprinting joint ANC–Indian Congress press releases and statements by campaign leaders, black newspapers disseminated this vocabulary and thus encouraged its appropriation by grassroots activists.

By late 1952, however, months of protests and repression began to take their toll and a growing antiwhite sentiment found its voice among ANC's supporters. In response, the ANC and Indian Congress issued a call for a "parallel white organization" to support the campaign.[93] This request eventually led to the formation of the Congress of Democrats (a small organization largely, but not exclusively, composed of

Communist Party supporters) and created the basis for the Congress Alliance, which became the main coordinating structure for the antiapartheid struggle of the 1950s. The alliance initially included the ANC, the Indian Congress, the Congress of Democrats, and the Coloured People's Organization—although the last group struggled to build a national following and possessed little presence in Natal. The Federation of South African Women (formed in 1954) served as a parallel and allied organization, since its membership consisted of female members of the Congress Alliance organizations.[94] After the formation of the South African Congress of Trade Unions in 1955, the nonracial trade union federation joined the alliance as a full member. By the late 1950s, the Liberal Party, which organized protests and released statements with the ANC and Indian Congress, effectively functioned as an alliance partner in Natal.[95]

Drawing on East African debates over group representation in colonial legislatures, the alliance's critics—most importantly the Africanist current within the ANC—argued that it embraced a form of multiracialism that subordinated the ANC to minority organizations and reproduced colonial racial categories.[96] A variant of this argument, especially the latter point, was refined by left-wing critics of the ANC such as Neville Alexander.[97] This polemic reads the structure of the alliance as the direct expression of the ANC's position on the "national question," rather than as a flexible (and provisional) strategy capable of incorporating different constituencies and ideological positions. While some presentations of the alliance did reify racial groups, the critique of multiracialism missed its mark in two respects. First, the alliance was predicated on the recognition of African leadership: its structure and symbolism combined the primacy of the ANC with an affirmation of a heterogeneity that was not just racial, but included class and (with the formation of the Federation of South African Women) gender. [98] The fundamental emphasis was on *unity* and many leading Congress members, included Monty Naicker and Luthuli, believed in the eventual fusion of the racially based organizations. Multiracialism, a term introduced into the debate by the ANC's opponents, poorly captures this ethos.

Second, the argument that the federated structure of the alliance recapitulated colonial racial categories misrecognizes the importance of the Native Question. The assertion of a modern African subject, moreover one that could lead whites and Indians, was a forceful rejection of the Native Question's relegation of Africans to the domain of "tribal custom" and therefore their exclusion from the very concept of the political. (It is worth recalling that the use of the term African, rather than Bantu or Native, was still an act of political opposition in the 1950s.) In turn, the Congress Alliance reflected the conviction that the African liberation struggle could create the framework for a single movement that included a multiplicity of interconnected identities. As Mbembe observes, "The desire for difference is not necessarily the opposite of the project of the in-common. In fact, for those who have been subjected to colonial domination, or for those whose share of humanity was stolen at a given moment in history, the recovery of that share often happens in part through the proclamation of difference."[99] In assuming that difference—no matter how it was articulated and structured—was necessarily colonial in origin, the critique of "multiracialism" conflated apartheid categories with political subjectivities developed in opposition to the logic of discrete identities enforced by white supremacy.

THE DEFIANCE CAMPAIGN AND THE NATAL ANC

When Luthuli called the Natal ANC executive together in March 1952, he issued a challenge: the leadership should not summon the people to protest unless they were "sure of the road and prepared to travel along it ourselves."[100] He then invited the assembled men to pray. Yengwa remembered the evening as a turning point. Long an advocate of the gradual path to freedom, Luthuli committed himself to the campaign "damn the consequences as long as he was advancing the cause of the movement."[101] Yengwa, recently elected provincial secretary, would later become Natal's volunteer in chief for Africans.[102] In a pen portrait of Luthuli published that August, Dhlomo (who served on the provincial joint-action committee) claimed that Natal's newly elected president endorsed the campaign for the sake of preserving the greater unity of the ANC. As a committed democrat, he acceded to the decision of the national majority despite the "extremely awkward and delicate position this would place him in the province," including—Dhlomo added rather gnomically—in his personal life.[103] It was an audacious decision. His opponents, including supporters of Champion's defeated faction, immediately accused him of "selling out" to the Indians.[104] Stoking the flames of controversy, the editor of *Ilanga*'s isiZulu pages, R. R. R. Dhlomo, used his column inches to undermine cooperation with the Indian Congress and denounced the campaign. Readers weighed in on both sides.[105]

Luthuli's notebooks from this period show that he faced opposition at the branch and provincial levels. In late October, a debate occurred in a meeting of the Lower Tugela ANC (which Luthuli attended on a regular basis) over the terminology for the alliance. Although nearly impossible to decipher, Luthuli's notes indicate that some branch members objected to the term "Indo-African," intimating that this designation referred to a fantastical creature. Their point was that no such amalgam existed. "Our name is African": the statement hangs on the page, categorical and unattributed. This dispute over nomenclature may have served as a proxy for critics who did not want to oppose Luthuli's leadership in his home branch. Whatever the case, their warning was clear: "ishela bulungu" (the membership will dry up or burn). The meeting endorsed "non-European" as a compromise. This discussion represented a significant enough challenge to Luthuli that he urged the adoption of separate motions supporting the campaign and the leadership of the ANC.[106]

In some form, the fight continued. Two weeks later, Luthuli tabled a resolution in the ANC's Natal branch that expressed "unshakable solidarity with our allies, the South African Indian Congress."[107] It is not clear whether Luthuli faced open dissent from the membership or—more likely—he was preempting the metastasis of an organized anti-Indian faction. In either case, the atmosphere was charged enough that the order of words became dear. In his minutes, he scratched out the phrase "Indo-African Alliance" and replaced it with the unwieldy coinage "Africo-Indian."[108] Luthuli was still searching for a way to defend the multiracial alliance in terms compatible with the nationalist conviction that Africans must achieve freedom through their own independent efforts.

The Natal ANC was at pains to emphasize the nationalist credentials of the campaign. Not only did members of the Zulu royal house and a number of chiefs stress the "positive" aspects of apartheid (including the protection of Africans from exploitation by Indians), some Africans believed that the Group Areas Act applied primarily to Indians.[109] More than any other section of the population, Indian traders resided among other racial groups: a naïve understanding of apartheid concluded that it would regularize existing residential patterns by ejecting anomalous individuals and enterprises. In this context, the Natal working committee decided that volunteers would protest the "burning issue" of the pass—an old and deeply hated institution. Pass laws, of course, did not apply to Indians.

During this period, Luthuli began speeches defending the campaign by invoking the ANC's most authoritative endorsement of African nationalism, 1949 Programme of Action.[110] Insisting on the principal of African leadership, he was scathing toward the paternalism of claims that African resisters were "toys" of the Indian merchant.[111] At moments, his dignity bristled. When *Ilanga* printed an editorial alleging that Indians and communists had pushed the ANC into defiance, Luthuli declared that the piece represented an insult "to us as men."[112] The invocation of African masculinity was deliberate: Luthuli's statements played with the racially charged binary of man/boy. Anti-Indian agitation, he implied, was counterfeit nationalism. It assumed that Africans were helpless children. He also inverted this charge by accusing his opponents of believing in an Indian "bogey."[113] These fights transformed Luthuli's understanding of the alliance. Previously he had argued for African-Indian cooperation on particular questions while criticizing and opposing "the Indians for the harm that they have done us."[114] He now advocated unity as a matter of principle. "We should carry on," he declared in response to *Ilanga*'s editorial, "even if others fall away."[115] Significantly, the fact that Luthuli conceptualized the alliance in terms of the mutual recognition of black manhood would help set the stage for later conflicts between the Natal ANC leadership and some militant supporters of the ANC Women's League.[116]

The approach of the campaign accentuated Natal's political divisions. The ANC and Indian Congress held separate meetings in April to announce the launch of the campaign.[117] According to *Bantu World*, a few hundred Indians and only a "hand full" of Africans attended the inaugural rally. Less than a hundred people listened to speeches by Luthuli and Yengwa at the Bantu Social Centre.[118] Predictably, the Unity Movement—which claimed a significant following among Indian activists in northern Natal—denounced the congresses for holding "apartheid rallies."[119] At a meeting held in the small town of Dundee,

Chota Motala and Omar Essack (Unity Movement cadre who had participated in the Indian anticolonial struggle) attacked passive resistance based on its alleged failure to drive British imperialism from South Asia. "Peace and non-violence leads you nowhere," Essack declared.[120]

The ANC and Indian Congress prepared for the campaign in parallel.[121] At the Port Elizabeth planning meeting, Yengwa had insisted that Africans and Indians should organize separately due to popular animosity toward collaboration—Natal's racial dynamics thus helped determine the national form of the campaign and the subsequent alliance.[122] The Natal ANC clearly envisioned the Defiance Campaign as an African-led movement that Indians could support in "associated *action*."[123] Indian Congress members were taken aback. In a letter to his father, the Transvaal activist Joe Mathews (who was traveling the country on behalf of the ANC Youth League) captured the atmosphere: "You see that the Indians are perturbed over the fact that throughout this campaign the Congress is not leaning on them at all. Our organization is entirely independent, and if anything is giving orders to them."[124] (Mathew's rather biting suggestion was that some Indians were rather too used to giving orders to Africans.) On the ground, the campaign encountered skepticism from most Indians. After two years of personal sacrifice during the mid-1940s, working-class Indians were ill disposed to volunteer for another campaign that promised hardship and dubious results.[125] Other fears were present as well. While activists did not discuss 1949 publically, the experience of the Riots was raw.

Despite these tentative beginnings, the spirit of defiance spread during the first months of the campaign. When the initial batch of volunteers emerged from prison, a massive gathering saluted them with cries of "Afrika" and then marched through central Durban. *Indian Opinion* reported: "As the procession made its way thousands of spectators witnessed an orderly march with Africans and Indians singing the resistance songs of Mayibuye Africa [Let Africa return]."[126] In its special Dewali issue, *Indian Opinion* (which rarely included news photographs) ran a quarter page image of the march led by Naiker and Ashwin Choudree (who carried an ANC flag). "It was," the caption commented, "the first great march of Africans and Indians in Durban in recent times."[127] The crowd of thousands stretched down West Street—a major thoroughfare in the "white" downtown—until it faded from view. *Indian Opinion* also printed photographs of working-class

Africans pressing through crowds to donate their "humble" coins to the defiance fund, Luthuli addressing a mass meeting with his arms raised high, a young Mavis Kumalo (smiling and eyes toward heaven) waiting for arrest at the Berea train station while others prayed and sang, groups of African and Indian protestors giving the thumbs-up salute from the backs of police lorries, and batches of resisters emerging from prison with their fists in the air.

In one of the most iconic images of the campaign, an Indian and an African activist (the one wearing a brilliantly white sari; the other sporting a trench coat, scarf, and heels) walked out of the female jail side by side, their right arms straight in salute, and their faces rapt with joy. Behind them, two other women followed, while an Indian boy—likely the child of a prisoner—watched from the corner. The photograph conveyed unity through their simultaneous release (evoking the powerful motif of a passage from imprisonment to freedom), their womanhood and implied motherhood, and their shared excitement. The photograph relied on the tension between two visual and temporal perspectives: the expectant viewer waiting for the moment of emergence and the protestors, prepared and self-conscious of their arrival, walking into the sight of the camera. Binding these two perspectives together was a shared sense of (historic, political, and personal) moment. More subtly, the presence of the child suggested a generational reciprocity between viewer and those viewed. If racial difference remained visible, it was nevertheless subsumed by the converging themes that gave the photograph its force. African and Indian identities (the latter highlighted by the tell-tale symbol of the sari) found their common fulfillment in the integrating narrative of the struggle.

In describing the prisoners simply as "women," *Indian Opinion* touched on an idea that would find its realization two years later in the formation of the Federation of South African Women and the famous 1956 women's anti-pass demonstration in Pretoria. Efforts to organize a conference on the role of women in the national liberation struggle began in the Eastern Cape after the conclusion of the Defiance Campaign. This group reached out to Natal and solicited the involvement of Indian Congress and ANC members, including Fatima Seedat, Fatima Meer, and Bertha Mkize (the last two were elected to the federation's executive board at its first meeting).[128] Held at the Trades Hall in Johannesburg on 17 April 1954, the founding conference adopted a Woman's Charter that insured that the questions of women's oppression and sexual equality would appear (in however limited a fashion) in later ANC statements. The Women's Charter declared: "We shall teach the men they cannot hope to liberate themselves from the evils of discrimination and prejudice as long as they fail to extend to women complete and unqualified equality in law and practice."[129] As Shireen Hassim observes, this declaration made the transformation of patriarchal relationships within black communities and organizations a necessary precondition for liberation.[130] It also invoked a nonracial category of woman that, combined with a southern African tradition of public motherhood, could underpin a powerful vision of solidarity and (by extension) national unity.[131] This vision of women's unity would operate as a significant, if contested and sometimes marginalized, intellectual current in the Congress Alliance and beyond.

"THE ROAD TO FREEDOM IS VIA THE CROSS"

In August 1952, Luthuli received a letter from the Native Affairs Department outlining claims that he was advocating opposition to government schemes in rural areas. After contesting the account's inaccuracies, Luthuli replied: "The African National Congress, which I [lead] in Natal, was engaging in campaign involving the defiance of certain laws and regulations, including the culling of cattle."[132] Soon afterward, he received an order to appear in Pretoria. In his memoir *Let My People Go*, Luthuli describes being ushered into the presence of W. W. M. Eiselen (the secretary for Native Affairs), the deputy secretary, and the Natal chief Native commissioner. They interrogated him regarding his opposition to government land rehabilitation schemes, influx control, and his obligation to enforce the law as a chief. In his answers, Luthuli outlined the failures of segregationist policies in considerable detail and underlined their basis in the systematic discrimination faced by Africans. Since the Defiance Campaign was a political demonstration against "criminal laws," he saw no conflict between his espousal of civil disobedience and the position of chief. Eiselen gave Luthuli a week to desist political activity.[133]

Tailored for a foreign audience, the account in *Let My People Go* does not capture the audacity of Luthuli's performance. Luthuli had dared to speak directly to the single most powerful government official with regards to African affairs and unapologetically rejected the entire framework of apartheid policy. Writing in *Indian Opinion*, Ngubane offered a breathless account of Luthuli's interview. "The hours he spent in Dr. Eiselen's office," Ngubane exclaimed, "where some of the most uncomfortable for the Department of Native Affairs; for rarely has its head been told the truth so plainly; so courageously and by so eminent an African authority."[134] Luthuli's stance, which would become the stuff of legend, transformed him into a national political figure and began to shift his reputation among a younger generation of activists.[135] When the department sent a demand that Luthuli resign either his chieftaincy or ANC presidency, Luthuli refused to comply. After some delay, the Native Affairs Department stripped Luthuli's chieftaincy.

Most accounts describe Luthuli's famous response to the government, "The Road to Freedom Is via the Cross," as a powerful defense of nonviolent civil disobedience and Christian piety. It was certainly both things—and considerably more. In this widely published text, Luthuli announced a break with the gradualist mode of politics that he had pursued for more than three decades. This rupture was both strategic and philosophical. In a scathing self-critique, he wrote these now famous words: "Who will deny that 30 years of my life have been spent knocking in vain, patiently, moderately and modestly at a closed and barred door?" (In a draft version, Luthuli demanded: "Who will dare deny." The final document removed the word "dare," cushioning his anger and allowing some readers to imagine an appeal rather than a challenge.)[136] The main concern of Luthuli's text was the nature of the chieftaincy and political leadership in general. In this respect, he was intervening into a venerable debate over the office of the *inkosi*—in effect, a debate over the existence and nature of precolonial African political culture—that had been reignited by the introduction of the Bantu Authorities Act in 1951. Reflecting an administrative conception of chieftainship, the act treated chiefs as government appointees responsible for "native law or custom": they were the enforcers of local regulations on behalf of an external sovereign. In the official statement on his dismissal, the Native Affairs Department reiterated that a chief "was part of the government of the country" and claimed that Luthuli's political activities had led him to neglect "his duties to his tribe."[137] The communiqué simply assumed that African political culture was essentially tribal (or antinational), predemocratic, and authoritarian.

Luthuli responded that he had decided to participate in the Defiance Campaign as a response to the call of his—the African—people: "I have joined my people in the new spirit of revolt that moves them today."[138] Attacking the authoritarian view of chieftainship, he asserted that chiefs were "part and parcel" of the tribe: they were the voice and servant of the people in local affairs.[139] It was therefore impossible for a chief to limit himself to local matters when the well-being of a tribe was closely bound to the common interests of the African people as a whole. In crafting this argument, Luthuli invoked a powerful set of Christian motifs—vocation and service—in articulating the relationship between leadership and his understanding of nation. The result was what the Mexican philosopher Enrique Dussel (a thinker deeply influenced by liberation theology) has called an "obediential" concept of power. According to this concept, true political authority derives from advancing "the demands, claims, and needs" of the nation through service.[140] Rejecting the opposition between local and national interests (and therefore the dichotomy between custom and modern politics), Luthuli depicted tribe as enfolded within the larger national subject: the African people existed both as individuated groups (represented by chiefs) and a greater whole (embodied by the democratically elected leaders of Congress). Implicit to Luthuli's argument was a conception of the people as a multiplicity.

The most important image in Luthuli's text was martyrdom. If the different segments of the African people were united through their leaders, the truest form of leadership was sacrifice: "It is inevitable that in the working for freedom some individuals and some families have to take the lead and suffer. The road to freedom is via the cross."[141] In a surviving draft, the final sentence was a clause linked to the previous idea by a colon ("lead and suffer: the road to freedom is via the cross."), further underscoring that Christianity did not appear here as instrumental means. Rather than representing the direct avenue to freedom (that is, redemption through faith), the cross illustrated and symbolized the responsibilities of political leadership: self-negation and struggle in the service of higher ideals. During the mid-1950s, he would express this understanding with a phrase drawn from the seventeenth-century Quaker theologian William Penn: "No Cross, No Crown."[142] Writing while imprisoned in the Tower of London (a historical resonance that would not have been lost on the ANC's president), Penn's tract described the cross as humanity's daily struggle for spiritual awareness against the beguiling lure of materialism.[143] In Luthuli's use, cross and crown were not sequential, but coterminous.

Luthuli's rejection of gradualism informed a second major theme in "The Road to Freedom Is via the Cross": his departure from "what liberal minded people rightly regarded as the path of moderation." Not only had decades of African political and economic efforts failed to secure citizenship, the last thirty years had witnessed the intensification of racist laws. The door, as Luthuli memorably declared, "was closed and barred."[144] In drawing this conclusion, Luthuli recalled his years of work with liberal organizations and government bodies, including the Christian Council of South Africa, the Joint Councils movement, and the Native Representative's Council. His moderate collaborators, he conceded, might find his new path "foolish and disappointing."[145] Nevertheless, his message to them was clear: it was time to embrace the people's spirit of revolt.

After announcing this break, Luthuli then turned, paused, and extended a hand to his erstwhile allies, many of whom had publically refused to support the Defiance Campaign. "This is no parting of the ways," he explained, citing Luke 5:4, "but a 'launching further into the deep.'"[146] The suggestion that liberals, both black and white, follow the initiative of the African people reversed the terms of trusteeship: it was the rebellion of the masses against racist laws, not gradualist efforts at uplift and reform, that would demonstrate the meaning of justice. This was a mischievous gesture. His former allies should "*join us* in our unequivocal pronouncement of all legitimate African aspirations," that is, they should support and identify with the political claims of African nationalism.[147] There would be a place for liberals in the freedom struggle only when they accepted that they could no longer dictate terms to the African people. They would, in effect, have to stop being moderates and gradualists.

This mode of disarming invitation would become a hallmark of Luthuli's political leadership. Faced with divisive questions, Luthuli attempted to neutralize conflicts and potential antagonists by transforming the grounds of the dispute. During preparations for the Defiance Campaign, Luthuli repeatedly encountered arguments against the alliance based on the exploitative practices of the Indian. Rather than deny these grievances, Luthuli reframed the debate by emphasizing the rational for common struggle. Whatever privileges Indians enjoyed, he contended, derived from laws enacted by white governments that oppressed *both* groups. In effect, he invited opponents of the alliance to ally with Indians to destroy the forms of privilege that made the exploitative practices of some Indians possible.

It is worth emphasizing that Luthuli was not downplaying or ignoring Natal's racial divisions, which were painfully evident to anyone who wished to see them. Rather, he was defending a major conquest of African nationalism: its redefinition of the problem space of South African politics. With the adoption of the 1949 Programme of Action, the ANC affirmed that the "South African dilemma" was neither a question of civilizational difference (the liberal framework of the Native Question) nor conflict between modernizing national groups (the Nationalist Party's apartheid). The fundamental truth of South African politics was the antagonism between democracy, represented by African nationalism, and white supremacy. However important, any conflict that obscured this understanding—whether between Indians and Africans, or Liberals and Communinists—directly threatened the ideological foundation of the liberation struggle. Luthuli's defence of chieftainship and the African-Indian allaince (both elaborated through his experiences during the Defiance Campaign) gave him the resources to conceptualize a political community that encompassed contradictions within a larger project of sacrifice for this national ideal.

PRESIDENT CHIEF

Within two months of Luthuli's dismissal from the Groutville chieftainship, the national ANC elected him to its highest office, the general presidency. This act was a ringing answer to the government and an assertion of the African people's right to choose their leaders through a democratic process. Across the country, ANC members began to refer to him as "chief." In a praise song for the occasion of Luthuli's Nobel Prize, his friend Alan Paton wrote: "Luthuli, they took your name of chief . . . Now they discover / You are more chief than ever."[148] In conversations before she died in 2012, the Indian Congress and later ANC stalwart Phyllis Naidoo—chain-smoking and cursing the record of the ANC in power—lovingly used this sobriquet nearly sixty years after Luthuli had lost his title. This too was an act of defiance.

At the point that Luthuli assumed office, the ANC had grown to a mass organization with support across the country, firmly established itself as the leader of opposition to the apartheid government, and embraced a strategic alliance with the Indian Congress. On these levels, the Defiance Campaign was a resounding success that augured a new direction for the fifty-year-old organization. For Luthuli, the Defiance Campaign resolved the "political and spiritual crisis" that followed the 1949 Durban Riots. In "The Road to Freedom Is via the Cross," he articulated a modality of politics that fused national liberation with a Christian critique of materialism: struggle as sacrifice for the ideal. After the transformative experience of the campaign, Luthuli was now in an authoritative position to interpret and shape the ANC's still inchoate trajectory. Until Sobukwe's election to the presidency of the Pan Africanist Congress in 1959, no other black leader rivaled either his public visibility or popularity. It was an unprecedented moment. In articles, interviews, policy documents, and speeches, Luthuli would spend the next decade defending a philosophy of African nationalism compatible with the Congress Alliance and the new image of a multiracial South Africa.

6 ↳ The Natal Synthesis

Inclusive Nationalism and the Unity of the ANC

IN JULY 1959, *Drum* magazine ran an article on the renewal of Luthuli's banning order entitled "Freedom in the Air."[1] Accompanied by Ian Berry's candid photographs of the ANC president, this piece—in the grand *Drum* style—trafficked in incongruities and jarring contrasts. After his previous banning order had expired, Luthuli traveled to Johannesburg in order to deliver an address to a mass meeting of the ANC. The security police intercepted him immediately before his arrival and delivered an expanded set of restrictions. If the author began by sketching this melancholy scene, it was only to convey the futility of the government's measures. Although the state appeared obsessed and even panicked—assigning scores of police to watch an old man whose grey hair was turning slowly to white—Luthuli himself was sanguine: "They are frightened. But how can they hope to stop the awakening of the people? They can't." Later, he continued: "I can smell freedom in the air. And they can smell it to." To illustrate these words, *Drum* published a photographic spread depicting the crowds that greeted Luthuli's car in downtown Johannesburg: wizened retirees in three-piece suits leaped and cheered; women clasped their hands in public prayer; and ANC members laughed, sang, and shouted while surrounding the automobile and waving the organization's tricolor flag. The atmosphere of the Defiance Campaign had returned. Under an image of a large conference hall waiting to hear Luthuli, *Drum* informed its readers that the meeting proceeded in the president's absence. The message was clear. The state could banish the ANC's leaders, prevent them from appearing publically, and confiscate their writings. But it could not arrest the spirit of resistance that Luthuli represented.

To convey this point, the editor decided to begin the article with a diptych: two side-by-side portraits of Luthuli taken moments apart. By the end of the 1950s, Luthuli's likeness had become a recognizable political symbol. Photographs of the banned leader appeared behind the rostrum at ANC events and protestors carried his image as a banner during marches and rallies. The effect of the *Drum* article, however, was different. Rather than a militant icon staring forward in defiance (say, an African version of a Lenin bust), the two photographs showed Luthuli with sharply contrasting expressions—and their juxtaposition gave both images a sense of animation. On the left, a tight-faced and arch-eyed Luthuli turned his hands outward as if making an emphatic point. On the right, Luthuli's famously round smile spread across a broad face while his eyes flashed at the camera. Presidential authority, worn with stately ease, flanked unencumbered joy. The cheeky caption read: "These are the faces of a banned chief. Serious? Sometimes. Happy? Yes. Despondent? No!" The lighthearted celebration of resilience mirrored the tone of Luthuli's statements. It implied that the state's failure to break his optimism about South Africa's future represented the ultimate limit of its power. It also invoked a representation of Luthuli's leadership style, which first developed during the Defiance Campaign—and which *Drum* itself had no small part in promoting. According to this depiction, Luthuli's greatness derived from his ability to reconcile contradictions: tradition and modernity, joy and political militancy, national unity and racial diversity.

There was something else notable about these portraits: Luthuli's dress. In addition to a brimless, tapering cap, he wore a Mandarin collar and a large-buttoned jacket with matching pants. These items constituted, as Raymond Suttner observes, the uniform of the Congress *voluntiyas*. An institution derived from the Defiance Campaign, the volunteers were "a special group of highly disciplined members" willing "to make unlimited sacrifices."[2] The provenance of Luthuli's headwear was unmistakable. Internationalized by Nehru's fame as a world statesman, this style of cap entered into Indian nationalist politics when Gandhi promoted it during the first Non-Cooperation Campaign of 1918–21 as a sign of resistance to the British Empire.[3] The high collar and button line strongly resembled the famous Nehru jacket.[4] By the time of the *Drum* story, the ensemble not only evoked the Indian independence struggle, but also (through the figure of Nehru the diplomat) the 1955 Bandung Conference of Afro-Asian states. Luthuli's uniform was evidence of a culture of struggle in which philosophical principles and a global vision of Afro-Asian solidarity were fused together in the everyday visual vocabulary of the movement.

In retrospect, Luthuli's optimism and *Drum*'s rebellious nonchalance were relics of an already-fading era. After their exclusion from the 1958 ANC national conference, the Africanist faction launched a rival political party with the formation of the Pan Africanist Congress on 6 April 1959. On 21 March of the following year, the PAC led a national anti-pass campaign. The state responded by massacring sixty-nine unarmed protestors near the Transvaal township of Sharpeville, declaring a national state of emergency, and banning the liberation organizations. As South Africa teetered on the brink of uncertainty, the Nobel committee announced that Luthuli would receive its peace prize. On 16 December 1961 (the day after Luthuli returned from the ceremony in Oslo), the ANC's armed wing initiated its first acts of sabotage against the South African state. Within three years, the preponderance of the ANC's leadership was arrested, banned, or abroad. Coordinated resistance to the regime virtually ceased to exist.

In *Long Walk to Freedom*, Mandela suggests that two main currents of thought prevailed in the ANC during the 1950s: one focused on the preparation for underground, insurrectionist activity and the other on mass mobilization.[5] After Youth League members like Mandela, Sisulu, Tambo, Joe Mathews, and Mji abandoned their opposition to working with Indians and Communists, they cultivated a revolutionary African nationalism that imagined overthrowing white supremacy through direct confrontation with the state. As Paul Landau shows, several members of this group (including Mandela) joined the Communist Party and eventually used the organization as their vehicle for pushing the ANC onto the path of armed struggle.[6] If this faction endorsed the alliance with the Indian Congress, they saw the question of "minorities" as subordinate: the majority's struggle for liberation was the driving force of the national democratic revolution.[7] Their outlook resonated with, and likely influenced, the South African Communist Party's (SACP) endorsement of a majoritarian African nationalism during this same period.[8]

The second tendency, embodied in the campaigns of the 1950s, identified the ANC's strength with its public activities and mass support. Luthuli, as the *Drum* article illustrated, was the most important advocate of this position. Drawing on the experience of the Defiance

Campaign, he articulated a philosophy that heavily influenced the ANC's political culture through its insistence on the constructive role of African nationalism in the creation of a broad South African identity, the primacy of ideals in the creation of national unity, and the centrality of collective symbols to the liberation struggle. While the Sharpeville Massacre, the banning of the ANC, and the launch of Umkhonto we Sizwe (MK) resulted in the eclipse of this second current by the first, it nevertheless survived as a tradition and a diffuse archive that later generations could resuscitate and rework.

This chapter focuses on the development of the second outlook. Following his leadership of the Defiance Campaign in Natal, Luthuli's election to the presidency of the ANC made him the most prominent interpreter of the African-Indian alliance. Abandoning his faith in liberal gradualism, Luthuli began to develop a new philosophy of African nationalism based on the form of multiracial unity developed during the course of struggle. These views formed the basis of the Natal synthesis and represented a distinct intellectual current within the ANC: an inclusive interpretation of African nationalism reflected in Luthuli's presidential statements, Natal ANC policy documents, and the writings of his close supporters, including Ngubane and H. I. E. Dhlomo.

Luthuli's understanding of African nationalism combined his conception of collective service with two other ideas. First, Luthuli advanced a plural idea of peoplehood that drew explicitly on Zulu ideas of hospitality and layered social belonging. Second, Luthuli placed symbolism and ritual at the center of nation building. If the first idea emerged during his struggle with the Native Affairs Department over the nature of chieftainship, the second reflected his reading of the Defiance Campaign. At two levels, the Natal synthesis was propelled by the question of the also-colonized other. It was the trauma of the 1949 Riots that created the problem space for Luthuli's reconceptualization of nationalism: what understanding of unity could incorporate Indians while respecting the other's difference and autonomy? The Defiance Campaign provided the answer. By joining Africans and Indians in struggle around common ideals, the campaign affirmed the simultaneous unity and plurality of South Africa by creating a new image of nationhood.

After discussing Luthuli's campaign for the ANC presidency, this chapter shows how Luthuli's philosophy of nationalism came to influence the broader culture of the ANC through its use of political symbolism, exemplified by 26 June, or Freedom Day, and the campaign for the adoption of the 1955 Freedom Charter. If the aesthetic of the Defiance Campaign emerged in response to the also-colonized other, the Congress Alliance generalized this imagery to include all South Africans, including whites. To a certain degree, the fact that the African-Indian alliance formed the template for this vision resulted in the absorption of the "Indian question" into battles over the Congress Alliance, the Freedom Charter, and the place of African politics within the Cold War. This chapter concludes by exploring these battles. Defending his pluralistic concept of nation building, Luthuli organized an opposition in response to efforts by the Transvaal-based nationalist group, centered around the Tambo Constitution, to restructure and centralize the ANC. At the same time, he publically broke from Ngubane in 1956 over his collaborator's sacrifice of African unity to liberal anticommunism. These events, although less well-known than the 1958 Africanist schism, were critical moments in Luthuli's elaboration and defense of an inclusive African nationalism.

LUTHULI'S PRESIDENTIAL CAMPAIGN

If there were any lingering doubts that Luthuli planned on contesting the ANC presidency in 1952, Ngubane put them to rest in his *Indian Opinion* article on 28 November. Published in the first issue after "The Road to Freedom Is via the Cross", the article fulminated against a "clumsy" rumor campaign by Moroka's opponents designed to undermine his presidency.[9] Detailing these rumors served, of course, to make them even more widely known. With corrosive irony, Ngubane praised Moroka—who had taken separate council during the Defiance Campaign trial and publically renounced racial equality in an attempt avoid prison—as a man of courage who refused to balk at the gravest of decisions. Ngubane then dismissed the possible contenders for the presidency. The name missing from his list, Luthuli's, was the most important. This was vintage Ngubane and seasoned observers knew how to read the leaves. While preparing the ground for an election campaign, Ngubane was guarding against any suggestion that Luthuli intended to stand. A public commitment would have opened Luthuli to attack from Moroka and his supporters.

Since July, Ngubane and Dhlomo had been working to raise Luthuli's national profile without prematurely revealing their intentions.[10] Their moment came when the Native Affairs Department dismissed Luthuli. According to Ngubane, the government did not expect Luthuli to defy their ultimatum and initially suggested that he reconsider. After Luthuli refused, Ngubane wrote, "their anger almost knew no limits."[11] They stripped his chieftainship (including his salary and a scholarship for his son), restricted Luthuli to his magisterial district, and banned him from addressing public meetings. In response to these actions, Ngubane approached S. S. Lungongolo Mtolo (a Youth League stalwart who had been appointed Natal provincial treasurer in 1951) and urged him to float the possibility of supporting Luthuli for the national presidency in the Natal executive. "It was a government vote of no confidence in Luthuli," Ngubane later reflected. "The world was watching what we would do. We had to make it clear beyond all shadow of doubt that we had the fullest confidence in Luthuli."[12] Adopting his proposal, the provincial executive appointed Ngubane, along with Mtolo and Wits law student Hyacinth Bhengu, to lead Natal's delegation to the ANC national conference. A skilled orator, Bhengu focused on rousing floor speeches while Ngubane pressed their case on delegates. In the context of a conference divided along provincial and generational lines, Luthuli's Natal Youth League support likely made him an attractive compromise candidate. The conference elected Luthuli in a vote of 150 to 47.

In his acceptance speech, Luthuli declared that he would continue the ANC's policy as represented by the Defiance Campaign. Emphasizing the constructive aspect of the freedom struggle, Luthuli described the ANC's mission as making "the European and the African and the Indian rediscover one another in sharing a common nationhood and in feeling bound together by ideals held in common."[13] In *Indian Opinion*, Ngubane observed that Luthuli's election should reassure Europeans and Indians that Africans had thoroughly rejected the racialist politics of the Bantu National Congress. Ngubane also identified Luthuli's emphasis on "constructiveness" as a major turning point.[14] Historically, the ANC had championed the African cause by opposing racist laws and promoting the extension of citizenship rights to Africans. In his first words as president, Luthuli transformed this sectional vision into an ambitious, positive program: the African struggle for democracy was the means by which a unified South African nation would come into being.

While Ngubane and Dhlomo served as Luthuli's publicists, the organizer of Luthuli's campaign was Yengwa. Born in 1923, Yengwa's father (who was active in the 1919 anti-pass campaign) drove oxen and his mother taught primary school.[15] Like Lembede, Yengwa worked as a "houseboy." Employed as an organizer in an Indian Congress–led trade union during the early 1940s, Yengwa resented the inferior treatment of the "African section" (he could not use the lift at the union's office) and the sidelining of African workers by the use of English at "general meetings." He quit the union after he was passed over for promotion in favor of less qualified Indian and Coloured candidates.[16]

Despite these experiences, the 1946 Passive Resistance Campaign convinced Yengwa that Africans and Indians could unite in common struggle. In the mid-1940s, he served as the secretary of the Natal Youth League and masterminded the campaign that ousted Champion. After the November 1951 elections, he became the secretary of the Natal ANC. According to Suleman, Yengwa was Luthuli's "right-hand man."[17] At the same time, and demonstrating the contradictions of the Natal ANC leadership, he appears to have maintained ties with the Zulu Hlanganani organization in Cato Manor. Yengwa shared Luthuli's great love of Zulu culture: he was an *imbongi* (a praise poet) and sometimes recited *izibongo* (laudatory epics) for the Zulu kings at ANC meetings. Liz Gunner, who studied isiZulu with him in exile, remembers his personal lightness, vibrancy, and *isithunzi*: a dignity and weight of presence that transmitted itself to those around him.[18] It was Yengwa who read Luthuli's speeches at rallies when he was serving government banning orders.[19]

Yengwa's role in delivering Luthuli's speeches points to an important dimension of the ANC president's intellectual production. Not only were Luthuli's words often embodied in public by others, but his texts emerged out of a collective editorial process. From a comparison of Luthuli's notebooks with published writings, it is clear that Luthuli revised his drafts on the basis of extensive consultation: the final versions represented the collaborative thinking of a group within the Natal ANC.[20] While the composition of this circle evolved over time, one stalwart was Luthuli's wife, Nokukhanya. Active in the ANC at a branch level, Nokukhanya sometimes represented Luthuli at events, and she played a leading role in the women's cooperative, the Daughters of Africa. (She also, Luthuli reported in a letter from 1956, exerted herself so strongly in working their field that she suffered from agonizing pains all over her body. Banning had reduced their proud family to the edge of subsistence and her labor enabled Luthuli's political activism.[21]) After Nokukhanya had listened to drafts and made her contributions, Luthuli felt the confidence to deliver his addresses—an anecdote that underscores the extent to which his sense of leadership was based on ongoing dialogue with his family and immediate community.[22] Dhlomo, Yengwa, and Ngubane were other trusted collaborators.[23] In turn, ideas and language from these collectively produced statements were incorporated into ANC speeches, Natal policy documents, and, in the early 1950s, articles published by Ngubane and Dhlomo.[24] Supported by this textual economy, a distinct strand of African nationalism began to consolidate around Luthuli's presidency.

The coalescence of this intellectual current was linked to a second development: Luthuli's self-fashioning of a new public persona. Over the course of 1952, Luthuli began to understand that he could combine his various public roles into a mode of political leadership that appealed across racial lines. Although he never discussed this evolution explicitly, it was evident from his public appearances and the increasing emphasis in Dhlomo and Ngubane's writings on Luthuli's leadership style. Luthuli "the moderate" gave way to something considerably more complex. He now appeared as a media-friendly president who combined the roles of teacher, minister, and Zulu chief—authoritative, and frequently authoritarian, positions in rural African society—in order to advocate for the peaceful rebellion of the oppressed. He was, *Drum* claimed, "a conservative turned radical."[25] Significantly, these forms of African masculinity, each reflecting Luthuli's standing as a respected elder, appealed in a different way to African and liberal or white Christian constituencies. These latter groups often described him in grandfatherly (or even Christ-like) terms: humble, kind, generous, and devout.[26] Luthuli's persona not only welded conservative forms of cultural capital to nationalist militancy, it did so in a way that disarmed the racial fears of a small, but not insignificant, group of Indians and whites. In important respects, this combination foreshadowed Mandela's self-presentation after his release from prison in February 1990.[27] It also articulated the image of the African nation through the figure of the male leader, reinforcing the historically gendered character of the "national" political arena. If radical in many respects, Luthuli's performance still worked within the structure of feeling that Ciraj Rassool describes as "presidentialism": a political culture in which the image and biography of the president underwrote unity by embodying the liberation organization and (by implication) the nation.[28]

It was H. I. E. Dhlomo who first wrote about the almost counterintuitive aspect of Luthuli's appeal and suggested that it represented something unprecedented. In a two-part article published in *Bantu World* on 26 July and 2 August 1952 (and republished, by popular demand, in *Ilanga*), Dhlomo described Luthuli as incarnating—and, in an important sense, overcoming—the antagonisms of South African society:

> A paradox! A chief who is respected by officials, is not their blind tool, but a dauntless leader of his people. A faithful servant fighting against a system that produced him. An intellectual with an analytic, objective mind plunged into the rough and tumble of militant politics. An interpreter [of black views to the white minority] and a moderate participating in a campaign of defiance. . . .
>
> He still retains the respect of liberals, missionaries, educated Africans, rural people, moderates and fanatical nationalists. Here is a man asked . . . to interpret and represent these varied interests—his, theirs, ours, everybody's.[29]

In this depiction, Dhlomo replaced the classic liberal understanding of representation (the delegation of authority) with an essentially figurative conceptualization of national leadership (an individual's distillation of collective experiences). This substitution underlined the symbolic dimension of Luthuli's political practice. Embodying the experiences and ideals of multiple constituencies, Luthuli's persona allowed different audiences to identify with him even while they recognized that his presidency was emblematic of something larger. In his life, sufferings, and struggles, Dhlomo observed, Luthuli "contradicts contradiction."[30] It was a small step from this analysis to conclude—as Luthuli did in his presidential acceptance speech—that this contradictory unity was the defining characteristic of the South African nation.

As novel as it was, Dhlomo's article still represented the South African dilemma in terms of two distinct, but overlapping conflicts: African versus European and tradition versus modernity. If Luthuli's leadership represented something genuinely South African, it was because he embodied an African nationalism that synthesized Zulu culture with Western civilization. Significantly, this synthesis configured the Indian as exterior to Dhlomo's problematic—the reconciliation of African and white. At some level, he seems to have recognized this implication. In an aside to readers outside Natal, Dhlomo stressed the delicacy of the Indian question: white anti-Indian racism was virulent, propaganda against the African-Indian alliance circulated widely, and race riots remained a very real danger. Luthuli's courageous stance on the alliance, Dhlomo warned, threatened to undermine his support among the very constituencies (especially rural Africans) that held him in the highest regard.

While the article represented African-Indian relations as a fault line that could undermine Luthuli's synthesis, it consigned the potential disruption to the province, thus preserving the binary terms of its discourse at the national level. In contrast, the "constructive" breakthrough of Luthuli's presidential speech occurred when he situated the African-Indian alliance and the experience of the Defiance Campaign at the center of his philosophy of nation. Much like Dhlomo (and he certainly read Dhlomo's articles during this period), Luthuli concluded that a symbolic politics could reconcile the otherwise conflicting demands of national unity and racial plurality. However, the centrality of the also-colonized other meant that the resolution would take a different form. The figure of the president was preserved, but its singularity was displaced. Luthuli needed a means of incorporating racial difference and group autonomy—in other words, a politics of heterogeneity—inside of the nation itself.

LUTHULI'S PHILOSOPHY OF AFRICAN NATIONALISM

Following the 1949 Durban Riots, Luthuli began to question the normative presupposition that democracy necessitated social homogeneity. In speeches from this period, he argued that shared values, developed through interracial contact and Christian fraternity, could unite a society composed of separate racial groups. Breaking with liberal gradualism, "The Road to Freedom Is via the Cross" reworked this proposal in militant and philosophically idealist terms. Sacrifice in the service of eternal values, exemplified by the crucifixion, could provide the foundations for a national movement. If he initially formulated this position while confronting his dismissal, he soon generalized it into a conceptualization of the relationship between struggle and political community. Luthuli's realization was that a national identity could simultaneously respect and transcend racial difference if it emerged through the collective subordination of self to the pursuit of eternal values such as justice, equality, magnanimity, and fellowship.[31] In other words, service and sacrifice—the active surrender to the ideals that define a community—could provide the organizing structure of nation.

The resulting philosophy of nationalism combined three elements: the project of African nation building, philosophical idealism, and the logic of active inclusion. According to Luthuli's vision, the goal of nation building was not the creation of a new sociological entity that somehow eliminated racial, ethnic, or religious identities. Consequently, nationalism was not the expression of a circumscribed political community. Redefining the structure of nation in terms of a people's pursuit of eternal ideals, Luthuli understood nationalism as the development of a shared loyalty through participation in an ethical-political project. Constituted in the very process of striving for freedom, this project derived its power from radical openness.

Luthuli summarized this position in a 1955 message to the ANC's annual conference: "It is also fair to infer that the African National Congress, having accepted the fact of the multiracial nature of our country, envisaged an all-inclusive African nationalism which, resting on the principle of freedom for all in the country, unity for all in the country, embraced all people under African nationalism, regardless of their racial or geographic origin who resided in Africa and gave their undivided loyalty and allegiance."[32] Inclusion, as the above quote indicated, presupposed an act of welcoming by *someone*. If the African people derived its cohesiveness from a common experience of oppression and struggle, the embodiment of this history in shared values meant that African nationalism could welcome outsiders—and incorporate social, cultural, and political heterogeneity—without threatening its fundamental basis of unity. For the means of this incorporation was the same structure that made African nationalism historically possible: the willing subordination of self to the common pursuit of eternal values. In an important and genuinely radical sense, this vision challenged the belief that a nation was an exclusive or autonomous entity.

If Luthuli expressed this concept in abstract or even platitudinous terms, a careful reading of his speeches and notebooks reveals that his thinking was based on the consideration of personal experiences. Far from Anderson's "confidence of community in anonymity," Luthuli's nationalism was a deeply felt attachment grounded in the immediacy of interpersonal relationships.[33] Echoing Lembede, Luthuli's discussions of nationalism are filled with references to emotion: nationhood required a shared *feeling* of belonging that emerged from living and actively participating in local communities.[34] It is hard not to imagine that Luthuli's experiences as the democratically elected chief of the Groutville mission reserve informed this understanding. Over the course of seventeen years, he adjudicated disputes over every possible matter of land ownership (the legal and customary terms of belonging) while guiding his community through the everyday challenges of living side by side and sharing inadequate resources. When he motivated international sanctions against South Africa in *Let My People Go*, Luthuli elaborated a parable based on the legal and ethical responsibilities that existed between neighbors.[35] A second model for a nation founded on ideals was the ecumenical vision of the Christian church. For just as Christianity included a multiplicity of denominations and orders whose integrity rested on individual belief, the African nation-building project could encompass different communities, organized on their own terms, but united by common values. Luthuli explicitly compared the diverse unity of the ANC to the Catholic Church.[36] The most important model for this idea of African nationalism, however, was the Defiance Campaign.

Unlike his earlier vision of gradual assimilation into settler civil society, Luthuli's nation-building project existed within the present rather than in an indeterminate future. It therefore provided the basis for an immediate claim to democracy and full citizenship rights. At the same time, Luthuli possessed a deeply Christian understanding of humanity's relationship with the transcendental. If the ongoing struggle to live by common values could bind diverse peoples together, no society would ever embody these values fully. In this respect, Luthuli's nationalism resembled an ethical process rather than a site of arrival: living with and across difference would necessitate the elaboration of new forms of unity—intellectual, political, cultural.[37] To invoke Judith Butler's reading of Edward Said: Luthuli's position *affirmed* "the irresolution of identity."[38] The ideals of nation, which Luthuli believed were the true foundation of "civilization," were not limited to Christianity or the West, but were universal. When writing *Let My People Go*, he stressed that South Africa would also build on the values of "the east— let us not forget our great debt to India."[39]

Although these views differed in important respects from Lembede, Luthuli's embrace of a nationalism based on philosophical idealism suggests that he read and reworked the writings of his former student as well as early Youth League policy documents. In terms that resonated strongly with Lembede's thinking, Luthuli repeatedly identified the struggle against apartheid with the defense of human freedom against materialism: the reduction of humanity to economic utility, rule by force, and spiritual impoverishment.[40] The defense of a spiritual humanism became the bedrock of Luthuli's philosophy. In notes for a 1952 speech to the Natal Indian Congress, he went so far as to suggest that the partition of South Africa between races would be preferable to the triumph of a materialist conception of wellbeing in African politics.[41] Freedom was only possible when human beings could develop their capacities in all arenas of life: political, social, and religious.[42] While Luthuli worked closely with Communists within the ANC (including his deeply respected friend Moses Kotane), he believed that their philosophical differences would necessarily lead to the formation of separate political parties and conflict after liberation.[43]

Perhaps the most striking aspect of this vision was that Luthuli, while sometimes warning against an overemphasis on nationalism, did not dissolve the African political subject into a broader nonracial identity. In notes made in late 1952, he expressed this program in stages: "1. Large[r] unity of race[s] in union. 2. First step is unity of Africans."[44] He elaborated this schema the following year. In notes for a speech to the Natal ANC, Luthuli advanced that there were two methods of building a multiracial united front against white supremacy. The first strategy continued the legacy of the ANC's founders by unifying "the tribes under the banner of African NATIONALISM." He hastened to add that this progressive nationalism would embrace cooperation with other communities based on their "intense desire" for freedom. The second strategy involved the creation of a multiracial front "with those who *respecting us as a people* share our democratic aspirations."[45] These stages were clearly interdependent. Together they implied a layered conception of identity.

At several points, Luthuli made it clear that he saw this form of nationalism as a historic innovation: it challenged the then-prevalent liberal assumption that both nationhood and democracy presupposed a homogenous people. In a 1958 speech to the South African Congress of Democrats, Luthuli explained:

> It is often suggested, quite rightly, that democracy was developed in homogenous communities—in Europe, possibly in Asia to an extent—in communities that were homogenous in colour. Here in South Africa we are not a homogenous community, not as far as race and coulour are concerned, nor possibly even in culture. . . . But I personally believe that here in South Africa, with all our diversities of colour and race, we will show the world a new pattern of democracy. . . .What is important is that we can build a homogenous South Africa not on the basis of colour but of human values.[46]

In a 1958 telegraph sent to congratulate Julius Nyerere on becoming Prime Minister of Tanganiyka, Luthuli predicted "destiny has preserved for Africa the task of building such a democracy in which all races participate."[47] Writing in isiZulu, he described his vision in these words: "kulelizwe siyizizwe eziningi" ("In this land/nation, we are a nation of many nations" or "In this land/nation, we are many nations").[48] In English, he translated this concept as "the multiracial nation." The main force of this concept was not, as later critics have sometimes suggested, that South Africa was composed of four discrete national groups.[49] Luthuli rarely invoked the distinct racial categories of African, Indian, white, and Coloured per se. (In contrast, newspapers produced by the Communist Party, like *Guardian* and the *New Age*, did organize their coverage of resistance politics according to these units.)

Luthuli's general emphasis was on the incorporation of difference and plurality into the idea of *African* nationalism rather than on the discrete character of identities. In effect, he challenged the deeply held idea, which the philosopher Isaiah Berlin traces from Kant to German Romanticism, that nations are in some sense autonomous, self-contained, and *singular* subjects. "It is this collective self," Berlin explains, "that generates the form of life lived by individuals, and gives meaning and purpose to all its members."[50] If the Romantic notion understood *self*-determination in terms of independence and *self*-rule, Luthuli reformulated nation in terms of an ethical-political relationship with others who were an inextricable part of the same society and, in a profound sense, part of one's very being.

This form of nationalism, he believed, possessed deep roots in precolonial African history. Defending the democratic character of Africans societies, he invoked the hospitality that Africans gave outsiders such as early European missionaries and underlined aspects of Zulu culture—including a strong sense of community, spirituality, and rituals such the harvest ceremony dedicated to the goddess Nomkubhulwana—that might have provided the basis for the development of an autochthonous nationalism.[51] In this respect, Luthuli's vision drew on a southern African political tradition of hospitality, alliance building, and inclusive notions of kinship that—as Jan Vansina and Landau show—stretched across millennia.[52] At the same time, Luthuli insisted that colonial conquest had disorganized African society, resulting in the perversion and death of its political institutions.[53] The ANC would have to develop the same principles on different foundations: a multiracial society, the universal values contained in Christianity and other religions, and democratic socialism. Even as he drew on earlier political traditions in his theorization of nation, Luthuli—like Ngubane and H. I. E. Dhlomo—opposed the vision of restoration that was a common theme of shack land politics and the millenarian Christian churches.[54]

Although Luthuli never elucidated his philosophy in a systematic form, he advanced each of its component ideas repeatedly after mid-1952. At one level, this presentation was strategic. By insisting on principles rather than rigid theories, Luthuli could defend an overall approach to nation building while attempting to minimize doctrinal disputes that might reinforce divisions within the ANC. At another level, Luthuli's insistence on principle and his avoidance of a single definition of nation directly reflected his pluralistic conception of nationalism. In contrast to the Youth League and Communist Party's attempts to develop a theoretical resolution of the "National Question" (in other words, to determine the nature and boundaries of nation in South Africa), Luthuli's approach did not attempt to establish an a priori delineation of either an African or a South African identity.[55] To the contrary, he sought to show how African nationalism could incorporate multiple communities within an open-ended ethical and political process.

If the ANC refrained from adopting an official position on the national question in the 1950s, this decision reflected (at least in significant part) the philosophy articulated by Luthuli and his co-thinkers in Natal.[56] In other words, the refusal of a single, decisive formulation of the national question reflected a specific approach to nation building. This stance built on a tradition that understood the ANC as a national movement rather than a political party. According to Sylvia Neame, this view developed as early as the 1920s and promoted the idea of the ANC as "a broad church" or "parliament" that contained numerous, often competing, tendencies.[57] However, Luthuli did something considerably more profound than extend this organizational culture to include other racial groups. After his election to the ANC presidency, Luthuli's greatest accomplishment was the development of a philosophy of African nationalism compatible with the political aesthetic of the Defiance Campaign.

SYMBOLIC CONSTITUTIONALISM

As president of the ANC, Luthuli drew two major conclusions from his philosophy of African nationalism. First and perhaps most radically, Luthuli developed a critique of the majoritarian conception of democracy. Because he understood nation in terms of the pursuit of eternal values, he rejected the premise that democratic governments derive their legitimacy from the will of the majority. As Lodge observes, Luthuli generally expressed the ANC's goals in terms of "participation" or "partnership in the government on the basis of equality" rather than self-determination.[58] To some degree, this phrasing reflected the ANC's political strategy during the 1950s. Committed to nonviolent methods of struggle, the ANC employed language that underscored their inclusive vision—for example, leaders generally referred to the "sections" of South African society rather than majority and minorities—and left open the possibility of power sharing with white parties as a transitional stage to universal adult suffrage.[59]

In Luthuli's case, however, discomfort with the idea of majority rule was more than a rhetorical stance. Before democratic institutions could represent something like the popular will or general interest, the African majority needed to convince other groups that its nation-building project represented their shared future. In other words, the relationship between majority and minority could not be expressed in terms of a right exercised over or against other groups—for example, the right to self-determination. In a multiracial society, the invocation of rights presupposed something more fundamental: each group had to embrace equality and interdependency within the nation of nations. The affirmation of this mutual entanglement, which Luthuli described in a 1957 letter as "a common society," was an essential demand of the liberation struggle.[60] In developing this vision, Luthuli extrapolated from the process of building the Congress Alliance to his understanding of democracy and its preconditions. The alliance did not rest on formal structures so much as the trust that developed among individuals and organizations in the course of struggle. He believed that the same principle would hold in a democratic society: elections and liberal institutions would remain hollow unless they rested on a dynamic relationship of trust and mutual recognition among racial groups. In this sense, Luthuli saw the ethical life of the nation as something that existed outside of and exceeded its realization in the formal institutions of a democratic state.

Defending the African-Indian alliance at the 1952 conference of the Natal ANC, Luthuli explicitly rejected the idea that a demographic majority possessed a greater claim to national belonging. Democracy, he insisted, did not apportion freedom on the basis of numerical weight. He expressed his argument first in isiZulu and then glossed it in English: "Umqondo wokwahlukaniselana kawukho kulendaba ngaba asilwi impi ezoba nempango *** yabiwe, kodwa yimpi yokuthola amathuba aphelele, nenkululeko. Lamanani awabiwa ayasetshenziswa ngothandayo. (Freedom is enjoyed with others, and not mathematically and proportionally shared with them: it is to each according to his talent and ability.)"[61] After affirming the multiracial character of South Africa, Luthuli argued that the ANC was not fighting a war or impi for something that could be divided. Freedom must be enjoyed collectively: it existed only when everyone possessed the opportunity for personal and spiritual development. The speech then proceeded to establish a direct link to Luthuli's idea of an inclusive African nationalism. These values, he explained, cannot be exclusively possessed. They existed so that anyone who wished could make use of them. Returning to isiZulu, he stated that he was confident that both Africans and Indians would pursue these ideals if given the opportunity. The alliance's critics, such as R. R. R. Dhlomo in *Ilanga*, were therefore wrong to ask which group would benefit more from cooperation. The question devalued freedom by treating it as a material good.

Luthuli's second major conclusion related to the practice of nation building. Once again drawing on the experience of the Defiance Campaign, Luthuli placed the conscious elaboration of symbols at the center of resistance politics. In this respect, he helped shape a broader political culture within the ANC that directly linked struggle, commemoration, and the encouragement of the local appropriation and refashioning of national symbols. (During the 1980s, the United Democratic Front resuscitated this strategy as well as the symbolism of the 1950s—most notably, the Freedom Charter and the figure of Mandela—in the effort to build the broadest possible unity of antiapartheid forces.)[62] The cornerstone of this culture was the commemoration of 26 June. First marked as a national day of mourning for workers killed on 1 May 1950, Freedom Day fused political action with remembrance: both the Defiance Campaign's launch and the 1955 Congress of the People occurred on this date. Mapped onto this annual calendar, new struggles not only continued and commemorated earlier battles (and their losses), but the very act of protest reinscribed the date into a shared history. This cyclical temporality allowed South Africans to participate in a living process of national self-fashioning. By the mid-1950s, this symbolism had become part of the ANC's everyday functioning. Tambo—now the national general secretary—signed his letters "Remember our national day—June 26th."[63]

In an important 1953 statement on the meaning of Freedom Day, Luthuli connected the ritualization of 26 June with the logic of inclusive African nationalism. After recounting the history and significance of the commemoration, Luthuli advised ANC supporters to light a fire or place a candle outside their homes while they gathered all members of the household in vigil. This ritual would begin across the country at 9 p.m. Luthuli instructed: "Let the older members of the household tell the younger, so far as they know it, the story of the struggle of the African

people in particular and the non-European in general for their liberation both in the area in which they are located and elsewhere in the
country."[64] By observing this ceremony, each household would participate in a national structure of feeling while actively nurturing a historical
consciousness based on the struggles of local communities. Although he
addressed this message primarily to Africans, Luthuli envisioned this ritual as a way that "other communities associated with us in our struggle"
could participate in an African day of national rededication.

Luthuli's proposal can be described as a form of *symbolic constitutionalism*. Rather than a founding charter or body of law, he envisioned
a shared set of symbols—produced by the liberation struggle but appropriated and reworked from below—uniting the diverse experiences of
a heterogeneous people. By adopting and mobilizing symbols in their
own way, a multitude of communities could write themselves into the
unfolding story of nationhood. In other words, Luthuli conceptualized
symbolism as a political technology for building a multiracial nation
based on shared values. As Dhlomo observed in his analysis of Luthuli's leadership style, symbolism could enable the emergence of a
contradictory unity that simultaneously transcended and respected racial identities.

This strategy, at least in its broadest outline, became widely accepted among the ANC leadership. In the National Executive's 1959
annual report, the Transvaal-based lawyer and Communist Party member Duma Nokwe identified key anniversaries, including Freedom
Day and the fiftieth anniversary of the Union of South Africa, that the
ANC could utilize in planning the next year's campaigns. Echoing Luthuli, he recognized that the leadership might select the dates, but success ultimately relied on the independent initiative of local branches.[65]
Intriguingly, the ANC leadership appears to have drawn inspiration for
annual 26 June rituals from the traditions of different groups. While the
1952 idea of candle burning and recitation clearly reflected Biblical
and Jewish influences (combining elements of Passover and Yom Kip-
pur), the 1959 commemoration drew on Gandhian themes. ANC supporters were to engage in acts of self-denial—the form was left to local
initiative—that would promote discipline, endurance, and renewed
determination.[66]

By placing heterogeneity and symbolism at the center of nation
building, Luthuli helped set the terms for the subsequent political

struggles within the ANC. These conflicts took the form of competing interpretations of the Defiance Campaign's political aesthetic. Insisting on the singular character of the nationalist subject, the Africanist current rejected the very possibility of Luthuli's multiracial nationalism. They argued that the idea of a multiracial nation entailed distinct, race-based claims to sovereignty. "Multiracialism" implied either the right of collective representation within the state ("a democratic apartheid") or the country's literal partition. At a more visceral level, the Africanists objected to the prominence of Indians and whites during the Defiance Campaign and the organizational structure of the Congress Alliance. In their view, these developments undermined African independence and therefore eroded the unifying power of African nationalism as an instrument of popular mobilization.[67]

In contrast, the underground Communist Party championed the image of the multiracial nation in the newspapers *Guardian* and *New Age*. Organizing its coverage of resistance politics along racial lines, these papers celebrated individual leaders (usually party cadre) and social struggles such as strikes, boycotts, and political protests as exemplifying "communities" as a whole. In the pages of the Communist Party's press, the African majority and the oppressed minorities (along with sympathetic whites) found unity through an aspirational civic nationalism: the struggle for democracy and human rights, exemplified by shared institutions, provided the content for a South African identity.[68] If Luthuli's symbolic constitutionalism distinguished between the ethical life of the nation and political representation through the state, the Africanist current and *New Age*—albeit working from opposed premises—collapsed this space in their interpretation of the alliance. Translating the political aesthetics of the Defiance Campaign into existing theories of nation, both tendencies reaffirmed the singularity of the nationalist subject, whether understood in ethno-nationalist or civic-political terms.

THE FREEDOM CHARTER

At the Cape annual conference in August 1953, Luthuli's long-time friend and former colleague at Adams, Z. K. Mathews, proposed that the ANC call a national assembly: "I wonder whether the time has not come for the ANC to convene a national convention, a congress of the people, representing all of the people of this country irrespective of race or colour, to draw up a Freedom Charter for a democratic South Africa of the future."[69] Endorsed at the ANC's annual conference in December, Mathews's suggestion launched one of the longest and, in some respects, most audacious campaigns undertaken by the Congress Alliance. Initially, Mathews conceived of the Congress of the People as a South African estates general: the campaign would divide the country into districts that would then elect delegates to a "people's parliament."[70] Confronted with the logistical difficulties of convening such an assembly, the campaign evolved into a call for political demands that would be incorporated into a national proclamation—comparable to the British Magna Carta or the American Declaration of Independence[71]—and ratified by a gathering of delegates from across the country.

Over the course of eighteen months, the ANC and its allies held regional conferences to popularize the idea of the charter, groups of volunteers went door-to-door soliciting ideas, and individuals mailed in suggestions from across the country. According to Luthuli, nothing in the ANC's history—not even the Defiance Campaign—had so thoroughly captured the imagination of the masses. Until the very last minute, items for the charter continued to arrive "on homespun strips of paper, on pieces of cardboard, envelopes and cigarette boxes."[72]

In two respects, the campaign incorporated the mode of symbolic politics elaborated by Luthuli in his statement on 26 June. First, the idea of a people's charter provided a unifying framework that allowed a multiplicity of actors to insert themselves into a collective process of self-definition. If the leadership provided the idea, the campaign was nevertheless conceived as a structure whose success required animation and definition from below. According to Congress of Democrats activist Norman Levy, the first meeting of the planning committee (held in Stanger so that Luthuli, its chairman, could attend) determined the decentralized and locally driven character of the campaign.[73] As an initial step, the Congress Alliance encouraged the formation of local committees across the country. These groups called meetings where people would gather, discuss their grievances, and propose demands. The same committees would later elect delegates to attend the Congress of the People. According to this strategy, thousands of autonomous initiatives from every region and group in the country—much like the self-organized vigils of Luthuli's 26 June proposal—would participate in determining the charter's content and the composition of the congress. It was a structure that allowed for the direct expression of South Africa's multiplicity within the creation of a new national compact.[74]

Second, both the campaign and the Congress of the People operated according to a logic of radical inclusion. This openness was insured by the self-determining character of committees and the practice of mailing suggestions. Anyone and everyone could contribute to the process: the only criteria for eligibility was participation in the campaign itself. Reaffirming an inclusive practice of nation building, the campaign invited the United Party and South African Liberal Party—neither of which supported universal adult suffrage—to attend the gathering (neither came). There were no political limitations to national belonging. In July 1954, the organizing committee wrote South Africa's Prime Minister, D. F. Malan, and requested his presence.[75]

More than any other event of the 1950s, the Congress of the People embodied the political aesthetic of the Congress Alliance. Convened near Kliptown (a small shack settlement then outside of Soweto) on 25 and 26 June 1955, over three thousand delegates listened to the presentation of the charter in English, Sesotho, and isiXhosa and approved its contents by acclamation. While the majority was African, several hundred Indian, Coloured, and white delegates were present as well. Flags and scarves boasting the ANC's green, gold, and black permeated the gathering, while speakers stood in front of a giant banner of the four-spoke wheel representing the ANC and its four allied organizations.[76] Between discussions of the charter's clauses, Women's League leader Ida Mntwana led the crowd in stirring renditions of freedom songs. The staging of nation was meticulous. Throughout the proceedings, provincial and national leaders of each organization sat together on the speaker's platform, presenting an image of "South Africa in miniature."[77] In a 1955 speech on the significance of the Congress of the People, Mandela quoted the following remarks sent by Luthuli to the gathering: "Why will this assembly be significant and unique? Its size, I hope, will make it unique. But above all its multi-racial nature and its noble objectives will make it unique, because it will be the first time in the history of our multi-racial nation that its people from all walks of life will meet as equals, irrespective of race, colour, and creed to formulate a freedom charter for all people in the country."[78]

The event incorporated the defining elements of the Defiance Campaign: the collective mobilization of diverse groups under the ANC's leadership and emblems, the conscious elaboration of an image of heterogeneous unity, and the nearly euphoric feeling of collective participation in the making of history. This sense of moment was heightened by the presence of the security police, who encircled the gathering and watched the proceedings until they disbanded the crowd on the afternoon of the second day. In his statement, Luthuli described the Congress of the People in terms of reversing the betrayal of democracy committed by the framers of the 1910 Act of Union. Claiming the authority to speak for *the* people (the singular of its title was in and of itself a powerful statement), the gathering sought to re-establish South Africa according to a radically different logic. In Luthuli's words, it was "a true partnership of all communities making up its multi-racial nature."[79] The Indian continued to embody the assembly's—and therefore the nation's—multiplicity. Contemporary observers waxed eloquent about "young Indian wives with glistening saris and shawls embroidered in Congress colours [and] smooth Indian lawyers and business men, moving confidently through the crowd in well-cut suits."[80] In Dadoo's absence, the gathering awarded him—along with Luthuli and Father Trevor Huddleston—the honorary title of Isitwalandwe (an award for heroism that translates as "the one who wears the plumes of the rare bird"). His elderly mother accepted on his behalf.

The Freedom Charter's relationship to the multiracial image of nation was complex and, ultimately, ambiguous. Alongside Luthuli and the Congress Alliance itself, the charter became a symbol of the ANC's inclusive nationalism and the ethos of the 1950s. Its first incantatory lines declared: "We, the People of South Africa, declare for all our country and the world to know: That South Africa belongs to all that live in it, black and white, and that no government can justly claim authority unless it is based on the will of the people."[81] In many people's eyes, the charter exemplified the multiracial nationalism that developed out of the political aesthetic of the Defiance Campaign. At the same time, the text of the charter did not articulate a definitive position on the national question—African, multiracial, nonracial, or otherwise. Drawing on the 1943 *African's Claims in South Africa* and the 1954 Women's Charter, the document presented a set of economic and political demands, including for universal education and the transfer of mineral wealth "to the ownership of the people." As both Luthuli's statement and editorials in *New Age* indicate, the campaign's leadership imagined the Freedom Charter as possessing constitutive force: the charter would provide South Africans with a common ethics and mode of life absent from the existing "caste society."[82] On the whole, the document addressed the question of race in the negative. While guaranteeing that groups would be protected from insult and given the equal opportunity to develop their cultures, it did not identify separate racial or national groups. The words "Indian" and "Coloured" appeared nowhere in the text and the authors used "African" only within the capacious phrase "South African."

Adopting the form of a manifesto, the charter's overwhelming emphasis was on the expression of a single national will: "we, the people of South Africa, black and white, *together*."[83] The unity of the national subject was thus enacted through the charter's voicing of a shared desire for freedom. This heavy reliance on rhetorical structure, however, left important questions unanswered. What would be the constitutional status of racial groups within a new state? Would a single ethnocultural identity develop out of South Africa's diverse society? What was the relationship between African nationalism and the charter's universalizing language of civic nationalism? While this calibrated ambiguity reflected the fact the ANC and its allies had not adopted an official position on the national question, it also served strategic ends by allowing different groups to read their aspirations into the document. In this respect, the charter drew on the mode of symbolic politics that had developed through the 26 June commemorations.

The ANC soon drew a direct connection between the Congress of the People and the idea of Afro-Asian unity celebrated by the April 1955 Bandung Conference. Composed of twenty-nine independent states, the majority of which had recently obtained independence from colonial rule, the Bandung Conference captured a moment when it fleetingly appeared that decolonization could radically transform global structures of power.[84] In his opening address, the Indonesian president Sukarno eulogized the religious, cultural, and political diversity of the gathering. He presented the conference's capacity to gather innumerable forms of differences as evidence of the gift that the Afro-Asian bloc offered to world affairs: the establishment of peace on a recognition of individual and national interdependence. Capturing the romance of the moment, Vijay Prashad suggests that the ability for Indonesia to create a nation from diverse people spread across hundreds of islands showed the potential for Bandung to provide a new model of political community.[85]

The conference excluded the South African government. However, Kotane and Indian Congress member Maulvi Cachalia traveled to Bandung in secret and attended as observers. *New Age* published an article announcing their arrival in Bandung as well as a report by Kotane that focused on Sukharno's opening speech.[86] At the end of the year, the Natal ANC executive invoked Bandung in defense of the African-Indian alliance: "Africa and Asia, as was seen in Bandung Conference in April, 1955, are coming together; how could we, in the home front, discourage and belittle this spirit of co-operation between Africa and Asia?"[87] In notes for his autobiography, Luthuli listed the conference as the second major event—following the case against South Africa at the UN—that connected "the outside world and *our* struggle."[88] This association of the ANC's policies and Bandung was not limited to one faction. In a 1957 editorial, *Liberation* (a journal associated with the Communist Party) proclaimed: "A new force in world politics has emerged, the Afro-Asiatic bloc of powers, holding the balance of world power between the lands of socialism and the lands of imperialism."[89] The 1958 ANC Handbook included Afro-Asian Day (April 24) in the Congress's official calendar.

The Africanist current interpreted the charter in terms of the organizational structure of the Congress Alliance. Arguing that the federated structure of the alliance gave "minority organizations" (and through them the Communist Party) power over ANC decisions, the Africanists concluded that the charter legitimated a parallel arrangement in a future state: group representation and minority veto power over African decisions. In the *Africanist*, Ufford Khoruha and Kwame Lekwame warned that the charter's invocation of "the people" was a dangerous abstraction. The assertion that "South Africa belongs to all who live in it" implicitly denied "the fundamental right of the African people to control their own country." Invoking the language of Marxian political economy, the authors postulated the identity of national oppression and economic exploitation. By recognizing racial groups, the charter not only denied the "common community of man," it accepted the colonial social relations that provided the foundations of racial identities.

In practice, this sociological analysis of race served as an a priori indictment. In Africanist polemics, racially defined blocs—African, Indian and European—functioned as the protagonists of South African history, their scripts determined by the confluence of material interest and historical origin. In order to protect their group identities and material privileges, according to this logic, the whites and Indians involved in drafting the charter *necessarily* sought to preserve the underlying economic foundations of settler colonialism. No member of the "ruling class" (i.e., whites and Indians) could consciously undermine the foundations of their own existence. Regarding Indians, they wrote: "The elements [at Kliptown] were the Indian Merchant Class who though politically repressed are in fact not oppressed. They are an exploiting alien group whose material interests are in direct conflict with those of the Indian masses." For the "alien" to become a "national," the authors concluded, they must abandon their racial privileges and undergo a moral transformation. This rebirth could not happen, as the Freedom Charter seemed to suggest, by proclamation. After the destruction of racial hierarchies, a government of the African majority would grant citizenship to loyal whites and Indians as individuals.[90]

The Natal ANC leadership also raised concerns regarding the document adopted at the Congress of the People. Meeting in January 1956, the provincial committee mandated that the Freedom Charter be discussed by the branches. While the carefully worded motion avoided taking a position on the charter's contents, it emphasized that a broader debate was necessary given the "important principles of economics involved" and the possibility of the charter's acceptance or rejection by "important" but "dissimilar" sections of the people such as workers, chiefs, and peasants.[91] Underlining the fact that the Natal executive saw the version approved at Kliptown as a draft, the motion reiterated a basic principle of the campaign: the final document should express the nation's unity in diversity. In later statements, including his 1960 memoir *Let My People Go*, Luthuli reiterated these concerns about the "by no means perfect" document. (The very fact that the ANC's president would register such objections publically indicates the weight that Luthuli gave to the matter.) Criticizing the inclusion of "variable details" in an "all-time document," Luthuli emphasized that the charter was a powerful embodiment of the desire for freedom. In other words, he sought to reaffirm the charter's status as a national symbol and dissociate this function from its specific political demands.

Luthuli's public statements regarding the charter were guarded and the surviving notes fragmentary. Read in the context of his philosophy of African nationalism, however, the depth of his concerns become apparent. As Luthuli made clear on several occasions, he did not disagree with what many in the ANC saw as the charter's most controversial clause, the call for the popular ownership of the mines and banks. He personally supported a democratic socialism comparable to the postwar policies of the British Labour government. However, Luthuli seems to have objected to the incorporation of this potentially divisive policy into a document that was meant to articulate the common values of national life. As an organization including all political currents, the ANC could not adopt one group's platform without undermining its basis of unity. Some of Luthuli's notes from this period suggest that he may have also worried that the charter's focus on economic demands implied a materialistic understanding of freedom. The eternal values that provided the foundations of inclusive nationalism transcended their realization in any one set of politics. The fact that the adoption of the charter was plagued by irregularities only compounded his alarm. By the first months of 1956, Luthuli concluded that party members within the alliance were attempting to circumvent the branch structures and transform the ANC into "a leftist organization under the domination of the Communist Party."[92] In Luthuli's reading, the Freedom Charter confused, perhaps deliberately, national ideals and the left's political goals. If this distinction was subtle, he nevertheless saw it as fundamental. Over the course of the next year, Luthuli staked his presidency on its defense.

THE TAMBO CONSTITUTION

In the early 1950s, the Natal ANC's star was ascendant. In addition to the ANC's national president, the Natal leadership included two of the country's best-known journalists—Ngubane and H. I. E. Dhlomo—and well-respected members from the ANC Youth League, the left, and the Old Guard. Flushed with the recent success of the Defiance Campaign, *Drum* celebrated the inauguration of a new era. Its headline declared "Congress Moves to Natal."[93]

State repression, personal tragedy, and renewed factional intrigue cut this promise short. In mid-1953, Luthuli received his first banning order.

Although he could still meet with the national executive committee, the order interrupted his efforts to visit branches outside of Natal and effectively cut him off from direct contact with the ANC's rank and file.[94] The following year the government reasserted these restrictions and confined Luthuli to the lower Tugela magisterial district for a period of two years.[95] In an unpublished memoir, Ngubane describes his concern during this period over Luthuli's mounting anger—at white South Africans, the government, and the passivity of many Africans, especially the educated middle class.[96] The combination of resentment and stress (Luthuli operated under constant police surveillance) seems to have taken its toll. Early in 1955, Luthuli's blood pressure increased to dangerous levels and he suffered a debilitating stroke. For the remainder of the year, Z. K. Mathews served as the ANC's acting president. During the period of Luthuli's first banning order, H. I. E. Dhlomo began to withdraw from an active role in Congress politics due to illness. In 1956, he died on the operating table in the middle of heart surgery.

When Luthuli resumed the duties of president in the later part of 1955, he confronted two major proposals by the Transvaal-based ANC leadership. The first was the introduction of a new constitution. Drafted by a committee headed by Oliver Tambo and known as the "Tambo Constitution," the initiative responded to the ANC's well-known organizational failings, including the near complete divorce between local branch activities and the national leadership. As Luthuli observed in 1955: "There does seem to be laxity in the machinery of the congress resulting in lack of sound disciplinary behavior at some congress levels."[97] According to a memo circulated with the draft, the proposal sought to restructure the ANC according to a particular vision of the liberation struggle: a single, centrally coordinated movement aimed at "the seizure of political power" in order to "govern this country in the name of the people in the shortest possible time."[98] The enemy of this vision was the province. While the memo conceded that provincial bodies were necessary at one stage, its author argued that they undermined the emergence of a collective political vision and encouraged a reactive style of leadership. The abolition of the provincial congresses would centralize decision-making in a Transvaal-based secretariat: "The Congress will function more nearly as one man than before."[99] Second, the outgoing meeting of the 1955 national executive passed a motion adopting the Freedom Charter (which the ANC had not yet formally discussed) as the basis for cooperation with other political groups.

Taken together, these proposals represented a fundamentally different vision of the liberation struggle than Luthuli's inclusive nationalism and the decentralized politics of the Congress of the People. By opposing national unity to the organizational and political diversity of Congress, the Tambo Constitution resurrected the vision of a disciplined revolutionary subject—the singular subject of nationalism that Luthuli had rejected following the 1949 Durban Riots. Luthuli clearly saw the larger philosophical implications of this shift. During the final discussion of the 1955 national executive, he successfully fought against the disbanding of provincial structures and won amendments to the draft constitution, including: "Clause 2: (e) Delete 'To support struggle for national independence'—To support the struggle for making South Africa a true democracy."[100] As he indicated in other contexts, Luthuli identified the language of independence, which implied the assertion of an African political subject against outside domination, with the threat of South Africa's partition.[101]

Luthuli initially supported the adoption of the Freedom Charter as the basis of cooperation with other organizations. However, subsequent events led him to reevaluate this suggestion in terms of the growing influence of the Communist Party—which he then conflated with the centralizing drive of the Tambo Constitution. After the elections at the 1955 annual conference, the national executive committee included an increased number of Transvaal-based party supporters and trade unionists. Although the new executive coopted three members from Natal, the elections produced concern among provincial leaders, including Luthuli. In early March 1956, Tambo wrote Luthuli with the suggestion that the draft constitution be presented for discussion at a special conference called for the end of the month to ratify the Freedom Charter.[102] Given the disorder caused by the banning of provincial leaders and the growing strength of the Africanist opposition, Tambo must have realized that the prospect of circulating the charter and draft constitution to the branches for ratification threatened chaos.

Whatever Tambo's motivations, Luthuli reacted with alarm. Viewing the March conference as a device for the subversion of the ANC's democratic processes, he responded to Tambo by requesting that the charter and draft constitution receive a full hearing within the ANC's branches. Behind the scenes, Luthuli prepared for war. In a letter to the Cape General secretary, T. E. kaTshunungwa, he declared: "people are taking advantage of the fact that I cannot move about to exert my influence."[103] Urging kaTshunungwa to secure the reelection for himself and his co-thinkers, Luthuli warned that the "left wing" would attempt to capture the provincial executives. It was necessary, he urged, for Natal, Cape, and the Orange Free State to prepare for a "show down" with the current leadership at the 1956 annual conference. In a shrewd calculation, he encouraged the Cape to boycott the March conference: the province's absence would undermine the meeting's authority to approve a new constitution.

Luthuli rejected centralization because he saw it as incompatible with the essential pluralism of democracy. "Power must be shared," he wrote to the ANC's national treasurer Arthur Letele, "or else you create dictators."[104] In response to the draft constitution, Luthuli suggested coopting provincial secretaries to the national executive in order to allow for the direct representation of the provinces.[105] His opposition to accepting the Freedom Charter as the basis of cooperation was, if anything, even stronger. In the letter to kaTshunungwa, Luthuli speculated that the Congress of Democrats was behind the idea. If the ANC adopted the charter as it stood, the document's radical economic policies would prevent cooperation between Congress and other white groups. He did not need to spell out the result: this outcome would permanently isolate the ANC from the majority of white South Africans. More fundamentally, the insistence on a political — rather than a broad national — basis of unity would transform the very nature of the organization. In separate letters to kaTshunungwa and Letele, Luthuli threatened to resign if these policies were adopted: "If the annual conference in December approves of these things I may have to consider seriously whether or not I can continue as President General."[106] Reports of Luthuli's views began to circulate within the ANC and black press. Invoking the president's authority, a Natal Youth League meeting attacked the Freedom Charter.[107] In May 1956, the Natal executive felt compelled to deny rumors that the province would secede if Luthuli was not reelected.[108]

THE NATAL COLD WAR

Even as Luthuli positioned himself against the Transvaal leadership, he recognized a cognate danger: an anticommunist backlash could threaten the Congress Alliance, especially the relationship between the ANC and Indian Congress in Natal. By the mid-1950s, the Natal ANC had polarized into two broadly defined factions. During much of this time, the day-to-day leadership of the province rested in the hands of a group of trade unionists and Communist Party supporters, including Moses Mahdiba, Stephen Dlamini, and Archie Gumede. Strongly committed to the alliance, this group centered its energies on union organizing among Africans and developed a strong base of working-class support by the late 1950s. They were aided in these activities by a younger generation of Indian Communist Party members, including Billy Nair and Ebrahim Ismail Ebrahim. In the aftermath of the 1949 Durban Riots, the membership of the NIC atrophied: its activists largely focused on supporting Congress Alliance campaigns, selling the left-wing *New Age*, and securing financial support for the ANC from sympathetic Indian businessmen.[109]

In opposition to the alliance, a second, more loosely knit "nationalist" faction developed that drew its support from ANC branches in the shack lands, especially Cato Manor. In many respects, this group sought to encourage forms of local activity that, Noor Nieftegodien argues, inspired the growing militancy of urban African politics: buyer's collectives, bus boycotts, rent strikes, and the fights for residency and land rights.[110] In Natal's shack lands, however, these modes of struggle challenged, directly or indirectly, Indian shopkeepers, bus drivers, and landowners. The nationalist faction believed, not without reason, that the pro-alliance ANC leadership sought to avert campaigns that threatened the economic interests of Indians. According to Ngubane's memoirs, the ANC leadership intervened to prevent bus boycotts against Indian-owned companies on two occasions in the late 1950s, once by convincing the operators not to raise fares in African areas.[111] Perhaps most damagingly, the Natal ANC refused to endorse the demand of African Cato Manor residents for urban land rights since it entailed the expropriation of property owned by Indians. Partially based on a defense of the alliance in principle, the calculations behind this position were likely complex: a bus boycott, for example, might devolve into violence, drive larger sections of the Indian community into the arms of the conservative forces, fracture the alliance in the Transvaal, provoke a new round of state repression, frighten white allies, and alienate badly needed international support. Nevertheless, the cost was high.

Until the end of the decade, ANC membership remained stagnant in Natal despite Luthuli's popularity.[112]

After the apartheid government announced its intention to require African women to carry passes in September 1955, a wave of protest swept the country as women mobilized in opposition. Cherryl Walker captures the scale this response: "The anti-pass campaign that followed was the most militant and sustained of any of the campaigns waged by the Congress Alliance of the 1950s."[113] Although Luthuli recognized this movement as a major turning point (it was the focus of his message to the March 1956 ANC meeting), these grassroots actions revealed the disconnect between the ANC leadership and the organization's increasingly militant following among poor and rural women. In Natal, the role of the Communist Party in supporting the alliance insured that the women's anti-pass campaign became entangled with Cold War anticommunism and popular anti-Indian sentiment. In 1956, two leaders of the Natal ANC, including the widely respected Bertha Mkhize, established a rival women's organization with the tacit support of some provincial ANC executive members.[114] Allying themselves with the remnants of the Bantu National Congress, they actively campaigned against cooperation with the Indian Congress.

In a series of organizers' reports from early 1956, Florence Mkhize (another ANC cadre) describes debating her former comrades in front of groups of women in neighborhoods such as Newlands, Clairmont, and Cato Manor. On one occasion, she almost came to blows with someone who claimed that Luthuli gave up his chieftainship because he was in the pay of Indians and that she was a Communist. Describing a meeting with domestic workers in Musgrave, Florence Mkhize wrote that the women would support the ANC's anti-pass campaign, but they would not become members: "They said they did not want to run the risk of being defiled as women in love with Indians as this propaganda had taken root in the mind of the people." On another occasion, she reported that Bertha Mkhize and G. Kuzwayo claimed "Congress Girls were in love with Indians during the Defiance Campaign." The trope of "being in love" suggests the surrender of self to another.[115] In the subaltern nationalism of Durban's shack lands, Communism, the Indian, and the sacrifice of female virtue—an emblem of urban independence—fused together.

Not only do these scenes convey the depth of anti-Indian sentiment that persisted within the ANC, they capture the weakness of the political aesthetic built around the Congress Alliance. Constructed through the personae of largely middle-class and self-consciously cosmopolitan men, this imagery could be read as replicating the structures of urban dispossession that informed popular anti-Indian discourse. The Congress Alliance's declarations of solidarity were performative: its leaders sought to create a unity in action that did not yet exist. In turn, many Africans perceived these declarations as a willful denial of Indian exploitation and the antipathy between the groups. If Luthuli sought to create symbols that would allow constituencies to write themselves into the nation, the already-racialized character of this narrative facilitated its rejection. In short, the policy of the mostly male ANC leadership appeared out of touch to many of its followers, especially men and women trying to build homes and maintain their independence in Durban's shack lands.[116] In their eyes, only deceit or corruption—only the willful surrender to the other's seduction—could explain this blindness to the lived experiences of so many Africans. In polemics from this period, the Africanist current alleged that the Freedom Charter's declaration "South Africa belongs to all who live in it" denied African indigeneity and erased the land's expropriation by the settler.[117] Mobilizing the language of feminine virtue, the claims that ANC women were "giving" themselves to the Indian expressed a similar sense of moral outrage and shock. In its celebration of plurality, inclusive nationalism could not register the suffering and deep anger that infused the subjectivity of many activists.[118]

THE BREAK WITH NGUBANE

The identification of the Indian with the Communist became a central theme in the writings of one of Luthuli's closest collaborators: Ngubane. In 1950, Ngubane stood down from the presidency of the Natal Youth League to focus on editorial work. Although he maintained close contact with Luthuli, Ngubane's role in the ANC diminished and he drew near to Manilal Gandhi and liberal circles. By the early 1950s, *Indian Opinion* had evolved into a platform for the publication of prominent liberals and Ngubane persisted in this direction when he assumed editorship after Gandhi's death in April 1956. Initially, this path would not have set Ngubane against Luthuli. The ANC president also developed close relationships with Natal liberals, including Paton, and Indian Congress members joined the Natal Liberal Party.

Over time, however, Ngubane embraced a Cold War worldview predicated on the struggle of democracy against dictatorship. This reading of politics inflected his evaluation of the Indian Congress. In his unpublished memoirs, Ngubane recalled: "Indian and Communist interests converged at the point of wanting to dominate the ANC in such a way that we found it difficult to draw the line between the two."[119]At first, Ngubane tried to convince the ANC and Indian Congress leadership that the appearance of Indian domination strengthened the hand of the government-supported Bantu National Congress. In a terse exchange with Dadoo that appeared in *Indian Opinion* between July and September 1953, Ngubane suggested that Dadoo and the Communist Party were inadvertently sabotaging the alliance: "Dadooism is the policy by which the Afro-Indian alliance is manipulated to create situations—some awkward, some embarrassing—where our Indian ally, in particular the Dadoo wing of the South African Indian Congress, wields an influence on events out of all proportion to the Indian's actual contribution to the struggle we wage jointly."[120]

His most serious allegation was that Dadoo's "followers" in the ANC—African party members—had publically questioned the ANC's commitment to nonviolence. In suggesting that nonviolence was merely tactical, Ngubane warned, they risked damage to the ANC's standing overseas, especially with India. Imprecating against "Dadooism," Ngubane was attempting to fight the Communist Party within the ANC without endangering Congress by publically fingering senior leaders (such as Sisulu and Mandela) as "card-carrying" members. At the same time, he sought to embarrass Dadoo in front of the Indian government (in the pages of *Indian Opinion*, no less) so that he would reign in nascent discussions about armed struggle. The line between this type of political intrigue and Cold War paranoia was thin—and Ngubane soon crossed it. His writings increasingly incorporated the classic elements of the "paranoid style": grandiosity, theories of persecution, and an apocalyptic vision that treated politics as a cosmic battle between clearly divided and mortally opposed protagonists.[121]

The break came in June 1956. After Luthuli's recovery, Ngubane repeatedly visited him and raised concerns regarding growing Communist Party influence. According to Ngubane's memoirs, Luthuli shared these worries but was prevented from confronting the party by his isolation, high-minded idealism, and the ANC's desperate need for international allies. Blinded by his belief in the principled unity of the ANC, Ngubane reasoned, Luthuli failed to understand the extent of the Communist effort to isolate him and seize control. "The naiveté astounded me," he later pronounced.[122] The naiveté was Ngubane's. In revealing his anxieties to Ngubane (although not his broader strategy), Luthuli may well have been planting information that he hoped would appear in the press. That had been Ngubane's specialty: he was the publicist that aired the views of the Natal leadership while preserving the public image of Congress's unanimity. This time, Ngubane failed to play along. Writing in *Indian Opinion*, he positioned himself as Luthuli's confidant (robbing the ANC president of plausible deniability) while presenting Luthuli as the unwitting figurehead of a leftwing faction that he was unable to control. In publically cornering Luthuli, Ngubane probably hoped to force him into an open confrontation with the Communist Party.

The strategy backfired. Published over the course of four issues in *Indian Opinion*, Luthuli's seething rejoinder to Ngubane was the product of extensive collaboration.[123] Luthuli treated Ngubane's allegations not only as a personal insult, but also as an aspersion against his loyalty to the ANC. Ngubane's redbaiting, Luthuli countered, was both unfounded and a threat to the ANC's existence given the 1950 Suppression of Communism Act. Dismissing the alleged divisions, Luthuli invoked the long record of Communist Party members serving in Congress leadership: at no point had their presence threatened to transform the organization into an instrument of Moscow. Luthuli's response emphasized the democratic character of the ANC's traditions and political structure. It was Ngubane's public attacks, which bypassed the organization's branches and democratically elected leadership bodies, that represented the real effort to undermine Congress democracy. Ngubane, he concluded, was conducting a wrecking operation on behalf of the Liberal Party. In response to the suggestion that the Communist Party had somehow undercut his presidency, Luthuli stridently denied that he belonged to a moderate faction closer to the liberals than the Marxist left. He was, he insisted, the president of a liberation movement that embodied the national aspirations of the African people as a whole.

There was no question that Luthuli's article directly contradicted views that he had expressed in private. The dismay that Ngubane expressed after reading the attack was probably genuine. As he confessed in his own series of responses, Ngubane could not bring himself to believe that his friend and close collaborator of the past decade had written the piece. More than anything else, Ngubane's surprise reflected the vast distance between the two men's basic political philosophies. Trapped in the worldview of a liberal Cold Warrior, Ngubane projected his own conspiratorial vision of politics onto the Communist Party and Indian Congress. As his notebooks reveal, Luthuli believed that Ngubane had become so blinded by his anti-communism that he viewed all Congress politics through this one question.[124] In contrast, Luthuli's primary concern was maintaining the unity of the ANC. In his eyes, the more immediate peril was that centralization and ideological rigidity would transform the ANC into the vehicle of a single current, negating its national character. In this respect, Ngubane's public attacks against Congress ironically mirrored the danger posed by adopting the Freedom Charter as the basis for cooperation. By encouraging a partisan struggle within the ANC, Ngubane rejected the "omnibus" character of Congress and therefore risked sacrificing the unity of the African people to the defense of an ideology. In other words, Ngubane's interventions threatened to reconfigure the problem space of African politics: they subordinated the struggle between African nationalism and white supremacy to a Cold War paradigm based on a liberal conception of democracy. Ngubane's nonracialism was agonistic in its basic structure. His ideal of nonracial democracy presupposed the division between liberalism and its enemies: the also-colonized other and the problem of difference were subsumed within a conception of politics defined as ideological warfare.

Refusing this dichotomous vision, Luthuli countered with a reassertion of the ethical dimension of nationalism: "The overriding interest of the African National Congress is in creating an atmosphere of trust in our multiracial nation."[125] This language was not in the least bit rhetorical. It was the slowly earned and often fragile confidence among individuals, and through them communities, that held the Congress Alliance together. The political aesthetic of the Defiance Campaign and the Congress of the People, more than any other element, had centered on a euphoric atmosphere of celebration that collectively affirmed this feeling of unity. Luthuli was arguing that this bond, based on the struggle for the ideals of justice and freedom, was the tenuous—and yet powerful—foundation of a common society.

The great "constructive" challenge of the liberation struggle, Luthuli realized, was the extension of these ties beyond the partisans of African nationalism and their few, precious allies. Given the opposition of the majority of white South Africans (and many Indians and Coloureds) to full African enfranchisement, a conception of democracy resting on majority rule alone would legitimate the domination of the majority over minority groups. Even if the antiapartheid struggle was able to force this result, it would not resolve the underlying problem of national unity. If a common South African identity was to emerge, something further was necessary. The ANC had to convince other groups that the African nation-building project ultimately represented their interests *and* that they could become active participants in the creation of a different South Africa. This was the fundamental problem that Ngubane's liberalism and his politics of suspicion could not resolve. As Luthuli explained:

> The African National Congress is not interested in making its African majority a tyranny to other groups. It appreciates that the essence of true democracy lies in the majority seeking through discussion rather than the mere counting of heads to accommodate to the utmost the legitimate wishes of the minority. The African National Congress has no desire to make the African majority the "tyranny of numbers." It is only interested in establishing a true bond of friendship amongst all sections of the South African population on the basis of true democracy.[126]

There was an echo of Gandhi's conception of satyagraha in Luthuli's assertion that democracy required the majority's accommodation of the minority. Like Gandhi, Luthuli believed that struggle must create and then affirm an ethical relationship between the oppressed and the oppressor. This relationship would not come into existence through an abstract assertion of right. Nor would it come solely through the oppressed groups' moral appeal. In Gandhian politics, the steadfastness and suffering of the satyagrahi ultimately (at least in theory) results in the moral enlightenment of the oppressor. For Luthuli, sacrifice served a different end: it affirmed that collective values alone could unite a nation of nations. This affirmation, joyous in the midst of sacrifice, functioned as an unconditional invitation.

CONCLUSION

At 4 a.m. on 5 December 1956, police awoke Luthuli at his Groutville home and presented him with the charge of high treason. Over the next few days, the state arrested 156 Congress leaders across the country. In his memoirs, Luthuli describes the scene that awaited him at the Johannesburg fort after he was flown to the Transvaal: "In the cells we met not just a few professionals and laborers, priests and laymen, Muslims, Christians, Hindus, infidels, Africans, Indians, Coloureds. And although, according to their fantasy about colour, the authorities did not allow us to glimpse them, we learned in no time that Europeans had been arrested too."[127] Although the state eventually released the accused on bail, the trial consumed the attention of the Congress leadership over an extended period.

Yet the overall effect of the trial was an unexpected boon. First, the combination of people charged, the spectacle of the trial, and the resulting international defense campaign reaffirmed the multiracial character of the resistance to apartheid under the ANC's leadership. Inadvertently, the state created a stage for the Congress Alliance to defend the image of nation that had inspired the Congress of the People. Second, the gathering of the Congress Alliance leadership (many of whom, as Luthuli observed, were not of the "travelling classes") created a genuinely unprecedented opportunity for discussion, debate, and consultation. Luthuli compared the experience to a sustained executive meeting.

While in prison, Luthuli, Monty Naicker, and Z. K. Mathews organized their membership into a regular routine of debates, lectures, worship services, and the singing of freedom songs (foreshadowing the structures later developed by prisoners on Robben Island). One of Mandela's memories of these events was Luthuli leading the assembled prisoners in dance and chanting after Yengwa performed Shaka's praise songs.[128] These experiences strengthened Luthuli's relationships with the Transvaal ANC leadership and allayed his suspicions regarding the Communist Party's motivations. In his notebooks, Luthuli listed the names of Communists Bram Fischer and Joe Slovo among his most trusted contacts.[129] He was also reassured regarding Tambo's leadership. In 1958, Luthuli gave his approval to the adoption of a revised version of the Tambo Constitution that maintained provincial structures and (although it would not be implemented until the ANC went into exile) opened membership to non-Africans. The following year, Luthuli strongly endorsed Tambo's leadership at the Natal provincial congress.[130] The breach had been fixed, temporarily.

On 29 March 1961, the court ruled that the government had failed to establish that the ANC had pursued a policy of overthrowing the state. By this point, events were developing rapidly. A year and eight days earlier, police shot and killed sixty-nine unarmed protestors during a protest against pass laws led by the Pan Africanist Congress. The Sharpeville massacre was followed by a nationwide state of emergency and the ban of liberation organizations. These events strengthened the position of Mandela's insurrectionist current within the ANC. After years of low-level discussions, the Congress Alliance executives came together to discuss the possibility of armed struggle at two meetings held outside of Stanger in June 1961. Over the course of two evenings of intense debate, advocates of sabotage—led by Mandela—argued for a change of policy against those who defended nonviolence and the modes of struggle developed since the Defiance Campaign. The philosophical differences within the Congress Alliance were given full expression. The line of division seems to have been generational more than organizational. Some older African members of the Communist Party opposed the new course; younger members of the Indian Congress were among its most steadfast advocates. Gandhi's ideas and precedent were invoked, debated, and invoked again. Toward dawn on the second night, the meeting broke fifty years of ANC tradition and voted to allow the creation of a new organization, Umkhonto we Sizwe, for the purpose of armed struggle.

Luthuli argued against this new course. Although he denied the charge that he was a pacifist during the gatherings ("If anyone thinks I am a pacifist, let him take my chickens, and he will know how wrong he is!"[131]), Luthuli nevertheless believed that nonviolence was an inviolable principle of the ANC. In a direct reprisal of the debates surrounding the Tambo Constitution and Freedom Charter, he argued that it would be undemocratic for the leadership to impose a new direction without consulting the membership. According to Mandela, Luthuli authored the compromise accepted by the second meeting: the ANC would maintain its policy of nonviolence while permitting the creation of an underground organization, separate but answerable to the ANC, that would prepare for the campaign of sabotage.[132]

In effect, Luthuli's proposal gave organizational expression to two major competing philosophies of African nationalism within the ANC. Given the conditions of illegality and Luthuli's refusal to condemn his comrades publically, it is impossible to reconstruct his position with complete certainty. Whatever other reasons informed his initial opposition, his stance should be understood in terms of his philosophy of African nationalism. First, Luthuli defended a practice of nation building founded on a pluralistic conception of political organization. Enabled by the collective pursuit of transcendental ideals, Luthuli's nationalism was embodied in the tradition of an all-inclusive ANC. The embrace of armed struggle, and the resulting transformation of the ANC into a clandestine organization, risked bringing this tradition to an end. Second, the turn to violence had direct implications for the symbolic politics of the Congress Alliance and the ANC's historic commitment to a common South African identity. Lutuli may have believed that violence would lead to the permanent hardening of racial divisions, rendering impossible the ethical vision of inclusive nationalism and the aspiration of a unified South Africa. Luthuli refused to condemn "the brave, just men" who launched Umkhonto we Sizwe.[133] But in his public statements, he never stopped defending the hope of nonviolent transformation.

Epilogue

How do we imagine and struggle for a democracy that . . . does not need enemies for its sustenance?[1]

—Angela Davis

We have to stand close enough to breathe one another's breath. It is the only thing that will save us from having to burn ourselves anew each time we rage.[2]

—Sisonke Msimang

On 9 June 1993, Mandela delivered a speech at the unveiling of a statue in Pietermaritzburg that commemorated the hundredth anniversary of Gandhi's failure to leave a first-class train compartment on the request of a white traveler.[3] His subsequent ejection from the train became narrated and memorialized (first and foremost by Gandhi himself) as a turning point in his life. According to Gandhi, this direct confrontation with racial prejudice provoked his first act of nonviolent resistance: the refusal to abandon his seat. When Mandela invoked these events one hundred years later, he did so in a context where the questions of nonviolence and compromise were being widely debated in the liberation struggle. In the early 1990s, the Pietermaritzburg region witnessed spiraling armed conflict between supporters of the ANC and the Inkatha Freedom Party, a Zulu-nationalist force based in the Kwa-Zulu Bantustan and covertly supported by the South African security forces. While the ANC negotiated the terms and date of the first election with the Nationalist Party, segments of the deep state fomented "black on black" conflict to undermine negotiations. Targeted by a coordinated campaign of terror and assassination, many grassroots supporters of the antiapartheid movement demanded a resumption of the armed struggle — unilaterally suspended by the ANC in 1991 — and weapons for self-defense units. More broadly, the government's stonewalling and double dealing challenged many people's already tenuous faith in a negotiated settlement.[4]

In this context, Mandela decided to speak on the importance of Gandhi to the ANC's tradition. After outlining Gandhi's early struggles against Indian disenfranchisement, Mandela described his attempt to build Hindu-Muslim unity through the Indian Congress and a "non-exploitative way of life" on Tolstoy Farm. "The Mahatma is an integral part of our history," Mandela enumerated, "because it is here that he first experimented with truth; here that he demonstrated his characteristic firmness in pursuit of justice; here that he developed Satyagraha as a philosophy and method of struggle." Allegorizing liberation history as an illustration of these principles, Mandela asserted the centrality of Gandhi's ideas to the ANC: "The Congress Movement was strongly influenced by this Gandhian philosophy," he stressed. "It was a philosophy that achieved the mobilization of millions of South Africans during the 1952 Defiance Campaign which established the ANC as a mass-based organization." The ANC only abandoned this strategy, he emphasized, painfully and reluctantly. The obstinacy of the oppressor forced the liberation struggle to take up arms to prevent "the destruction of our people through genocide."

Mandela presented the struggle as composed of multiple strands united by the common goal of a peaceful, unified South Africa: the guerilla actions of the ANC's armed wing, protests in the townships and countryside, the international campaign of sanctions, and the willingness of ordinary people to oppose an unjust system. In this narrative, Gandhi served as a model for a strategy that transpired on multiple fronts, including through negotiation "in good faith and without bitterness."[5] While this speech warned the Nationalist Party of the ANC's willingness to resume insurrectionary activity unless an election date was set, it also served as a reminder to militant factions that negotiation and compromise was a long-recognized mode of political struggle within the Congress tradition.

In arguing for the importance of India and the Indian diaspora to the antiapartheid struggle, *Internal Frontiers* locates the problem of the also-colonized other at the heart of the ANC's adoption of an inclusive African nationalism. In the midst of the Second World War, intellectuals within the ANC such as Lembede and Xuma began to conceptualize a vision of the national subject beyond empire and settler civil society. In different fashions, Indian independence provided a model for these efforts to reimagine peoplehood and sovereignty. India signified both a new global legal order founded on the nation-state and a heterogeneous, non-Western people united by the power of the national ideal. Because India emerged as a key ally in internationalizing the struggle against South Africa's racist policies, the ANC's relationship with the Indian Congress (and its understanding of the place of the diaspora within a future South Africa) became a question of strategic importance. In the mid-1940s, the debate among members of the ANC, Youth League, Communist Party, Indian Congress, and Unity Movement over "cooperation" versus "non-European unity" raised fundamental questions regarding the external and internal frontiers of an African nationalist project. At the same time, the launch of the momentous 1946 Passive Resistance Campaign not only challenged the common prejudice that Indians were incapable of defying the state, it also provided a living model of militant struggle to a younger generation of African nationalists.

The debate over unity was interrupted by two events. First, the partition of India and Pakistan severely damaged the credibility of Nehru's Indian National Congress among many Africans thinkers at a time when disillusionment was growing with regard to robust UN action against the South African government. In the pages of the African press, the violence of Partition resonated within a larger global moment—including events such as the Greek Civil War, the founding of Israel, and (most immediately) the election of the Nationalist Party in 1948—and foreshadowed the dangers of national self-determination in a profoundly divided country. If India provided African intellectuals with a model for conceiving nation beyond empire, Partition represented a crisis for this paradigm and forced a grappling with the limitations of majoritarian nationalism.

Second, the outbreak of the 1949 Durban Riots profoundly shocked the national ANC leadership, revealed the dangers of Natal's racial polarization, and sounded the death knell for an older style of conservative politics in Natal. Among a group of intellectuals in the Youth

League and Natal ANC, the Riots resulted in an urgent self-reflection on the racial underpinnings of their conception of nationalism and inaugurated a reconsideration of the nature of the African political subject. For a younger generation of activists leading the Indian Congress, the Riots made it clear that securing a future for Indians in South Africa required their support for the African liberation struggle—a decision that made an implicit claim to inclusion within an expanded idea of nation.

In the aftermath of the Riots, the Natal Youth League engineered the candidacy of Luthuli for president of the province. A gradualist known for his years of work as a teacher and then chief in rural Natal, Luthuli was already grappling with the philosophical implications of the Riots when he assumed the Natal leadership of the 1952 Defiance Campaign. The Riots provoked the question of how to unite South Africa while respecting difference; the African-Indian alliance provided an answer. Service and sacrifice for a common ideal could bind together an otherwise heterogeneous people. As Luthuli understood, this idealist conception of nationhood represented a break from the liberal assumption that democracy presupposed social homogeneity grounded in settler civil society. Drawing on Christianity, African ideas of inclusive kinship, and Lembede's philosophical idealism, Luthuli and his Natal co-thinkers developed a philosophy of inclusive nationalism that stressed its capacity to incorporate, but not assimilate, the also-colonized other while retaining its core African identity. For Luthuli, inclusive nationalism was less a solution to the "national question" (it was not a circumscribed idea of community that would find expression in an independent state—than a way of living nation in the middle of the divisions, frictions, and misrecognitions of a necessarily ongoing struggle.

This philosophy envisioned the African liberation struggle as a "constructive" force that simultaneously enabled the self-development of other communities and created the overarching framework for a shared national identity. Through the Defiance Campaign, Luthuli came to believe that this identity could be expressed, and therefore shaped, through symbols and political rituals. The Defiance Campaign, the Congress Alliance, and their representation within the black press (especially *Drum*) created a new image of a multiracial, African nation that reconciled the competing claims of unity and diversity in a new political aesthetic.

These ideas were widely influential. The Natal Group's understanding of inclusive nationalism and symbolic constitutionalism informed the political mobilizations of the ANC through the celebration of Freedom Day and the mobilization for the 1955 Congress of the People. Despite the significant ideological differences between the Natal Group and other factions (the Communist Party, the Africanists, and the Transvaal ANC leadership), Luthuli's conception of a "constructive" African nationalism found echoes in the party's idea of the National Democratic Revolution and Sobukwe's nonracial Africanism. Although they understood the dynamics of revolutionary struggle differently, these positions held that a common identity could emerge out of the African people's struggle for freedom and the collective embrace of democratic ideals. Within the ANC, the experience of multiracial organizing and the aesthetic of the Congress Alliance contributed to the formation of a political culture that transcended, at least to a degree, competing positions on the national question.

In important respects, 1960 cut off these discussions and resulted in the eclipse of Luthuli's ideas. The Sharpeville Massacre and the banning of the liberation organizations significantly restricted the space for debate and political mobilization, including the forms of mass, nonviolent civil resistance that embodied Luthuli's vision. Despite Luthuli's efforts to preserve this strategic orientation after the turn to violence, the campaign of sabotage resulted in the transformation of the ANC into an underground organization while provoking new waves of repression that further constricted political space. When the ANC and its allied organizations regrouped abroad, the ideological influence of the Communist Party grew significantly as the ANC's security culture, developed in response to police infiltration and the strains of exile, curtailed discussion and internal dissent.[6]

While some older cadre continued to adhere to the principles of Gandhi and Luthuli, the ANC's leadership concluded that the Sharpeville Massacre and the launch of Umkhonto we Sizwe had eliminated, at least for the foreseeable future, the possibility of a peaceful transition to democracy. Within South Africa, the forced removals mandated by the Group Areas Act transformed South Africa's cities and destroyed the iconic neighborhoods of the cosmopolitan moment: Fietas, District Six, and Sophiatown. Although urban spaces of African-Indian interaction did not vanish, they were reduced in number and significantly transformed. After the 1960s, South African cities far more closely resembled the (ultimately futile) apartheid program of the strict correlation of race with space.[7]

Nevertheless, the Natal synthesis did not disappear. As Mandela's remarks in Pietermaritzburg show, Gandhi, the Defiance Campaign, and an ethical ideal of nation remained significant reference points for the ANC, especially for a section of its senior leadership. These earlier moments of struggle persisted as part of a common tradition and strategic repertoire that the ANC could invoke in the form of political allegory. Raymond Suttner observes that the ANC developed a system of education that utilized individual figures (such as Luthuli) and periods of the struggle (such as the 1950s) to embody the principles of its complex and variegated heritage.[8] Even if earlier "stages" had been surpassed, they remained central to the official narrative of the ANC's history and represented ideals that the organization continued to promote—at least in theory. Indeed, this conscious deployment of symbols and iconic figures to embody political values itself represented, to a considerable degree, the contribution of the Youth League and the Natal Group's philosophical idealism to the ANC's political culture. Within South Africa, Luthuli's ideas survived among an older generation of cadres. They were also preserved in a few centers of education and debate such as the Phoenix Settlement. When the pro-ANC United Democratic Front launched in 1983, it included a broad cross spectrum of political positions—ranging from liberal Christians to revolutionary Marxists—and it mobilized these diffuse currents around symbols drawn from the 1950s, most significantly the Freedom Charter. After sections of the ANC leadership returned from exile or Robben Island in the early 1990s, they drew on the ideas and imagery of the cosmopolitan moment, which was also (in many cases) the formative period of their own political development, to move beyond the armed struggle and articulate a politics of nation building.

Today, these ideals are dead within South Africa's ruling party. Since assuming power in 1994, the ANC has evolved from a mass, revolutionary movement into an increasingly brutal mechanism for absorbing and redistributing state resources.[9] Whatever its accomplishments in dismantling apartheid and promoting socioeconomic transformation, the ANC's flagrant corruption, open attacks against democracy, and its defense of neoliberal capital have vitiated its former claims to represent a national movement. Among a younger generation of South African activists, the very words "negotiation" and "compromise" have become synonymous with its betrayals.[10] If Luthuli once imagined African nationalism as an ethical community that would exceed its realization within the state, the ANC promoted a statist project of transformation that gradually substituted the party and then the state for the nation itself.[11] The result has been the resurgence of majoritarian and increasingly racialized conceptions of the nation, which, moreover, have infused South African political culture with an aggressive and misogynist form of masculinity.[12] Divorced from struggle and its connection with the multitude, symbolic constitutionalism has hardened into the presidential nationalism of "big man" politics. Although this racial and sexual authoritarianism draws on elements from the ANC's long and contested history (early Africanism, Stalinist vanguardism, patriarchal neotraditionalism), the outcome of the South African struggle reflects a larger, late-twentieth-century phenomenon: the absorption of social movements by the neoliberal state. This process now coexists with a global crisis of the liberal order and an international resurgence of ethno-nationalist, right-wing populism in the name of reclaiming "the nation."

In exploring this period in the ANC's history, *Internal Frontiers* is not promoting a return to an earlier moment in the Congress tradition. Nor does it try to resurrect the dead to authorize a contemporary politics: a form of rhetorical necrophilia. If anything, the mode of historical reconstruction employed by this book underlines the impossibility of a simplistic restoration. The Natal Group's understanding of African nationalism developed in response to a specific intellectual problem space: the imperative of thinking nation beyond empire and settler civil society while incorporating, but not assimilating, the also-colonized other. The philosophical idealism of the Natal synthesis, and its elaboration of a political aesthetic that affirmed unity-in-difference, facilitated its appropriation, reworking, and extension in multiple contexts. Nevertheless, it was still an idea of nation that privileged one cluster of questions at the expense of others. Even in the context of the 1950s, this problem space was necessarily limited.

Some of its failings, particularly around gender and class, were present from its formulation. Beyond the endorsement of formal equality and the recognition of women's importance to the liberation struggle, the Natal Group did not grapple with the centrality of gender and its effects for the thinking of political community. They certainly did not assimilate the assertion of the Women's Charter that the destruction of patriarchal relationships in black communities and political movements was a necessary precondition of true liberation.[13] Moreover, this generation of male intellectuals was largely unaware of the different ways that apartheid's white supremacy was also a project of neotraditional patriarchal rule and sexual governance.[14] In theory, the Natal synthesis's heterogeneous and ethical conception of the African political subject—a partial anticipation of feminist ideas of relationality—could have created the space for thinking about the interplay between different logics of difference and their ethical-political demands. This missed opportunity has facilitated its appropriation by more conservative forms of presidential nationalism.

If Lembede and Luthuli's idealism reflected their revolt against capitalism's materialist epistemology, their thinking only partially and empirically addressed race's articulation with both class and the structural violence of settler civil society. They believed in the need for some type of socialism, but they never explored the relationship between an idealist conception of nation and the critique of capitalist political economy. This separation reflected a larger weakness within the ANC's intellectual tradition. Despite some notable exceptions, the ANC's theoretical production largely focused on the problem of nation rather than the questions of democracy, capitalism, and the nature of the South African state.[15] While the emphasis on the national question and political symbolism facilitated a broad unity during the antiapartheid struggle, this tradition has been an inadequate resource for confronting the problems of transformation after 1994.[16]

The eventual crisis of the Natal synthesis and Luthuli's leadership came from yet another direction. The Natal synthesis generalized from the African-Indian alliance to the structure of an inclusive South African nationalism. In this respect, Luthuli's thinking was infused with the generosity and optimism of mid-century African liberation struggles. Like many of his contemporaries, he believed that the also-colonized other and the settler—when confronted with the prospects of international isolation and imminent civil war—would abandon power and/or privilege to embrace living in a common African society. Indeed, Luthuli envisioned struggle as an ongoing invitation to participate in shared nationhood.

The ANC fought against its opponents—not just the apartheid regime, but ultimately all South Africans who opposed universal citizenship rights—to uphold the vision of living side-by-side and among its opponents in a democratic society. In essence, this position refused the friend/enemy distinction that underwrites the conceptualization of politics, especially nationalist and revolutionary politics, as warfare.[17] Whatever strategy the ANC adopted, it had to preserve the possibility of reconciling with and then embracing its former adversaries within a common, national community. This insistence was a way of refusing to mirror the world view of the oppressor in the values of the liberation struggle. Unless one envisions the expulsion or destruction of one's enemies, struggle creates (a necessarily asymmetrical) relationship: it redefines both parties in terms of how they recognize and reciprocate the other's humanity. What happens if the other refuses this invitation? After a decade of nonviolent struggle in the 1950s, white South Africa—with precious exceptions—continued to support the Nationalist Party or the opposition United Party, a stance that hardened after the 1960 Sharpeville Massacre and the resulting state of emergency. Even after the 1994 elections, white economic power and social separation largely endures: one example of the global persistence of institutionalized white supremacy. What could the Natal synthesis, joyous in its unembarrassed optimism, offer in the face of militarized and recalcitrant whiteness beyond the power of sacrifice and faith?

Despite its shortcomings, Luthuli's inclusive African nationalism represented a significant moment in one of the twentieth century's greatest (and most imperiled) achievements: the replacement of the fantasy of nation as homogenous community with an understanding of nation as the name of an open question. What project of community can draw its strength from multiple forms of difference?. Although they recognized partial exceptions, most nineteenth- and early twentieth-century thinkers held that a heterogeneous nation was an impossibility. Even those theorists who understood nation in idealist terms stressed the fundamental unity of the collective will: behind the "everyday referendum" of nation was a singular subject forged through the forgetting of historical violence and difference.[18] In accounts of Western political thought, the movement away from ethno-nationalism is frequently identified with the development of liberal multiculturalism. However, multiculturalism (which presupposes private property and the institutions of settler civil society) was only one local and generally conservative strand of a global effort to reimagine nation after the Second World War.

Through its reading of Indian independence and the trauma of the Durban Riots, the Natal Group extrapolated from the question of the also-colonized other to a new ideal of peoplehood while developing a critique of the implicit racialism that continued to inform anticolonial nationalism. Although Luthuli's philosophy receded after 1960, the political aesthetic of a multiracial, African subject remained integral to inform the culture of the ANC. In turn, the ANC's vision was internationalized in multiple waves: Luthuli's Nobel prize in 1960, the global solidarity movement of the 1980s, and the tremendous attention produced by Mandela's release and the first democratic elections in April 1994. In ways that still reverberate today, the antiapartheid struggle refracted and transformed the philosophical event of Indian independence. However profound its limitations and bitter its many reversals, this "South African moment" must continue.

Notes

INTRODUCTION

1. Jordan Ngubane, "Bambulaleleni Ugandhi?," *Inkundla ya Bantu*, 19 February 1948. The author is a major figure in the story that follows.

2. George M. Fredrickson, *Black Liberation: A Comparative History of Black Ideologies in the United States and South Africa* (New York: Oxford University Press, 1995), 230.

3. D. D. T. Jabavu, *E-Indiya Nase East Africa: Uhambo lomNgqika eMpumalanga* (Lovedale, Ind.: Lovedale Mission Press, 1951).

4. Isabel Hofmeyr and Uma Dhupelia-Mesthrie, "South Africa/India: Re-imagining the Disciplines," *South African Historical Journal* 57 (2007): 1–11; Isabel Hofmeyr, "The Black Atlantic Meets the Indian Ocean: Forging New Paradigms of Transnationalism for the Global South–Literary and Cultural Perspectives," *Social Dynamics* 33 (2007): 3–32; and Uma Dhupelia-Mesthrie, "The Place of India in South African History: Academic Scholarship, Past, Present and Future," *South African Historical Journal* 57 (2007): 12–34.

5. Oliver Tambo, "Mandela and Nehru," in *Preparing for Power: Oliver Tambo Speaks*, ed. Adelaide Tambo (London: Heinemann, 1987), 193–99.

6. E. S. Reddy, "How the 'Long Walk to Freedom' Began," *South African History Online*, 2013. http://www.sahistory.org.za/archive/how-"long-walk-freedom"%C2%9D-began-es-reddy.

7. Franco Barchiesi, "Imagining the Patriotic Worker: The Idea of 'Decent Work' in the ANC's Political Discourse," in *One Hundred Years of the ANC: Debating Liberation Histories Today*, ed. Arianna Lissoni et al. (Johannesburg: Wits University Press, 2012), 111–34; and Barchiesi, "The Problem with 'We': Affiliation, Political Economy, and the Counterhistory of Non-racialism," in *Ties that Bind: Race and the Politics of Friendship in South Africa*, ed. Shannon Walsh and Jon Soske (Johannesburg: Wits University Press, 2016), 125–66.

8. Pixley Ka Isaka Seme, "The Regeneration of Africa," *Journal of the Royal African Society* 17 (1906): 404–8.

9. Heather Hughes, *The First President: A Life of John Dube, Founding President of the ANC* (Cape Town: Jacana Media, 2011).

10. Peter Limb, *The ANC's Early Years: Nation, Class and Place in South Africa before 1940* (Pretoria: Unisa Press, 2010).

11. Robert Trent Vinson, *The Americans Are Coming!: Dreams of African American Liberation in Segregationist South Africa* (Athens: Ohio University Press, 2012), 6.

12. The formulation of liberal political theory most important to the ANC during the 1940s and '50s was R. F. A. Hoernlé's *South African Native Policy and the Liberal Spirit* (Johannesburg: Witwatersrand University Press, 1945). For Hoernlé's impact on the ANC (which was mediated through the publications of the South African Institute of Race Relations), see Jon Soske, "The Impossible Concept: Settler Liberalism, Pan-Africanism, and the Language of Non-racialism," *African Historical Review* 47, no. 2 (2015): 1–36.

13. For the concept of "problem space," see David Scott, *Conscripts of Modernity: The Tragedy of Colonial Enlightenment* (Durham: Duke University Press, 2004), 4.

14. The original phrase is "homogenous, empty time," taken from Walter Benjamin. Benedict Anderson, *Imagined Communities: Reflections on the Origin and Spread of Nationalism*, rev. ed. (London: Verso Books, 2006), 24.

15. The term "liberated sovereignty" comes from Ariella Azoulay's discussion of Hannah Arendt. Azoulay, *The Civil Contract of Photography*, trans. Rela Mazali and Ruvik Danieli (New York: Zone Books, 2008), 48.

16. See John Kelly and Martha Kaplan, "Nation and Decolonization toward a New Anthropology of Nationalism," *Anthropological Theory* 1, no. 4 (2001): 419–37.

17. Aamir Mufti, *Enlightenment in the Colony: The Jewish Question and the Crisis of Postcolonial Culture* (Princeton: Princeton University Press, 2007).

18. Ibid., 13.

19. Eric Hobsbawm, *Nations and Nationalism since 1780: Programme, Myth, Reality* (Cambridge: Cambridge University Press, 2012).

20. Benjamin Harshav, *The Polyphony of Jewish Culture* (Palo Alto: Stanford University Press, 2007), 27.

21. Paul Gilroy, *'There Ain't No Black in the Union Jack': The Cultural Politics of Race and Nation* (Chicago: University of Chicago Press, 1987), 156.

22. Dipesh Chakrabarty, *Provincializing Europe: Postcolonial Thought and Historical Difference* (Princeton: Princeton University Press, 2009). This argument is stated in a more programmatic form in Chakrabarty, "Provincializing Europe: Postcoloniality and the Critique of History," *Cultural Studies* 6, no. 3 (1992): 337–57.

23. Ashis Nandy, *The Intimate Enemy: The Psychology of Colonialism* (Oxford: Oxford University Press, 1989).

24. Mahmood Mamdani, "Beyond Settler and Native as Political Identities: Overcoming the Political Legacy of Colonialism," *Comparative Studies in Society and History* 43, no. 4 (2001): 651–64.

25. For discussions of idealism in anticolonial thought, see: Souleymane Bachir Diagne, *African Art as Philosophy: Senghor, Bergson, and the Idea of Negritude,* trans. Chike Jeffers (London: Seagull Books, 2011); Pankaj Mishra, *From the Ruins of Empire: The Intellectuals Who Remade Asia* (New York: Farrar, Straus, Giroux, 2012); Faisal Devji, *Muslim Zion: Pakistan as a Political Idea* (London: Hurst Publishers, 2013); and Gary Wilder, *Freedom Time: Negritude, Decolonization, and the Future of the World* (Durham: Duke University Press, 2014).

26. Michael Adas, "Contested Hegemony: The Great War and the Afro-Asian Assault on the Civilizing Mission Ideology," *Journal of World History* 15, no. 1 (2004): 31–63.

27. Ibid., 61.

28. Mishra, *From the Ruins of Empire,* 302.

29. Achille Mbembe, *Sortir de la grande nuit: essai sur l'Afrique décolonisés* (Paris: La Découverte, 2010), 10.

30. Vijay Prashad, *The Darker Nations: A Biography of the Short-Lived Third World* (New Delhi: LeftWord Books, 2007).

31. Fred Ho and Bill V. Mullen, eds., *Afro-Asia: Revolutionary Political and Cultural Connections between African Americans and Asian Americans* (Durham: Duke University Press, 2008); Christopher Lee, ed., *Making a World after Empire: The Bandung Moment and its Political Afterlives* (Athens: Ohio University Press, 2010); and Nico Slate, *Colored Cosmopolitanism: The Shared Struggle for Freedom in the United States and India* (Cambridge, MA: Harvard University Press, 2012).

32. Amitov Ghosh, "Confessions of a Xenophile," *Chimurenga* 14 (2009): 35–41.

33. For nostalgic futurism as an aesthetic strategy, see Sukhdev Sandhu's essay on the Otolith Group. Sandhu, "O Navigators," in *South-South: Interruptions and Encounters,* ed. Tejpal S. Ajji and Jon Soske (Toronto: Justina M. Barnike Gallery, 2009), 54.

34. See Isabel Hofmeyr, "Africa as a Fault Line in the Indian Ocean," in *Eyes Across the Water: Navigating the Indian Ocean,* ed. Pamila Gupta, Isabel Hofmeyr, and Michael Pearson (Pretoria: UNISA Press, 2010), 99–106.

35. James R. Brennan, *Taifa: The Making of Race and Nation in Urban Tanzania* (Athens: Ohio University Press, 2012).

36. Sana Aiyer, *Indians in Kenya: The Politics of Diaspora* (Cambridge, MA: Harvard University Press: 2015), 12–17.

37. Antoinette Burton, *Africa in the Indian Imagination: Race and the Politics of Postcolonial Citation* (Durham: Duke University Press, 2016).

38. For an unsparing critique of solidarity, see Frank Wilderson III, *Red, White, and Black: Cinema and the Structure of U.S. Antagonism* (Durham: Duke University Press, 2010).

39. For a critique of liberal multiracialism and its underlying racism, see Jared Sexton, *Amalgamation Schemes: Antiblackness and the Critique of Multiracialism* (Minneapolis: University of Minnesota Press, 2008).

40. For a broader reflection on the politics of entanglement, see Sarah Nuttall, *Entanglement: Literary and Cultural Reflections on Post-apartheid* (Johannesburg: Witwatersrand University Press, 2009).

41. Thank you to Paul Landau for help with this formulation.

42. Gillian Rose, *Mourning Become the Law* (Cambridge: Cambridge University Press, 1996), 100.

43. This form of vulnerability is explored in Jacqueline Rose, *The Last Resistance* (London: Verso, 2013), especially 43–45.

44. For a reflection on the diffuse and relational character of sovereignty in West African nationalist thinking, see Frederick Cooper, *Citizenship between Empire and Nation: Rethinking France and French Africa 1945–1960* (Princeton: Princeton University Press, 2014).

45. Pádraig Ó Tuama interviewed by Krista Tippett, *On Being*, 2 March 2017, https://onbeing.org/programs/padraig-o-tuama-belonging-creates-and-undoes-us-both/.

46. Patrick Wolfe, "Settler Colonialism and the Elimination of the Native," *Journal of Genocide Research* 8, no. 4 (2006): 387–409.

47. For an overview, see Andrew Duminy and Bill Guest, eds., *Natal and Zululand from Earliest Times to 1910: A New History* (Pietermaritzburg, Zaf.: University of Natal Press, 1989); for a more recent analysis of Natal through the framework of settler colonialism, see T. J. Tallie, "Limits of Settlement: Racialized Masculinity, Sovereignty, and the Imperial Project in Colonial Natal, 1850–1897" (PhD diss., University of Illinois at Urbana-Champaign, 2014).

48. Shula Marks, "Patriotism, Patriarchy, and Purity: Natal and the Politics of Zulu Ethnic Consciousness," in *The Creation of Tribalism in Southern Africa*, ed. Leroi Vail (Berkeley: University of California Press, 1989), 215–40; Jeff Guy, *The Maphumulo Uprising: War, Law and Ritual in the Zulu Rebellion* (Scottsville: University of KwaZulu-Natal Press, 2005); and Michael Mahoney, *The Other Zulus: The Spread of Zulu Ethnicity in Colonial South Africa* (Durham: Duke University Press, 2012).

49. See Benedict Carton, John Laband, and Jabulani Sithole, eds., *Zulu Identities: Being Zulu, Past and Present* (New York: Columbia University Press, 2008).

50. Bhana and Brain note that some planters reportedly brought a small number of Indian workers earlier at their own expense. Surendra Bhana and Joy Brain, *Setting Down Roots: Indian Migrants and South Africa, 1860–1922* (Johannesburg: Witwatersrand University Press, 1990), 15.

51. Ashwin Desai and Goolam Vahed, *Inside Indian Indenture: A South African Story, 1860–1914* (Cape Town: HSRC Press 2010).

52. For a discussion of language in indentures, see Rajend Mesthrie, *Langue in Indenture: A Sociolinguistic History of Bhojpuri-Hindi in South Africa* (London: Routledge, 1991).

53. Desai and Vahed, *Inside Indian Indenture*, 423–38.

54. Surendra Bhana and Goolam Vahed, *The Making of a Political Reformer: Gandhi in South Africa, 1893–1914* (New Delhi: Manohar, 2005), 14–15.

55. Uma Dhupelia-Mesthrie, "The Passenger Indian as Worker: Indian Immigrants in Cape Town in the Early Twentieth Century," *African Studies* 68, no. 1 (2009): 111–34.

56. Ibid.

57. Brij Maharaj, "The Group Areas Act in Durban: Central Local State Relations" (PhD diss., University of Natal, 1992), 3.

58. Important contributions include: Maureen Swan, *Gandhi: The South African Experience* (Johannesburg: Ravan Press, 1985); Jonathan Hyslop, "Gandhi 1869–1915: The Transnational Emergence of a Public Figure," in *The Cambridge Companion to Gandhi*, ed. Judith M. Brown and Anthony Parel (Cambridge: Cambridge University Press, 2011), 30–51; Joseph Lelyveld, *Great Soul: Mahatma Gandhi and His Struggle with India* (New York: Vintage, 2011); and Isabel Hofmeyr, "Seeking Empire, Finding Nation: Gandhi and Indianness in South Africa," in *Routledge Handbook of the South Asian Diaspora*, ed. Joya Chatterji and David Washbrook (Routledge: London, 2014), 153–65.

59. Isabel Hofmeyr, *Gandhi's Printing Press: Experiments in Slow Reading* (Cambridge, MA: Harvard University Press, 2013).

60. Desai and Vahed, *Inside Indian Indenture*, 371–95.

61. For an overview, see Uma Dhupelia-Mesthrie, "Satyagraha in South Africa: Principles, Practice and Possibilities," *Historia* 54, no. 1 (2009): 13–33.

62. Gary Younge, *The Speech: The Story behind Dr. Martin Luther King Jr.'s Dream* (Chicago: Haymarket Books, 2013), 114.

63. See Raghavan Iyer, *The Moral and Political and Political Thought of Mahatma Gandhi* (New Delhi: Oxford University Press, 2000), 269–92.

64. M. K. Gandhi, *An Autobiography, or the Story of My Experiments with Truth* (Boston: Beacon Press, 1993), 315.

65. Ashwin Desai and Goolem Vahed, *The South African Gandhi: Stretcher-Bearer of Empire* (Palo Alto: Stanford University Press, 2015).

66. Quoted in Lelyveld, *Great Soul*, 54.

67. Hofmeyr, "Seeking Empire," 157.

68. Lelyveld, *Great Soul*, 61–65.

69. Barchiesi, "The Problem with 'We,'" 147.

70. Essop Pahad, "The Development of Indian Political Movements in South Africa 1924–1946" (PhD diss., University of Sussex, 1972); Parvathi Raman, "Yusuf Dadoo: Transnational Politics, South African

Belonging," *South African Historical Journal* 50, no. 1 (2004): 27–48; and Ashwin Desai and Goolam Vahed, *Monty Naicker: Between Reason and Treason* (Pietermaritzburg, Zaf.: Shuter, 2010).

71. Bill Freund, *Insiders and Outsiders: The Indian Working Class of Durban, 1910–1990* (Portsmouth: Heinemann, 1995), 57–58, 61–62.

72. In addition to the literature cited in note 23 above, see: Edward Said, *Culture and Imperialism* (New York: Vintage, 1993); Sylvia Wynter, "Unsettling the Coloniality of Being/Power/Truth/Freedom: Towards the Human, after Man, Its Overrepresentation–An Argument," *New Centennial Review* 3, no. 3 (2003): 257–337; Andrew Sartori, *Bengal in Global Concept History: Culturalism in the Age of Capital* (Chicago: University of Chicago Press, 2008); Aishwary Kumar, *Radical Equality: Ambedkar, Gandhi, and the Risk of Democracy* (Stanford: Stanford University Press, 2015); and Lisa Lowe, *The Intimacies of Four Continents* (Durham: Duke University Press, 2015).

73. Hamid Dabashi, *Can Non-Europeans Think?* (London: Zed, 2015).

74. For a trenchant critique of this mode of theory, see McKenzie Wark, *The Spectacle of Disintegration: Situationist Passages Out of the Twentieth Century* (London: Verso Books, 2013).

75. For a development of this argument, see Judith Butler "Restaging the Universal: Hegemony and the Limits of Formalism," in *Contingency, Hegemony, and Universality*, ed. Judith Butler, Ernesto Laclau, and Slavoj Žižek (London: Verso, 2000), 11–43.

76. The idea of community as a site and medium for philosophy plays a significant role in recent writing on blackness and political thought: Paul Gilroy, *The Black Atlantic: Modernity and Double Consciousness* (Cambridge, MA: Harvard University Press, 1993); Nikhil Pal Singh, *Black is a Country* (Cambridge, MA: Harvard University Press, 2004), and Richard Iton, *In Search of the Black Fantastic: Politics and Popular Culture in the Post–Civil Rights Era* (Oxford: Oxford University Press, 2010).

77. The literature on this question in various contexts is now extensive. For a useful discussion of press, gender, and nationalist public culture in South Africa, see Meghan Healy-Clancy, "The Politics of New African Marriage in Segregationist South Africa," *African Studies Review* 57, no. 2 (2014): 7–28.

78. Ntongela Masilela, "Theorizing the Modernist Moment of the New African Intellectuals," in *New African Intellectuals and New African Political Thought in the Twentieth Century*, ed. Mbukeni Herbert Mnguni (New York: Waxman, 2015), 51.

79. From 1932 to 1952, the editor of the *Bantu World* was Richard Victor Selope Thema, who played an active role in the All Africa Convention and the ANC until he formed the Nationalist Bloc (with R. G. Baloyi) in opposition to the ANC's collaboration with Communists and Indians.

80. For more on this idea, see Stephanie Newell, *The Power to Name: A History of Anonymity in Colonial West Africa* (Athens: Ohio University Press, 2013), 35; and Masilela, "Theorizing the Modernist Moment," 52.

81. David Everatt, *The Origins of Non-racialism: White Opposition to Apartheid in the 1950s* (Johannesburg: Wits University Press, 2010).

82. See the discussion of Mandela's views on the national question in Crain Soudien, "Robben Island University Revisited," in Lissoni et al., *One Hundred Years of the ANC*, 211–32.

83. Gail Gerhart, *Black Power in South Africa: The Evolution of an Ideology* (Berkeley: University of California Press, 1979).

84. This contradiction is explored at length in Benjamin Pogrund, *How Can Man Die Better: Sobukwe and Apartheid* (London: Halban, 1990).

85. With the exception of Anton Lembede, who moved to Johannesburg in 1943 and died in 1947. After 1959, Ngubane joins the PAC to encourage a rapprochement with the Liberal Party, but he publicly criticizes its mobilization of racial anger.

86. See, for example, Julie Frederikse, *The Unbreakable Thread: Non-racialism in South Africa* (Johannesburg: Ravan Press, 1990).

87. Michael MacDonald, *Why Race Matters in South Africa* (Cambridge, MA: Harvard University Press, 2006), 92–123.

88. Soske, "Impossible Concept," 29–30.

89. It is notable that major statements of the ANC's position, for example Tambo's 1976 address to the UN general assembly, do not contain the term. For a discussion of the ANC's failure to clarify the meaning of non-racialism in exile, see Gerhard Maré, "'Non-racialism' in the Struggle against Apartheid," *Society in Transition* 34, no. 1 (2003): 13–37.

90. Philip Bonner, "Fragmentation and Cohesion in the ANC: The First 70 Years," in Lissoni et al., *One Hundred Years of the ANC*, 7.

91. See Burton, *Africa in the Indian Imagination*, 1–5.

92. Jacques Rancière, *The Politics of Aesthetics*, trans. Gabriel Rockhill (New York: Continuum, 2004).

93. Ismail Meer, *A Fortunate Man* (Cape Town: Zebra Press, 2002), 84.

94. Nelson Mandela, *Long Walk to Freedom* (Boston: Little, Brown and Company, 1994), 104.

95. I. Meer, *A Fortunate Man*, 84. My thanks to M. Neelika Jayawardane for pushing me to think more about the curry and Amina Pahad's part in this story.

CHAPTER 1

1. Hilda Kuper, *Indian People in Natal* (Pietermaritzburg, Zaf.: Natal University Press, 1960), xiii.

2. C. C. Majola interviewed by A. Manson and D. Collins, 20 June 1979, Killie Campbell Oral History Project (KCAV 142), Killie Campbell Africana Library, Durban (hereafter KCAL).

3. See Goolam Vahed, "The Making of 'Indianess': Indian Politics in South Africa during the 1930s and 1940s," *Journal of Natal and Zulu History* 17 (1997): 1–36.

4. E. P. Thompson, *The Making of the English Working Class* (New York: Vintage, 1963), 10–13.

5. For an overview, see Paul Maylam, "Explaining the Apartheid City: 20 Years of South African Urban Historiography," *Journal of Southern African Studies* 21, no. 1 (March 1995): 19–38.

6. Thomas Blom Hansen, *Melancholia of Freedom: Social Life in an Indian Township in South Africa* (Princeton: Princeton University Press, 2012), 7. The classic account of the contradictory and ultimately unrealizable character of apartheid is Deborah Posel, *The Making of Apartheid 1948–1961* (Oxford: Oxford University Press, 1991).

7. C. A. Woods, *The Indian Community of Natal: Their Economic Position*, vol. 9 of *Natal Regional Survey* (Cape Town: Oxford University Press, 1954), 13; and Paul La Hausse, "Drink and Cultural Innovation in Durban: The Origins of the Beerhall in South Africa 1902–16," in *Liquor and Labor in South Africa*, ed. Charles Amber and Jonathan Crush (Athens: Ohio University Press, 1993).

8. See University of Natal Economics Department, *Durban Housing Survey: A Study of Housing in a Multi-racial Community*, Natal Regional Survey, Additional Report no. 2 (Pietermaritzburg, Zaf.: University of Natal Press, 1952), 19.

9. This phrase comes from Antoinette Burton, *Brown over Black: Race and the Politics of Postcolonial Citation* (Delhi: Three Essays Collective, 2012).

10. Sander Gilman, *Difference and Pathology: Stereotypes of Sexuality, Race, and Madness* (Ithaca: Cornell University Press, 1985), 18.

11. See Brackette F. Williams, *Stains on My Name, War in My Veins: Guyana and the Politics of Cultural Struggle* (Durham: Duke University Press, 1991), 127–54.

12. This argument has been powerfully made in Zine Magubane, "Which Bodies Matter? Feminism, Poststructuralism, Race, and the Curious Theoretical Odyssey of the 'Hottentot Venus,'" *Gender and Society* 15, no. 6 (2001): 816–34.

13. For the idea of "transcript" as tool for analyzing the performative dimensions of racialized interactions, see Robin D. G. Kelley, *Race Rebels: Culture, Politics, and the Black Working Class* (New York: Free Press, 1994).

14. For a discussion of this conflict in a context where the parties are not racialized, see E. P. Thompson, "The English Crowd in the Eighteenth Century," *Past and Present* 50, no. 1 (February 1971). For a more recent elaboration of this argument in comparative terms, see Yuri Slezkine, *The Jewish Century* (Princeton: Princeton University Press, 2004), 4–39. This argument also has a long Marxist lineage: Abram Leon, *The Jewish Question: A Marxist Interpretation* (New York: Pathfinder, 1970).

15. Francois Petrus Van den Heever, *Report of the Commission of Enquiry into Riots in Durban* (Pretoria: Government Printer, 1949), 15. For an earlier

example of this discourse, see the following statement from 1903: "Money was brought by Europeans. We had none. Natives should not have been given money because they do not know its use. They should be paid in clothing and cattle. But coolies, Arabs, and Chinese understand money. Let contracts exist between them." James Stuart, *The James Stuart Archive of Recorded Oral Evidence Relating to the History the Zulu and Neighbouring People*, vol. 3, ed. and trans. C. de B. Webb and J.B. Wright (Pietermaritzburg, Zaf.: University of Natal Press, 1976), 29.

16. Quoted in Leo Kuper, *An African Bourgeoisie: Race, Class, and Politics in South Africa* (New Haven: Yale University Press, 1965), 300.

17. For an exploration of this theme, see the special issue, "Everyone Has Their Indian," *Chimurenga* 14 (2009).

18. L. Kuper, *African Bourgeoisie*, 303; and Pierre L. Van den Berghe, "Race Attitudes in Durban, South Africa," *Journal of Social Psychology* 57 (1962): 58.

19. Hansen, *Melancholia of Freedom*, especially chapter 3.

20. See my discussion in chapter 3.

21. Gilman, *Difference and Pathology*, 18.

22. Vahed, "Making of 'Indianness,'" 10–11. See also Woods, *Indian Community of Natal*, 56; S. L. Kirk, "The 1949 Durban Riots—A Community in Conflict" (MA thesis, University of Natal, January 1983), 29; and University of Natal Economics Department, *Studies of Indian Employment in Natal*, vol. 11 of *Natal Regional Survey* (Cape Town: Natal University Press, 1961), 33.

23. "In Durban in 1951, only 4.6 percent of gainfully employed Indians were engaged in agriculture, mining and associated occupations; the percentage for manufacturing industries, commerce, and services being 37.3, 21.1 and 28.7 respectively." University of Natal Economics Department, *Indian Employment in Natal*, 4.

24. Jay Naidoo, *Coolie Location* (London: South African Writers, 1990), 84.

25. See "As We Were," *Ilanga lase Natal*, 30 April 1949.

26. C. C. Majola interview, 20 June 1979, KCAV 142, KCAL.

27. For a brief survey of different patterns of Indian segregation in Natal, see Woods, *Indian Community of Natal*, 12–13.

28. Ibid., 8.

29. Vahed, "Making of 'Indianness,'" 3. This generalization is complicated by the fact that there also existed a large group of indentured laborers from the Ganges Valley and a small stratum of south Indian merchants, who were sometimes Muslim.

30. Ibid., 4.

31. Fatima Meer, *The Ghetto People: A Study in the Effects of Uprooting the Indian People of South Africa* (London: Africa Publications Trust, 1975), 2.

32. C. G. Maasdorp and N. Pillay, *Urban Relocation and Racial Segregation: The Case of Indian South Africans* (Durban, Zaf.: University of Natal Department of Economics, 1977), 80.

33. Maynard W. Swanson, "'The Asiatic Menace': Creating Segregation in Durban, 1879–1900," *International Journal of African Historical Studies* 16, no. 3 (1983): 403.

34. Freund, *Insiders and Outsiders*, 33.

35. According to Fatima Meer: "The Indian people, although poor, had accumulated substantial freehold property. A door-to-door survey conducted by the Natal Indian Congress of six Indian neighbourhoods in 1944 had found 56% of the houses to be owned by the occupants." Meer, *The Ghetto People*, 4. The University of Natal 1943–44 housing survey (based on a one in twenty sample of all structures listed on the 1941 valuation roll of the municipality) provides a lower number of 36 percent of houses owned by occupants. University of Natal Economics Department, *Durban Housing Survey*, 252.

36. For the example of Clairwood, see Dianne Scott, "The Destruction of Clairwood: A Case Study on the Transformation of Communal Living Space," in *The Apartheid City and Beyond: Urbanization and Social Change in South Africa*, ed. David M. Scott (London: Routledge, 1992), 91.

37. In Freund's words, Indian areas were composed of "networks of community linked together through dense human contacts that tied into family relationships and a myriad of economic connections." Freund, *Insiders and Outsiders*, 75.

38. H. Kuper, *Indian People in Natal*, xv.

39. See Paul la Hausse, "'Mayihlome!': Towards an Understanding of Amalaita Gangs in Durban, 1900–1939," in *Regions and Repertoires: Topics in South African Politics and Culture*, ed. Stephen Clingman (Braamfontein, Zaf.: Ravan Press, 1991), 33.

40. For the "enclave city," see Setha M. Low, "The Anthropology of Cities: Imagining and Theorizing the City," *Annual Review of Anthropology* 25 (1996): 387–90.

41. H. Kuper, *Indian People in Natal*, xii. Some sources provide a higher estimate.

42. Ashwin Desai, "A Context for Violence: Social and Historical Underpinnings of Indo-African Violence in a South African Community" (PhD diss., Michigan State University, 1993), 63.

43. Paul Maylam, "The 'Black Belt': African Squatters in Durban 1935–1950," *Canadian Journal of African Studies*, vol. 17, no. 3 (1983): 414–15.

44. The revised census figures for 1951 were: Europeans: 131,430; Coloureds: 16,104; Indians: 145, 744; and Africans: 132,841. University of Natal Economics Department, *Durban Housing Survey*, 35.

45. See "Weekly Review and Commentary," *Ilanga lase Natal*, 27 July 1946.

46. University of Natal Economics Department, *Durban Housing Survey*, 27.

47. It is a striking aspect of Durban's racial discourse during this period that while Coloureds appear not infrequently in sources such as Indian and

African newspapers, discussions of African-Indian relations rarely mention Coloureds. The major exception, as discussed in chapter 4, is the reference to Coloured children in representations of interracial sex. There is a significant amount of research that needs to be done both on the history of the Coloured community in Natal and the place of Coloureds within the thinking of African nationalist intellectuals. Sharad Chari's important ethnographic work on the neighborhood of Wentworth has started to address some of these questions. See, inter alia, Chari, "Photographing Dispossession, Forgetting Solidarity: Waiting for Social Justice in Wentworth, South Africa," *Transactions of the Institute of British Geographers* 34, no. 4 (2009): 521–40. For Coloured identity in contemporary Natal, see Fileve Tlaloc Palmer, "Through a Coloured Lens: Post-apartheid Identity Formation amongst Coloureds in KZN" (PhD thesis, Indian University, 2015). For the larger phenomenon of marginalizing Coloureds within narratives of South African history, see Mohamed Adhikari, *Not White Enough, Not Black Enough: Racial Identity in the South African Coloured Community* (Athens: Ohio University Press, 2005), 33–35; and Gabeba Baderoon, *Regarding Muslims: From Slavery to Post-apartheid* (Johannesburg: Wits University Press, 2014), 16–17.

48. Jordan Ngubane, *Unpublished Autobiography*, 41, Historical Papers, William Cullen Library, University of the Witwatersrand, Johannesburg (hereafter HP, WCL).

49. See Jon Soske, "The Life and Death of Dr. Abu Baker 'Hurley' Asvat, 23 February 1943 to 27 January 1989," *African Studies* 70, no. 3 (2011): 337–58.

50. See chapter 5, this book.

51. Madoda Ncayiyana interviewed in *African-Indian Odyssey*, directed by Hina Saiyada and Jon Soske (Johannesburg: CISA, 2010).

52. See Iain Edwards, "Mkhumbane, Our Home: African Shantytown Society in Cato Manor Farm" (PhD diss., University of Natal, Durban, 1989).

53. "Benoni Indians Attacked after Death of Youth," *Bantu World*, 12 July 1952.

54. Omar Badsha interviewed in *African-Indian Odyssey*, directed by Hina Saiyada and written by Jon Soske (Johannesburg: CISA, 2010).

55. This is a significant theme, for example, in the poetry of the Durban antiapartheid activist Mafika Gwala. See "Grey Street," reprinted in *Imperial Ghetto: Ways of Seeing in a South African City*, by Omar Badsha (Pretoria: South African History Online, 2001), 3; and his homage to the veteran Marxist, Indian Congress activist, and purveyor of banned books A. K. M. Docrat, "A Stalwart—August 1977," in *No More Lullabies*, ed. Mafika Gwala (Johannesburg: Ravan Press, 1982), 60–61.

56. Van den Heever, *Report of the Commission*, 4; and I. Meer, *A Fortunate Man*, 116.

57. For a depiction of this world, see: Riason Naidoo, *The Indian in DRUM Magazine in the 1950s* (Cape Town: Bell-Roberts Publishing, 2008);

and chapter 5 of this book. See chapter 4 for a discussion of the trope of the "Coloured girlfriend."

58. For an introduction to Durban's cinemas, see Vashna Jagarnath, "The Politics of Urban Segregation and Indian Cinema in Durban," in *City Flicks: Indian Cinema and the Urban Experience*, ed. Preben Kaarsholm (Calcutta: Seagull Books, 2004), 211–22.

59. Woods, *Indian Community of Natal*, 20. See also H. Kuper, *Indian People in Natal*, 57.

60. Bill Freund, "Indian Women and the Changing Character of the Working Class Indian Household in Natal, 1860–1990," *Journal of Southern African Studies* 17, no. 3 (1991): 414–29.

61. Iain Edwards, "Swing the Assegai Peacefully? 'New Africa,' Mkhumbane, the Co-operative Movement and Attempts to Transform Durban Society in the Late Nineteen-Forties," *Holding Their Ground: Class, Locality and Culture in 19th and 20th Century South Africa*, ed. Philip Bonner et al. (Johannesburg: Witwatersrand University Press and Ravan Press, 1989), 67.

62. Fredrick Dube, "The Riots," letter, *Ilanga lase Natal*, 29 January 1949.

63. See "Ezika Msimbithi Induku Engaphukiyo Umfana we Khishi," *Ilanga lase Natal*, 7 June 1947.

64. G. R. Moya, "Indians and Segregation," letter, *Ilanga lase Natal*, 7 September 1946. See also Rolling Stone, "On Segregation," *Ilanga lase Natal*, 1 March 1947.

65. H. I. E. Dhlomo, "How Long, O Lord!," *Ilanga lase Natal*, 22 January 1949.

66. Edwards, "Mkhumbane, Our Home," 21.

67. Tunya Dlamini interviewed by B. T. C. Mkhize, 14 June 1981, Kwa Mashu, Killie Campbell Oral History Project (KCAV 305), KCAL.

68. "Be Warned of Sharks," *Ilanga lase Natal*, 16 February 1946.

69. Quoted in "How They Sell Air to the Natives," *Natal Mercury*, 26 March 1947. See also "Food," *Ilanga lase Natal*, 16 February 1946.

70. L. Kuper, *African Bourgeoisie*, 300.

71. "Rolling Stone on Umuthi," *Ilanga lase Natal*, 5 January 1946.

72. Karen Flint, "Indian-African Encounters: Polyculturalism and African Therapeutics in Natal, South Africa, 1820–1948," *Journal of Southern African Studies* 32, no. 2 (June 2006): 367–85.

73. Before the election of the Nationalist government, the municipality of Durban had only reserved two locations in the vicinity for African residence, Lamontville and Chesterville.

74. Surplus People Project, *Forced Removals in South Africa*, vol. 4, *Natal* (Cape Town: Surplus People Project, 1983), 198–99.

75. University of Natal Economics Department, *Durban Housing Survey*, 357–58. Other figures were closer to a third. In 1950, the mayor of Durban claimed that forty thousand Africans were living in shacks. Ibid., 361.

76. Maylam, "Black Belt," 418.

77. Ibid., 418–19; and University of Natal Economics Department, *Durban Housing Survey*, 232–39.

78. Thank you to Omar Badhsa for emphasizing the importance of this practice.

79. Dhlomo, "How Long, O Lord!," *Ilanga lase Natal*, 22 January 1949.

80. University of Natal Economics Department, *Durban Housing Survey*, 358–59.

81. Edwards, "Swing the Assegai Peacefully?," 82.

82. H. Kuper, *Indian People in Natal*, 63.

83. Mandela, *Long Walk to Freedom*, 149.

84. "Cato Manor Curse," typescript article draft, undated, A922/Ha13, HP, WCL.

85. Edwards, "Mkhubane, Our Home," 9. Some Africans lived more "respectable" areas or even the reserves and rented out their Cato Manor plots. See University of Natal Economics Department, *Durban Housing Survey*, 370.

86. "Cato Manor," *Ilanga lase Natal*, 26 April 1952.

87. See Memorandum by S. S. Brisker to the Riots Commission, 8 March 1949, A922/Ha4, HP, WCL. During the 1949 pogrom, Africans stoned and burned buses. After the pogrom, some bus owners hired Africans to drive the Cato Manor route. See A. Desai, "Context for Violence," 92–94; and Steven Selby interviewed by C. N. Shum, 12 August 1980, Killie Campbell Oral History Project (KCAV 366), KCAL.

88. S. S. Brisker to the Riots Commission, 8 March 1948, A922/Ha4, HP, WCL.

89. Louise Torr, "Lamontville: A History," in *The People's City: African Life in Twentieth Century Durban*, ed. Paul Maylam and Iain Edwards (Pietermaritzburg, Zaf.: University of Natal Press, 1996), 260–65.

90. "Evidence from Edendale Africans," *Ilanga lase Natal*, 15 June 1946.

91. Z. A. Ngcobo interviewed by Simeon Zulu, 13 September 1980, Killie Campbell Oral History Project (KCAV 361), KCAL.

92. Annual Report of the Local Road Transportation Board for the Period 1st April 1945 to 31 March 1946, quoted in S. S. Brisker to the Riots Commission, 8 March 1949, A922/Ha4, HP, WCL.

93. "Rolling Stone on Umunthi," *Ilanga lase Natal*, 5 January 1946.

94. "As We Were," *Ilanga lase Natal*, 30 April 1949.

95. Ibid.

96. Josephine Hadebe interviewed by L. Mabaso, 26 April 1981, Killie Campbell Oral History Project (KCAV 308), KCAL.

97. A. Desai, "Context for Violence," 256.

98. Dhlomo, "How Long, O Lord!," *Ilanga lase Natal*, 22 January 1949.

99. Van den Heever, *Report of the Commission*, 13. In a Zulu-language interview conducted in 1981, Dupha Mtshali expressed a similar idea: "The

government ended the enslavement of people [Indians] completely because it was useless. . . . The Indians are now masters. Don't you hear me saying that blacks are now living on their farms." Mtshali interviewed by A. M. Jili, 15 February 1981, Killie Campbell Oral History Project (KCAV 313), KCAL.

100. See, for example, the classic Elliott Rudwick, *Race Riot at East St. Louis, July 2, 1917* (Carbondale: Southern University of Illinois Press, 1964).

101. For a broader reflection on the issue of recognition and its denial in the context of slavery, see Orlando Patterson, *Slavery and Social Death* (Cambridge, MA: Harvard University Press, 1982).

102. "Ucongress Uyaphi?," *Ilanga lase Natal*, 13 February 1960.

103. Ibid.

104. Keyter, *Holiday and Travel Facilities for Non-whites in South Africa* [pamphlet] (Johannesburg: Institute of Race Relations, 1926), 18.

105. Letter from A. M. Rajab to Margaret Ballinger, 23 January 1959, A410/B2.7, HP, WCL; and "Application Shah Jehan Cinema, Indian, 275/9 Grey Street, 28 February 1959," A410/B2.7, HP, WCL.

106. "We Are the Tools of the Indians," *Ilanga lase Natal*, 27 August 1955.

107. Rolling Stone, "On Segregation," *Ilanga lase Natal*, 1 March 1947.

108. Peter Abrahams, "Can We Unite?," *Drum*, July 1952.

109. Kogila Moodley, "The Ambivalence of Survival Politics in Indian-African Relations," in *South Africa's Indians: The Evolution of a Minority*, ed. B. Pachai (Washington, DC: University Press of America, 1979), 451. See also Richman K. Mabika interviewed by E. N. Yenwa, 25 September 1981, Stanger, Killie Campbell Oral History Project (KCAV 321), KCAL.

110. Ngcobo interviewed by Zulu, 13 September 1980, KCAV 361, KCAL.

111. Mr. Drum [Henry Nxumalo], "Sugar Farms," *Drum*, February 1953.

112. University of Natal Economics Department, *Indian Employment in Natal*, 21.

113. Nxumalo, "Sugar Farms," *Drum*, February 1953.

114. See, for example, "A Girls Success," *Ilanga lase Natal*, 10 December 1955.

115. Edwards, "Swing the Assegai Peacefully?," 72.

116. Bertha Mkhize interviewed by J. Wells and H. Hughes, 20 August 1980, Killie Campbell Oral History Project (KCAV 354), KCAL.

117. Ranajit Guha, *History at the Limit of World-History* (New York: Columbia University Press, 2002).

118. Absolom Vilakazi with Bongani Mthethwa and Mthembeni Mpanza, *Shembe: The Revitalization of African Society* (Johannesburg: Skotaville Publishers, 1986), 57.

119. Moodley, "Ambivalence of Survival Politics," 449.

120. Africa Ambrose interviewed by C. N. Shum, 25 September 1980, Killie Campbell Oral History Project (KCAV 300), KCAL: "At Sinyameni some

young men used to stay who said they were not girls but played like they were girls [*Esinyameni kwakuhlala khona izinsizwa ezazithi azisiwo amantombazana zidla amantomgazane*]. Myafethe was an Indian who lived there."

121. A letter sent by the Natal Muslim Council to the chief constable in 1949 complained, "Most of the participants in these celebrations are African, Coloureds, Hindus and Muslims of the ignorant type." Quoted in Goolam Vahed, unpublished manuscript on Islam in Natal, chapter 3, Center for Research Libraries, University of Chicago (hereafter CRL). My thanks to Goolam for giving me permission to cite this work.

122. The major exception occurs in the autobiographies of political activists, where relationships between individual Indians and Africans involved in political struggle are extremely important.

CHAPTER 2

1. X. [H. I. E. Dhlomo], "On Durban," *Ilanga lase Natal*, 22 February 1947.

2. Document 39, "Joint Declarartion of Coopertaion," Statement by Dr. A. B. Xuma of the ANC, Dr. G. M. Naicker of Natal Indian Congress and Dr. Y. M. Dadoo of the Transvaal Indian Congress, 9 March 1947, in *Hope and Challenge, 1935–1952*, vol. 2 of *From Protest to Challenge*, ed. Thomas Karis and Gail Gerhart (Stanford: Hoover Institution, 1973), 272.

3. Susan Buck-Morss, *Hegel, Haiti, and Universal History* (Pittsburg: University of Pittsburgh Press, 2009).

4. For nationalism and universal history, see Prasenjit Duara, *Rescuing History from the Nation: Questioning Narratives of Modern China* (Chicago: University of Chicago Press, 1996), 19–51.

5. Mark Mazower, *No Enchanted Palace: The End of Empire and the Ideological Origins of the United Nations* (Princeton: Princeton University Press, 2009), 28–65.

6. For the early history of the ANC, see: Peter Walshe, *The Rise of African Nationalism in South Africa: The African National Congress 1912–1952* (London: C. Hurst and Company, 1970); Limb, *ANC's Early Years*; André Odendaal, *The Founders: The Origins of the ANC and the Struggle for Democracy in South Africa* (Cape Town: Jacana Media, 2012); and Martin Plaut, *Promise and Despair: The First Struggle for a Non-racial South Africa* (Cape Town: Jacana, 2016).

7. Sol Plaatje, *Native Life in South Africa* (Northlands, Zaf.: Picador Africa, 2007); Walshe, *Rise of African Nationalism*, 112–13; and "The Leadership of Educated Men," *Abantu-Batho*, March 1914, reprinted in *The People's Paper: A Centenary History and Anthology of "Abantu-Batho*," ed. Peter Limb (Johannesburg: Wits University Press, 2012), 349–51; "The Next Step in African Government II," *Abantu-Batho*, September 1915, reprinted in Limb, *The People's Paper*, 367–69; and "Cen. Smuts Answered," *Abantu-Batho*, December 1915, reprinted in Limb, *The People's Paper*, 372.

8. For unity as a theme in ANC history, see: Anthony Butler, *The Idea of the ANC* (Athens: Ohio University Press, 2012), 58–91; and Philip Bonner, "Fragmentation and Cohesion in the ANC: The First 70 Years," in Lissoni et al., *One Hundred Years of the ANC*, 1–11.

9. For a discussion of empire in these terms, see Laura Benton, *Law and Colonial Cultures: Legal Regimes in World History, 1400–1900* (Cambridge: Cambridge University Press, 2002); Hofmeyr, *Gandhi's Printing Press*, 1–29; and (in the French Empire) Cooper, *Citizenship between Empire and Nation*, 21.

10. In this respect, parallels with prewar West African nationalism are striking. See Cooper, *Citizenship between Empire and Nation*, 165–213; and Wilder, *Freedom Time*, 133–66.

11. Premesh Lalu, *The Deaths of Hintsa: Post-apartheid South Africa and the Shape of Recurring Pasts* (Cape Town: HSRC, 2009); and Barchiesi, "Imagining the Patriotic Worker," 114–19.

12. Premesh Lalu, "Restless Natives, Native Questions," *Mail and Guardian South Africa*, 28 August 2011, 3.

13. Jon Soske and Shannon Walsh, "Thinking about Race and Friendship in South Africa," in Walsh and Soske, *Ties that Bind*, 1–28.

14. For the relationship between progress, historicity, and civilization in nationalist thinking, see Duara, *Rescuing History from the Nation*, 27–30.

15. For a powerful statement of these arguments, see Plaatje, *Native Life in South Africa*, 21.

16. Hannah Arendt, *The Origins of Totalitarianism* (New York: Harcout, 1968), 177.

17. Hughes, *First President*, 195–97; and my sympathetic critique of her account in Jon Soske, "Review of *The First President: A Life of John L. Dube, Founding President of the ANC*," *South African Historical Journal* 66, no. 1 (2014): 200–203.

18. A. Butler, *Idea of the ANC*, 27.

19. Plaatje, *Native Life in South Africa*, 21.

20. R. V. Selope Thema, "Dingane ka Senzangakona," *Abantu-Batho*, 16 December 1920, reprinted in Limb, *The People's Paper*, 445; and "South Africa: The Next World Imbroglio?," *Abantu-Batho*, 14 August 1930, reprinted in Limb, *The People's Paper*, 476.

21. "Bantu Reminder to White World about Garvey," *Abantu-Batho*, 17 March 1927, reprinted in Limb, *The People's Paper*, 467.

22. Hughes, *First President*, 110; and Paul La Hausse, *Restless Identities: Signatures of Nationalism, Zulu Ethnicity, and History in the Lives of Petros Lamula (c. 1881–1948) and Lymon Maling (1889–c. 1936)* (Pietermaritzburg, Zaf.: University of Kwazulu Natal Press, 2000), 70–71, 84–85.

23. A. B. Xuma, "Bridging the Gap between White in Black in South Africa," in *A. B. Xuma: Autobiography and Selected Works*, ed. Peter Limb (Cape Town: Van Riebeeck Society, 2012), 266.

24. In a fascinating discussion, Nafisa Sheik argues that the late nineteenth century Natal state attempted to articulate the Indian and Native questions as isomorphic through the categories of gender, marriage, and custom. Ultimately, these efforts were undermined by the British Empire's invalidation of laws directly invoking racial categories with regards to Indians. See Nafisa Essop Sheik, "Colonial Rites: Custom, Marriage Law and the Making of Difference in Natal, 1830s–c. 1910," (PhD thesis, University of Michigan, 2012).

25. Tom Lodge, *Black Politics in South Africa since 1945* (London: Longman, 1983), 1.

26. Mandela, *Long Walk to Freedom*, 112–15.

27. This account Xuma's life is based on Steven Gish, *Alfred B. Xuma: African, American, South African* (New York: NYU Press, 2000); and Peter Limb, "Introduction," in *A. B. Xuma*, xii–xxv.

28. "A. B. Xuma to Reverend D Sibeko," in Limb, *A. B. Xuma*, 97–98.

29. "A. B. Xuma to R. T. Bokwe, 11 November 1941," in Limb, *A. B. Xuma*, 85; "Cable from A. B. Xuma to Paul Robeson, 1 May 1946," in Limb, *A. B. Xuma*, 106; and A. B. Xuma, "South West Africa: Annexation or United Nations Trusteeship?," in Limb, *A. B. Xuma*, 334–45.

30. A. B. Xuma, "The Bantu and Politics," in Limb, *A. B. Xuma*, 297.

31. Xuma Papers, AD843, HP, WCL.

32. Limb, "Introduction," xi.

33. "A. B. Xuma to R. T. Bokwe, 11 November 1941," 85. Xuma refers to the Indian Congress, but the context of his remarks suggests that he was thinking of the Indian National Congress, not the then rather moribund South African Indian Congress.

34. Iris Berger, "An African American 'Mother of the Nation': Madie Hall Xuma in South Africa, 1940–1963," *Journal of Southern African Studies* 27, no. 3 (2001): 547–66.

35. Limb, "Introduction," xxi.

36. Mandela, *Long Walk to Freedom*, 98.

37. Here I am extrapolating the development of Xuma's views from his later statements regarding Indian role in the United Nations. See Xuma, "Annexation or United Nations Trusteeship?," 334–45.

38. "A. B. Xuma to R.T. Bokwe, 11 November 1942," 85–86.

39. Azoulay, *Civil Contract of Photography*, 47–51.

40. Gish, *Alfred B. Xuma*, 121.

41. Ibid. I find Gish's assessment more convincing than Walshe's reading of *Africans' Claims* as the culmination of an earlier tradition in the ANC. Walshe, *Rise of African Nationalism*, 272–79.

42. The ANC's policy on the franchise was evolving in the early 1940s toward universal suffrage but it continued to advocate a transitional stage between the Native Representative system and full citizenship rights. Walshe, *Rise of African Nationalism*, 265–66.

43. African National Congress, "African Claims in South Africa," in *From Protest to Challenge: Documents of African Politics in South Africa*, vol. 2, *Hope and Challenge, 1935–1952*, ed. Thomas G. Karis and Gail M. Gerhart (Stanford: Hoover Institution, 1973), 217–23.

44. Mahmood Mamdani, *Citizen and Subject: Contemporary Africa and the Legacy of Late Colonialism* (Princeton: Princeton University Press, 1996), 4-6.

45. Xuma, "Annexation or United Nations Trusteeship?," 340, 344.

46. Ibid., 344.

47. Mandela, *Long Walk to Freedom*, 96.

48. Mary Benson, *South Africa: The Struggle for a Birthright* (Hamondsworth, Eng.: Penguin, 1966), 80.

49. Luyanda ka Msumza and Robert R. Edgar, Introduction, in *Freedom in Our Lifetime: The Collected Writings of Anton Muziwakhe Lembede*, ed. Robert R. Edgar and Luyanda ka Msumza (Athens: Ohio University Press, 1996), 5.

50. "An Address to the Nation on the Occasion of the Twelfth Anniversary of the Death of Anton Muziwakhe Lembede," *Africanist*, July/August 1959.

51. Msumza and Edgar, Introduction, 18–20.

52. "Congress Youth League Manifesto," in Edgar and Msumza, *Freedom in Our Lifetime*, 68.

53. A. M. Lembede, "National Unity among the Africans," *Ilanga lase Natal*, 6 October 1945, reprinted in Edgar and Msumza, *Freedom in Our Lifetime*, 90.

54. A. M. Lembede, "Some Basic Principles of African Nationalism," *Ilanga lase Natal*, 24 February 1945, reprinted in Edgar and Msumza, *Freedom in Our Lifetime*, 85.

55. W. E. B. Du Bois, "The Conservation of Races," in *The Oxford W.E.B. Du Bois Reader*, ed. Eric J. Sundquist (New York: Oxford University Press, 1996), 40.

56. Jacques Maritain, "Integral Humanism and the Crisis of Modern Times," *Review of Politics* 1, no. 1 (1939): 1-17.

57. "Africanism," *Transvaal African Students' Association Bulletin* 1, no. 2 (July 1944), reprinted in Edgar and Msumza, *Freedom in Our Lifetime*, 84.

58. A. M. Lembede, "In Defense of Nationalism," *Inkundla ya Bantu*, 27 February 1947.

59. Jawaharlal Nehru, *The Discovery of India* (Oxford: Oxford University Press, 1985), 53.

60. Ibid., 59.

61. Lembede, "In Defense of Nationalism," *Inkundla ya Bantu*, 27 February 1947.

62. A. M. Lembede, "Policy of the Congress Youth League," *Inkundla ya Bantu*, May 1946, reprinted in Edgar and Msumza, *Freedom in Our Lifetime*, 91.

63. "Nelson Mandela's Speech at the Unveiling of Gandhi Memorial, 6 June 1993," *South African History Online*, http://www.sahistory.org.za/archive/nelson-mandelas-speech-unveiling-gandhi-memorial-pietermaritzburg-6-june-1993.

64. For the effect of Lembede's illness, see "Address to the Nation," *Africanist*, July/August 1959.

65. A. M. Lemebede, "Fallacy of the Non-European Unity Movement," *Bantu World*, 11 August 1945, reprinted in Edgar and Msumza, *Freedom in Our Lifetime*, 119.

66. Lembede, "Policy of the Congress Youth League," 91.

67. Swan, *South African Experience*; and Vishnu Padayachee, Shahid Vawda, and Paul Tichmann, *Indian Workers and Trade Unions in Durban: 1930–1950* (Durban, Zaf.: Institute for Social and Economic Research, August 1985), 138–39.

68. "The Native Strike and Its Lesson," *Indian Opinion*, 23 August 1946.

69. Mabel Palmer, *The History of the Indian in Natal* (Cape Town: Oxford University Press, 1957), 127–32.

70. "Pandit Nehru's Message to South African Indians," *Indian Opinion*, 21 June 1946.

71. For a portrait of the Communist Party in Natal during this period, see Pauline Podbrey, *White Girl in Search of the Party* (Pietermaritzburg, Zaf.: Hadea Books, 1993).

72. Baruch Hirson, "A Trade Union Organizer in Durban: M. B. Yengwa, 1943–44," in *The Left in South Africa*, 207–19.

73. For the deployment of these struggles as a usable past, see Marie, *Divide and Profit: Indian Workers in Natal*, 38–61.

74. Padayachee, Vawda, and Tichmann, *Indian Workers and Trade Unions*, 107–9.

75. Freund, *Insiders and Outsiders*, 56–57.

76. I. Meer, *A Fortunate Man*, 59.

77. Ibid., 93.

78. Goolam Vahed, "Race or Class? Community and Conflict amongst Indian Municipal Employees in Durban, 1914–1949." *Journal of Southern African Studies* 27, no.1 (March 2001): 122. See also Freund, *Insiders and Outsiders*, 61–63.

79. Vahed, "Race or Class?," 122.

80. Baruch Hirson, "A Short History of the Non-European Unity Movement: An Insider's View," *Searchlight South Africa*, no. 12 (1995): 64–93.

81. Mohamed Adhikari, "Fiercely Non-Racial? Discourses and Politics of Race in the Non-European Unity Movement, 1943–70," *Journal of Southern African Studies* 31, no. 2 (2005): 403–18.

82. Robert Sobukwe interviewed by Gail M. Gerhart, 8 and 9 August 1970, 2422/A, HP WCL.

83. Patricia Van der Spuy and Lindsay Clowes, "'A Living Testimony of the Heights to Which a Woman Can Rise': Sarojini Naidu, Cissie Gool and the Politics of Women's Leadership in South Africa in the 1920s," *South African Historical Journal* 64, no. 2 (2012): 343–63.

84. Goolam Vahed, "Race, Empire, and Citizenship: Sarojini Naidu's 1924 Visit to South Africa," *South African Historical Journal* 64, no. 2 (2012): 319–42.

85. Surendra Bhana and Bridglal Pachai, eds, *A Documentary History of Indian South Africans* (Stanford: Hoover Institute Press, 1984), 77.

86. Gavin Lewis, *Between the Wire and the Wall: History of South African "Coloured" Politics* (Cape Town: David Philip Publishers, 1987), 198–204.

87. S. A. Javiva and E. Ramsdale to Dr. A. B. Xuma, 31 May 1945, AD843, HP, WCL.

88. Dr. A. B. Xuma to Dr. E. T. Dietrich, 10 August 1945, AD843, HP, WCL.

89. Dr. A. B. Xuma, Opening Address of the All-In-One Conference of the Non-white Trade Unions at Bloemfontein, 4 August 1945, AD843, HP, WCL.

90. For an example of this distinction, see "Dr. Xuma Questioned," *Ilanga lase Natal*, 17 April 1948.

91. Moses M. Kotane to Dr. A. B. Xuma, 14 November 1945, AD843, HP, WCL.

92. See Martin Legassick, *Class and Nationalism in South African Protest: The South African Communist Party and the "Native Republic" 1928–34* (Syracuse: The Program of Eastern African Studies, 1973).

93. Padayachee, Vawda, and Tichmann, *Indian Workers and Trade Unions*, 164.

94. I. Meer, *A Fortunate Man*, 67.

95. See Y. M. Dadoo, "The Non-European Unity," *Freedom* 4, no. 1 (February 1945), reprinted in *South Africa's Radical Tradition: A Documentary History*, vol. 2, *1943–1964*, ed. Allison Drew (Cape Town: University of Cape Town Press, 1997), http://www.sahistory.org.za/archive/document-10-y-m-dadoo-non-european-unity-freedom-41-february-1945.

96. "Resist . . . Indian Ghetto Act," AD 1710, HP, WCL.

97. Xuma made this argument explicitly. See Xuma, "Annexation or United Nations Trusteeship?," 342.

98. "UNO and Ourselves," *African National Congress Youth League Bulletin*, no. 1, AD 2186, La 3.2, HP, WCL.

99. See, for example, "An Indian Says Passive Resistance Has Not Failed," *Inkundla ya Bantu*, 22 October 1947; and H. I. E. Dhlomo, "Significance of the Passive Resistance Campaign," *Indian Opinion*, 12 July 1946.

100. Busy-Bee, "Weekly Review and Commentary," *Ilanga lase Natal*, 7 June 1947.

101. Goonam, *Coolie Doctor*, 109.

102. Fatima Meer, *Memories of Love and Struggle* (Cape Town: Kwela Books, 2017), 105.

103. "Intellectuals and Congress," *Ilanga lase Natal*, 2 November 1946.

104. Cl. A. W. Geo. Champion, "Call to African Women," *Ilanga lase Natal*, 20 April 1947.

105. "A Clarion Call to African Women," *Ilanga lase Natal*, 18 October 1947.

106. For a fuller examination of this idea, see chapter 4.

107. For an account by an Indian participant, see C. S. Jha, *From Bandung to Tashkent: Glimpses of India's Foreign Policy* (Madras: Sagam Books, 1983), 22–30.

108. Mazower, *No Enchanted Palace*, 151.

109. "Comments on Events," *Inkundla ya Bantu*, 20 February 1949.

110. "Comment on Events," *Inkundla ya Bantu*, first fortnight, January 1947.

111. "Mrs. Pandit, Dr. Xuma Address Meeting Honoring S. African Mine Workers," *New Africa* (Council on African Affairs Monthly Bulletin) 5, no. 11 (December 1946), 1.

112. "Comment on Events," *Inkundla ya Bantu*, first fortnight, January 1947.

113. "Dr. A. B. Xuma in Durban," *Ilanga lase Natal*, 13 February 1947.

114. Padayachee, Vawda, and Tichmann, *Indian Workers and Trade Unions*, 155–57.

115. "Significance of Passive Resistance," *Inkundla ya Bantu*, 8 October 1947.

116. "Indian Political Movements in South Africa," South Africa Police report for the Secretary of External Affairs, 30 January 1948, KCAL 308210, File 39.

117. "Natal Indians Divided," *Inkundla ya Bantu*, 8 May 1947.

118. "Comments on Events," *Inkundla ya Bantu*, 27 March 1947.

119. "Indian Political Movements," 30 January 1948, KCAL 308210, File 39.

120. "Weekly Review and Commentary," *Ilanga lase Natal*, 22 February 1947.

121. Minutes of a special meeting of the National Executive, 1 and 2 February 1947, a922/eb2, HP, WCL.

122. Minutes of the African National Congress National Executive, Bloemfontein, 1–2 February 1947, AD 2186/Bd3, HP, WCL. Note that these sets of minutes differ significantly in the amount of verbatim material they report.

123. "Joint Declarartion of Coopertaion," 272.

124. Xuma's papers include letters from Dadoo in his capacity as leader of the NEUF and leader of Nationalist Group of the TIC beginning in 1939. Dr. Y. Dadoo to "Dear Friend," 27 February 1939, AD843, HP, WCL; Dr.

Y. Dadoo to "Dear Friend," 30 March 1939, AD843, HP, WCL; and Dr. Y. Dadoo to Dr. A. B. Xuma, 28 February 1943, AD843, HP, WCL.

125. I. B. Tabata, *The Awakening of a People* (Nottingham, Eng.: Spokesman Books, 1974), 100; Walshe, *Rise of African Nationalism*, 398.

126. "Dr. Xuma to Wait and See," *Inkundla ya Bantu*, 5 May 1948.

127. Letter by Isharina [A. P. Mda], "Congress Going Communist?," *Inkundla ya Bantu*, 10 April 1947.

128. I owe this point to conversations with Premesh Lalu.

129. Kader Asmal and Adrian Hadland with Moira Levy, *Politics in My Blood: A Memoir* (Auckland Park, Zaf.: Jacana Media, 2011), 13

130. "Dr. Xuma to Wait and See," *Inkundla ya Bantu*, 5 May 1948.

131. R. S. Canca, "Unity in Words, Disunity in Action," *Inkundla ya Bantu*, 21 August 1948.

132. "Congress at Parting of the Ways," *Inkundla ya Bantu*, 11 June 1949.

133. I. Meer, *A Fortunate Man*, 90.

134. Heb. M. Ngcobo, "A Political Blunder," *Ilanga lase Natal*, 5 April 1947.

135. See the draft letter from Xuma to Champion, 17 April 1947, AD843, HP, WCL.

136. A. W. G. Champion to H. Selby Msimang, 21 July 1947, A922/Da74, HP, WCL.

137. Dr. A. B. Xuma to A. W. G. Champion, 19 April 1947, AD843, HP, WCL.

138. James A Calata to H. Selby Msimang, 27 June 1947, A922/Da62, HP, WCL.

139. H. Selby Msimang to James A. Calata, 30 June 1947, A922/Da63, HP, WCL.

140. A. W. G. Champion to the President General, 31 August 1947, a922/ Da83, HP, WCL.

141. Walshe, *Rise of African Nationalism*, 349–61; and Clive Glaser, *The ANC Youth League* (Athens: Ohio University Press, 2012).

142. Walshe, *Rise of African Nationalism*, 349–61.

143. Ibid., 355.

144. Tim Couzens, *The New African: A Study of the Life and Work of H. I. E. Dhlomo* (Johannesburg: Ravan Press, 1985), 262.

145. Glaser, *ANC Youth League*, 35.

146. Jordan K. Ngubane, *An Unpublished Biography*, Carter-Karis Collection, CRL, 143–45.

147. T. R. H. White, "Z. K. Mathews and the Formation of the ANC Youth League at the University College of Fort Hare," *African Historical Review* 27, no. 1 (1995): 124–44; and Donovan Williams, *A History of the University College of Fort Hare, South Africa, the 1950s: The Waiting Years* (Lewiston, ID: Edwin Mellen Press, 2001), 33–36.

148. Sobukwe interviewed by Gerhart, 8 and 9 April 1970, not verbatim, 2422/A, HP, WCL.

149. White, "Formation of the ANC Youth League"; Adam Sitze, "Mandela and the Law," in *The Cambridge Companion to Nelson Mandela*, ed. Rita Bernard (Cambridge: Cambridge University Press, 2014), 137; and Soske, "Impossible Concept," 6.

150. Graeme Rosenberg, "Auto/Biographical Narratives and the Lives of Jordan Ngubane," *Alternation* 7, no. 1 (2000): 62–96.

151. This pragmatism changed in exile, where Ngubane came under the influence of US Afrocentric philosophy. See his novel *Ushaba: The Hurtle to Blood-River* (Washington, DC: Three Continents Press, 1974).

152. Peter [A. P.] Mda, "Jordan K. Ngubane: Portraits in Bronze," *Drum* (July 1954).

153. Ibid.

154. Ngubane was the author of the article discussed at the beginning of the introduction, "Bambulaleleni uGandhi?," *Inkundla ya Bantu*, 19 February 1948. His views will be explored further below.

155. Couzens, *New African*, 198–99.

156. These plays have received substantial scholarly attention. See Bhekizizwe Peterson, *Monarchs, Missionaries and African Intellectuals: African Theatre and the Unmaking of Colonial Marginality* (Trenton: Africa World Press, 2000); and Jennifer Wenzel, "Voices of Spectral and Textual Ancestors: Reading Tiyo Soga alongside HIE Dhlomo's *The Girl Who Killed to Save*," *Research in African Literatures* 36, no. 1 (2005): 51–73.

157. Ntongela Masilela, *The Cultural Modernity of H. I. E. Dhlomo* (Trenton: Africa World Press, 2007).

158. X. [Dhlomo], "On Durban," *Ilanga lase Natal*, 22 February 1947.

159. "Significance of Passive Resistance," *Inkundla ya Bantu*, 8 October 1947.

160. For Dhlomo at the rally, see Bridglal Pachai, *The International Aspects of the South Africa Indian Question, 1860–1971* (Cape Town: C Struik, 1971), 190; and Azzim Hassim, *The Lotus People* (Durban, Zaf.: The Institute of Black Research/Madiba Publishers, 2002), 92. Meer remembers Dhlomo's role as key, but focuses on an article republished in *Forum*. I. Meer, *A Fortunate Man*, 121–22.

161. Elinor Sisulu, *Walter and Albertina Sisulu: In Our Lifetime* (Claremont, Zaf.: David Philip Publishers, 2003), 113.

162. Letter by Isharina [A. P. Mda], "Congress Going Communist?," *Inkundla ya Bantu*, 10 April 1947.

163. "Straight Thinking on the Indian Problem," *Inkundla ya Bantu*, 20 February 1947.

164. Sometimes this was in the form of a backhanded warning. See "Weekly Review and Commentary," *Ilanga lase Natal*, 1 June 1946.

165. R. M. Nkopo to Dr. A. B. Xuma, 13 August 1948, AD843, HP, WCL.

166. "Our Fight," AD 2186/Fa6, HP, WCL.

167. Anthony Sampson, *Mandela: The Authorised Biography* (London: Harper Collins, 1999), 62–63.

168. Philip Bonner and Noor Nieftagodien, *Alexandra: A History* (Johannesburg: Witwatersrand University Press, 2008), 129.

169. Gerhart, *Black Power in South Africa*, 145–64; Fredrickson, *Black Liberation*, 280–86; and Glaser, ANC *Youth League*, 51–66.

CHAPTER 3

1. Ngubane, *Unpublished Biography*, CRL, 133

2. See Kirk, "Community in Conflict"; L. K. Ladlua, "The Cato Manor Riots 1959–60" (MA thesis, University of Natal, 1985); Tim Nuttall, "'It Seems Peace but It Can Be War': The Durban 'Riots' and the Struggle for the City" (paper presented at the *12th National Conference* of the *South African Historical Society*, Pietermaritzburg, Zaf.: University of Natal, 1989); E. C. Webster, "The 1949 Durban 'Riots'—A Case Study in Race and Class," in *Working Papers in Southern African Studies*, ed. P. L. Bonner (Johannesburg: University of the Witwatersrand, 1977); and A. Desai, "Context for Violence."

3. Moodley, "Ambivalence of Survival Politics," 450.

4. Razia Timol and Tutuzile Mazibuko, *Soweto: A People's Response; Sample Survey of the Attitudes of People in Durban to the Soweto Violence of June 1976* (Durban, Zaf.: Institute for Black Research, 1976).

5. On Inanda, see Heather Hughes, "Violence in Inanda, August 1985," *Journal of Southern African Studies* 13, no. 3 (1987): 331–54.

6. See, for example, A. Hassim, *Lotus People*; I. Meer, *A Fortunate Man*; and Fatima Meer, *Portrait of Indian South Africans* (Durban, Zaf.: Avon House, 1969), 36.

7. Edwards, chapter 3 in "Mkhumbane, Our Home."

8. For the pogrom as the origin point of African initiative and business, see A. W. G. Champion, *The Views of Mahlathi: Writings of A.W.G. Champion a Black South African* , ed. M. W. Swanson, trans. E. R. Dahle (Pietermaritzburg, Zaf.: University of Natal Press, 1982), 68–69.

9. For an extended discussion of this problem, see Jonathon Glassman, *War of Words, War of Stones: Racial Thought and Violence in Colonial Zanzibar* (Bloomington: Indiana University Press, 2011), 230–63. I would like to thank Catherine Burns, Nafisa Sheik, and Julie Parle for pushing me to think more about the language of violence in this chapter.

10. "The Durban Riots," *Inkundla ya Bantu*, 22 January 1949.

11. Mufti, *Enlightenment in the Colony*,13.

12. Edwards, "Swing the Assegai Peacefully?," 63.

13. For the importance of African soldiers and foreign sailors, see ibid., 64.

14. See, for example, "Contrasts, Contradictions, and Impossibilities," *Ilanga lase Natal*, 31 July 1948.

15. See Rebecca Karl, *Staging the World: Chinese Nationalism at the Turn of the Twentieth Century* (Durham: Duke University Press, 2002).

16. "India's Independence and Africans," *Ilanga lase Natal*, 23 August 1947.

17. "In Durban and Other Parts," *Indian Opinion*, 22 August 1947.

18. "Celebrations in Johannesburg," *Indian Opinion*, 22 August 1947.

19. See, for example, "India and Ourselves," *Ilanga lase Natal*, 14 June 1947.

20. "India's Independence and Africans," *Ilanga lase Natal*, 23 August 1947.

21. An exception is the brief mention of the march from Natal to the Transvaal in Ngubane, "Bambulaleleni uGandhi?," *Inkundla ya Bantu*, 19 February 1948.

22. "Gandhi," *Inkundla ya Bantu*, 4 February 1948.

23. "Weekly Review and Commentary," *Ilanga lase Natal*, 7 February 1948.

24. See "Africans and the U.N.," *Ilanga lase Natal*, 8 March 1947.

25. "Comments on Events," *Inkundla ya Bantu*, first fortnight, April 1946.

26. "Policy on Dependent Territories, Note Written 15 September 1946, External Affairs Department File No. 6(76)-cc/46," pp. 31–34/n., National Archives of India. Reprinted in *Selected Works of Jawaharlal Nehru*, ser. 2, vol. 1, ed. S. Gopal (New Delhi: Jawaharlal Nehru Memorial Fund, 1984), 445–49.

27. "Pan-Asiatic Conference," *Inkundla ya Bantu*, 27 March 1947.

28. "India and Ourselves," *Ilanga lase Natal*, 14 June 1947.

29. Robert Mangaliso Sobukwe, "The 1959 Pan Africanist Manifesto," in *Speeches of Mangaliso Sobukwe from 1949–1959 and other Documents of the Pan-Africanist Congress of Azania* (New York: PAC of Azania Office, n.d.), 43.

30. Notes for autobiography in notebook entitled Draft Topics, 6 January 1960, Luthuli Papers (LP) file 12, Center for Research Libraries, University of Chicago (hereafter CRL). The underlining was in the original.

31. For examples of the Bantustan Policy discussed as Partition, see Cyril Ray, "Dr Malan's Mission," *Spectator*, 14 July 1950; "Partition by Colour in South Africa: Hatred Calls to Hatred," *Jerusalem Post*, 11 December 1952; Patrick Duncan, "Inside Strijdom's South Africa," *Africa Today* 3, no. 3 (1956): 2–6; and "Partition in South Africa?," *Jerusalem Post*, 6 November, 1959. My thanks to Lauren Laframboise for research assistance on this question.

32. Nelson Mandela, "Verwoerd's Tribalism," in *No Easy Walk to Freedom* (Cape Town: Kwela Books, 2013), 99–115.

33. See Luthuli on this score: "The Road to Freedom: Let Us Be Clear of Our Goals," draft address to the NIC, no date [late 1952?], LP 4, CRL.

34. According to one account: "When he arrived an Indian came and took a paper from Madonda. When he had taken the paper the India said when the boy asked him for the money, he said, 'Fuck off!' He took him and pushed him over there so that the boy crashed into a window." Dlamini interviewed

by Mkhize, 14 June 1981, KCAV 305, KCAL. The Riots Commission Report contains the following version: "A Native boy, 14 years of age, had words with an Indian shop assistant, 16 years of age, and slapped the latter's face. The Indian youth lodged a complaint with his employer, also an Indian, who came out of the Indian Market to Victoria Street and assaulted the Native boy. In the tussle, the Native's head accidentally crashed through the glass of a shop window." Van den Heever, *Report of the Commission*, 5. Basanth was later convicted on a charge of assault and sentenced to a fine £1 or seven days hard labor.

35. "Eye-Witness Account of the Durban Riots," *Inkundla ya Bantu*, 29 January 1949.

36. T. Nuttall, "It Seems Peace," 16.

37. Van den Heever, *Report of the Commission*, 4.

38. Z. A. Ngcobo interviewed by Simeon Zulu, 13 September 1980, Killie Campbell Oral History Project (KCAV 361), KCAL.

39. "Eye-Witness Account," *Inkundla ya Bantu*, 29 January 1949.

40. M. S. Manyathi interviewed by C. N. Shum, 16 September 1980, Killie Campbell Oral History Project (KCAV 327), KCAL.

41. H. Dhlomo, "How Long, O Lord!," *Ilanga lase Natal*, 22 January 1949.

42. See T. Nuttall, "It Seems Peace" 18; and David Hemson, "Class Consciousness and Migrant Workers: Dock Workers of Durban" (PhD diss., University of Warwick, 1979), 351–53.

43. "Race Rioting in Durban Inflicts Grave Damage to Indians," *Indian Opinion*, 21 January 1949.

44. These details are taken from interviews, in particular Hadebe interviewed by Mabaso, 26 April 1981, KCAV 308, KCAL. For an African whose mother sent him away out of fear he might be attacked, see William Maseko interviewed by E. N. Yengwa, 22 September 1981, Killie Campbell Oral History Project (KCAV 342), KCAL.

45. T. Nuttall, "It Seems Peace," 23.

46. "Eye-Witness Account," *Inkundla ya Bantu*, 29 January 1949.

47. "The NEUM on Riots," *Inkundla ya Bantu*, 19 February 1949. *Indian Opinion* reports violence in Pietermaritzburg occurring on Wednesday, 19 January. "Race Rioting in Durban," *Indian Opinion*, 21 January 1949.

48. "Riot Deaths and Figures," *Ilanga lase Natal*, 29 January 1949.

49. My gratitude to Julie Parle and Catherine Burns for pushing me to think through the stakes of the terms "riots" and "pogrom."

50. Kenneth Kirkwood, "Failure of a Report," in *The Durban Riots and After*, ed. Maurice Webb and Kenneth Kirkwood (Johannesburg: South Africa Institute of Race Relations, 1949), 19. See also Palmer, *The Indian in Natal*, 158.

51. This quote is a description of the Red Summer of 1919 from David Levering Lewis, *W. E. B. Du Bois: Biography of a Race, 1868–1919* (New York: Henry Holt, 1993), 579.

52. "Uthuthuva eThekwini," *Ilanga lase Natal*, 22 January 1949.

53. H. Dhlomo, "How Long, O Lord!," *Ilanga lase Natal*, 22 January 1947.

54. "Uthuthuva eThekwini," *Ilanga lase Natal*, 22 January 1949.

55. H. Dhlomo, "How Long, O Lord!," *Ilanga lase Natal*, 22 January 1947.

56. "Eye-Witness Account," *Inkundla ya Bantu*, 29 January 1949.

57. This is particularly stressed in Edward's account.

58. Manyathi interviewed by Shum, 16 September 1980, KCAV 327, KCAL.

59. See chapter 1, this book, for a discussion of arrogance as a trope.

60. Tanya Dlamini interviewed by B. C. Mkhize, 17 June 1981, Killie Campbell Oral History Project (KCAV 305), KCAL.

61. Hadebe interviewed by Mabaso, 26 April 1981, KCAV 308, KCAL.

62. "The Riots and Propaganda," *Inkundla ya Bantu*, 22 January 1949. See also "Eye-Witness Account," *Inkundla ya Bantu*, 29 January 1949.

63. Goonam, *Coolie Doctor: An Autobiography* (Durban, Zaf.: Madiba Publishers, 1991), 138–39.

64. Thank you to Liz Gunner for this information.

65. Goonam, *Coolie Doctor*, 138. Note that she reinforces the generalization of "African" violence by depicting the attackers in racial terms even while she argues against the involvement of all Africans.

66. "Eye-Witness Account," *Inkundla ya Bantu*, 29 January 1949. On the basis of her own experience, Moodley writes: "The writer's own memory of the riots brings to the fore the assistance many Africans, at risk to themselves, gave to Indians by shielding them from activists." Moodley, "Ambivalence of Survival Politics," 449.

67. "Heroes of the Riots," *Inkundla ya Bantu*, 5 February 1949.

68. "Weekly Review and Commentary," *Ilanga lase Natal*, 1 June 1946.

69. "Riots and Propaganda," *Ilanga lase Natal*, 29 January 1949.

70. The first sentence of the *Ilanga* editorial on the Riots is "The inevitable has happened."

71. A. Desai, "Context for Violence,"152.

72. Podbrey, *In Search of the Party*, 109.

73. "Statement issued by the Joint Meeting of African and Indian Leaders," 6 February 1949, in Karis and Gerhart, *From Protest to Challenge*, 2:287. The Transvaal ANC and Indian Congress released an earlier joint statement appealing for calm on 15 January. Press Statement signed by R. S. Ramohanne, 15 January 1949, A922/Ec5, HP, WCL.

74. Ngubane, *Unpublished Biography*, 136–37. According to Ngubane, Mda intended this address to be published, but it was later lost.

75. For an elaboration of this distinction, see chapter 2 of this book.

76. Luli Callinicos, *Oliver Tambo: Beyond the Engeli Mountains* (Claremont, Zaf.: David Philip Publishers, 2004), 165.

77. Sisulu, *Albertina and Walter Sisulu*, 120–22.

78. M. R. Sobukwe, "Address on Behalf of the Graduating Class at Fort Hare College, Delivered at the 'Completers' Social, October 21, 1949," in Karis and Gerhart, *From Protest to Challenge*, 2:335.

79. Ibid.

80. "Programme of Action, Statement of Policy Adopted at the ANC Annual Conference, December 17, 1949," in Karis and Gerhart, *From Protest to Challenge*, 2:337.

81. "Press Conference Held by Dr. Y. M. Dadoo, the President of the Transvaal Indian Congress," 27 January 1949, AD 843, HP, WCL.

82. Fatima Meer, "African and Indian in Durban," *Africa South in Exile* 4, no. 4 (July-September 1960): 30.

83. "The Racial Disturbances," *Indian Opinion*, 21 January 1949.

84. I discuss the coverage of the Riots in *Indian Opinion* and *Ilanga* more fully below.

85. Van den Heever, *Report of the Commission*, 5; and H. Dhlomo, "How Long, O Lord!," *Ilanga lase Natal*, 22 January 1949.

86. Ibid., 153.

87. "Indians and Africans Must Unite," *Inkundla ya Bantu*, 12 February 1949. The amount of aid was £3,500. The article also appears in *Indian Opinion*, 11 February 1949.

88. I. Meer, *A Fortunate Man*, 117.

89. "Durban Massacre—First Fruit of Apartheid," *Paravasi*, April 1949.

90. Several articles in the African press warned Africans against a newfound solicitousness on the part of Europeans: "All of a sudden the European community of Durban has discovered that the African has been cruelly exploited by the Indian; that he has been charged extortionate rentals by the Indian and that, after all, 'he is a better human being' than the Indian." "Timeo Danaos . . ." *Inkundla ya Bantu*, 12 February 1949.

91. H. Dhlomo, "How Long, O Lord!," *Ilanga lase Natal*, 22 January 1949.

92. Ibid.

93. For the prevalence of this narrative in the 1950s, see Edwards, "Mkhubane, Our Home," 50–51.

94. H. Dhlomo, "How Long, O Lord!," *Ilanga lase Natal*, 22 January 1949.

95. "Poisoning the Minds of Indians and Africans," *Indian Opinion*, 28 January 1949.

96. "Racial Disturbances," *Indian Opinion*, 21 January 1949.

97. Ibid. See the similar language in "Statement submitted by the Natal Indian Organization to the Chairman and Members of the Judicial Community Appointed to Enquire into the Durban Riots (1949)," KCAL, 3.

98. For the origins of the idea of "Indian industriousness" in the colonial economy of labor extraction, and its subsequent contrast to African "indolence" by the colonial state (and later Gandhi), see Sheik, "Colonial Rites," 241–43.

99. Ngubane, *Unpublished Autobiography*, 346, HP, WCL.

100. Uma Dhupelia-Mesthrie, *Gandhi's Prisoner?: The Life of Gandhi's Son Manilal* (Cape Town: Kwela Books, 2005), 336, 340–42, 372.

101. "Indo-African Friction and Oppressors," *Inkundla ya Bantu*, 19 February 1949.

102. After consulting with Indian leaders in Pietermaritzburg, Msimang discovered they were ignorant of Xuma's proposed meeting. He warned Xuma: "You will achieve very little in the way you are going about this delicate question." A subsequent letter reiterated the point: "The focus should be in Natal. To send the conference away from the explosive centre would be begging the question." H. Selby Msimang to Dr. A. B. Xuma, 31 January 1949, AD843, HP, WCL.

103. "Out-Moded Leadership" *Ilanga lase Natal*, 19 March 1949.

104. Mary Benson, *The African Patriots: The Story of the African National Congress of South Africa* (London: Faber and Faber, 1963), 153. Benson's source is unnamed.

105. "Out-Moded Leadership," *Ilanga lase Natal*, 19 March 1949.

106. "Indo-Africa Peace," *Inkundla ya Bantu*, 26 February 1949.

107. "Comments on Events," *Inkundla ya Bantu*, 26 February 1949.

108. "Durban Riots," *Inkundla ya Bantu*, 22 January 1949.

109. In particular, the Youth League harshly criticized the Doctors' Pact. "Plan to Stop the Riots: Statement by Working Committee of Congress Youth League," *Inkundla ya Bantu*, 26 February 1949.

110. "Joint Statement by Leaders," *Ilanga lase Natal*, 19 February 1949.

111. "Advisory Board Meeting: A Call to Africans," *Ilanga lase Natal*, 19 February 1949.

112. "A Strange, if Remarkable Meeting," *Ilanga lase Natal*, 26 February 1949.

113. Edwards, "Swing the Assegai Peacefully?," 73–74.

114. N. Nomnganga, "Is Natal Really Impossible Politically?," *Inkundla ya Bantu*, 5 February 1949.

115. "Lack of Foresight in Our Leadership," *Ilanga lase Natal*, 19 March 1949.

116. Zulu-language article in *Inkundla* from August 1949. Quoted in Ime J. Ukpanah, "Yearning to Be Free: *Inkundla ya Bantu* (Bantu Forum) as a Mirror and Mediator of the African National Struggle in South Africa, 1938–1951" (PhD diss., University of Houston, 1993), 192.

117. L. Kuper, *African Bourgeoisie*, 301–6.

118. "Statement to City Council by Native Representatives," 16 January 1949, KCAL 309059. These demands were subsequently publicized in *Ilanga*, which reported that Chief Isaac Zulu was among the representatives who addressed the Durban City Council. "African Leaders on the Riots," *Ilanga lase Natal*, 22 January 1949.

119. "Comments on Events," *Inkundla ya Bantu*, 26 February 1949.

120. Ukpanah, "Yearning to Be Free," 305–6.

121. Resolutions at Durban African Public Meeting about Riots, 8 March 1949, KCAL 309059. See also L. Kuper, *African Bourgeoisie*, 301–2.

122. "Durban Africans Rush to Become Traders," *Ilanga lase Natal*, 5 March 1949.

123. "Boycott of Indian Establishments, *Inkundla ya Bantu*, 12 February 1949.

124. L. Kuper, *African Bourgeosie*, 302.

125. "Communists Angry," *Inkundla ya Bantu*, 30 April 1949.

126. Edwards, "Mkhumbane, Our Home," 214–15.

127. Ibid., 214. Champion's own accounts of the Riots differed over the years, growing more anti-Indian with time. Champion, *Views of Mahlathi*, 68–69.

128. "Co-operation with Indians," *Inkundla ya Bantu*, 14 May 1949.

129. Quoted in Frederikse, *Unbreakable Thread*, 52.

130. Nomnganga, "Is Natal Really Impossible?," *Inkundla ya Bantu*, 5 February 1949. This style of politics is brilliantly analyzed in Shula Marks, *The Ambiguities of Dependence in South Africa: Class, Nationalism, and the State in Twentieth-Century Natal* (Baltimore: Johns Hopkins University Press, 1986).

131. See A. W. G. Champion to Mr. Moodley, 24 February 1949, A922/ c53, HP, WCL.

132. Ngubane, *Unpublished Memoir*, 138.

133. "Politicians, Publics Servants, Women, Herbalists All Meet in Bloemfontein," *Bantu World*, December 24, 1949.

134. Walshe, *Rise of African Nationalism*, 398.

135. Ngubane, *Unpublished Biography*, 139.

136. "The Annual Provincial Conference," *Inkundla ya Bantu*, 23 July 1949.

137. Ngubane, *Unpublished Biography*, 154.

138. Walshe, *Rise of African Nationalism*, 399–400.

139. L. Kuper, *African Bourgeoisie*, 303.

140. Ashwin Desai quotes a 1949 *Ilanga* article written by a cooperative movement leader: The cooperative movement was "much more powerful, in membership and accumulation of funds, than the Congress." A. Desai, "Context for Violence," 91.

141. Edwards, "Mkhumbane, Our Home," 200; and L. Kuper, *African Bourgeoisie*, 302–6.

142. Edwards, "Mkhumbane, Our Home," 201.

143. F. Meer, "African and Indian," 33.

144. Phyllis Naidoo, *Footprints in Grey Street* (Durban, Zaf.: Far Ocean Jetty, 2002), 29.

145. Moodley, "Ambivalence of Survival Politics," 450.

146. I. Meer, *A Fortunate Man*, 119.

147. Goonam, *Coolie Doctor*, 134.

148. Ngubane, *Unpublished Biography*, 138.

CHAPTER 4

1. Moodley, "Ambiguity of Survival Politics," 445.

2. "Letter from Jeremiah Sithole to the Manager, Native Affairs Department, Durban," 10 August 1951 (KCM 99/42/35a/64), S. St.I. Bourquin Papers (BP), KCAL.

3. "Evidence on the Causes of the Race Riots," January 1949 (KCM 99/42/33/11), BP, KCAL.

4. Kirk, "Community in Conflict," 114.

5. See, for example Dube, "The Riots," *Ilanga lase Natal*, 29 January 1949.

6. Goonam, *Coolie Doctor*, 138.

7. Edwards, "Mkhumbane, Our Home," 51.

8. See chapter 6.

9. Hemson, "Class Consciousness and Migrant Workers," 125.

10. Ibid., 163.

11. P. R. Maylam, "Aspects of African Urbanization in the Durban Area before 1940," in *Natal in the Union, 1931–1961: A Collection of Papers on Developments in Natal, Presented at a Workshop at the University of Natal, October 29–30, 1980* (Pietermaritzburg, Zaf.: Department of Historical and Political Studies, 1981), 11.

12. Maynard W. Swanson, "The Sanitation Syndrome: Bubonic Plague and Urban Native Policy in the Cape Colony," *Journal of African History* 18, no. 3 (1977): 387–410.

13. For a discussion of missionaries and the introduction of Victorian ideas of domesticity and female sexuality in South Africa, see Cherryl Walker, ed., *Women and Gender in Southern Africa to 1945* (Cape Town: David Philip Publishers, 1990), especially chapters 3, 5, and 8.

14. Marks, "Patriotism, Patriarchy and Purity," 217.

15. Ibid., 225. See also Shula Marks, *Not Either an Experimental Doll: The Separate Worlds of Three South African Women* (London: The Women's Press, 1987).

16. Jeff Guy, "The Destruction and Reconstruction of Zulu Society," in *Industrialisation and Social Change in South Africa: African Class Formation, Culture, and Consciousness, 1870–1930*, ed. Shula Marks and Richard Rathbone (London: Longman, 1982), 187.

17. Deborah Gaitskell, "'Wailing for Purity': Prayer Unions, African Mothers and Adolescent Daughters, 1912–1940," in Shula and Rathbone, *Industrialisation and Social Change*, 341.

18. Marks, "Patriotism, Patriarchy and Purity," 225–30.

19. Ukpanah, "Yearning to Be Free," 167.

20. "Weekly Review and Commentary," *Ilanga lase Natal*, 23 July 1949.

21. Timothy Nuttall, "Class, Race and Nation: African Politics in Durban, 1929–1949" (PhD diss., University of Oxford, 1991), 260. See also "Homes for African Women," *Ilanga lase Natal*, 10 August 1946.

22. "Woman," *Ilanga lase Natal*, 25 May 1946.

23. "Weekly Review and Commentary," *Ilanga lase Natal*, 4 March 1950.

24. See L. Kuper, *African Bourgeoisie*, 113.

25. "Rolling Stone on Nurse Jane Maplank," *Ilanga lase Natal*, 24 February 1945; and "Rolling Stone on Nurse Jane Maplank," *Ilanga lase Natal*, 2 June 1945.

26. "Weekly Review and Commentary," *Ilanga lase Natal*, 16 February 1946.

27. A parallel discourse can be found in Indain newspapers. See "Liberals and Indians," *Indian Opinion*, 19 July 1946.

28. "Weekly Review and Commentary," *Ilanga lase Natal*, 1947.

29. "The African Family," *Ilanga lase Natal*, 25 September 1948.

30. "A Painless World?," *Ilanga lase Natal*, 8 May 1948.

31. For a discussion of this ideal in France, see Kristen Ross, *Fast Cars and Clean Bodies: Decolonization and the Reordering of French Culture* (New York: October Books, 1995). For southern Africa, see Timothy Burke, *Lifebuoy Men, Lux Women: Commodification, Consumption, and Cleanliness in Modern Zimbabwe* (Durham: Duke University Press, 1996).

32. "Women's Corner," *Ilanga lase Natal*, 22 November 1947.

33. Lynn M. Thomas, "The Modern Girl and Racial Respectability in 1930s South Africa," *Journal of African History* 47 (2006): 461–90.

34. Edwards, "Mkhumbane, Our Home," 9.

35. Vilakazi with Mthethwa and Mpanza, *Revitalization of African Society*, 24–25, 32–35. For the importance of Shembe's teaching on adultery, see Gerald O. West, "Reassessing Shembe 'Remembering the Bible': Isaiah Shembe's Instructions on Adultery," *Neotestamentica* 40, no. 1 (2006): 157–84.

36. Bengt G. M. Sundkler, *Bantu Prophets in South Africa*, 2nd ed. (London: Oxford University Press, 1964), 338–42.

37. Isaiah Shembe and Londa Shembe, "The Prayer to Confess Their Sins on Behalf of His Nation," in *The Scriptures of the amaNazaretha of EkuphaKameni: Selected Writings of the Zulu Prophets Isaiah and Londa Shembe*, ed. Irving Hexham, trans. Londa Shembe and Hans-Jürgen Becken (Calgary, Can.: University of Calgary Press, 1994), 46.

38. Isaiah Shembe, "The First Words of Advice of Shembe at Rosboom," in *The Man of Heaven and the Beautiful Ones of God*, ed. and trans. Liz Gunner (Durban, Zaf.: University of KwaZulu-Natal Press, 2004), 111. Thank you to Liz Gunner for bringing this sermon to my attention.

39. "Sithole to the Manager," 10 August 1951, KCM 99/42/35a/64.

40. H. Kuper, *Indian People in Natal*, xii.

41. See chapter 1, this book; and Bill Freund, "Indian Women and the Changing Character of the Working Class Indian Household in Natal 186–1990," *Journal of Southern African Studies* 17, no. 3 (1991): 414–29.

42. H. Kuper, *Indian People in Natal*, 26.

43. F. Meer, *Portrait of Indian South Africans*, 87.

44. H. R. Burrows, "Indian Life and Labour in Natal," *Race Relations* 10, no. 1 (1943): 18; F. Meer, *Portrait of Indian South Africans*, 66–67; and H. Kuper, *Indian People in Natal*, 102.

45. H. Kuper, *Indian People in Natal*, xv.

46. See University of Natal Economics Department, *Durban Housing Survey*, 293; Maasdorp and Pillay, *Urban Relocation and Racial Segregation*, 85; F. Meer, *Portrait of Indian South Africans*, 66; and H. Kuper, *Indian People in Natal*, 97–102.

47. Freund, *Insiders and Outsiders*, 37. See also P. D. Hey, *The Rise of the Natal Indian Elite* (Pietermaritzburg, Zaf.: The Natal Witness, 1961), 17.

48. See Freund, "Indian Women," 421; "School for Indian Girls," *Indian Opinion*, 25 July 1935; and Molnira Banu, "Muslim Women in South Africa," *Great Ramadan*, no date [mid-1950s] (KCM 17060), KCAL.

49. F. Meer, *Portrait of Indian South Africans*, 115.

50. H. Kuper, *Indian People in Natal*, 139.

51. Susan Bayly, *Caste, Society, and Politics in India: From the Eighteenth Century to the Modern Age* (Cambridge: Cambridge University Press, 1999), 7. See also Nicholas B. Dirks, *Castes of Mind: Colonialism and the Making of Modern India* (Princeton: Princeton University Press, 2001); C. J. Fuller, Introduction to *Caste Today*, ed. C. J. Fuller (Dehli: Oxford University Press, 1997), 5–7; and David Washbrook, "Progress and Problems: South Asian Economic and Social History c1720–1860," *Modern Asian Studies* 22, no. 1 (1988): 81–82.

52. S. Bayly, *Caste, Society, and Politics in India*, 187–90.

53. H. Kuper, *Indian People in Natal*, 18–43; Birbal Rambiritch and Pierre L. van den Berghe, "Caste in a Natal Hindu Community," *African Studies* 20 (1961): 217–25; Mesthrie, *Language in Indenture*, 8; and Rehana Ebr.-Valley, *Kala Pani: Caste and Colour in South Africa* (Cape Town: Kwela Books, 2001). This approach has several problems in the South African context. First, it fails to address the regional differences in caste understandings in India. Second, it assumes that all Indian migrants equally understood and accepted the Brahminical construction of caste hierarchy. Third, this approach fails to historicize caste in terms of changes occurring within India both before and, especially, after the experience of migration. Fourth, this approach conflates the experiences and attitudes of indentured and passenger Indians.

54. Sidney Mintz and Richard Price, *The Birth of African-American Culture: An Anthropological Approach* (Boston: Beacon Press, 1992).

55. Vasanth Kannabiran and Kalpana Kannabiran, "Caste and Gender: Understanding Dynamics of Power and Violence," in *Gender and Caste*, ed.

Anupama Rao (New Delhli: Kali for Women, 2003), 254. See also Sumit Sarkar, *Writing Social History* (New Delhi: Oxford University Press, 1997), 220.

56. Historians point to a number of factors leading to the attenuation of rigid caste orthodoxy. For a summary of debate over caste in Trinidad, see Tejaswini Niranjana, *Mobilizing India: Women, Music and Migration between India and Trinidad* (Durham: Duke University Press, 2006), 38–41.

57. H. Kuper, *Indian People in Natal*, 30–32.

58. See Agehananda Bharati, *The Asians in East Africa: Jayhind and Uhuru* (Chicago: Nelson Hall Company, 1972), 23–94; and H. S. Morris, *The Indians in Uganda: Caste and Sect in a Plural Society* (Hertfordshire, Eng.: Weidenfield and Nicolson, 1968), 60–62.

59. H. Kuper, *Indian People in Natal*, 32.

60. Ibid., 36.

61. Rambiritch and van den Berghe as well as H. Kuper describe the persistence of endogamy within varnas. However, it appears that both studies simply assign varna status to their non-elite informants. Kuper states that only 23 percent of Durban high school students could provide a "traditional caste name" in one survey. Ibid., 39.

62. Rajend Mesthrie, *English in Language Shift: The History, Structure and Sociolinguistics of South African Indian English* (Cambridge: Cambridge University Press, 2006).

63. See chapter 2 for the importance of women in the Passive Resistance Campaign. For a discussion of the place of women and gender during the period of Gandhi's campaigns, see Radhika Mongia, "Gender and the Historiography of Gandhian *Satyagraha* in South Africa," *Gender and History* 18, no. 1 (2006): 130–49.

64. Pachai, *International Aspects*, 119. See also "Memorandum on Indian Marriages" submitted by the Natal Indian Organization to the Protector of Indian Immigrants, Stanger Street, Durban, 17 January 1951, KCAL.

65. See Swan, *South African Experience*.

66. Freund, "Indian Women," 422–23.

67. Hey, *Natal Indian Elite*, 22–23.

68. Kalpana Hiralal, "Married to the Struggle: For Better or Worse; Wives of Indian Antiapartheid Activists in Natal; The Untold Narratives," *New Contree*, no. 70, spec. ed. (2014): 89.

69. S. Coopan and B. A. Naidoo, "Indian Adjustments to Urbanization," *Race Relations* 22, no. 1 (1955): 15.

70. Birbal Rambiritch, "An Investigation into Some Aspects of the Education of Indian Girls in Natal" (MA thesis, University of Natal, 1955), 52–53.

71. See H. Kuper, *Indian People of Natal*; and Gavin Maasdorp, *A Natal Indian Community: A Socio-economic Study in the Tongaat-Verlun Area* (Pietermaritzburg, Zaf.: University of Natal Department of Economics, 1968).

72. Freund, "Indian Women," 418.

73. M. Sirkari Naidoo, "As an Indian Sees Natal," in *The Indian — Citizen or Subject?*, ed. Maurice Webb and M. Sirkari Naidoo (Johannesburg: South Africa Institute of Race Relations, 1947), 29.

74. "Resolutions Passed by the South African Indian Youth Culture Conference Held at Gandhi Hall, Johannesburg on the 9 April, 1944," A410, HP, WCL. This conference received greetings from Hindu organizations throughout South Africa and India, as well as Yusuf Dadoo for the Transvaal Indian Congress, the South African government, and African Youth League.

75. Achin Vanaik, *The Furies of Indian Communalism: Religion, Modernity, and Secularism* (London: Verso, 1997), 31. See also Aijaz Ahmad, *Lineages of the Present: Ideology and Politics in Contemporary South Asia* (London: Verso, 2000).

76. Ayesha Jalal, "Exploding Communalism: The Politics of Muslim Identity in South Asia," in *Nationalism, Democracy, and Development*, ed. Sugata Bose and Ayesha Jalal (New Delhi: Oxford University Press, 1998), 78.

77. See "Mixed Marriages," *Inkundla ya Bantu*, 4 June 1949; and Van den Heever, *Report of the Commission*, 14.

78. M. Naidoo, "As an Indian Sees Natal," 29. See also S. Coopan and A. D. Lazarus, "The Indian as an Integral Part of South African Society," in *The Indian as a South African* (Johannesburg: South African Institute of Race Relations, 1956), 67; and Palmer, *The Indian in Natal*, 27.

79. G. Monty Naicker, *A Historical Synopsis of the Indian Question in South Africa* (Durban, Zaf.: Killie Campbell Africana Library, 1993), 29.

80. "Statement Submitted by the Natal Indian Organisation to the Chairman and Members of the Judicial Commission Appointed to Enquire into the Durban Riots, 1949," KCAL.

81. For this discourse, see Mohamed Adhikari, "'God Made the White Man, God Made the Black Man . . .': Popular Racial Stereotyping of Coloured People in Apartheid South Africa," *South African Historical Journal* 55, no. 1 (2006): 142–64. See also Baderoon, *Regarding Muslims*, 87–89.

82. "Tools of the Indians," *Ilanga lase Natal*, 27 August 1955.

83. H. Dhlomo, "How Long, O Lord!," *Ilanga lase Natal*, 22 January 1949.

84. For more on Katherine Mayo, see Mrinalini Sinha, Editor's Introduction in *Selections from Mother India*, by Katherine Mayo, ed. Mrinalini Sinha (New Delhi: Kali for Women, 1998), 1–61.

85. "Rolling Stone on Coloureds," *Ilanga lase Natal*, 9 March 1946.

86. Quoted in Kirk, "1949 Durban Riots," 83.

87. L. Kuper, *African Bourgeoisie*, 221, 306.

88. For parallel debates in India, see Tanika Sarkar, *Hindu Wife, Hindu Nation: Community, Religion, and Cultural Nationalism* (New Delhi: Permanent Black, 2001), 81.

89. X. [H. I. E. Dhlomo], "Stopping the Bus," *Ilanga lase Natal*, 10 January 1948.

90. Van den Heever, *Report of the Commission*, 14.

91. "Registration of Indian Marriages," *Indian Opinion*, 30 August 1935.

92. University of Natal Economics Department, *Experiment at Edendale: An Economic Survey of a Peri-urban Settlement of Africans and Indians in Natal* (Pietermaritizburg, Zaf.: University of Natal Press, 1951), 36.

93. "United Front or Separate Ways?," *Ilanga lase Natal*, 26 March 1949.

94. "Durban Exposed," *Drum*, July 1952.

95. Personal communication from Omar Badsha, Pretoria, 25 April 2006.

96. An African witness before the riots commission, for example, reported that "his sister-in-law as robbed and ravished by an Indian bus-driver and his friends." Van den Heever, *Report of the Commission*, 13.

97. For discussions of rumor see: Ranajit Guha, *Elementary Aspects of Peasant Insurgency in Colonial India* (Delhi: Oxford University Press, 1983); Steven Hahn, "'Extravagant Expectations' of Freedom: Rumour, Political Struggle, and the Christmas Insurrection Scare of 1865 in the American South," *Past and Present* 157 (1997): 122–58; and George Rude, *The Crowd in the French Revolution* (Oxford: Oxford University Press, 1959).

98. "University Celebrations and the Riots," *Ilanga lase Natal*, 26 March 1949.

99. Edwards, "Mkhumbane, Our Home," 213. See also chapter 6.

100. Institute for Social Research, *Baumannville: A Study of an Urban African Community*, Natal Regional Survey, report 6 (Cape Town: Oxford University Press, 1959), 68–70.

101. "Indian Men and African Women," *Ilanga lase Natal*, 30 August 1955.

102. "Ladies, Please Beware!," *Ilanga lase Natal*, 24 September 1955.

103. H. Dhlomo, "How Long, O Lord!," *Ilanga lase Natal*, 22 January 1949. See also Moya, "Indians and Segregation," *Ilanga lase Natal*, 7 September 1946; and "Rolling Stone on Segregation," *Ilanga lase Natal*, 1 March 1947.

104. "Indo-African Race Relations," *Ilanga lase Natal*, 17 January 1953.

105. Shalini Puri, "Race, Rape, and Representation: Indo-Caribbean Women and Cultural Nationalism," *Cultural Critique*, Spring 1997, 127

106. Maurice Webb, "The Indian in South Africa: Towards a Solution of Conflict," pamphlet reprinted from *Race Relations* 11, no. 1 (1944): 9.

107. Moodley, "Ambiguities of Survival Politics," 450

108. Personal communication, Vishnu Padayachee, 26 May 2006; and J. Naidoo, *Coolie Location*, 5.

109. Ngcobo interviewed by Zulu, 13 September 1980, KCAV 361, KCAL.

110. Personal communication, Phyllis Naidoo, Durban, 24 May 2006.

111. For an example from West Bengal, see Urvashi Butalia, *The Other Side of Silence: Voices from the Partition of Indian* (Durham: Duke University Press, 2000), 31.

112. Moodley, "Ambiguities of Survival Politics," 450.

113. F. Meer, *Portrait of Indian South Africans*, 116.

114. Letter to S. Borquin, 28 April 1965 (KCM 99/42/35/29), BP, KCAL.

115. Letter to S. Borquin, no date (KCM 99/42/35a/32), BP, KCAL.

116. See Jacklyn Cock, *Maids and Madams: Domestic Workers under Apartheid*, rev. ed. (London: The Women's Press, 1989), 79–81.

117. Abrahams, "Can We Unite?," *Drum*, July 1952.

CHAPTER 5

1. Quoted in Goolam Vahed, "In the End It Was Academic: Responses to the Establishment of the University College for Indians," *Journal of Natal and Zulu History* 31 (2013): 22.

2. Ebr.-Valley, *Kala Pani*.

3. Albert Luthuli, "Some Aspect of the Apartheid Union Laws and Policy as Affecting Africans," paper presented to the Conference on the Group Areas Act convened by the Natal Indian Congress, 5–6 May 1956, LP file 4, CRL.

4. "Readers Forum," *Bantu World*, 10 May 1952.

5. "Readers Forum," *Bantu World*, 4 October 1952.

6. "Readers Forum," *Bantu World*, 10 May 1952.

7. "Readers Forum," *Bantu World*, 24 May 1952. Nhaplo responds in "Readers Forum," *Bantu World*, 31 May 1952.

8. Benjamin Pogrund, Draft article on Madyzuna [1962?], reel 2, document 477, Gerhart Papers (GP), CRL.

9. Peter Rodda, "Africanists Cut Loose," *Africa South*, July 1959, 23.

10. Veit Erlmann, *Nightsong: Performance, Power, and Practice in South Africa* (Chicago: University of Chicago Press, 1996), 61, 72, 76; and Gwen Ansell, *Soweto Blues: Jazz, Popular Music, and Politics in South Africa* (London: A&C Black, 2005), 59.

11. Can Themba, "Requiem for Sophiatown," in *Requiem for Sophiatown* (Johannesburg: Penguin Books, 2006), 54.

12. Nat Nakasa, "Quiet a Place, Fourteenth Street," in *The World of Nat Nakasa*, ed. Essop Patel (Johannesburg: Ravan Press, 1975), 9–11.

13. Lewis Nkosi, "Racialism Is an Evil that Must Be Fought," *Bantu World*, 12 November 1955.

14. See chapter 6, this book.

15. Logan Naidoo, *In the Shadow of Chief Albert Luthuli: Reflections of Goolam Suleman* (KwaDukuza, Zaf.: Luthuli Museum, 2010), 47.

16. This phrase comes from Rancière, *Politics of Aesthetics*. I want to thank Patricia Hayes for many helpful conversations about the concept of political aesthetics.

17. Walshe, *Rise of African Nationalism*, 16; and Scott Couper, *Albert Luthuli: Bound by Faith* (Scottsville, Zaf.: University of KwaZulu-Natal Press, 2012), 24.

18. "Freedom in the Air," *Drum*, July 1959.

19. Sebastian C. H. Kim, "The Kingdom of God versus the Church: The Debate at the Conference of the International Missionary Council, Tambaram, 1938," in *Interpreting Contemporary Christianity: Global Processes and Local Identities*, ed. Ogbu Kalu and Alaine Low (Grand Rapids: Wm. B. Eerdmans Publishing, 2008), 131–48.

20. Albert Luthuli, *Let My People Go* (London: Collins, 1962), 78–81.

21. L. Naidoo, *In the Shadow*, 7, 46. Naidoo references speeches on this topic in 1938 and 1945.

22. Mahtma Gandi [*sic*] Memorial on the Occasion of the Centenary Celebrations of the Washington University, USA, Luthuli Museum (LM), LutMus 2005.02.001. Couper suggests that this piece of writing was a speech delivered at Howard University during Luthuli's trip to the United States in 1948. Couper, *Bound by Faith*, 49–50. However, Luthuli concluded the document with "signed" and included his signature, indicating a draft meant for retyping rather than a speech. It was most likely a statement requested by the event organizers. Furthermore, the date of Luthuli's trip does not correspond with Howard's centenary (1967). Luthuli may have confused University of District Columbia (founded in 1951) with Washington, DC University. It is more likely, however, that the statement was written during the last months of his life. Luthuli refers to US Congressional support for civil rights. He is probably referring to the Civil Rights Act of 1964. My thanks to Yasmine Mosimann for research assistance on this question.

23. Luthuli, *Let My People Go*, 81.

24. Desai and Vahed, *Inside Indian Indenture*, 179.

25. Heather Hughes, "'The Coolies Will Elbow Us Out of the Country': African Reactions to Indian Immigration in the Colony of Natal, South Africa," *Labour History Review* 72 (2007): 155–68.

26. Albert Luthuli, Notes on chief meeting, Lower Tugela, 25 September 1951, LP file 8, CRL.

27. L. Naidoo, *In the Shadow*, 17.

28. I owe this point to conversations with Vishnu Padayachee and Rajend Mesthrie.

29. L. Naidoo, *In the Shadow*, 2–5.

30. Ibid., 7.

31. Ibid., 11.

32. Ibid., 38–42.

33. Ngubane, *Unpublished Biography*, 108.

34. Ibid., 147.

35. L. Naidoo, *In the Shadow*, 24.

36. Ibid., 27–29.

37. Soske, "Impossible Concept," 6–8.

38. Albert Luthuli, "How to Develop a Unified South Africa?," LP file 1, CRL. Luthuli quotes sections of an earlier speech, indicating that these notes were written after 1949. Luthuli, "The Christian and Political Issues," in

The Christian Citizen in a Multi-racial Society: A Report of the Rosettenville Conference (Cape Town: The Christian Council of South Africa, 1949), 70–77.

39. "Booker T. Washington Delivers the 1895 Atlanta Compromise Speech," *History Matters: The U.S. Survey Course on the Web*, http://historymatters.gmu.edu/d/39/.

40. Luthuli, "A Unified South Africa?"

41. Jatinder Mann, "The Introduction of Multiculturalism in Canada and Australia, 1960s–1970s," *Nations and Nationalism* 18, no. 3 (2012): 483–503. For the philosophical origins of value pluralism, see William Arthur Galston, *Liberal Pluralism: The Implications of Value Pluralism for Political Theory and Practice* (Cambridge: Cambridge University Press, 2002).

42. Luthuli, "A Unified South Africa?"

43. Lodge, *Black Politics in South Africa*, 33. See also chapter 2, this book.

44. Sampson, *Mandela: The Authorised Biography*, 63; and Mandela, *Long Walk to Freedom*, 101.

45. Benson, *Struggle for a Birthright*, 131.

46. "Abaholi BakaKhongolosi Abathola Amatiye EmaNdiyeni," *Bantu World*, 3 May 1952.

47. Benson, *Struggle for A Birthright*, 132.

48. Sobukwe interviewed by Gerhart, 8 and 9 April 1970, 2422/A, HP, WCL.

49. Mandela, *Long Walk to Freedom*, 79.

50. Nelson Mandela, Forward in I. Meer, *Fortunate Man*, vii.

51. Sampson, *Mandela: The Authorized Biography*, 86.

52. Ibid., 65, 216.

53. Mandela, *Long Walk to Freedom*, 123.

54. Ibid.

55. Sisulu, *Walter and Albertina Sisulu*, 120–21.

56. "Report of the Joint Planning Council of the African National Congress and the South African Indian Congress," presented to the 39th Annual Conference of the African National Congress, 15 to 17 December 1951, AD 2186/Ba2, HP, WCL.

57. Ibid.

58. Gerald Pillay, ed., "His Life," in *Albert Luthuli: Voices of Liberation*, 2nd ed. (Cape Town: HSRC Press, 2012), 12; and Couper, *Bound by Faith*, 55.

59. "At Bloemfontein Africans Choose between—Congress and Convention," *Drum*, February 1952.

60. "Msimang Queries Present Congress Policy," *Bantu World*, 5 January 1952.

61. "Weekly Review and Commentary," *Ilanga lase Natal*, 23 February 1952.

62. "Gandhi Fasts—and Talks with DRUM," *Drum*, May 1952.

63. T. N. Naidoo, "Reply to Gandhi," *Drum*, May 1952.

64. Mandela, *Long Walk to Freedom*, 127.

65. Callinicos, *Oliver Tambo*, 180.

66. The quote is from Tambo's later account of the campaign. Oliver Tambo, "Passive Resistance in South Africa," in *Mandela, Tambo, and the African National Congress: The Struggle against Apartheid, 1948–1990; A Documentary Survey*, ed. Sheridan Johns and R. Hunt Davis Jr. (Oxford: Oxford University Press, 1991), 134.

67. Neither Gandhi nor passive resistance were mentioned in the initial proposal (above), the published speeches of Mandela and Luthuli, or the flyer issued by the ANC (Transvaal) and the Transvaal Indian Congress, "April 6: People's Protest Day," flyer, in Karis and Gerhart, *From Protest to Challenge*, 2:482–83.

68. Benson, *Struggle for a Birthright*, 140.

69. Quoted in Baruch Hirson, "The Defiance Campaign, 1952: Social Struggle or Party Stratagem?," in *A History of the Left in South Africa: Writings of Baruch Hirson* (London: I. B. Tauris, 2005), 144.

70. See, for example, Albert Luthuli, Notes for a speech motivating Passive Resistance, date unreadable, notebook dedicated to ANC Tugela branch notes, LP file 8, CRL.

71. For a clear-eyed account of Dube and Gandhi, see Hughes, *First President*, 107–13.

72. Tambo, "Passive Resistance in South Africa," 134.

73. Fredrickson, *Black Liberation*, 241, 243.

74. While ANC leaders were aware of Gandhi's opposition to collaboration and probably knew of his disparaging statements regarding Africans, I have not seen any evidence as to what role these facts might have played in their reading and reception of Gandhi during this period. It is notable that some ANC leaders, like Moroka and Luthuli, must have consciously "set aside" these views in their appropriation of Gandhi. Mandela's much later evaluation was that Gandhi's statements refelected his time and circumstances, and that Gandhi later outgrew his earlier prejudices as he matured politically and spiritually. See E. S. Reddy, "Some of Gandhi's Early Views on Africans Were Racist. But That Was Before He Became Mahatma," *Wire*, 18 October 2016, https://thewire.in/73522/gandhi-and-africans/.

75. "Dr. Malan's Statement on India's Attitude towards South Africa," *Indian Opinion*, 7 November 1952; and "Dr. Malan," *Indian Opinion*, 21 November 1952.

76. "Sisulu Arrested in Boksburg," *Bantu World*, 27 June 1952.

77. Ibid.

78. "The Beginning of the Campaign," *Bantu World*, 27 June 1952.

79. "Volunteers Welcomed at Trades Hall," *Bantu World*, 2 August 1952.

80. Benson, *Struggle for a Birthright*, 140–56.

81. Ibid., 147–48.

82. "Code for A.N.C. Volunteers," *Bantu World*, 27 June 1952.

83. Benson, *Struggle for a Birthright*, 149–50.

84. Ibid., 150.

85. For a fictionalized portrayal, see Nadine Gordimer, "The Smell of Death and Flowers," in *Selected Stories* (New York: Penguin, 1983), 122–44.

86. My gratitude to the late Ismail Nagdee for emphasizing this point in discussions.

87. See Dhlomo's comments in chapter 4 and chapter 6, this book.

88. Victor Sifore interviewed by Gail Gerhart, Ga-Rankuwa, Pretoria, 19 October 1972, A2422/a, HP, WCL; and Charles Lakaje, "Unpublished Autobiographical Notes," Nairobi, February 1970, A2422/a, HP, WCL.

89. African National Congress and Natal Indian Congress, *Flash*, AD 2186/Hb1.6, HP, WCL.

90. Albert Luthuli, "Wake Up, Africans! Wake Up!," in Pillay, *Voices of Liberation*, 45.

91. J. L. Z. Njongwe, *Leader*, 7 November 1952, quoted in Goolam Vahed, "'Gagged and Trussed Rather Securely by the Law': The 1952 Defiance Campaign in Natal," *Journal of Natal and Zulu History* 31, no. 2 (2014): 89.

92. Nelson Mandela, "No Easy Walk to Freedom," in *No Easy Walk to Freedom: Articles, Speeches and Trial Addresses*, ed. Ruth First (London: Heinemann, 1965), 28.

93. Everatt, *Origins of Non-racialism*, 98.

94. However, this structure generated significant confusion and contestation between the ANC and the federation. Cherryl Walker, *Women and Resistance in South Africa* (Cape Town: David Philip Publishers, 1991), 171–72, 257.

95. Chizuko Sato, "Liberal Opposition to Forced Removals and Non-racialism in South Africa," *Ritsumeikan Annual Review of International Studies* 6, no. 1 (2007): 79–102.

96. For the importance of East Africa for debates over the Congress Alliance, see Soske, "Impossible Concept," 23–26.

97. No Sizwe [Neville Alexander], *One Azania, One Nation: The National Question in South Africa* (London: Zed Press, 1979).

98. Contrary to a popular misunderstanding, for example, the spokes of the Congress Alliance wheel did not symbolize the four race-based organizations: the ANC was the center that united the three race-based organizations and the South African Congress of Trade Unions. Frederikse, *Unbreakable Thread*, 59.

99. Achille Mbembe, "There is Only One World," *Con*, 19 July 2017, http://www.theconmag.co.za/2017/07/19/there-is-only-one-world/.

100. Benson, *Struggle for a Birthright*, 145. Benson provides no date for this meeting. Luthuli's public call for defiance dates the Natal ANC's

endorsement of the national decision as occurring on 15 March 1952, over three months after the delegation had returned from the ANC national congress. Luthuli, "We Go to Action," LP file 3, CRL.

101. Benson, *Struggle for a Birthright*, 145.

102. Executive Meeting, ANC Natal Branch, 16 August 1952, [Luthuli's handwritten minutes], LP file 3, CRL.

103. H. I. E. Dhlomo, "Pen Portrait: Chief A. J. Lutuli," part 1, *Bantu World*, 26 July 1952.

104. H. I. E. Dhlomo, "Pen Portrait: Chief A. J. Lutuli," part 2, *Bantu World*, 2 August 1952.

105. Vahed, "1952 Defiance Campaign in Natal," 73.

106. Luthuli, Notes on Lower Tugela Branch meeting, 18 October 1952, LP file 8, CRL.

107. Resolutions, African National Congress (Natal Branch), 1 November 1952, LP file 10, CRL.

108. Ibid.

109. Luthuli, "Apartheid Union Laws and Policy," 5–6 May 1956, LP file 4, CRL.

110. Luthuli, Motivating Passive Resistance, date unreadable, LP file 8, CRL.

111. Albert Luthuli, Draft Resolutions Made in Red Square, LP file 13, CRL.

112. Luthuli, "Let Us Be Clear," 23–24 November 1952, LP file 4, CRL.

113. Albert Luthuli, The Presidential Address at the Annual Conference of the African National Congress, Natal Branch, 31 October to 1 November 1953, LP file 3, CRL.

114. Luthuli, "Wake Up, Africans!," 47.

115. Luthuli, "Let Us Be Clear," 23–24 November 1952, LP file 4, CRL.

116. See chapter 6, this book.

117. *Ilanga lase Natal*, 12 April 1952, quoted in Vahed, "1952 Defiance Campaign in Natal," 75.

118. "5,000 Met at Protest Gathering in Fordsburg," *Bantu World*, 12 April 1952; and "How April 6 Was Observed," *Indian Opinion*, 11 April 1952.

119. "From Other Parts," *Bantu World*, 27 June 1952; and Vahed, "1952 Defiance Campaign in Natal," 75.

120. Vahed, "1952 Defiance Campaign in Natal," 74. Vahed notes that Motola and Essack later switched their alliance to the NIC and formed a strong alliance with ANC stalwart Archie Gumede.

121. Executive Meeting, 16 August 1952, LP file 3, CRL.

122. Callinicos, *Beyond the Engeli Mountains*, 183.

123. Executive Meeting, 16 August 1952, LP file 3, CRL. Emphasis in original.

124. Quoted in Hirson, "Defiance Campaign, 1952" 142.

125. Vahed, "1952 Defiance Campaign in Natal," 74.

126. "News of the Campaign," *Indian Opinion*, 3 October 1952.

127. "The Defiance Campaign," *Indian Opinion*, Special Diwali number, 1952.

128. Walker, *Women and Resistance*, 140.

129. "The Women's Charter," South African History Online, 17 April 1954, http://www.sahistory.org.za/topic/womens-charter.

130. Shireen Hassim, *Women's Organizations and Democracy in South Africa: Contesting Authority* (Madison: University of Wisconsin Press, 2006), 25.

131. Meghan Healy-Clancy, "The Family Politics of the Federation of South African Women: A History of Public Motherhood in Women's Antiracist Activism," *Signs: Journal of Women in Culture and Society* 42, no. 4 (2017): 843–66.

132. Luthuli, *Let My People Go*, 119–23; and Couper, *Bound by Faith*, 65–62.

133. The deadline was later amended to fourteen days.

134. Jordan Ngubane, "Africa Teachers Become Political Commissars," *Indian Opinion*, 5 December 1952.

135. Ngubane, *Unpublished Biography*, CRL,145.

136. "A Personal Statement on His Dismissal from the Chieftainship of the AbaseMakolweni Tribe in the Umvoti Mission Reserve, Groutville, Lower Tugela District by Albert John Luthuli," LP file 1, CRL.

137. "Official Statement on Dismissal of Chief Luthuli," *Bantu World*, November 1952.

138. Albert Luthuli, "The Road to Freedom Is via the Cross," in Pillay, *Voices of Liberation*, 52.

139. Ibid., 53.

140. Enrique Dussel, *Twenty Theses on Politics*, trans. George Ciccariello-Maher (Durham: Duke University Press, 2008), 26.

141. Luthuli, "Road to Freedom," 52.

142. Albert Luthuli, Draft special message to the ANC national congress, 16 December 1955, LP file 8, CRL; and Luthuli, "The African National Congress in Recent Years," in Pillay, *Voices of Liberation*, 85.

143. William Penn, *No Cross, No Crown: A Discourse Shewing the Nature and Discipline of the Holy Cross of Christ. And that the Denial of Self, and Daily Bearing of Christ's Cross, Is the Alone Way to the Rest and Kingdom of God* (Boston: Rogers and Fowle, 1747).

144. Luthuli, "Road to Freedom," 52.

145. Ibid.

146. Ibid.

147. Ibid. Emphasis added.

148. Alan Paton, "Praise Song for Luthuli," appendix C in L. Naidoo, *In the Shadow*, 88.

CHAPTER 6

1. "Freedom in the Air," *Drum*, July 1959.

2. Raymond Suttner, "Periodisation, Cultural Construction and Representation of ANC Masculinities through Dress, Gesture and Indian Nationalist Influence," *Historia* 54, no. 1 (May 2009): 66. In the *Drum* photographs, marshals and some crowd members wore a different version of the uniform, which included turn-downed collars on the jacket, shoulder straps, berets instead of the Gandhi cap, and (in some cases) neck ties. I suspect that Luthuli was wearing a special version of the volunteer uniform meant to indicate his status as president.

3. Emma Tarlo, *Clothing Matters: Dress and Identity in India* (Chicago: University of Chicago Press, 1996), 82–84.

4. Suttner questions this association on the basis of difference in color and wear. Influence, however, does not require identity.

5. Mandela, *Long Walk to Freedom*, 170.

6. Paul Landau, "The ANC, MK, and 'The Turn to Violence' (1960–1962)," *South African Historical Journal* 64 (2012): 538–63.

7. Soudien, "Robben Island University Revisited," 211–32.

8. For a general discussion of the SACP's evolution during this period, see Everatt, *Origins of Non-racialism*, 82–86.

9. Jordan K. Ngubane, "Whispering Campaign against Dr. Moroka," *Indian Opinion*, 28 November 1952.

10. See, especially, Dhlomo, "Chief A. J. Luthuli," part 1, *Bantu World*, 26 July 1952; and Dhlomo, "Chief A. J. Luthuli," part 2, *Bantu World*, 2 August 1952.

11. Ngubane, *Unpublished Biography*, 166.

12. Ibid.

13. Jordan K. Ngubane, "Change in Congress Leadership," *Indian Opinion*, 2 January 1953. While this quote is Ngubane's paraphrase, it is very much Luthuli's language and Ngubane's use of this argumentation is a novelty. Throughout this article, Ngubane is consciously popularizing the language that Luthuli used at the conference.

14. Ibid.

15. Baruch Hirson, "A Trade Union Organizer in Durban: M. B. Yengwa, 1943–44," in *The Left in South Africa*, 207–19.

16. Ibid.

17. L. Naidoo, *In the Shadow*, 31.

18. Letter from Liz Gunner to author, 22 February 2016.

19. L. Naidoo, *In the Shadow*, 31.

20. For example, compare Luthuli, To the ANC national congress, 16 December 1955, LP file 8, CRL to Luthuli, "Congress in Recent Years," 83–87. The latter version is based on the text from the Carter-Karis Collection.

21. Luthuli to friend [Mary L. Hooper], 2 July 1956, LP file 1, CRL.

22. Raymond Suttner, "Chief Albert Luthuli and the 'Gospel of Service,'" *Daily Maverick*, 12 March 2014, http://www.dailymaverick.co.za/article/2014-03-11-chief-albert-luthuli-and-the-gospel-of-service/#.V1DNg2MSBg0. Suttner gives Luthuli's daughter as his source.

23. Luthuli, for example, describes cowriting his statement on Bantu Education with Ngubane. Luthuli, *Let My People Go*, 157.

24. See, for example: *Mayibuye I Afrika: Iphephe-Ndaba Lika Khongolosi Wesifunda* [Bulletin of the Natal ANC], issue 2, volume 1, 1955, LP file 2, CRL; and Jordan Ngubane, "Durban Diary," *Drum*, March 1953.

25. "Congress Moves to Natal," *Drum*, February 1953.

26. See, for example, Couper, *Bound by Faith*, 163–64.

27. For useful discussions of Mandela's performance of masculinity, see Brenna Munro, "Nelson, Winnie, and the Politics of Gender," in Bernard, *Cambridge Companion to Nelson Mandela*, 92–114; and Raymond Suttner, "Nelson Mandela's Masculinities," *African Identities* 12 (2014): 342–56.

28. Ciraj Rassool, "The Individual, Auto/Biography and History in South Africa" (PhD diss., University of the Western Cape, 2004), 384–94.

29. Dhlomo, "Chief A. J. Luthuli," part 1, *Bantu World*, 26 July 1952; and Dhlomo, "Chief A. J. Luthuli," part 2, *Bantu World*, 2 August 1952.

30. Dhlomo, "Chief A. J. Luthuli," part 2, *Bantu World*, 2 August 1952.

31. For the centrality of ideals or (Luthuli's preferred term) values to civilization and democracy, see, inter alia: Albert Luthuli, undated Notes for a greeting to the annual conference of the Congress of Democrats [1956], LP file 10, CRL; Luthuli, Draft address to Special Conference of the ANC, 31 March–1 April 1956, LP file 10, CRL; and "Chief Luthuli Speaks to White South Africans: 'Freedom Is the Apex'" (Congress of Democrats Pamphlet, 1959), LP file 12, CRL.

32. Luthuli, "Congress in Recent Years," 86.

33. Anderson, *Imagined Communities*, 35.

34. Luthuli most often used the terms *loyalty*, *trust*, or *friendship* to describe this feeling. See Luthuli, "Congress in Recent Years," 86; Luthuli, "Letter to the Prime Minister, J. G. Strigdom, 28 May 1957," in Pillay, *Voices of Liberation*, 106; and Luthuli, "A Reply to Mr. Jordan K. Ngubane's Attacks on the African National Congress," *Indian Opinion*, 13 July 1956.

35. Luthuli, *Let My People Go*, 207–8.

36. "The African Viewpoint," *Bantu World*, 9 February 1952.

37. Albert Luthuli, "Our Version of a Democratic Society," in Pillay, *Voices of Liberation*, 116–17.

38. Judith Butler, *Parting Ways: Jewishness and the Critique of Zionism* (New York: Columbia University Press, 2013), 31.

39. Luthuli, Draft manuscript of *Let My People Go*, LP 4, CRL. For a valuable account of Luthuli's concept of civilization, see Scott Everett Couper, "Chief Albert Luthuli's Conceptualisation of Civilisation," *African Studies* 70, no. 1 (2011): 46–66. I differ with Couper in that I understand Luthuli's stress

on the ideal, rather than material, foundation of civilization as a break from his earlier liberal progressivism. Luthuli's idealism was therefore a critique of nineteenth-century European conceptualizations of progress, such as Hegel's. Couper also elides the key role of African nationalism in creating Luthuli's new civilizational synthesis and therefore his complex debt to Lembede.

40. For a strong statement of this position, see Luthuli, Notes for a greeting, [1956], LP file 10, CRL.

41. Luthuli, "Let Us Be Clear," no date [late 1952?], LP 4, CRL.

42. Albert Luthuli, *Fifty Years of Union—Political Review* (Johannesburg: South Africa Institute of Race Relations, 1960).

43. L. Naidoo, *In the Shadow*, 21.

44. Albert Luthuli, Notes for a speech, undated [October or November 1952], notebook dedicated to ANC Tugela branch notes, LP file 8, CRL.

45. Luthuli, Presidential Address at the Annual Conference, 31 October to 1 November 1953, LP file 3, CRL.

46. Luthuli, "Version of a Democratic Society," 115.

47. "Luthuli Sends Message to Nyerere," *New Age*, 3 November 1960. See also Luthuli, "Letter to the Prime Minister," 102–10.

48. Albert Luthuli, Inkulumo Yomongameli we African National Congress e Natal, Lekulumo Yensizwe Umhlanganweni Woyaka Wesifunda sika Congress Sase Natal Obushangete Ethekwini, ngo 1 November, no. 2 1952, LP file 5, CRL.

49. For an influential articulation of this critique, see Alexander, *One Azania, One Nation*.

50. Isaiah Berlin, "Kant as an Unfamiliar Source of Nationalism," in *The Sense of Reality: Studies in Ideas and Their History*, ed. Henry Hardy (New York: Farrar, Straus, and Giroux, 1996), 244.

51. "An Unbecoming Statement from Dr. Malherbe," LP file 4, CRL; and Albert Luthuli, Notes from 1956 [?] in notebook titled Research, LP file 11, CRL.

52. Jan Vansina, *Paths in the Rainforests: Toward a History of Political Tradition in Equatorial Africa* (Madison: University of Wisconsin Pres, 1990); and Paul Landau, *Popular Politics in the History of South Africa, 1400–1948* (Cambridge: Cambridge University Press, 2010). My gratitude to Paul Landau for helping me fully appreciate this influence on Luthuli.

53. Albert Luthuli, Draft manuscript of *Let My People Go*, p. 34, LP file 3, CRL; and Luthuli, *Fifty Years of Union*.

54. For the extension of this argument to the Bantustans, see Couper, "Luthuli's Conceptualisation of Civilisation," 59–60.

55. For the debate over the national question, see Maria van Diepen, ed., *The National Question in South Africa* (London: Zed Books, 1988).

56. For the ANC's failure to adopt an official position on the national question, see Neville Alexander's quotation of Benjamin Turok in Alexander, "Class Structure and National Ideology in South Africa," in *One

Azania, One Nation, 163; and Immanuel Wallerstein, "The Construction of Peoplehood: Racism, Nationalism, Ethnicity," *Sociological Forum* 2 (1987): 373–88.

57. Sylvia Neame, *The Congress Movement: CU, ANC, CP and Congress Alliance*, 3 vols. (Cape Town: HSRC Press, 2015).

58. Lodge, *Black Politics in South Africa*, 68.

59. Soske, "Impossible Concept," 16.

60. Luthuli, "Letter to the Prime Minister," 106.

61. Luthuli, Inkulumo Yomongameli we African National Congress e Natal, LP file 5, CRL.

62. For the revival of 1950s ideas and practices as the basis of "broad unity," see Bill Freund's (quite critical) "Some Unasked Questions on Politics: South African Slogans and Debates," *Transformation* 1 (1986): 119.

63. O. R. Tambo to Dear Sir, 7 May 1956, LP file 9, CRL.

64. Albert Luthuli, "Message by Albert Luthuli for the Observance of South Africa Freedom Day, 15 June 1953," http://www.anc.org.za/content/message-albert-luthuli-observance-south-africa-freedom-day.

65. Executive Report Submitted to the African National Congress, annual National Conference, December 1959, LP file 9, CRL.

66. Ibid.

67. Gerhart, *Black Power in South Africa*, 150–64; and Fredrickson, *Black Liberation*, 282–86.

68. This current of thinking is well analyzed by MacDonald, although he too-quickly attibutes it to the ANC as a whole. MacDonald, *Why Race Matters*, 108–9.

69. Z. K. Mathews, *Freedom for My People: The Autobiography of Z. K. Mathews* (London: R. Collings in association with David Philip Publishers, 1990), 173.

70. Norman Levy, *The Final Prize: My Life in the Anti-apartheid Struggle* (Cape Town: SAHO, 2011), 166.

71. The comparison is commonplace in Congress statements. See "Three Weeks to Go," *New Age*, 9 June 1955.

72. Levy, *Final Prize*, 176.

73. Ibid., 164.

74. This echoed the mode of direct representation that Luthuli defended in "The Road to Freedom Is via the Cross." See chapter 5, this book.

75. "Congress to Draw Up Charter," *Bantu World*, July 1954.

76. Mandela, *Long Walk to Freedom*, 173.

77. The phase is Benson's description of the gathering. Benson, *Struggle for a Birthright*, 175.

78. Quoted in Nelson Mandela, "Freedom in Our Life Time," in First, *Articles, Speeches and Trial Addresses*, 55.

79. Albert Luthuli, Message to the Congress of the People, LP file 8, CRL.

80. Quoted in *From Protest to Challenge: A Documentary History of African Politics in South Africa, 1882–1990*, vol. 3, *Challenge and Violence, 1953–1964*, ed. Thomas Karis and Gail Gerhart (Stanford: Hoover Institution, 1977), 61.

81. Raymond Suttner and Jeremy Cronin, *50 Years of the Freedom Charter* (Pretoria: Unisa Press, 2006), 12.

82. "Three Weeks to Go," *New Age*, 9 June 1955.

83. "The Freedom Charter," adopted by the Congress of the People, 26 June 1955, in Karis and Gerhart, *Protest to Challenge*, 3:205. Emphasis added.

84. Lee, *World after Empire*.

85. Prashad, *Darker Nations*, 49.

86. "Kotane and Cachalia Arrive for Asia-Africa Conference," *New Age*, 21 April 1955; and "Moses Kotane Reports from Indonesia," *New Age*, 5 May 1955.

87. Report of the Natal Provincial Executive for the Year Commencing November 1, 1954 and Ending September 30th, 1955, LP file 13, CRL.

88. Albert Luthuli, Notes for autobiography in notebook entitled Draft Topics, 6 January 1960, LP file 12, CRL. Emphasis in original.

89. Editorial, "The Weakest Link," *Liberation* 25 (June 1957).

90. Ufford Khoruha and Kwame Lekwame [Peter Raboroko and Robert Sobukwe?], "The Kliptown Charter," *Africanist* 11, no. 4 (June/July 1958).

91. Minutes of the Meeting of the Provincial Committee of the African National Congress, Natal Branch, Held at Groutville in the 21st and 22nd January 1956, LP 2, CRL.

92. Albert Luthuli, Letter to Provincial Secretary, Cape ANC, Confidential [handwritten draft], 20 March 1956, LP file 2, CRL.

93. "Congress Moves to Natal," *Drum*, February 1953.

94. Luthuli, *Let My People Go*, 145.

95. Ibid., 151.

96. Ngubane, *Unpublished Biography*, 121.

97. Albert J. Luthuli, "The African National Congress in Recent Years," *Voices of Liberation*, 86.

98. "Memo on Draft Constitution," LP file 6, CRL.

99. Ibid.

100. Albert Luthuli, Notebook entitled Comments on Draft Constitution, 1955 and Other Agenda Items, 19 November 1955, LP file 12, CRL.

101. Luthuli, "The Road to Freedom," no date, LP file 4, CRL.

102. Albert Luthuli, Handwritten draft letter to the Secretary General of the ANC, 19 March 1956, LP file 2, CRL. Luthuli's handwriting is unclear and his files do not include Tambo's letters. Tambo's letter may have been dated 9 February.

103. Luthuli, Letter to Provincial Secretary, 20 March 1956, LP file 2, CRL.

104. Luthuli, Draft letter to Dr. Letele, Treasurer General ANC, date unclear [22 March 1956], LP file 2, CRL.

105. Albert Luthuli, Draft letter to the Secretary General, 24 March 1956, LP file 2, CRL.

106. Luthuli, letter to Letele, 22 March 1956, LP file 2, CRL.

107. Luthuli, Draft letter to Jordan Ngubane, 20 June 1956, LP file 2, CRL. Although Luthuli later dissociated himself from this rebellion, it indicates that his views on the Freedom Charter were widely known, and to some extent shared, within the Natal ANC.

108. Handwritten minutes of the Natal Provincial Executive, 12–13 May 1956, LP file 4, CRL.

109. Bernard Magubane et al., "The Turn to Armed Struggle," in *Road to Democracy in South Africa*, vol. 1, *1960–1970*, ed. South African Democracy Education Trust (Cape Town: Zebra, 2004), 109; Natoo Babenia and Iain Edwards, *Memoirs of a Saboteur: Reflections on My Political Activity in India and South Africa* (Bellville: Mayibuye Books, 1995), 75; and Jon Soske, "'Wash Me Black Again': African Nationalism, the Indian Diaspora, and Kwa-Zulu Natal, 1944–1960" (PhD diss., University of Toronto, 2009), 231–34.

110. Noor Nieftagodien, "Popular Movements, Contentious Spaces and the ANC, 1943–1956," in Lissoni et al., *One Hundred Years of the ANC*, 135–62.

111. Ngubane, *Unpublished Autobiography*, 154.

112. However, ANC membership expanded dramatically in 1959 in response to the struggles against the Group Areas Act, rural relocations, and the extension of passes to women. For these events, see Soske, "Wash Me Black Again," 234–37.

113. Walker, *Women and Resistance*, 186.

114. Edwards, "Mkhumbane, Our Home," 258–59.

115. Organizational Report, Organizer Florence Mkhize, LP file 7, CRL.

116. For more on these tensions, see Edwards, "Mkhumbane, Our Home," 258–60.

117. Khoruha and Lekwame, "Kliptown Charter."

118. For an extended reflection on suffering and ontologies of black experience, see Wilderson, *Red, White, and Black*, 54–91.

119. Ngubane, *Unpublished Biography*, 152.

120. Y. M. Dadoo, "'Smear Tactics Again'—Some Queries," *Indian Opinion*, 2 August 1953; and Jordan K. Ngubane, "Dadoo and Dadoo-ism," *Indian Opinion*, 4 September 1953.

121. Richard Hofstadter, "The Paranoid Style in American Politics," in *The Paranoid Style in American Politics and Other Essays* (Cambridge, MA: Harvard University Press, 1964), 4.

122. Ngubane, *Unpublished Autobiography*, CRL, 174.

123. Albert Luthuli, "A Reply to Mr. Jordan K. Ngubane Attacks on the African National Congress," *Indian Opinion*, 13 July 1956; Jordan Ngubane, "Comment on Mr. Luthuli's Reply—II," *Indian Opinion*, 13 July 1956; Albert Luthuli, "A Reply to Mr. Jordan K. Ngubane Attacks on the African National

Congress," *Indian Opinion*, 20 July 1956; and Jordan Ngubane, "Comment on Mr. Luthuli's Reply—III," *Indian Opinion*, 27 July 1956.

124. Albert Luthuli, Notebook entitled Ngubane reply, 17 May 1956, LP file 13, CRL.

125. Luthuli, "Reply to Mr. Jordan."

126. Ibid.

127. Luthuli, *Let My People Go*, 165.

128. Mandela, *Long Walk to Freedom*, 202.

129. Luthuli, Notes for autobiography, 6 January 1960, LP file 12, CRL.

130. Callinicos, *Oliver Tambo*, 240.

131. Mandela, *Long Walk to Freedom*, 272.

132. Ibid.

133. Luthuli, "On the Rivonia Trial," 12 June 1964, in *Voices of Liberation*, 138.

EPILOGUE

1. Angela Davis, *The Meaning of Freedom* (San Francisco: City Lights Books, 2012), 149.

2. Sisonke Msimang, "Shutdown—On the Death of Compromise in South Africa," *Africa Is a Country*, 11 October 2016.

3. Nelson Mandela, "Speech at the Unveiling of the Gandhi Memorial," 6 June 1993, http://www.anc.org.za/content/nelson-mandelas-speech-unveiling-gandhi-memorial.

4. For this period, see: Stephen Ellis, "The Historical Significance of South Africa's Third Force," *Journal of Southern African Studies* 24, no. 2 (1998): 261–99; Jill Elizabeth Kelly, "'Only the Fourth Chief': Conflict, Land, and Chiefly Authority in 20th Century KwaZulu-Natal, South Africa" (PhD diss., Michigan State University, 2012); and Frank Wilderson III, *Incognegro: A Memoir of Exile and Apartheid* (Durham, NC: Duke University Press, 2015.)

5. Mandela, "Unveiling of the Gandhi Memorial."

6. For the ANC in exile, see: Arianna Lissoni, "The South African Liberation Movements in Exile, c. 1945–1970" (PhD. diss., University of London, 2008); Hugh Macmillan, *The Lusaka Years: The ANC in Exile in Zambia, 1963 to 1994* (Cape Town: Jacana Media, 2013); and Rachel Sandwell, "Building a State in Exile: Women in the African National Congress, 1960-1990" (Phd diss., McGill University, 2014).

7. Laurine Platzky and Cherryl Walker, *The Surplus People: Forced Removals in South Africa* (Johannesburg: Ravan Press, 1985).

8. Raymond Suttner, "The Character and Formation of Intellectuals within the ANC-Led South African Liberation Movement," in *African intellectuals. Rethinking Politics, Language, Gender and Development*, ed. Thandika Mkandawire (London: Zed Books, 2005), 117–54.

9. John Saul, "Cry for the Beloved Country: The Post-apartheid Denouement," *Review of African Political Economy* 28, no. 89 (2001): 429–60;

and Roger Southall, "The ANC and Black Capitalism in South Africa," *Review of African Political Economy* 31, no. 100 (2004): 313–28.

10. Msimang, "Death of Compromise in South Africa"; and Joy Shan, "The Return of Winnie Mandela," *Africa Is a Country*, 20 December 2015, http://africasacountry.com/2015/12/the-return-of-winnie-mandela/.

11. Jon Soske, "Open Secrets, Off the Record: Audience, Intimate Knowledge, and the Crisis of the Post-apartheid State," *Historical Reflections/ Reflexions Historiques* 38, no. 2 (2012): 55–70.

12. Pumla Gqola, "The Difficult Task of Normalizing Freedom: Spectacular Masculinities, Ndebele's Literary/Cultural Commentary and Post-Apartheid Life," *English in Africa* 36, no. 1 (2009): 61–76; and Shireen Hassim, "Democracy's Shadows: Sexual Rights and Gender Politics in the Rape Trial of Jacob Zuma," *African Studies* 68, no. 1 (2009): 57–77.

13. S. Hassim, *Contesting Authority*, 25.

14. This is explored subtly and at length in Mark Hunter, *Love in the Time of AIDS: Inequality, Gender, and Rights in South Africa* (Bloomington: Indiana University Press, 2010).

15. A major exception is the work of Harold Wolpe and his students, who attempted to ground the idea of colonialism as a special type and the national democratic revolution in a more rigorous account of South Africa's political economy and state. See Steven Friedman, *Race, Class and Power: Harold Wolpe and the Radical Critique of Apartheid* (Pietermaritzburg: UKZN Press, 2015).

16. Bill Freund warned about this weakness in the mid-1980s. See Freund, "Some Unasked Questions on Politics." Through our discussions, he has helped me appreciate the shortcoming of framing the problem space of South African politics in terms of the "national question."

17. For the friend/enemy distinction as the foundation of the political, see Carl Schmitt, *The Concept of the Political*, expanded ed. (Chicago: University of Chicago Press, 2008). In significant ways, Gandhi and Luthuli's politics can be characterized as "anti-Schmittian": their founding gesture is the refusal of the friend/enemy distinction by affirming the reciprocity created through struggle as an ethical relationship. For reflections on the friend/ enemy distinction in later anticolonial thinking, see Mahmood Mamdani, "An African reflection on Tahrir Square," Globalizations 8, no. 5 (2011): 559-566.

18. Ernest Renan, *Qu'est-ce qu'une nation?* [What is a nation?] (Toronto: Tapir, 1996).

Selected Bibliography

ARCHIVES

KILLIE CAMPBELL AFRICANA
LIBRARY, DURBAN (KCAL)

BP: S. St.I. Bourquin Papers
NP: George Heaton Nicholls Papers

UNIVERSITY OF THE WITWATERSRAND, WILLIAM
CULLEN LIBRARY, HISTORICAL PAPERS (HP)

AD 2186: ANC Papers
A410: Ballinger Papers
A922: A.W.G. Champion Papers
AD 1710: Hassim Seedat Papers
AD 843: A.B. Xuma Papers

CENTER FOR RESEARCH LIBRARIES,
UNIVERSITY OF CHICAGO (CRL)

CKP: Carter-Karis Papers
GP: Gerhart Papers
LP: Luthuli Papers

INTERVIEWS

KILLIE CAMPBELL ORAL HISTORY PROJECT,
KILLIE CAMPBELL AFRICANA LIBRARY (KCAV)

Tape No. 142, Interview with C. C. Majola by A. Manson and D. Collins, Durban, 20 June 1979.
Tape No. 300, Interview with Africa Ambrose by C. N. Shum, Durban, 25 September 1980.
Tape No. 305, Interview with Tunya Dlamini by B. T. C. Mkhize, Kwa Mashu, 14 June 1981.

Tape No. 305, Interview with Tunya Dlamini by B. T. C. Mkhize, Kwa Mashu, 17 June 1981

Tape No. 308, Interview with Josephine Hadebe by L. Mabaso, Durban, 26 April 1981.

Tape No. 313, Interview with Dupha Mtshali by A. M. Jili, Durban, 15 February 1981.

Tape No. 321, Interview with Richman K. Mabika by E. N. Yenwa, Durban, 25 September 1981.

Tape No. 327, Interview with M. S. Manyathi by C. N. Shum, Durban, 16 September 1981.

Tape No. 342, Interview with William Maseko by E. N. Yengwa, Durban, 22 September 1981.

Tape No. 354, Interview with Bertha Mkhize by J. Wells and H. Hughes, Durban, 20 August 1980.

Tape No. 361, Interview with Z. A. Ngcobo by Simeon Zulu, Durban, 13 September 1980.

Tape No. 366 Interview with Steven Selby interviewed by C. N. Shum, Durban, 12 August 1980.

WILLIAM CULLEN LIBRARY, HISTORICAL PAPERS, UNIVERSITY OF THE WITWATERSRAND (HP)

A2422: Gerhart Papers, PAC Interviews.
Interview with Charles Lakaje, Nairobi, February 1970.
Interview with Joe Matthews, Gaberone, 15 August 1970.
Interview with Peter Molotsi, New York City, 15 August 1969.
Interview with Peter Molotsi, New York City, 17 August 1969.
Interview with Peter Molotsi, New York City, 25 August 1969.
Interview with Mathew Nkoana, London, September 1969. (Not verbatim)
Interview with Victor Sifore, Ga-Rankuwa, Pretoria, 19 October 1972.
Interview with Robert Sobukwe, Kimberly, 8 August 1970.
Interview with Robert Sobukwe, Kimberly, 9 August 1970.

NEWSPAPERS AND PERIODICALS

Africa South
Africa South In Exile
Africanist
Afrika: Newsletter of the African National Congress and Natal Indian Congress
Bantu World
Drum
Ilanga Lase Natal
Indian Opinion
Inkundla ya Bantu
Liberation
Natal Mercury

New Africa
New Age
Paravasi
Race Relations Journal

GOVERNMENT REPORTS

Union of South Africa. *Interim Report of Commission of Enquiry into Matter Affecting the Indian Population of the Province of Natal.* Cape Town: Government Printer, 1945.

Van den Heever, Francois Petrus. *Report of the Commission of Enquiry into Riots in Durban.* Pretoria: Government Printer, 1949.

UNPUBLISHED MANUSCRIPTS

Ngubane, Jordan K. *Unpublished Autobiography.* Historical Papers. William Cullen Library, University of the Witwatersrand, Johannesburg.

Ngubane, Jordan K. *An Unpublished Biography.* Carter-Karis Collection, Center for Research Libraries, University of Chicago.

Vahed, Goolam. Unpublished manuscript on Islam in Natal. Center for Research Libraries, University of Chicago.

PAPERS, REPORTS, AND THESES

Desai, Ashwin. "A Context for Violence: Social and Historical Underpinnings of Indo-African Violence in a South African Community." PhD diss., Michigan State University, 1993.

Edwards, Iain. "Mkhumbane, Our Home: African Shantytown Society in Cato Manor Farm." PhD diss., University of Natal, 1989.

Ginwala, Frene. "Class, Consciousness and Control: Indian South Africans, 1860–1956." PhD diss., Oxford University, 1974.

Hemson, David. "Class Consciousness and Migrant Workers: Dock Workers of Durban." PhD diss., University of Warwick, 1979.

Kelly, Jill Elizabeth. "'Only the Fourth Chief': Conflict, Land, and Chiefly Authority in 20th Century KwaZulu-Natal, South Africa." PhD diss., Michigan State University, 2012.

Kirk, S. L. "The 1949 Durban Riots—A Community in Conflict." MA thesis, University of Natal, January 1983.

Ladlua, L. K. "The Cato Manor Riots 1959–60." MA thesis, University of Natal, 1985.

Lissoni, Arianna. "The South African Liberation Movements in Exile, c. 1945–1970." PhD diss., University of London, 2008.

Maharaj, Brij. "The Group Areas Act in Durban: Central Local State Relations." PhD diss., University of Natal, 1992.

Nuttall, Timothy Andrew. "Class, Race and Nation: African Politics in Durban, 1929–1949." PhD diss., University of Oxford, 1991.

———. "'It Seems Peace but It Can Be War': The Durban 'Riots' and the Struggle for the City." Paper presented at the 12th National Conference of the South African Historical Society, Pietermaritzburg, University of Natal, 1989.

Pahad, Essop. "The Development of Indian Political Movements in South Africa 1924–1946." PhD diss., University of Sussex, 1972.

Palmer, Fileve Tlaloc. "Through a Coloured Lens: Post-apartheid Identity Formation amongst Coloureds in KZN." PhD diss., Indiana University, 2015.

Rambiritch, Birbal. "An Investigation into Some Aspects of the Education of Indian Girls in Natal." MA thesis, University of Natal, 1955.

Rassool, Ciraj. "The Individual, Auto/Biography and History in South Africa." PhD diss., University of the Western Cape, 2004.

Sandwell, Rachel. "Building a State in Exile: Women in the African National Congress, 1960–1990." PhD diss., McGill University, 2014.

Sheik, Nafisa Essop. "Colonial Rites: Custom, Marriage Law and the Making of Difference in Natal, 1830s–c. 1910." PhD diss., University of Michigan, 2012.

Soske, Jon. "'Wash Me Black Again': African Nationalism, the Indian Diaspora, and Kwa-Zulu Natal, 1944–1960." PhD diss., University of Toronto, 2009.

Tallie, T. J. "Limits of Settlement: Racialized Masculinity, Sovereignty, and the Imperial Project in Colonial Natal, 1850–1897." PhD diss., University of Illinois at Urbana-Champaign, 2014.

Ukpanah, Ime John. "Yearning to be Free: Inkundla ya Bantu [Bantu Forum] as Mirror and Mediator of the African Nationalist Struggle in South Africa, 1938–1951." PhD diss., University of Houston, 1993.

COLLECTIONS OF PUBLISHED DOCUMENTS

Drew, Allison, ed. *South Africa's Radical Tradition: A Documentary History.* Vol. 1, *1907–1950.* Cape Town: Mayibuye Books, 1996.

———, ed. *South Africa's Radical Tradition: A Documentary History.* Vol. 2, *1943–1964.* Cape Town: Cape Town University Press, 1997.

Karis, Thomas G., and Gail M. Gerhart, eds. *Challenge and Violence, 1953–1964.* Vol. 3 of *From Protest to Challenge: A Documentary History of African Politics in South Africa, 1882–1990.* Stanford: Hoover Institution, 1977.

———, eds. *Hope and Challenge, 1935–1952.* Vol. 2 of *From Protest to Challenge: A Documentary History of African Politics in South Africa, 1882–1990.* Stanford: Hoover Institution, 1973.

———, eds. *Nadir and Resurgence, 1964–1979.* Vol. 5 of *From Protest to Challenge: A Documentary History of African Politics in South Africa, 1882–1990.* Bloomington: Indiana University Press, 1997.

Stuart, James. *The James Stuart Archive of Recorded Oral Evidence Relating to the History of the Zulu and Neighboring People*. Edited and translated by C. de B. Webb and J. B. Wright. 3 vols. Pietermaritzburg, Zaf.: University of Natal Press, 1976.

PAMPHLETS

African National Congress. *Forward to Freedom: Strategy, Tactics and Programme of the African National Congress, South Africa*. Pamphlet. 1969.

Keyter, Carl. *Holiday and Travel Facilities for Non-whites in South Africa*. Johannesburg: Institute of Race Relations, June 1962.

Kirkwood, Kenneth. "Failure of a Report." In *The Durban Riots and After*, edited by Maurice Webb and Kenneth Kirkwood. Johannesburg: South Africa Institute of Race Relations, 1949.

Natal Indian Organization. *Statement Submitted by the Natal Indian Organization to the Chairman and Members of the Judicial Community Appointed to Enquire into the Durban Riots*. Natal Indian Organization, 1949.

Pan Africanist Congress. "The 1959 Pan Africanist Manifesto." In *The Basic Documents of the Pan Africanist Congress*, 21–22. Lusaka: Secretary, Publicity and Information, Pan Africanist Congress of South Africa, 1965.

BOOKS AND ARTICLES

Adas, Michael. "Contested Hegemony: The Great War and the Afro-Asian Assault on the Civilizing Mission Ideology." *Journal of World History* 15, no. 1 (2004): 31–63.

Adendorff, R. "Fanakalo—A Pidgin in South Africa." In *Language in South Africa*, edited by Rajend Mesthrie, 179–98. Cambridge: Cambridge University Press, 2002.

Adhikari, Mohamed. "Fiercely Non-racial? Discourses and Politics of Race in the Non-European Unity Movement, 1943–70." *Journal of Southern African Studies* 31, no. 2 (2005): 403–18.

———. "'God Made the White Man, God Made the Black Man...': Popular Racial Stereotyping of Coloured People in Apartheid South Africa." *South African Historical Journal* 55, no. 1 (2006): 142–64.

African National Congress. "African Claims in South Africa." In Karis and Gerhart, *From Protest to Challenge*, 2:217–23.

Aiyer, Sana. *Indians in Kenya: The Politics of Diapsora*. Cambridge, MA: Harvard University Press: 2015.

Aijaz Ahmad. *Lineages of the Present: Ideology and Politics in Contemporary South Asia*. London: Verso, 2000.

Alexander, Neville. "Approaches to the National Question in South Africa." *Transformation*, no. 1 (1986): 77–80.

———. *An Ordinary Country: Issues in the Transition from Apartheid to Democracy in South Africa*. New York: Berghahn Books, 2003.

Aloysius, G. *Nationalism without a Nation in India*. Oxford: Oxford University Press, 1997.

Anderson, Benedict. *Imagined Communities: Reflections on the Origins and Spread of Nationalism*. Rev. ed. London: Verso, 2006.

Ansell, Gwen. *Soweto Blues: Jazz, Popular Music, and Politics in South Africa*. London: A and C Black, 2005.

Arendt, Hannah. *The Origins of Totalitarianism*. New York: Harcout, 1968.

Asad, Talal. *Genealogies of Religion: Discipline and Reasons of Power and Christianity and Islam*. Baltimore: The Johns Hopkins University Press, 1993.

Asmal, Kader, and Adrian Hadland with Moira Levy. Politics in *My Blood: A Memoir*. Auckland Park, Zaf.: Jacana Media, 2011.

Azoulay, Ariella. *The Civil Contract of Photography*. New York: Zone Books, 2008.

Babenia, Natoo, and Iain Edwards. *Memoirs of a Saboteur: Reflections on My Political Activity in India and South Africa*. Bellville: Mayibuye Books, 1995.

Baderoon, Gabeba. *Regarding Muslims: From Slavery to Post-apartheid*. Johannesburg: Wits University Press, 2014.

Barchiesi, Franco. "Imagining the Patriotic Worker: The Idea of 'Decent Work' in the ANC's Political Discourse." In Lissoni et al., *One Hundred Years of the ANC*, 111–34.

———. "The Problem with 'We': Affiliation, Political Economy, and the Counterhistory of Non-racialism." In Walsh and Soske, *Ties that Bind*, 125–66.

Bayly, C. A. *The Birth of the Modern World*, 1780–1914. Oxford: Blackwell Publishing, 2004.

Bayly, Susan. *Caste, Society, and Politics in India: From the Eighteenth Century to the Modern Age*. Cambridge: Cambridge University Press, 1999.

Benjamin, Walter. "On Some Motifs in Baudelaire." In *Illuminations*. Edited by Hannah Arendt. Translated by Harry Zohn. New York: Fontana Press, 1973.

Benson, Mary. *The African Patriots: The Story of the African National Congress of South Africa*. London: Faber and Faber, 1963.

———. *South Africa: The Struggle for a Birthright*. Hamondsworth, Eng.: Penguin, 1966.

Berger, Iris. "An African American 'Mother of the Nation': Madie Hall Xuma in South Africa, 1940–1963." *Journal of Southern African Studies* 27, no. 3 (September, 2001): 547–66.

Berlin, Isaiah. "Kant as an Unfamiliar Source of Nationalism." In *The Sense of Reality: Studies in Ideas and Their History*, edited Henry Hardy, 231–48. New York: Farrar, Straus, and Giroux, 1996.

Bernard, Rita, ed. *The Cambridge Companion to Nelson Mandela*. Cambridge: Cambridge University Press, 2014.

Bhana, Surendra. Gandhi's Legacy: *The Natal Indian Congress 1894–1994*. Pietermaritzburg, Zaf.: University of Natal Press, 1997.

Bhana, Surendra and Joy Brain. *Setting Down Roots: Indian Migrants and South Africa, 1860–1922*. Johannesburg: Witwatersrand University Press, 1990.

Bhana, Surendra, and Bridglal Pachai, eds. *A Documentary History of Indian South Africans*. Stanford: Hoover Institute Press, 1984.

Bhana, Surendra, and Goolam Vahed. *The Making of a Political Reformer: Gandhi in South Africa, 1893–1914*. New Delhi: Manohar, 2005.

Bharati, Agehananda. *The Asians in East Africa: Jayhind and Uhuru*. Chicago: Nelson Hall Company, 1972.

Bonner, Philip. "Fragmentation and Cohesion in the ANC: The First 70 Years." In Lissoni et al., *One Hundred Years of the ANC*, 1–12.

Bonner, Philip, Peter Delius, and Deborah Posel, eds. *Apartheid's Genesis: 1935–1962*. Braamfontein, Zaf.: Ravan Press, 1993.

Bonner, Phillip, and Noor Nieftagodien. *Alexandra: A History*. Johannesburg: Witwatersrand University Press, 2008.

Bose, Sugata. *A Hundred Horizons: The Indian Ocean in the Age of Global Empire*. Cambridge, MA: Harvard University Press, 2006.

Brennan, James. *Taifa: The Making of Race and Nation in Urban Tanzania*. Athens: Ohio University Press, 2012.

Benton, Laura. *Law and Colonial Cultures: Legal Regimes in World History, 1400–1900*. Cambridge: Cambridge University Press, 2002.

Buck-Morss, Susan. Hegel, Haiti, and Universal History. Pittsburgh: University of Pittsburgh Press, 2009.

Burke, Timothy. *Lifebuoy Men, Lux Women: Commodification, Consumption, and Cleanliness in Modern Zimbabwe*. Durham, NC: Duke University Press, 1996.

Burrows, H. R. "Indian Life and Labour in Natal." *Race Relations* 10, no. 1 (1943): 18.

Burton, Antoinette. *Africa in the Indian Imagination: Race and the Politics of Postcolonial Citation*. Durham, NC: Duke University Press, 2016.

———. *Brown over Black: Race and the Politics of Postcolonial Citation*. Delhi: Three Essays Collective, 2012.

Butalia, Urvashi. *The Other Side of Silence: Voices from the Partition of India*. Durham, NC: Duke University Press, 2000.

Butler, Anthony. *The Idea of the ANC*. Athens: Ohio University Press, 2012.

Butler, Judith. *Parting Ways: Jewishness and the Critique of Zionism*. New York: Columbia University Press, 2013.

———. "Restaging the Universal: Hegemony and the Limits of Formalism." In *Contingency, Hegemony, and Universality*, edited by Judith Butler, Ernesto Laclau, and Slavoj Zizek, 11–43. London: Verso, 2000.

Callinicos, Luli. *Oliver Tambo: Beyond the Engeli Mountains*. Claremount: David Phillip Publishers, 2004.

Carton, Benedict, John Laband, and Jabulani Sithole, eds. Zulu Identities: *Being Zulu, Past and Present*. New York: Columbia University Press, 2008.

Chhabra, Hari Sharan. *Nehru and Resurgent Africa*. New Delhi: Africa Publications, 1989.

Champion, A.W.G. *The Views of Mahlathi: Writings of A. W. G. Champion a Black South African*. Edited by M. W. Swanson. Translated by E. R. Dahle. Pietermaritzburg, Zaf.: University of Natal Press, 1982.

Chakrabarty, Dipesh. *Provincializing Europe: Postcolonial Thought and Historical Difference*. Princeton: Princeton University Press, 2009.

———. "Provincializing Europe: Postcoloniality and the Critique of History." *Cultural Studies* 6, no. 3 (1992): 337–57.

Chari, Sharad. "Photographing Dispossession, Forgetting Solidarity: Waiting for Social Justice in Wentworth, South Africa." *Transactions of the Institute of British Geographers* 34, no. 4 (2009): 521–40.

Healy-Clancy, Meghan. "The Family Politics of the Federation of South African Women: A History of Public Motherhood in Women's Antiracist Activism." *Signs: Journal of Women in Culture and Society* 42, no. 4 (2017): 843–66.

———. "The Politics of New African Marriage in Segregationist South Africa." *African Studies Review* 57, no. 2 (2014): 7–28.

Cock, Jacklyn. *Maids and Madams: Domestic Workers under Apartheid*. Rev. ed. London: The Women's Press, 1989.

Colenso, Rev. J.W. *Zulu-English Dictionary*. Natal: Vause, Slater and Co., 1905.

Coopan, S., and A. D. Lazarus. "The Indian as an Integral Part of South African Society." In *The Indian as a South African*. Johannesburg: South African Institute of Race Relations, 1956.

Coopan, S., and B. A. Naidoo. "Indian Adjustments to Urbanization." *Race Relations* 22, no. 1 (1955).

Cooper, Frederick. *Citizenship between Empire and Nation: Rethinking France and French Africa 1945–1960*. Princeton: Princeton University Press, 2014.

Couper, Scott. *Albert Luthuli: Bound by Faith*. Scottsville, Zaf.: University of KwaZulu-Natal Press, 2012.

Couzens, Tim. *The New African: A Study of the Life and Work of H. I. E. Dhlomo*. Johannesburg: Ravan Press, 1985.

Dabashi, Hamid. *Can Non-Europeans Think?* London: Zed, 2015.

Dadoo, Y. M. "The Non-European Unity." *Freedom* 4, no. 1 (February 1945). Reprinted in *South Africa's Radical Tradition: A Documentary History*. Vol. 2, 1943–1964, edited by Allison Drew, 123. Cape Town: University of Cape Town Press, 1997.

Davin, Anna. "Imperialism and Motherhood." In *Tensions of Empire: Colonial Cultures in a Bourgeois World*, edited by Frederick Cooper and Ann Laura Stoler, 87-151. Berkeley: University of California Press, 1997.

Davis, Angela. *The Meaning of Freedom*. San Francisco: City Lights Books, 2012.

Desai, Ashwin, Vishnu Padayachee, Krish Reddy, and Goolam Vahed. *Blacks in Whites: A Century of Cricket Struggles in KwaZulu-Natal*. Pietermaritzburg, Zaf.: University of Natal Press, 2002.

Desai, Ashwin, and Goolam Vahed. *Inside Indian Indenture: A South African Story, 1860–1914*. Cape Town: HSRC Press, 2010.

———. *Monty Naicker: Between Reason and Treason*. Pietermaritzburg, Zaf.: Shuter, 2010.

———. *The South African Gandhi: Stretcher-Bearer of Empire*. Palo Alto: Stanford University Press, 2015.

Desai, Radhika. "The Cast(e) of Anti-secularism. " In *Will Secular India Survive?*, edited by Mushirul Hasan, 175–209. Dhaka, Bgd.: University Press, 2004.

Devji, Faisal. *Muslim Zion: Pakistan as a Political Idea*. London: Hurst Publishers, 2013.

Diagne, Souleymane Bachir. *African Art as Philosophy: Senghor, Bergson, and the Idea of Negritude*. Translated by Chike Jeffers. London: Seagull Books, 2011.

Dirks, Nicholas B. *Castes of Mind: Colonialism and the Making of Modern India*. Princeton: Princeton University Press, 2001.

Dhupelia-Mesthrie, Uma. "The Passenger Indian as Worker: Indian Immigrants in Cape Town in the Early Twentieth Century." *African Studies* 68, no. 1 (2009): 111–34.

———. "The Place of India in South African History: Academic Scholarship, Past, Present and Future." *South African Historical Journal* 57 (2007): 12–34.

———. "Satyagraha in South Africa: Principles, Practice and Possibilities." *Historia* 54, no. 1 (2009): 13–33.

Döhne, Jacob L. *A Zulu-Kafir Dictionary: Etymologically Explained with Copious Illustrations and Examples*. Cape Town: G. J. Pike's Machine Print Office, 1857.

Duara, Prasenjit. *Rescuing History from the Nation: Questioning Narratives of Modern China*. Chicago: University of Chicago Press, 1996.

Du Bois, W. E. B. "The Conservation of Races." In *The Oxford W. E. B. Du Bois Reader*, edited by Eric J. Sundquist, 38–47. New York: Oxford University Press, 1996.

Duminy, Andrew, and Bill Guest, eds. *Natal and Zululand from Earliest Times to 1910: A New History*. Pietermaritzburg, Zaf.: University of Natal Press, 1989.

Duncan, Patrick. "Inside Strijdom's South Africa." *Africa Today* 3, no. 3 (1956): 2–6.

Dussel, Enrique. *Twenty Theses on Politics*. Translated by George Ciccariello-Maher. Durham, NC: Duke University Press, 2008.

Ebr.-Valley, Rehana. *Kala Pani: Caste and Colour in South Africa*. Cape Town: Kwela Books, 2001.

Edgar, Robert R., and Luyanda ka Msumza, eds. *Freedom in Our Lifetime: The Collected Writings of Anton Muziwakhe Lembede*. Athens: Ohio University Press, 1996.

Editorial. "The Weakest Link." *Liberation* 25 (June 1957).

Edwards, Iain. "Swing the Assegai Peacefully? 'New Africa,' Mkhumbane, the Co-operative Movement and Attempts to Transform Durban Society in the Late Nineteen-Forties." In *Holding Their Ground: Class, Locality and Culture in 19th and 20th Century South Africa*, edited by Philip Bonner, Isabel Hofmeyr, Deborah James, and Tom Lodge, 59–103. Johannesburg: Witwatersrand University Press and Ravan Press, 1989.

Ellis, Stephen. "The Historical Significance of South Africa's Third Force." *Journal of Southern African Studies* 24, no. 2 (1998): 261–99.

Erlmann, Veit. *Nightsong: Performance, Power, and Practice in South Africa*. Chicago: University of Chicago Press, 1996.

Everatt, David. *The Origins of Non-racialism: White Opposition to Apartheid in the 1950s*. Johannesburg: Wits University Press, 2010.

Fair, T. J. D., and N. Manfred Shaffer. "Population Patterns and Policies in South Africa,1951–1960." *Economic Geography* 40, no. 3 (July 1964): 261–74.

Feit, Edward. *South Africa: The Dynamics of the African National Congress*. London: Oxford University Press, 1962.

Fields, Barbara Jeanne. "Race, Slavery and Ideology in the United States of America." *New Left Review* I/181 (May-June 1990): 95–118.

Flint, Karen. "Indian-African Encounters: Polyculturalism and African Therapeutics in Natal, South Africa, 1820–1948." *Journal of Southern African Studies* 32, no. 2 (June 2006): 367–85.

Frederikse, Julie. *The Unbreakable Thread: Non-racialism in South Africa*. Johannesburg: Ravan Press, 1990.

Fredrickson, George M. *Black Liberation: A Comparative History of Black Ideologies in the United States and South Africa*. New York: Oxford University Press, 1995.

Freund, Bill. "Contrasts in Urban Segregation: a Tale of Two Cities, Durban (South Africa) and Abidjan (Côte d'Ivoire)." *Journal of Southern African Studies* 27, no. 3, Special Issue for Shula Marks (September 2001): 527–46.

———. "Indian Women and the Changing Character of the Working Class Indian Household in Natal, 1860–1990." *Journal of Southern African Studies* 17, no. 3 (1991): 414–29.

———. *Insiders and Outsiders: The Indian Working Class of Durban, 1910–1990*. Portsmouth: Heinemann, 1995.

———. "Some Unasked Questions on Politics: South African Slogans and Debates," *Transformation* 1 (1986): 119.

Friedman, Steven. *Race, Class and Power: Harold Wolpe and the Radical Critique of Apartheid.* Pietermaritzburg, Zaf.: UKZN Press, 2015.

Fuller, C. J. Introduction to Caste Today. Edited by C. J. Fuller. Delhi: Oxford University Press, 1997.

Gaitskell, Deborah. "'Wailing for Purity': Prayer Unions, African Mothers and Adolescent Daughters, 1912–1940." In Marks and Rathbone, *Industrialisation and Social Change*, 338–73.

Galston, William. *Liberal Pluralism: The Implications of Value Pluralism for Political Theory and Practice.* Cambridge: Cambridge University Press, 2002.

Gandhi, M. K. *An Autobiography, or the Story of My Experiments with Truth.* Boston: Beacon Press, 1993.

Gerhart, Gail M. *Black Power in South Africa: The Evolution of an Ideology.* Berkeley: University of California Press, 1979.

Gilman, Sander. *Difference and Pathology: Stereotypes of Sexuality, Race, and Madness.* Ithaca: Cornell University Press, 1985.

Gilroy, Paul. *The Black Atlantic: Modernity and Double Consciousness.* Cambridge: Harvard University Press, 1993.

——. *'There Ain't No Black in the Union Jack': The Cultural Politics of Race and Nation.* Chicago: University of Chicago Press, 1987.

Glaser, Clive. *The ANC Youth League.* Athens: Ohio University Press, 2012.

Glassman, Jonathan. "Slower than a Massacre: The Multiple Sources of Racial Thought in Colonial Africa." *American Historical Review* 109, no. 3 (June 2004): 720–54.

——. *War of Words, War of Stones: Racial Thought and Violence in Colonial Zanzibar.* Bloomington: Indiana University Press, 2011.

Gluckman, Max. "The Kingdom of the Zulu of South Africa." In *African Political Systems*, edited by Meyer Fortes and E. E. Evans-Pritchard, 25–54. London: Oxford University Press, 1940.

Dr. Goonam. *Coolie Doctor: An Autobiography.* Durban, Zaf.: Madiba Publishers, 1991.

Gordimer, Nadine. "The Smell of Death and Flowers." In *Selected Stories.* New York: Penguin, 1983.

Gregory, Robert G. *Quest for Equality: Asian Politics in East Africa, 1900–1967.* Hyderabad: Orient Longman, 1993.

Ghosh, Amotiv. "Confessions of a Xenophile." *Chimurenga* 14 (2009): 35–41.

Gish, Steven. *Alfred B. Xuma: African, American, South African.* New York: NYU Press, 2000.

Guha, Ranajit. *Elementary Aspects of Peasant Insurgency in Colonial India.* Delhi: Oxford University Press, 1983.

——. *History at the Limit of World-History.* New York: Columbia University Press, 2002.

Guy, Jeff. "The Destruction and Reconstruction of Zulu Society." In Marks and Rathbone, *Industrialisation and Social Change*, 167–94.

———. *The Maphumulo Uprising: War, Law and Ritual in the Zulu Rebellion.* Scottsville, Zaf.: University of KwaZulu-Natal Press, 2005.

Gqola, Pumla. "The Difficult Task of Normalizing Freedom: Spectacular Masculinities, Ndebele's Literary/Cultural Commentary and Post-apartheid Life." *English in Africa* 36, no. 1 (2009): 61–76.

Gwala, Mafika. "Grey Street." Reprinted in Omar Badsha, *Imperial Ghetto: Ways of Seeing in a South African City*, 3. Maroelana, Zaf.: South African History Online, 2001.

Hahn, Steven. "'Extravagant Expectations' of Freedom: Rumour, Political Struggle, and the Christmas Insurrection Scare of 1865 in the American South." *Past and Present* 157 (November 1997): 122–58.

Hall, Stuart. "Race, Articulation and Societies Structured in Dominance." In *Sociological Theories: Race and Colonialism*, 305–45. Paris: UNESCO, 1980.

Hansen, Thomas Blom. *Melancholia of Freedom: Social Life in an Indian Township in South Africa.* Princeton: Princeton University Press, 2012.

Harries, Patrick. *Work, Culture, and Identity: Migrant Laborers in Mozambique and South Africa*, c. 1860–1910. Portsmouth: Heinemann, 1994.

Harshav, Benjamin. *The Polyphony of Jewish Culture.* Palo Alto: Stanford University Press, 2007.

Hassim, Azzim. *The Lotus People.* Durban, Zaf.: The Institute of Black Research/Madiba Publishers, 2002.

Hassim, Shireen. "Democracy's Shadows: Sexual Rights and Gender Politics in the Rape Trial of Jacob Zuma." *African Studies* 68, no. 1 (2009): 57–77.

———. *Women's Organizations and Democracy in South Africa: Contesting Authority.* Madison: University of Wisconsin Press, 2006.

Hey, P. D. *The Rise of the Natal Indian Elite.* Pietermaritzburg, Zaf.: The Natal Witness, 1961.

Hirson, Baruch. "The Defiance Campaign, 1952: Social Struggle or Party Stratagem?" In *The Left in South Africa*, 134–55.

———. *A History of the Left in South Africa: Writings of Baruch Hirson.* London: I. B. Tauris, 2005.

———. "A Short History of the Non-European Unity Movement: An Insider's View." *Searchlight South Africa* 12 (1995): 64–93.

———. "A Trade Union Organizer in Durban: M. B. Yengwa, 1943–44." In *The Left in South Africa*, 207–19.

Ho, Fred, and Bill V. Mullen, eds. *Afro-Asia: Revolutionary Political and Cultural Connections between African Americans and Asian Americans.* Durham, NC: Duke University Press, 2008.

Hobsbawm, Eric. *Nations and Nationalism since 1780: Programme, Myth, Reality.* Cambridge: Cambridge University Press, 2012.

Hoernlé, R. F. A. *South African Native Policy and the Liberal Spirit.* Johannesburg: Witwatersrand University Press, 1945.

Hofmeyr, Isabel. "Africa as a Fault Line in the Indian Ocean." In *Eyes across the Water: Navigating the Indian Ocean*, edited by Pamila Gupta, Isabel Hofmeyr, and Michael Pearson, 99–106. Pretoria: UNISA Press, 2010.

———. "The Black Atlantic Meets the Indian Ocean: Forging New Paradigms of Transnationalism for the Global South – Literary and Cultural Perspectives." *Social Dynamics* 33, no. 2 (2007): 3–32.

———. *Gandhi's Printing Press: Experiments in Slow Reading.* Cambridge, MA: Harvard University Press, 2013.

———. "Seeking Empire, Finding Nation: Gandhi and Indianness in South Africa." In *Routledge Handbook of the South Asian Diaspora*, edited by Joya Chatterji and David Washbrook, 153–65. London: Routledge, 2014.

Hofmeyr, Isabel, and Uma Dhupelia-Mesthrie. "South Africa/India: Re-imagining the Disciplines." *South African Historical Journal* 57 (2007): 1–11.

Hofstadter, Richard. "The Paranoid Style in American Politics." In *The Paranoid Style in American Politics and Other Essays.* Cambridge, MA: Harvard University Press, 1964.

Hughes, Heather. "'The Coolies Will Elbow Us Out of the Country': African Reactions to Indian Immigration in the Colony of Natal, South Africa." *Labour History Review* 72 (2007): 155–68.

———. "Doubly Elite: Exploring the Life of John Langalibalele Dube." *Journal of Southern African Studies* 27, no. 3 (September 2001): 445–58.

———. *First President: A Life of John Dube*, Founding President of the ANC. Cape Town: Jacana Media, 2011.

———. "Violence in Inanda, August 1985." *Journal of Southern African Studies* 13, no. 3 (1987): 331–54.

Hunter, Mark. *Love in the Time of AIDS: Inequality, Gender, and Rights in South Africa.* Bloomington: Indiana University Press, 2010.

Hyslop, Jonathan. "Gandhi 1869–1915: The Transnational Emergence of a Public Figure." In *The Cambridge Companion to Gandhi*, edited by Judith M. Brown and Anthony Parel, 30–51. Cambridge: Cambridge University Press, 2011.

Institute for Social Research. *Baumannville: A Study of an Urban African Community.* Natal Regional Survey, report 6. Cape Town: Oxford University Press, 1959.

Iton, Richard. *In Search of the Black Fantastic: Politics and Popular Culture in the Post–Civil Rights Era.* Oxford: Oxford University Press, 2008.

Iyer, Raghavan. The Moral and Political and Political Thought of Mahatma Gandhi. New Delhi: Oxford University Press, 2000.

Jabavu, D. D. T. *E-Indiya Nase East Africa: Uhambo lomNgqika eMpumalanga.* Lovedale, IN: Lovedale Mission Press, 1951.

Jalal, Ayesha. "Exploding Communalism: The Politics of Muslim Identity in South Asia." In *Nationalism, Democracy, and Development*, edited by Sugata Bose and Ayesha Jalal, 76–103. New Delhi: Oxford University Press, 1998.

Jha, C. S. *From Bandung to Tashkent: Glimpses of India's Foreign Policy*. Madras: Sagam Books, 1983.

Jagarnath, Vashna. "The Politics of Urban Segregation and Indian Cinema in Durban." In *City Flicks: Indian Cinema and the Urban Experience*, edited by Preben Kaarsholm, 211–22. Calcutta: Seagull Books, 2004.

Johns, Sheridan, and R. Hunt Davis Jr.. *Mandela, Tambo, and the African National Congress: The Struggle against Apartheid, 1948–1990; A Documentary Survey*. New York: Oxford University Press, 1991.

Kannabiran, Vasanth, and Kalpana Kannabiran. "Caste and Gender: Understanding Dynamics of Power and Violence." In *Gender and Caste*, edited by Anupama Rao, 249–60. New Delhi: Kali for Women, 2003.

Karl, Rebecca E. *Staging the World: Chinese Nationalism at the Turn of the Twentieth Century*. Durham, NC: Duke University Press, 2002.

Kelly, John, and Martha Kaplan. "Nation and Decolonization toward a New Anthropology of Nationalism." *Anthropological Theory* 1, no 4 (2001): 419–37.

Kelley, Robin D. G. *Race Rebels: Culture, Politics, and the Black Working Class*. New York: Free Press, 1994.

Khoruha, Ufford, and Kwame Lekwame [Peter Raboroko and Robert Sobukwe?]. "The Kliptown Charter." *Africanist* 11, no. 4 (June/July 1958).

Kim, Sebastian C. H. "The Kingdom of God versus the Church: The Debate at the Conference of the International Missionary Council, Tambaram, 1938." In *Interpreting Contemporary Christianity: Global Processes and Local Identities*, edited Ogbu Kalu and Alaine Low, 131–48. Grand Rapids: Wm. B. Eerdmans Publishing, 2008.

Kimble, Judy, and Elaine Unterhalter. "'We Opened the Road for You, You Must Go Forward': ANC Women's Struggles, 1912–1982." *Feminist Review* 12 (1982): 11–35.

Kumar, Aishwary. *Radical Equality: Ambedkar, Gandhi, and the Risk of Democracy*. Stanford: Stanford University Press, 2015.

Kuper, Hilda. *Indian People in Natal*. Pietermaritzburg, Zaf.: Natal University Press, 1960.

Kuper, Leo. *An African Bourgeoisie: Race, Class, and Politics in South Africa*. New Haven: Yale University Press, 1965.

Laband, John. "'Bloodstained Grandeur': Colonial and Imperial Stereotypes of Zulu Warriors and Zulu Warfare." In *Zulu Identities: Being Zulu, Past and Present*, edited by Benedict Carton, John Laband, and Jabulani Sithole,168–76. Scottsville, Zaf.: University of KwaZulu-Natal Press, 2008.

La Hausse, Paul. "Drink and Cultural Innovation in Durban: The Origins of the Beerhall in South Africa 1902–16." In *Liquor and Labor in South Africa*, edited by Charles Amber and Jonathan Crush, 78–114. Athens: Ohio University Press, 1993.

———. "'Mayihlome!': Towards an Understanding of Amalaita Gangs in Durban,1900–1939." In *Regions and Repertoires: Topics in South African*

Politics and Culture, edited by Stephen Clingman, 30–59. Braamfontein, Zaf.: Ravan Press, 1991.

——. *Restless Identities: Signatures of Nationalism, Zulu Ethnicity, and History in the Lives of Petros Lamula (c. 1881–1948) and Lymon Maling (1889–c. 1936)*. Pietermaritzburg, Zaf.: University of KwaZulu-Natal Press, 2000.

Lalu, Premesh. *The Deaths of Hintsa: Post-apartheid South Africa and the Shape of Recurring Pasts*. Cape Town: HSRC, 2009.

Landau, Paul. "The ANC, MK, and 'The Turn to Violence' (1960–1962)." *South African Historical Journal* 64 (2012): 538–63.

——. *Popular Politics in the History of South Africa, 1400–1948*. Cambridge: Cambridge University Press, 2010.

Lee, Christopher, ed. *Making a World after Empire: The Bandung Moment and Its Political Afterlives*. Athens: Ohio University Press, 2010.

Legassick, Martin. *Class and Nationalism in South African Protest: The South African Communist Party and the "Native Republic" 1928–34*. Syracuse: The Program of Eastern African Studies, 1973.

——. "Myth and Reality in the Struggle against Apartheid." *Journal of Southern African Studies* 24, no. 2 (June 1998): 443–58.

Lelyveld, Joseph. *Great Soul: Mahatma Gandhi and His Struggle with India*. New York: Vintage, 2011.

Leon, Abram. *The Jewish Question: A Marxist Interpretation*. New York: Pathfinder, 1970.

Levy, Norman. *The Final Prize: My Life in the Anti-apartheid Struggle*. Cape Town: SAHO, 2011.

Lewis, David Levering. *W. E. B. Du Bois: Biography of a Race, 1868–1919*. New York: Henry Holt, 1993.

Lewis, Gavin. *Between the Wire and the Wall: History of South African "Coloured" Politics*. Cape Town: David Philip Publishers, 1987.

Limb, Peter, ed. *A. B. Xuma: Autobiography and Selected Works*. Cape Town: Van Riebeeck Society, 2012.

——. *The ANC's Early Years: Nation, Class and Place in South Africa before 1940*. Pretoria: Unisa Press, 2010.

——, ed. *The People's Paper: A Centenary History and Anthology of "Abantu-Batho."* Johannesburg: Wits University Press, 2012.

Lodge, Tom. *Black Politics in South Africa since 1945*. London: Longman, 1983.

——. *Mandela: A Critical Life*. Oxford: Oxford University Press, 2006.

Low, Setha M. "The Anthropology of Cities: Imagining and Theorizing the City." *Annual Review of Anthropology* 25 (1996): 383–409.

Lowe, Lisa. *The Intimacies of Four Continents*. Durham, NC: Duke University Press, 2015.

Luckhardt, Ken, and Brenda Wall. *Organize or Starve! The History of the South African Congress of Trade Unions*. London: Lawrence and Wishart, 1980.

Lumpkins, Charles L. *American Pogrom: The East St. Louis Race Riot and Black Politics*. Athens: Ohio University Press, 2008.

Luthuli, Albert. "The African National Congress in Recent Years." In *Pillay, Voices of Liberation*, 85.

———. "The Christian and Political Issues." In *The Christian Citizen in a Multi-racial Society: A Report of the Rosettenville Conference*, 70–77. Cape Town: The Christian Council of South Africa, 1949.

———. *Fifty Years of Union — Political Review*. Johannesburg: South Africa Institute of Race Relations, 1960.

———. "The Implications of the Freedom Charter." In *Pillay, Voices of Liberation*, 82–85.

———. *Let My People Go*. London: Collins, 1962.

———. "Letter to the Prime Minister, J. G. Strigdom." In Pillay, *Voices of Liberation*, 106.

———. "Our Version of a Democratic Society." In Pillay, *Voices of Liberation*, 116–17.

———. "Resist Apartheid! — July 11, 1954." In Pillay, *Voices of Liberation*, 72–75.

———. *The Road to Freedom Is via the Cross*. London: Publicity and Information Bureau, African National Congress, 1970s [exact date unknown].

———. "The Road to Freedom Is via the Cross." In Pillay, *Voices of Liberation*, 52.

———. "Wake Up, Africans! Wake Up!" In Pillay, *Voices of Liberation*, 45.

Maasdorp, Gavin. *A Natal Indian Community: A Socio-economic Study in the Tongaat-Verlun Area*. Pietermaritzburg, Zaf.: University of Natal Department of Economics, 1968.

Maasdorp, Gavin, and Nesen Pillay. *Urban Relocation and Racial Segregation: The Case of Indian South Africans*. Durban, Zaf.: University of Natal Department of Economics, 1977.

Macmillan, Hugh. *The Lusaka Years: The ANC in Exile in Zambia, 1963 to 1994*. Cape Town: Jacana Media, 2013.

Magubane, Bernard, Philip Bonner, Jabulani Sithole, Peter Delius, Janet Cherry, Pat Gibbs, and Thozama April. "The Turn to Armed Struggle." In *The Road to Democracy in South Africa*, vol. 1, 1960–1970, edited by South African Democracy Education Trust, 53–146. Cape Town: Zebra Press, 2004.

Magubane, Zine. "Which Bodies Matter? Feminism, Poststructuralism, Race, and the Curious Theoretical Odyssey of the 'Hottentot Venus.'" *Gender and Society* 15, no. 6 (2001): 816–34.

Mahoney, Michael. *The Other Zulus: The Spread of Zulu Ethnicity in Colonial South Africa*. Durham, NC: Duke University Press, 2012.

Mamdani, Mahmood. "Beyond Settler and Native as Political Identities: Overcoming the Political Legacy of Colonialism." *Comparative Studies in Society and History* 43, no. 4 (2001): 651–64.

———. *Citizen and Subject: Contemporary Africa and the Legacy of Late Colonialism*. Princeton: Princeton University Press, 1996.

Mann, Jatinder. "The Introduction of Multiculturalism in Canada and Australia, 1960s–1970s." *Nations and Nationalism* 18, no. 3 (2012): 483–503.

Mandela, Nelson. Forward to *A Fortunate Man*, by Ismail Meer. Cape Town: Zebra Press, 2002.

———. "Freedom in Our Life Time." In *First, Articles, Speeches and Trial Addresses*, 55–60.

———. *Long Walk to Freedom*. Boston: Little, Brown and Company, 1994.

———. *No Easy Walk to Freedom*. Cape Town: Kwela Books, 2013.

———. "No Easy Walk to Freedom." In *First, Articles, Speeches and Trial Addresses*, 21–31.

———. *No Easy Walk to Freedom: Articles, Speeches and Trial Addresses*. Edited by Ruth First. London: Heinemann, 1965.

Maré, Gerhard. "'Non-racialism' in the Struggle against Apartheid." *Society in Transition* 34, no. 1 (2003): 13–37.

Marks, Shula. *The Ambiguities of Dependence in South Africa: Class, Nationalism, and the State in Twentieth Century Natal*. Baltimore: The Johns Hopkins University Press, 1986.

———. *Not Either an Experimental Doll: The Separate Worlds of Three South African Women*. London: The Women's Press, 1987.

———. "Patriotism, Patriarchy and Purity: Natal and the Politics of Zulu Ethnic Consciousness." In *The Creation of Tribalism in Southern Africa*, edited by Leroi Vail, 215–40. Berkeley: University of California Press, 1991.

Marks, Shula, and Richard Rathbone, eds. *Industrialization and Social Change in South Africa: African Class Formation, Culture, and Consciousness, 1870–1930*. New York: Longman, 1982.

Masilela, Ntongela. *The Cultural Modernity of H. I. E. Dhlomo*. Trenton: Africa World Press, 2007.

———. "Theorizing the Modernist Moment of the New African Intellectuals." In *New African Intellectuals and New African Political Thought in the Twentieth Century*, edited by Mbukeni Herbert Mnguni, 25–110. New York: Waxman, 2015.

Mathews, Z. K. *Freedom for My People: The Autobiography of Z. K. Mathews*. London: R. Collings in association with David Philip Publishers, 1990.

Maylam, P. R. "Aspects of African Urbanization in the Durban Area before 1940." In *Natal in the Union, 1931–1961: A Collection of Papers on Developments in Natal, Presented at a Workshop at the University of Natal, October 29–30, 1980*, 1–15. Pietermaritzburg, Zaf.: Department of Historical and Political Studies, 1981.

———. "The 'Black Belt': African Squatters in Durban 1935–1950." *Canadian Journal of African Studies* 17, no. 3 (1983): 413–28.

———. "Explaining the Apartheid City: 20 Years of South African Urban Historiography." *Journal of Southern African Studies* 21, no. 1 (March 1995): 19–38.

———. "The Struggle for Space in Twentieth-Century Durban." In Maylam and Edwards, *People's City*, 1–30.

Maylam, Paul, and Iain Edwards, eds. *The People's City: African Life in Twentieth-Century Durban*. Pietermaritzburg, Zaf.: University of Natal Press, 1996.

Marie, Shamim. *Divide and Profit: Indian Workers in Natal*. Durban, Zaf.: Worker Resistance and Culture Publications, 1986.

Mazower, Mark. *No Enchanted Palace: The End of Empire and the Ideological Origins of the United Nations*. Princeton: Princeton University Press, 2009.

Mbembe, Achille. *Sortir de la Grande Nuit: Essai sur L'Afrique décolonisés*. Paris: La Découverte, 2010.

MacDonald, Malcolm. *Why Race Matters in South Africa*. Cambridge, MA: Harvard University Press, 2006.

Mann, Jatinder. "The Introduction of Multiculturalism in Canada and Australia, 1960s–1970s." *Nations and Nationalism* 18, no. 3 (2012): 483–503.

Meer, Ismail. *A Fortunate Man*. Cape Town: Zebra Press, 2002.

Meer, Fatima. "African and Indian in Durban." *Africa South in Exile* 4, no. 4 (July-September 1960): 30–41.

———. *The Ghetto People: A Study in the Effects of Uprooting the Indian People of South Africa*. London: Africa Publications Trust, 1975.

———. *Memories of Love and Struggle*. Cape Town: Kwela Books, 2017.

———. *Portrait of Indian South Africans*. Durban, Zaf.: Avon House, 1969.

Mesthrie, Rajend. *English in Language Shift: The History, Structure and Sociolinguistics of South African Indian English*. Cambridge: Cambridge University Press, 1992.

———. *Language in Indenture: A Sociolinguistic History of Bhojpuri-Hindi in South Africa*. London: Routledge, 1991.

Mintz, Sidney, and Richard Price. *The Birth of African-American Culture: An Anthropological Approach*. Boston: Beacon Press, 1992.

Mishra, Pankaj. *From the Ruins of Empire: The Intellectuals Who Remade Asia*. New York: Farrar, Straus, Giroux, 2012.

Molema, S. M. *The Bantu: Past and Present*. Edinburgh: W. Green & Son, 1920.

Mongia, Radhika. "Gender and the Historiography of Gandhian Satyagraha in South Africa." *Gender and History* 18, no. 1 (2006): 130–49.

Moodley, Kogila. "The Ambivalence of Survival Politics in Indian-African Relations." In *South Africa's Indians: The Evolution of a Minority*, edited by B. Pachai, 441–63. Washington, DC: University Press of America, 1979.

Morris, H. S. *The Indians in Uganda: Caste and Sect in a Plural Society*. Hertfordshire, Eng.: Weidenfield and Nicolson, 1968.

Mufti, Aamir. *Enlightenment in the Colony: The Jewish Question and the Crisis of Postcolonial Culture*. Princeton: Princeton University Press, 2007.

Munro, Brenna. "Nelson, Winnie, and the Politics of Gender." In Bernard, *Cambridge Companion to Nelson Mandela*, 92–114.

Naicker, G. Monty. *A Historical Synopsis of the Indian Question in South Africa*. Durban, Zaf.: Killie Campbell Africana Library, 1993.

Naicker, M. P. *Defiance Campaign in South Africa 1952*. New Delhi: A Mainstream Publication, c. 1972 [exact date unknown].

Naidoo, Jay. *Coolie Location*. London: South African Writers, 1990.

Naidoo, Logan. *In the Shadow of Chief Albert Luthuli: Reflections of Goolam Suleman*. KwaDukuza, Zaf.: Luthuli Museum, 2010.

Naidoo, M. Sirkari. "As an Indian Sees Natal." In *The Indian—Citizen or Subject?*, edited by Maurice Webb and M. Sirkari Naidoo, 12–29. Johannesburg: South Africa Institute of Race Relations, 1947.

Naidoo, Phyllis. *Footprints in Grey Street*. Durban, Zaf.: Far Ocean Jetty, 2002.

Naidoo, Riason. *The Indian in DRUM Magazine in the 1950s*. Cape Town: Bell-Roberts Publishing, 2008.

Nandy, Ashis. *The Intimate Enemy: The Psychology of Colonialism*. Oxford: Oxford University Press, 1989.

Nakasa, Nat. "Quiet a Place, Fourteenth Street." In *The World of Nat Nakasa*, edited by Essop Patel, 9–11. Johannesburg: Ravan Press, 1975.

Neame, Sylvia. *The Congress Movement: CU, ANC, CP and Congress Alliance*. 3 vols. Cape Town: HSRC Press, 2015.

Nehru, Jawaharlal. *The Discovery of India*. Oxford: Oxford University Press, 1985.

———. *Selected Works of Jawaharlal Nehru*. Ser. 2, edited by S. Gopal. New Delhi: Jawaharlal Nehru Memorial Fund and Oxford University Press, 1984.

———. *Toward Freedom*. Boston: Beacon Press, 1963.

Newell, Stephanie. *The Power to Name: A History of Anonymity in Colonial West Africa*. Athens: Ohio University Press, 2013.

Ngubane, Jordan. *Ushaba: The Hurtle to Blood-River*. Washington, DC: Three Continents Press, 1974.

Nieftagodien, Noor. "Popular Movements, Contentious Spaces and the ANC, 1943–1956." In *Lissoni et al., One Hundred Years of the ANC*, 135–62.

Niranjana, Tejaswini. *Mobilizing India: Women, Music and Migration between India and Trinidad*. Durham, NC: Duke University Press, 2006.

No Size [Neville Alexander]. *One Azania, One Nation: The National Question in South Africa*. London: Zed Press, 1979.

Nuttall, Sarah. *Entanglement: Literary and Cultural Reflections on Post Apartheid*. Johannesburg: Witwatersrand University Press, 2009.

Odendaal, André. *The Founders: The Origins of the ANC and the Struggle for Democracy in South Africa*. Cape Town: Jacana Media, 2012.

Pachai, Bridglal. *The International Aspects of the South Africa Indian Question, 1860–1971*. Cape Town: C. Struik, 1971.

Padayachee, Vishnu, Shahid Vawda, and Paul Tichmann. *Indian Workers and Trade Unions in Durban: 1930–1950*. Durban, Zaf.: Institute for Social and Economic Research, 1985.

Palmer, Mabel. *The History of the Indian in Natal.* Cape Town: Oxford University Press, 1957.

Penn, William. *No Cross, No Crown: A Discourse Shewing the Nature and Discipline of the Holy Cross of Christ. And that the Denial of Self, and Daily Bearing of Christ's Cross, Is the Alone Way to the Rest and Kingdom of God.* Boston: Rogers and Fowle, 1747.

Peterson, Bhekizizwe. *Monarchs, Missionaries and African Intellectuals: African Theatre and the Unmaking of Colonial Marginality.* Trenton: Africa World Press, 2000.

Pillay, Gerald. *Albert Luthuli: Voices of Liberation.* 2nd ed. Cape Town: HSRC Press, 2012.

Plaatje, Sol. *Native Life in South Africa.* Johannesburg: Picador Africa, 2007.

Platzky, Laura, and Cherryl Walker. *The Surplus People: Forced Removal in South Africa.* Johannesburg: Ravan Press, 1985.

Plaut, Martin. *Promise and Despair: The First Struggle for a Non-racial South Africa.* Cape Town: Jacana, 2016.

Podbrey, Pauline. *White Girl in Search of the Party.* Pietermaritzburg, Zaf.: Hadea Books, 1993.

Pogrund, Benjamin. *How Can Man Die Better: Sobukwe and Apartheid.* London: Halban, 1990.

Posel, Deborah. *The Making of Apartheid 1948–1961.* Oxford: Oxford University Press, 1991.

Prashad, Vijay. *The Darker Nations: A Biography of the Short-Lived Third World.* New Delhi: LeftWord Books, 2007.

Puri, Shalini. "Race, Rape, and Representation: Indo-Caribbean Women and Cultural Nationalism." *Cultural Critique,* Spring 1997, 119–63.

Rambiritch, Birbal, and Pierre L. van den Berghe. "Caste in a Natal Hindu Community." *African Studies* 20 (1961): 217–25.

Raman, Parvathi. "Yusuf Dadoo: Transnational Politics, South African Belonging." *South African Historical Journal* 50, no. 1 (2004): 27–48.

Rancière, Jacques. *The Politics of Aesthetics.* Translated by Gabriel Rockhill. New York: Continuum, 2004.

Reyher, Rebecca Hourwich. *Zulu Woman: The Life Story of Christina Sibiya.* New York: Feminist Press, 1999.

Renan, Ernest. *Qu'est-ce qu'une nation?* [What is a nation?] Toronto: Tapir, 1996.

Rose, Gillian. *Mourning Become the Law.* Cambridge: Cambridge University Press, 1996.

Rose, Jacqueline. *The Last Resistance.* London: Verso, 2013.

Rosenberg, Graeme. "Auto/Biographical Narratives and the Lives of Jordan Ngubane." *Alternation* 7, no. 1 (2000): 62–96.

Ross, Kristen. *Fast Cars and Clean Bodies: Decolonization and the Reordering of French Culture.* New York: October Books, 1995.

Rude, George. *The Crowd in the French Revolution.* Oxford: Oxford University Press, 1959.

Rudwick, Elliott. *Race Riot at East St. Louis, July 2, 1917*. Carbondale: Southern University of Illinois Press, 1964.

Said, Edward. *Culture and Imperialism*. New York: Vintage, 1993.

Sampson, Anthony. *DRUM: The Newspaper that Won the Heart of Africa*. Boston: The Houghton Mifflin Press, 1957.

———. *Mandela: The Authorised Biography*. London: Harper Collins, 1999.

Sandu, Sukhdev. "O Navigators." In *South-South: Interruptions and Encounters*, edited by Tejpal S. Ajji and Jon Soske, 53–55. Toronto: Justina M. Barnike Gallery, 2009.

Sarkar, Sumit. *Writing Social History*. New Delhi: Oxford University Press, 1997.

Sarkar, Tanika. *Hindu Wife, Hindu Nation: Community, Religion, and Cultural Nationalism*. New Delhi: Permanent Black, 2001.

Sartori, Andrew. *Bengal in Global Concept History: Culturalism in the Age of Capital*. Chicago: University of Chicago Press, 2008.

Saul, John. "Cry for the Beloved Country: The Post-apartheid Denouement." *Review of African Political Economy* 28, no. 89 (2001): 429–60.

Schmitt, Carl. *The Concept of the Political*. Expanded ed. Chicago: University of Chicago Press, 2008.

Scott, David. *Conscripts of Modernity: The Tragedy of Colonial Enlightenment*. Durham, NC: Duke University Press, 2004.

Scott, Dianne. "The Destruction of Clairwood: A Case Study on the Transformation of Communal Living Space." In *The Apartheid City and Beyond: Urbanization and Social Change in South Africa*, edited by David M. Scott, 89–100. London: Routledge, 1992.

Seme, Pixley Ka Isaka. "The Regeneration of Africa." *Journal of the Royal African Society* 17 (1906): 404–8.

Sexton, Jared. *Amalgamation Schemes: Antiblackness and the Critique of Multiracialism*. Minneapolis: University of Minnesota Press, 2008.

Shembe, Isaiah, and Londa Shembe. *The Scriptures of the amaNazaretha of EkuphaKameni: Selected Writings of the Zulu Prophets Isaiah and Londa Shembe*. Edited by Irving Hexham. Translated by Londa Shembe and Hans-Jürgen Becken. Calgary, Can.: University of Calgary Press, 1994.

Shembe, Isaiah. "The First Words of Advice of Shembe at Rosboom." In *The Man of Heaven and the Beautiful Ones of God*, edited and translated by Liz Gunner, 111–13. Durban, Zaf.: University of KwaZulu-Natal Press, 2004.

Singh, Nikhil Pal. *Black Is a Country*. Cambridge, MA: Harvard University Press, 2004.

Sinha, Mrinalini. *Introduction to Selections from Mother India*, by Katherine Mayo. Edited by Mrinalini Sinha. New Delhi: Kali for Women, 1998.

Sisulu, Elinor. *Walter and Albertina Sisulu: In Our Lifetime*. Claremont, Zaf.: David Philip Publishers, 2003.

Sitze, Adam. "Mandela and the Law." In *The Cambridge Companion to Nelson Mandela*, edited by Rita Bernard, 134–61. Cambridge: Cambridge University Press, 2014.

Slate, Nico. *Colored Cosmopolitanism: The Shared Struggle for Freedom in the United States and India*. Cambridge, MA: Harvard University Press, 2012.

Slezkine, Yuri. *The Jewish Century*. Princeton: Princeton University Press, 2004.

Sobukwe, Robert Mangaliso. *Speeches of Mangaliso Sobukwe from 1949–1959 and Other Documents of the Pan-Africanist Congress of Azania*. New York: PAC of Azania Office, n.d.

South African Democratic Education Trust. *The Road to Democracy in South Africa*. Vol. 1. Cape Town: Zebra Press, 2004.

Southall, Roger. "The ANC & Black Capitalism in South Africa." *Review of African Political Economy* 31, no. 100 (2004): 313–28.

Soske, Jon. "The Impossible Concept: Settler Liberalism, Pan-Africanism, and the Language of Nonracialism." *African Historical Review* 47, no. 2 (2015): 1–39.

———. "The Life and Death of Dr. Abu Baker 'Hurley' Asvat, 23 February 1943 to 27 January 1989." *African Studies* 70, no. 3 (2011): 337–58.

———. "Open Secrets, Off the Record: Audience, Intimate Knowledge, and the Crisis of the Post-apartheid State." *Historical Reflections (Reflexions Historiques)* 38, no. 2 (2012): 55–70.

———. "Review of *The First President: A Life of John L. Dube, Founding President of the ANC*." *South African Historical Journal* 66, no. 1 (2014): 200–203.

Soske, Jon, and Shannon Walsh. "Thinking about Race and Friendship in South Africa." In *Walsh and Soske, Ties that Bind*, 1–28.

Soudien, Crain. "Robben Island University Revisited." In Lissoni et al., *One Hundred Years of the ANC*, 211–32.

Stoler, Ann Laura. *Carnal Knowledge and Imperial Power: Race and the Intimate in Colonial Rule*. Berkeley: University of California Press, 2002.

Sundkler, Bengt G. M. *Bantu Prophets in South Africa*. 2nd ed. London: Oxford University Press, 1964.

Surplus People Project. *Forced Removals in South Africa*. Vol. 4, Natal. Cape Town: Surplus People Project, 1983.

Suttner, Raymond. "The Character and Formation of Intellectuals within the ANC-led South African Liberation Movement." In *African Intellectuals. Rethinking Politics, Language, Gender and Development*, edited by Thandika Mkandawire, 117–54. London: Zed Books, 2005.

———. "Nelson Mandela's Masculinities." *African Identities* 12 (2014): 342–56.

———. "Periodisation, Cultural Construction and Representation of ANC Masculinities through Dress, Gesture and Indian Nationalist Influence." *Historia* 54, no. 1 (May 2009): 66.

Suttner, Raymond, and Jeremy Cronin. 50 Years of the Freedom Charter. Pretoria: Unisa Press, 2006.

Swan, Maureen. *Gandhi: The South African Experience*. Johannesburg: Ravan Press, 1985.

Swanson, Maynard W. "'The Asiatic Menace': Creating Segregation in Durban, 1879–1900." *International Journal of African Historical Studies* 16, no. 3 (1983): 401–21.

———. "The Sanitation Syndrome: Bubonic Plague and Urban Native Policy in the Cape Colony." *Journal of African History* 18, no. 3 (1977): 387–410.

Swanzy, Henry. "Quarterly Notes." *African Affairs* 53, no. 213 (October 1954): 271–302.

Tabata, I. B. *The Awakening of a People*. Nottingham: Spokesman Books, 1974.

Tambo, Oliver. "Mandela and Nehru." In *Preparing for Power: Oliver Tambo Speaks*, edited by Adelaide Tambo, 193–99. London: Heinemann, 1987.

———. "Passive Resistance in South Africa." In *Johns and Davis, Struggle against Apartheid*, 134–37.

Tarlo, Emma. *Clothing Matters: Dress and Identity in India*. Chicago: University of Chicago Press, 1996.

Themba, Can. *Requiem for Sophiatown*. Johannesburg: Penguin Books, 2006.

Thomas, Lynn M. "The Modern Girl and Racial Respectability in 1930s South Africa." *Journal of African History* 47, no. 3 (2006): 461–90.

Thompson, E. P. "The English Crowd in the Eighteenth Century." *Past and Present* 50, no. 1 (February 1971): 76–136.

———. *The Making of the English Working Class*. New York: Vintage Books, 1966.

Timol, Razia, and Tutuzile Mazibuko. *Soweto: A People's Response; Sample Survey of the Attitudes of People in Durban to the Soweto Violence of June 1976*. Durban, Zaf.: Institute for Black Research, 1976.

Tleane, Console. "Is There Any Future in the Past? A Critique of the Freedom Charter in the Era of Neoliberalism." In *Articulations: A Harold Wolpe Memorial Lecture Collection*, edited by Amanda Alexander, 157–80. Trenton: Africa World Press, 2006.

Torr, Louise. "Lamontville: A History." In Maylam and Edwards, *People's City*, 260–65.

Tyler, Josiah. *Forty Years among the Zulu*. Cape Town: C. Struik, 1971.

University of Natal Economics Department. *Durban Housing Survey: A Study of Housing in a Multi-racial Community*. Natal Regional Survey, Additional Report no. 2. Pietermaritzburg, Zaf.: University of Natal Press, 1952.

———. *Experiment at Edendale: An Economic Survey of a Peri-urban Settlement of Africans and Indians in Natal*. Pietermaritzburg, Zaf.: University of Natal Press, 1951.

———. *Studies of Indian Employment in Natal*. Vol. 11 of Natal Regional Survey. Cape Town: Natal University Press, 1961.

Vahed, Goolam. "'Gagged and Trussed Rather Securely by the Law': The 1952 Defiance Campaign in Natal." *Journal of Natal and Zulu History* 31, no. 2 (2014): 68–89.

———. "In the End It Was Academic: Responses to the Establishment of the University College for Indians." *Journal of Natal and Zulu History* 31 (2013): 22–44.

———. "The Making of 'Indianess': Indian Politics in South Africa during the 1930s and 1940s." *Journal of Natal and Zulu History* 17 (1997): 1–36.

———. "Race or Class? Community and Conflict amongst Indian Municipal Employees in Durban, 1914–1949." *Journal of Southern African Studies* 27, no. 1 (March 2001): 105–25.

———. "Race, Empire, and Citizenship: Sarojini Naidu's 1924 Visit to South Africa." *South African Historical Journal* 64, no. 2 (2012): 319–42.

Van den Berghe, Pierre L. "Race Attitudes in Durban, South Africa." *Journal of Social Psychology* 57 (1962): 58.

Van der Spuy, Patricia, and Lindsay Clowes. "'A Living Testimony of the Heights to Which a Woman Can Rise': Sarojini Naidu, Cissie Gool and the Politics of Women's Leadership in South Africa in the 1920s." *South African Historical Journal* 64, no. 2 (2012): 343–63.

van Diepen, Maria, ed. *The National Question in South Africa*. London: Zed Books, 1988.

Vanaik, Achin. *The Furies of Indian Communalism: Religion, Modernity, and Secularism*. London: Verso, 1997.

Vansina, Jan. *Paths in the Rainforests: Toward a History of Political Tradition in Equatorial Africa*. Madison: University of Wisconsin Press, 1990.

Vilakazi, Absolom. *Zulu Transformations: A Study of the Dynamics of Social Change*. Pietermaritzburg, Zaf.: University of Natal Press, 1962.

Vilakazi, Absolom, Bongani Mthethwa, and Mthembeni Mpanza. *Shembe: The Revitalization of African Society*. Johannesburg: Skotaville Publishers, 1986.

Vinson, Robert Trent. *The Americans Are Coming!: Dreams of African American Liberation in Segregationist South Africa*. Athens: Ohio University Press, 2012.

Wacquant, Loïc J. D. "For an Analytic of Racial Domination." *Political Power and Social Theory* 11:221–34.

Walker, Cherryl, ed. *Women and Gender in Southern Africa to 1945*. Cape Town: David Philip Publishers, 1990.

———. *Women and Resistance in South Africa*. Cape Town: David Philip Publishers, 1991.

Wallerstein, Immanuel. "The Construction of Peoplehood: Racism, Nationalism, Ethnicity." *Sociological Forum* 2 (1987): 373–88

Walsh, Shannon, and Jon Soske, eds. *Ties that Bind: Race and the Politics of Friendship in South Africa*. Johannesburg: Wits University Press, 2016.

Walshe, Peter. *The Rise of African Nationalism in South Africa: The African National Congress 1912–1952*. London: C. Hurst and Company, 1970.

Wark, McKenzie. *The Spectacle of Disintegration: Situationist Passages Out of the Twentieth Century*. London: Verso Books, 2013.

Washbrook, David. "Progress and Problems: South Asian Economic and Social History c1720–1860." *Modern Asian Studies* 22, no. 1 (1988).

Webb, Maurice. "The Indian in South Africa: Towards a Solution of Conflict." *Race Relations* 11, no.1 (1944).

Weber, Eugen. *Peasants into Frenchmen: The Modernization of Rural France, 1870–1914*. Stanford: Stanford University Press, 1976.

Webster, E. C. "The 1949 Durban 'Riots'—A Case Study in Race and Class." In *Working Papers in Southern African Studies*, edited by P. L. Bonner, 1–54. Johannesburg: University of the Witswatersrand, 1977.

Wenzel, Jennifer. "Voices of Spectral and Textual Ancestors: Reading Tiyo Soga alongside HIE Dhlomo's *The Girl Who Killed to Save*." In *Research in African Literatures* 36, no. 1 (2005): 51–73.

West, Gerald O. "Reassessing Shembe 'Remembering the Bible': Isaiah Shembe's Instructions on Adultery." *Neotestamentica* 40, no. 1 (2006): 157–84.

White, T. R. H. "Z. K. Mathews and the Formation of the ANC Youth League at the University College of Fort Hare." *African Historical Review* 27, no. 1 (1995): 124–44.

Williams, Donovan. *A History of the University College of Fort Hare, South Africa, the 1950s: The Waiting Years*. Lewiston, ID: Edwin Mellen Press, 2001.

Wilder, Gary. *Freedom Time: Negritude, Decolonization, and the Future of the World*. Durham, NC: Duke University Press, 2014.

Wilderson, Frank, III. *Incognegro: A Memoir of Exile and Apartheid*. Durham, NC: Duke University Press, 2015.

———. *Red, White, and Black: Cinema and the Structure of U.S. Antagonism*. Durham, NC: Duke University Press, 2010.

Williams, Brackette F. *Stains on My Name, War in My Veins: Guyana and the Politics of Cultural Struggle*. Durham, NC: Duke University Press, 1991.

Williams, Gavin. "Celebrating the Freedom Charter." *Transformation*, no. 6 (1988): 73–86.

Woods, C. A. *The Indian Community of Natal: Their Economic Position*. Vol. 9 of Natal Regional Survey. Cape Town: Oxford University Press, 1954.

Wolfe, Patrick. "Settler Colonialism and the Elimination of the Native." *Journal of Genocide Research* 8, no. 4 (2006): 387–409.

Wylie, Dan. *Savage Delight: White Myths of Shaka*. Pietermaritzburg, Zaf.: University of Natal Press, 2000.

Wynter, Sylvia. "Unsettling the Coloniality of Being/Power/Truth/Freedom: Towards the Human, after Man, Its Overrepresentation–An Argument." *New Centennial Review* 3, no. 3 (2003): 257–337.

Xuma, A. B. "The Bantu and Politics." In Limb, *A. B. Xuma*, 297.

———. "Bridging the Gap between White in Black in South Africa." In Limb, A. B. Xuma, 266.

———. "South West Africa: Annexation or United Nations Trusteeship?" In Limb, A. B. Xuma, 334–45.

Younge, Gary. *The Speech: The Story behind Dr. Martin Luther King Jr.'s Dream.* Chicago: Haymarket Books, 2013.

Index

African-Indian relations (*cont'd*)
alliances and, 24, 64, 65, 71, 92, 104, 170–71, 219–22; antagonism in, 5, 40, 50, 62–63, 126, 128, 175; antiapartheid struggle and, 237–46; debates over, 65, 90; discourse of, 43, 105; Durban economics and, 60–64, 127; economics and, 50, 54, 55–56, 59–60; food and, 159; hierarchical relationship in, 39–40, 60–64, 136; Indian arrogance and, 60, 161; Indian exclusivity and, 45, 158; personalized, 56, 157; racial discourse, 28, 30, 117; sexuality and, 30, 120 (*see* sexual relations); "sister-continent" mentality and, 3, 88, 97; in urban settings, 27–28; wages and, 63–64

Africanism, 25, 26, 94; early, 99, 243; leadership of, 185, 225; nonracial, 216, 241; opposition to, 167, 168; racial foundations of, 27, 106, 116. *See also* nationalism, African

Africanist, 221, 229

African masculinity, 137, 188, 243

African National Congress (ANC), 2–3; 1949 Durban Riots and, 125–29; Advisory Boards, 128; Africanist faction of, 185, 199; alliances, 85, 119; communism in (*see* Communist Party of South Africa); constitution of, 73, 77; cooperation policy, 167; corruption in, 30, 242–43; crises within, 25, 92–94; on democracy, 70, 233; development of, 3–4, 24, 26, 68–71, 175–76; evolution of, 31, 170, 242–43, 246; Freedom Charter and, 217–18; Handbook, 221; iconography of, 31, 242; Indian relations in, 4–5, 28, 40, 80–81, 98–99; intellectualism and, 19, 180–81, 242; leadership of, 6, 10, 13, 29, 61, 83, 162; media and, 23–24, 71; national conferences, 178, 199; Nationalist Bloc, 166; Native Affairs Department, 169, 191–93, 200; Native Representative Council, 73, 130–31, 173, 194; Old Guard, 77,

223; on 1949 Durban Riots, 115, 125–27; opposition to, 20, 94, 174; policies of, 212, 221, 225–26; policy documents, 200, 209; Programme of Action, 117, 131, 184, 188, 195–96; and Radicals, 66; response to apartheid, 166–68; revitalization of, 71–76, 131; vision of nation, 27, 212–13; Women's League, 63–64, 73, 183–84, 188, 218. *See also* 1952 Defiance Campaign

African nationalism, 4–7, 24–27; changes in, 176, 200–201; complexities of, 10, 167, 168; counterfeit, 188–89; crisis of, 103–34; defense of, 78–79, 117, 196; endorsement of, 131, 188; fears of degeneration, 138, 181; gender and, 137–40, 141; inclusive, 13–14, 207–12, 213, 219, 229, 240; insurrectionist, 31; interpersonal relationships and, 208; philosophy of, 23, 31, 76, 172, 236; project of, 13, 72, 74, 207, 245; racial basis for, 67, 200; revolutionary, 184, 199; theorization of, 79, 109

African People's Organization, 83, 85

African politics, 133; culture of, 192, 200; localized, 18, 130, 132, 168; subjective, 3–4, 27, 70

Africans' Claims in South Africa, 74–75, 91–92, 219

African stereotypes, 31, 42, 106, 112; domestic break-ins and, 159–60; opposition to, 115, 119; Zulu, 120

African Teachers Association, 170

Afrikaans, xviii

Afro-Asianism, 11–14; Day of, 221

Afro-Caribbean culture, 146

Alexander, Neville, 185

Alexandra, South Africa, 50, 82, 99, 167

All African Convention (AAC), 73–74, 82

also-colonized other, ix, 3, 4, 10, 24, 25, 32, 68, 136, 169, 170, 200, 201, 206, 232, 239, 240, 243, 244, 246

alterity, 22, 25

amakula, 44, 59–60

amalaita gangs, 47

Ambedkar, B. R., 22
Amra, Cassim, 161
Amritsar massacre, 71
ANC. *See* African National Congress (ANC)
ANC Youth League, 23, 93–98, 116; 1944 Manifesto, 77; activists from, 6, 66, 130; debates within, 77, 83; intellectual life of, 4, 28–29, 94–95, 223; leadership of, 72, 76, 94, 133; publications from, 86; on Xuma, 106, 131–32
Anderson, Benedict, 7, 208
Andhra, India, 147
anthropology, 15, 50, 74, 150
antiapartheid, 2–3, 21; Indian diaspora and, 238–39; liberalism and, 110, 209; methods of, 117, 119, 160; symbolism of, 214–15
anticolonialism, 2; global struggle, 12, 71; radical, 20, 22; women and, 143, 148
anticommunism, 32, 88, 228
antisemitism, 43, 106, 167
apartheid: and 1949 Durban Riots, 122, 123; defense of, 14, 122, 156, 181, 188; democratic, 216; early years of, 38, 162, 173; fascism and, 167; legacy of, 63, 74; legislation of, 17, 165–66; postapartheid, 10, 30; structure of, xviii, 165–66, 188; tribal homelands and, 110; women and, 136, 228–29. *See also* antiapartheid
Arendt, Hannah, 70
Asiatic Land Tenure Act, 66, 85
Asiatic Question, 71, 91–92
Asiatic Registration Act, 18
assimilation, 9, 41, 69, 148; anti-, 166, 240; settler civil society, 208–9, 240; social, 68, 222
Asvat, Zainab, 21, 148
Atlanta, 72
Atlantic Charter, 5, 74, 75, 105
Atlantic Convention, 175
authoritarianism, 192; sexual, 243, 244

Badsha, Omar, 50

Baloyi, R. G., 89, 166, 177
Bamabatha rebellion, 173–74
Bandung Conference. *See* 1955 Bandung Conference
Bandung, Indonesia, 3, 12
Bantu National Congress, 132; on apartheid, 166, 230; on Indian relations, 156, 228
Bantu Social Centre, 50, 188; meetings, 126, 128–29
the Bantustans, 104, 110; Indian, 166; Kwa-Zulu, 237
Bantu World, 23, 95, 166; on anti-racialism, 50, 168; on national campaigns, 169, 182, 188
Barchiesi, Franco, 20–21
Basanth, Harilal, 110
Baummannville, South Africa, 156
Bayly, Susan, 146
Benson, Mary, 125, 177
Bergson, Bergson, 11
Berlin, Isaiah, 175, 211–12
Berry, Ian, 197
Bhengu, Hyacinth, 202
Bhojpuri, 16
Bhoola, Ahmed, 178
"Black Bulls," 95
Black Consciousness Movement, xvii
Black Republic, 85
Bloemfontein Conference, 89, 116, 131
Bombay, 107
Bonner, Philip, 30
Bose, Subash Chandra, 178
boycotts, 88, 131, 226, 227; economic, 19, 128, 174; Riots Commission, 128–30
Brazil, Russia, India China, and South Africa group (BRICS), 2
Brennan, James, 12
BRICS (Brazil, Russia, India, China, and South Africa group), 2
British Empire, 2, 15, 68, 74, 107, 198
British Labour Party, 223
British Royal Family, 88
Brookes, E. H., 136
Buck-Morrs, Susan, 67
Budapest, 72
Bulawayo, Zimbabwe, 170

Burton, Antoinette, 13
Bus Owners Association, 58
Butler, Anthony, 70
Butler, Judith, 209–10

Cachalia, Maulvi, 221
Cachalia, Y. A., 178
Calata, James, 73, 93
Calcutta, 16
Callinicos, Luli, 117–18
Cape Town, 39; District Six, 49, 168, 241
capitalism: critique of, 141, 244; global, 7, 8, 15; liberal, 69
the Caribbean, 16, 71
Carnegie Non-European Library, 95
caste, 16, 46, 145–48; literature on, 146–47; pan-Indian, 17, 146–47; untouchability in, 159
Catholicism, 11
Cato Manor, Durban, South Africa: and 1949 Durban Riots, 113; housing in (see Durban, South Africa, housing in, Cato Manor); Indian business in, 104, 128; politics of, 227; social work in, 149
Césaire, Aimé, 11
Ceylon, 171
Chakrabarty, Dipesh, 10
Champion, A. W. G., 87, 176, 186; on 1949 Durban Riots, 115, 126–27; African National Congress and, 92–93, 125; downfall of, 30, 203; on Indian relations, 57, 88; International Commercial Union and, 70; negotiations of, 54, 73; policies of, 129–31, 174
Chari, R. T., 119
chieftainship, 95, 169, 192–93, 195–96, 200; Luthuli's loss of, 200, 202, 228
China, 49
Choudree, Ashwin, 189
Christianity, 6, 193; Africanist, 137, 141–45, 171; converts of, 95, 171; denominations of, 171, 208; education in, 64, 72; liberal, 242; materialism and, 10, 77, 95, 194; missionaries of, 15, 68, 138, 181; other religions

and, 171, 211; political, 114, 176, 192–96; redemptionist, 77–78; traditions of, 11, 19, 193, 211
Churchill, Winston, 74
cinemas, 51, 61, 145; symbolism of, 61, 64, 168
citizenship, 8; concepts of, 22, 68; imperial, 68, 83, 91; loyalties of, 175; secular, 8; security of, 194; South African, 90; universal, 8, 75, 209
civil disobedience, 28, 131, 166. See also 1946; 1952 Defiance Campaign; passive resistance.
Clairwood, South Africa, 119
Cold War, 4, 12, 32; anti-pass campaign and, 228–29; in Natal, 226–29; paranoia, 230–31; worldview, 32, 181, 230–31, 231–32
collective victimization, 104
Colonial Born Indian Association, 16–17
colonialism: crime of, 11, 78; economics of, 6, 16, 222; governance of, 69, 185; ideology of, 7, 11, 97; "others" and, 3–4, 13, 136, 169; policies of, xvii, 42, 77; societies of, 5, 6, 69, 136. See also anticolonialism, postcolonialism
Coloured: housing of in South Africa, 48, 156, 179; politics of in South Africa, 65, 83, 166, 179, 183; segregation, 179; sexuality and, 62, 137, 152, 155, 179
Coloured People's Organization, 185
Combined Locations Advisory Board, 126
Commonwealth of Nations, 107
Communism: anti-Indianism and, 98; Indian, 94, 177; spread of, 81, 181. See also anticommunism
Communist Party of South Africa, 5, 21, 32; on 1949 Durban Riots, 115, 129; campaigns and, 32, 67, 71, 176; development of, 25; Doctors' Pact and, 90, 96; Indian, 227, 229; influence of, 81, 225, 241; leadership of, 23, 174; media of, 216, 221; nationalism and, 199, 209, 230; "Popular Front" period, 184;

identity and, 42–43, 136, 222; as new empire, 24–27, 109; unification of, 149–50

Indian migrants (Durban, South Africa), 37–65, 104; High School, 133; landlords, 54, 55–57, 60, 129; merchant class of, 50–55, 60, 126; Parsis population, 51; suburbs of, 145

Indian National Congress, 2, 28, 105; African National Congress and, 5, 93; Partition and, 4, 29, 109

Indian nationalism: gender and, 31, 148, 151; politics of, 4, 122, 198; rise of, 81, 108; symbols of, 133, 158

Indian Ocean, 4, 12, 14

Indian Opinion, 18, 73, 229; on 1949 Durban Riots, 106, 111, 118–19; on African issues, 80, 155, 189, 230; on Defiance Campaign, 189, 192; Ilanga lase Natal and, 119–25; on passive resistance, 19–20

Indian Representation Act of 1946, 85

Indian stereotypes, 40, 42; of arrogance, 60, 113, 120; merchant, 52, 98, 121; of corruption, 43, 62–63, 121, 166; perpetuation of, 130–31; of victimhood, 106, 112, 121

Indian Views, 81, 119

Indian women, 31, 59; and political activism, 86–87; construct of, 148–51, 158; dichotomies of, 149–50; social exclusion of, 157–58

Indian Youth Cultural Conference, 150, 151

indigeneity, 13, 97, 229

individualism, 14, 26, 59

Indo-African Alliance. See 1952 Defiance Campaign.

Indonesia, 220

industrial revolution, 18, 38

In India and East Africa, 2

Inkatha Freedom Party, 237

inkosi, 192

Inkundla ya Bantu, 1, 44; on 1949 Durban Riots, 111, 113, 114, 115; African anxiety in, 105, 109, 126, 139; "Bambulaleleni Ugandhi?," 1; columns from, 63, 92; editors of,

23, 94; "India Triumphant!," 88; Lembede and, 76, 78–79; warnings from, 108, 129

International Club, 54

International Commercial Union (ICU), 70, 83

interracial sexual relations: class and, 151, 156; politicization of, 62, 138, 140, 152–53, 155–56; prevention of, 136, 152; white supremacy and, 152–53, 160

interviews, xvii, 40, 43, 64

Iqbal, Mohammed, 11

Isharina. See Mda, A. P.

Isitwalandwe, 219

isiXhosa, 2, 218

isiZulu: arguments in, 32–33, 115, 213; newspapers in, 30; socioeconomic implications of, 53, 54–55

Islam, 8, 11, 21, 88–89; discrimination against, 1, 181; Indian, 6–7, 17, 46

Israel, 106, 239

Jabavu, D. D. T., 2, 83

Jawaharlal Nehru Award for International Understanding, 2–3

Jeeva, Dawood, 57

Johannesburg: activism in, 2, 26, 33; Alexandra, 50; Anderson Street Hall, 182; conferences in, 67, 90, 178; culture of, 24, 167; Indian migrants in, 18, 39, 57; organizations in, 76, 93; Sophiatown, 49, 168, 241; Trades Hall, 182; Vrederdorp ("Fietas"), 49, 168

Joint Council Movement, 54, 127, 194

Joshi, P. S., 150

Kajee, A. I., 80

kaMancinza, Bambatha, 20, 173

Kant, Immanuel, 211

Kashmir, 181

Kathrada, Ahmed, 184

kaTshunungwa, T. E., 226

Kenya, 13

Khoruha, Ufford, 221

Kimberley, South Africa, 125

King, Martin Luther, Jr., 19

Kliptown, 218, 222
Kotane, Moses, 84, 115, 176, 209, 221
Kumalo, Mavis, 190
Kuper, Hilda, 37, 47; on Durban, 50,
    145, 146
Kuper, Leo, 42–43
Kuzwayo, G., 228
Kwa-Mashu, South Africa, 45

Lalu, Premesh, 69
Landau, Paul, 199, 211
language: Bhojpuri, 16; of democracy
    (see democracy, language of);
    English (see English); Fanagalo, 53;
    Gujarati (see Gujarat, language of);
    Hindi, 50–51, 63; historical ap-
    proach to, 41–46; isiXhosa, 2, 218;
    isiZulu (see isiZulu); nationalist,
    184, 220; of oppression, 42, 60, 170;
    Portuguese, 146; racial, xvii, 41, 43;
    schools of, 51, 146; Sesotho, 218; of
    social structure, xvii, 41, 61; Tamil
    (see Tamil); Telugu (see Telugu);
    vernacular, 30, 150, 162
Lekwame, Kwame, 221
Lembede, Anton: on African national-
    ism, 5, 31, 116; on cultural differ-
    ences, 33, 239; on Doctors' Pact,
    96; education of, 26, 76, 94; as
    historian, 77–78; as idealist, 76–80;
    legacy of, 208; passive resistance
    and, 90; philosophy of, 23, 28; slo-
    gan, 7, 79; Youth League and, 6, 72
Lenin, Vladimir, 198
Letele, Arthur, 226
Let My People Go, 171, 191, 208, 209
Levy, Norman, 217
liberalism, 4, 5, 65, 232; colonial, 31, 78,
    176; empires and, 18, 20, 68; racial,
    26–27, 174; tradition of, 94, 205,
    213; white, 25, 73, 122, 148
Liberal Party, 185, 218
Liberation, 110
Liberia, 70
Lincoln, Abraham, 115
linguistics, 47, 78
literacy, 16, 68, 148
Locke, John, 22

Lodge, Tom, 71, 212–13
London, 73
Long Walk to Freedom, 3, 199
Luthuli, Albert: on 1949 Durban Riots,
    174, 240; on African nationalism,
    31, 206–12, 211–12; autobiography,
    171, 191; banning order, 197, 203;
    campaign, 201–6; and Christian
    politics, 192–96; on civil disobedi-
    ence, 13, 191, 235–36; collaborators
    with, 10, 203; on congresses, 185,
    219; and cosmopolitan moment,
    169–77; crisis of conscience of, 30;
    on Defiance Campaign, 179–80,
    188–89; Drum magazine writings,
    197–98; election of, 24, 26; as
    farmer, 170–71; on Freedom Char-
    ter, 222–26; on Gandhi, 2, 171–72;
    on gradualism, 186, 192, 194, 200;
    headwear of, 198–99; "How to De-
    velop a Unified South Africa," 175–
    76; imprisonment of, 234–36; on
    Indian relations, 54, 109; influence
    of, 32, 76, 192; memoir, 234–35;
    methods of activism, 191–96, 198,
    200, 204–5; as nationalist, 200–201;
    on Ngubane, 230–31; opposition to,
    79, 187–88, 226–29; philosophy of,
    23, 32, 174–75; as realist, 173; on
    symbolic constitutionalism, 24, 212;
    on white supremacy, 175
Luthuli, Martin, 170
Luthuli, Nokukhanya, 204–5

Madondo, George, 110
Madras Christian College, 171
Madras, India, 15–16
Madzunya, Josiah, 167
Magna Carta, 217
Mahatma Gandhi Memorial Society,
    171
Mahdiba, Moses, 227
Mahomed, E. V., 173
Majola, C. C., 37; on Indian relations,
    45
Malan, D. F., 178, 181, 218
Malaysia, 49
Mamdani, Mahmood, 10

Third World, 3, 10, 12, 74; nationalism in (*see* nationalism, Third World)
Thompson, E. P., 38
Tolstoy Farm, 238
Transkei, South Africa, 72
Transvaal, 17, 19, 27, 81
Transvaal Indian Congress, 67, 80, 89, 176; mandates of, 93
Transvaal Youth League, 98–99, 126, 177; on passive resistance, 180
Treason Trial, 183
tribalism, 139, 192; customs of, 186, 192; gender and, 153
Trotskyism, 82
Tugela district, 224
Tuskegee Institute, 72

Umgeni River, South Africa, 55
Umkhonto we Sizwe (MK), 200, 235, 236, 241
Umvoti Reserve, 170, 172
UN. *See* United Nations (UN).
United Democratic Front, 214, 242; opposition to, 245
United Nations (UN): Charter of Rights and Freedoms, 90, 105; Committee against Apartheid, 3, 166; as Court of Appeal, 75–76; foundation of, 28, 67, 74; General Assembly, 3, 28, 75–76; on Indian treatment, 66, 87; Indian victory at, 109, 181; Partition Plan for Palestine, 105; passive resistance and, 85–89; South Africa and, 93, 239
United Party, 218
United States (US), 70, 73; universities in, 72
University of Minnesota, 72
University of Natal, 152
University of the Witwatersrand, 33, 73, 202
urbanization, 30, 37–65, 43; displacement and, 118, 162; gender and, 137–40; imaginations of, 41, 53; Indian, 47, 136; patterns of, 45–49, 168
US. *See* United States (US)

Vahed, Goolam, 16, 20, 46, 82

vanguardism, 243
Vansina, Jan, 211
vegetarianism, 18
venereal disease, 137, 138, 141
Victorianism, 140
Vinson, Robert, 6
violence: anti-Indian, 99, 103–34 (*see also* 1949 Durban Riots); class-based and sexual, 155; colonial, 15, 244, 245; communal, 29, 88, 109; justification for, 60, 105, 130; nonviolence, 19, 123, 174, 227; Partition, 239; racialized, 104–5, 166; reactions to, 30, 114; sexual, 103, 111, 114, 136; state, 14, 199

Walker, Cherryl, 228
warfare: industrialized, 11, 27; political, 176, 232; race, 112
Washington, Booker T., 72, 175
weltanschauung, 77
Wentworth oil refinery, 55
Western Cape, 17, 65
Western civilization, 6, 10; African culture and, 96, 119, 144; criticisms of, 62, 67; philosophy of, 11, 18, 22
white supremacy, 3, 5; as common enemy, 96–97, 156–57; defenders of, 166, 181–82; democracy and, 195–96; disavowing of, 13, 22–23, 175; economics and, 17–18; institutionalized, 38; interracial sex and, 152–53, 160–61, 244; multiracialism and, 69, 209; opposition to, 25, 199, 232 (*see also* 1952 Defiance Campaign); persistence of, 77, 245
"Why did they kill Gandhi?," 1
Wolfe, Patrick, 15
women, activism and, 148, 161–62, 190–91; antiapartheid, 228–29; feminist, 244; pro-imperialist, 153
Women's Charter. *See* 1954 Women's Charter.
Woods, C. A., 52
World War I, 10, 37, 71, 112
World War II, 27, 67, 86; globalization and, 106–10; impact of, 112, 239; post-, 71–76

Wynter, Sylvia, 22

xenophilia, 12
Xuma, A. B., 5, 28, 72; African National Congress and, 71–76, 125; African National Congress Youth League and, 94–95; criticism of, 30, 89, 106; Doctors' Pact and, 89–91; on Indian relations, 67, 87–88, 107; on Native Question, 71, 239; Non-European Unity Movement and, 84–85; response to Durban Riots, 131–32
Xuma-Dadoo-Naicker Pact. *See* Doctors' Pact.

Yengwa, M. B., 133, 203, 234; African National Congress and, 26, 94, 186; collaborators with, 130, 204; negotiations of, 54, 189
Young Men's Christian Association (YMCA), 72, 153

Zondizitha Buying Club, 132
zoology, 72
Zulu Hlanganani, 130, 132, 156, 203
Zulu Kingdom, 15, 20; advisors to royal family, 26; as house of Senzanga-khona, 142, 143; battle cry of, 111; Christianity in, 64, 135; culture of, 95, 203, 206, 211; martial traditions, 113; poetry, 95; royal family, 58, 187; working class, 47

www.ingramcontent.com/pod-product-compliance
Lightning Source LLC
Chambersburg PA
CBHW021847020426

42334CB00013B/226